W9-AXN-588

EDUCATION AND TRANSFORMATION

Education and Transformation
Marianist Ministries in America
since 1849

CHRISTOPHER J. KAUFFMAN

Foreword by
Joseph P. Chinnici, O.F.M.

Afterword by
David J. Fleming, S.M.

A Herder & Herder Book
The Crossroad Publishing Company
New York

The Crossroad Publishing Company
370 Lexington Avenue, New York, NY 10017

Printed in the United States of America

Library of Congress Cataloging-in-Publication Data

Kauffman, Christopher J., 1936–
    Education and transformation : Marianist ministries in America
since 1849 / by Christopher J. Kauffman ; foreword by Joseph P.
Chinnici ; afterword by David J. Fleming.
        p.   cm.
    Includes bibliographical references.
    ISBN 0-8245-1574-9
    1. Marianists–United States—History.   I. Title.
BX3784.Z5U65   1999
271'.79—dc21   98-44258
                                                                   CIP

1   2   3   4   5   6   7   8   9   10   04   03   02   00   99

For my Sister, Peggy Abel,
my Brother, Dan, and
the Memory of our Brother, Jack

Contents

Acknowledgments

OVER THE PAST TWENTY-FIVE YEARS I HAVE HAD MANY VERY
rewarding experiences as I placed religious communities on the historical
topography, a process that requires several consultants within each of these
communities who, because they had reflected on the historical dimensions
of the ministry, spirituality, and governance, provided insights, direction,
and support. In researching and writing this history I have worked closely
with Brother Lawrence Cada, S.M., who has been teaching Marianist history to novices for many years and has been director of the North American
Conference on Marianist Studies (NACMS). He has been *the* resource person and proofreader/editor par excellence. The accuracy of this book owes a
great deal to Brother Cada. Thanks, Larry!

I am also grateful to Father Joseph Lackner, S.M., who shared his many
insights into Marianist history. He and Brother Cada helped to make my
research trips to Dayton very enjoyable experiences. I have also been gra-
ciously assisted by many other Marianists and colleagues, without whom I
could never have undertaken this history with a sense of confidence and
clarity.

Archivists provide the basic sustenance for historians. Many thanks to
Brother Ben Laurinaitis, archivist of the Cincinnati Province, to Brothers
Paul Novasal and Earl Leistikow of the St. Louis Province, Father Joseph
Stefanelli of the Pacific Province, Brother Frank O'Donnell and Father
Robert E. Backherns of the New York Province, Brother Ambrogio Albano
of the General Administration in Rome, and Ms. Kerrie Moore, archivist of
the University of Dayton. Thanks to Brother Leistikow for his splendid list
of Marianist communities in Appendix II.

I am gratefully indebted to the Marianist Conference for their support and direction over the years. Thanks especially to Brother Thomas Giardino, Brother Joseph Kamis, and Father George Cerniglia, not only for their liaison efforts between the conference and me but also for proofreading the text. Many thanks to all those Marianists whom I interviewed, particularly Fathers Norbert Brockmann, Bertrand Buby, George Cerniglia, Philip Eichner, David Fleming, James Heft, Philip Hoelle, Christian Janson, Francis Keenan, Willis Langlinais, John McGrath, James Mifsud, George Montague, Patrick Tonry, Stephen Tutas, and Adolf Windisch, and Brothers Bill Bolts, George Dury, Stephen Glodek, Donald Hebeler, John McCluskey, Paul Novasal, John Samaha, James Wipfield, and James Wood. Though I did not cite each of them in the text, they shared experiences, ideas, and insights that permeated the background of several topics and themes included in this work. I gratefully acknowledge the historians of the St. Louis and Pacific Provinces: Gerald J. Schnepp and Charles G. Boglitz. Thanks also to Carol Quinn, director of the North American Center for Marianist Studies, for her friendly support.

Several other archivists provided assistance with interest and professional concern: Father Carl Hoegerl, C.SS.R, archivist of the Baltimore Province of the Redemptorists, located at Our Lady of Good Counsel Residence in Brooklyn, was very helpful; Father Gary Heinecke, C.SS.R., was a splendid host at Villa Redeemer in Glenview, Illinois. The archivist there, John J. Treanor, is also archivist of the archdiocese of Chicago. Mr. Treanor not only acquainted me with both the Redemptorists' and the Chicago archives but also kindly met me at the airport and drove me to Glenview. I am grateful to Brother Joseph Grabenstein, F.S.C., of the archives at LaSalle University in Philadelphia and Brother Robert Werle, F.S.C., of the Midwest Province located in Memphis. These archivists of the Christian Brothers kindly provided materials for the Marianist story in Baltimore and a Christian Brothers' manual of pedagogy, a work comparable to the Marianist publication. I am indebted to several diocesan archivists: Jeffrey Burns in San Francisco, John Treanor in Chicago, Charles Nolan in New Orleans, Christine Krosel of Cleveland, and Roman P. Godzak of Detroit. Many thanks to the Sulpician provincials Gerald Brown, S.S., and Ronald Witherup, S.S., for allowing me to keep my office at the Sulpician archives.

John Bowen, S.S., archivist emeritus of the Sulpician archives and a good friend, has proofread everything I have written since 1986, including this Marianist history, with precision and concern. Thanks again, John. I am pleased to be associated with and grateful to Robert Schindle and Janine Bruce, assistant archivists. Thanks also to historians Thomas Spalding,

C.F.X., Joseph M. White, Elizabeth McKeown, and Philip Gleason, each of whom made valuable suggestions to improve the manuscript. Justus George Lawler, editor, mentor, and friend has had an enormous impact upon my life and work for many years. The author of many books on such topics as poetics, literature and theology, higher education, and nuclear war, Lawler has a command of the intersection of religion and culture that is widely recognized. Thanks, George, especially for your editorial commentary on this work. I am very grateful to Joseph P. Chinnici, O.F.M., for his advice and inspiration, his critique of the manuscript, and for his foreword to this work. Of course, I am grateful to David Fleming, S.M., for his afterword, as well as for suggestions for improving the historical accuracy of my manuscript. I gratefully acknowledge James Hennesey, S.J., whose life and works continue to be sources of inspiration for me.

Many other colleagues have been supportive over the years; thanks to the CLIO group, historians of the American Catholic experience: Dorothy Brown, Emmet Curran, John Farina, Maureen Harp, Dolores Liptak, R.S.M., Elizabeth McKeown, Timothy Meagher, Paul Robechaud, C.S.P., and William Portier.

This book originated as a handwritten text that Denise McCord was able to decipher and place in the computer. She not only is a super professional but is abundant with grace and intelligence. Thanks so very much, Denise.

I am grateful to be associated with fine colleagues in the Department of Church History: the late Robert Eno, S.S., Jacques Gres-Gayer, Nelson Minnich, and Robert Trisco have been consistent sources of encouragement. Patrick Lynch and Patrick McNamara, graduate assistants over the years, were diligent bibliographers, gathering secondary works related to topics of this book. I sincerely appreciate your splendid work. Our administrative assistant, Gloria Wilkenson, provides valuable service.

Helen and our children, Jane, Christopher, and Kathryn Ann, have created a family melody that resounds as a rhapsody on the themes of love and concern; I join them with songs of gratitude, love, and affection. I am proud to be associated with two fine men, Robert Marinelli and Luis Maldonado, the husbands of Jane and Katie. Now there is Michael Robert Kauffman Marinelli, our first grandson; what a blessing to behold! To him and to all my family-friends, Peace!

Foreword

ON OCTOBER 28, 1965, THE SECOND VATICAN COUNCIL ISSUED *Perfectae Caritatis*, the decree on the up-to-date renewal of religious life. The seismic consequences of this call for revitalization have rippled through the church's interior life, its understanding of its identity, its relationships in society, and its mission in the world. In the immediate aftermath of the council, members of religious orders held extraordinary chapters of renewal, revised their constitutions, reexamined their apostolates, and entered into an extended period of experimentation designed to recapture the spirit of the founders in the light of contemporary "signs of the times." Generally viewed as concluding with the publication of the new code of canon law in 1983 and the approval of definitive texts of constitutions, this initial period has been followed by more focused attempts at institutional restructuring and refounding in accord with the conciliar experience. A very prevalent pattern has been that of diminished numbers, a pluralistic understanding of ministries, and a growing desire to meet the demands of a now global church. Many of these themes have found a three-fold synthesis in the 1994 document issued by the Congregation for Institutes of Consecrated Life and Societies of Apostolic Life, "Fraternal Life in Community," the discussions surrounding the world Synod of Bishops on the consecrated life, and the Apostolic Exhortation *Vita Consecrata* (March 25, 1996). Indeed this last papal teaching can be said both to bring the proximate postconciliar period of renewal to an end and to initiate a much longer, more difficult process of global appropriation of the charism of religious life in the experience of the church in the modern world.

In this context and after the initial research in most religious communities focused almost exclusively on the recovery of the intentions and structures of the founding period, many groups are now searching for a much longer perspective, one that can successfully root the contemporary experience of change, renewal, and refounding in the much deeper soil of a living religious tradition. Part of the postconciliar journey has been the rediscovery, particularly in the American church, that a well-founded identity needs to take seriously both the founding moment and its subsequent reception and transmission over time. The recently published *Encyclopedia of American Catholic History* (1997) gives ample testament to this more historical view of change in significant articles on American women and men religious. The author of this present book, Christopher J. Kauffman, has already contributed significantly to our understanding of these developments with studies on the founder of the Glenmary Home Missioners, the histories of the Alexian Brothers and the Sulpicians in the United States, and the important role of women religious in the development of health care in American society and church. The Society of Mary, or Marianists, is fortunate indeed to have a historian of this caliber present a thoroughly researched and well-documented history, so sensitive to the development of a living religious tradition in the context of our contemporary retrieval. They themselves are to be commended for opening themselves to a historical analysis that does justice to their rich heritage in both its high and low moments, its periods of retraction and its times of great expansion and vision. Here, indeed, is a human history full of grace, a living witness to the centrality of Christ in the symbol of Joseph and Mary at Nazareth.

As I read *Education and Transformation: Marianist Ministries in America since 1849*, I am struck by its well-told and synthesized story. In addition, some of the underlying themes open up new dimensions of research and understanding for both the historian and the vowed religious in the United States. Let me give three examples. First, many religious groups in the immediate postconciliar period experienced disorientation and a loss of values, the collapse of an internal system of pedagogy and wisdom. The analysis presented by Dr. Kauffman in chapter 7 of this work is one of the first to analyze this period from a well-substantiated documentary base. Yet, seen as a whole, the book gives testimony to the importance of viewing a living religious tradition in the church as a "community of wisdom," imparting from generation to generation insights and a witness to the gospel expressed through the institutional carriers of legal documents, manuals of pedagogy, styles of governance, ministries, and formative relationships. The transmission of this inheritance, as a living and organic reality, necessarily involves growth and decline, conflict and resolution, continuity and discontinuity, inherited and novel expressions. It may encompass, as this book makes evident, theological conflicts between more rigorous and more flexible views of religious life, or for the 1920s and 1960s intergenerational conflicts of some magnitude. At times, disagreements led to alienation from the community, as in the case of the founder himself, to ideological attempts to control historical interpretations, or to the painful formation of a new province, as happened in the 1970s. Still, a true knowledge of one's history grants perspective and gives rootage to this always developing and relational identity. Thus, Kauffman makes clear that the primitive spirit of William Joseph Chaminade (1761–1850), continually reinterpreted and sometimes muted, perdured and in some measure found its embodied expression in the constitutions of 1839 and 1891, the 1899 English version of *Manual of Christian Pedagogy*, the successive biographies of the late nineteenth and twentieth centuries, and the work of William Ferree both before and after Vatican II. It is usually in the persons of their respected ones that communities of wisdom find their true compass. The Marianists have been blessed with many of these people, and their history itself provides vision in the midst of change.

Second, *Education and Transformation*, as might be expected from a historian of such wide-ranging interests, points to an understanding of a religious group as a mediating institution in the context of church and society. This is a helpful development which properly moves beyond the internally focused perspective so often presented in the histories of religious orders, or the more broadly accepted notion of the antipathy between Catholicism and secularity. This reader was struck repeatedly by the significant relationships established between the Marianists and developments in secular education, the reformulation of their curriculum in the light of the emerging humanistic studies in the sciences and psychology, their grappling with the problems of institutional racism in the 1950s and 1960s. In addition, running through this work is an analysis of the sodality or religious confraternity, a key institution mediating between church and society, the religious and lay worlds, the sacred and secular dimensions of life. As a social institution, the sodality is now receiving intensive historical attention among European scholars, and the Society of Mary, perhaps because of its emergence from a lay confraternal base, provides a key example of the importance of this structure and its vitality in the history of American religion. General developments among the Marianists thus coincide with the historical rewriting that has occurred with the analysis of the mediating functions of the Sister Formation Movement and Catholic social institutions.

Examining religious institutions as mediating structures is, it could be argued, a historiographical viewpoint that takes seriously the conciliar insights of *Gaudium et Spes* and presents the relationship between the church and the world in dialogic fashion. This perspective has the potential to change the general picture of American Catholic studies, give religious historians a place at the table of our secular counterparts, and help provide a historical past in the struggle for a contemporary American Catholic identity. Conceiving of religious life as a "primary mediating force" between the institutional church and social developments can perhaps also move religious themselves beyond the categorical structural conflict of "monastic" and "apostolic," which is really rooted in juridicism, and which has plagued the history of the church and that of the Marianists themselves. Christopher Kauffman's own works are an indication of the general path that needs to be followed. Especially in this area, creative vistas remain before us in retrieving a living tradition.

Lastly, this detailed presentation of the history of the Marianists in the United States, a unique group by virtue of its mixed lay and clerical character, sheds important historical light on contemporary ecclesiological issues. Clearly, members of the Society of Mary have taken key leadership roles in the National Catholic Educational Association, the educational branch of the National Catholic Welfare Conference, the Black Catholic Clergy Caucus, and the Conference of Major Superiors of Men. Through primary, secondary, and college education they have had a considerable influence on the formation of lay leadership in church and society. Several have served as important spokesmen articulating to bishops and Vatican personnel the developments in the American church. In addition, the mixed character of the society (from 10 percent clerical in the nineteenth century to 30 percent after 1970), its struggles over clericalization and tensions with Rome, the maternal character of its spirituality, and the confraternal focus on egalitarian membership in the Body of Christ provide threads for writing a deeper history of ecclesiology in the American church, one that moves beyond more juridical and hierarchical preoccupations into an analysis of public and private roles and relationships. Perhaps it may be possible here to build a bridge with the insights emerging from feminist historical scholarship and the postconciliar emphasis on the role of the laity. Here is a history that has common coinage and is more inclusive of the realities of the church's past. A religious group such as the Marianists can serve as a laboratory for reconceptualizing and retrieving a living tradition for a contemporary audience.

Christopher Kauffman has once again written narrative history with a difference. *Education and Transformation* combines solid scholarship and insightful synthesis with an interpretation that points beyond itself to the importance of a living tradition, a broader view of religion in society, and a deeper understanding of the American Catholic ecclesiological tradition. It is to the great credit of the Marianists that they have made this complex and substantial history available to the rest of the church. It comes at a good time.

Joseph P. Chinnici, O.F.M.
Franciscan School of Theology
Berkeley, California
September 1, 1998

Introduction

TWO RECENT WORKS ON THE RELIGIOUS LIFE, *LIVING IN THE Meantime*, edited by Paul J. Philibert, O.P., and "Between the Times," an article by Elizabeth Johnson, C.S.J., capture the historical consciousness of women and men religious on the ecclesial and cultural changes from the 1960s through the 1980s.[1] As the titles of these works clearly symbolize, Johnson, Philibert, and others are consciously situated in the postlude of one period and the prelude to another; the language of transformation, hope, freeing the charism, and Johnson's metaphor—the advent season—convey the anticipation of the birth of new forms of religious life. Free from the distorted lens of nostalgia, they share a common perception of the vital relationships among the areas of church, society, and the developmental character of religious life. Though Elizabeth Johnson's article is a systematic theological analysis of contemporary and historical aspects of religious life within the context of the modern and postmodern eras, other reflections meld the historical with the autobiographical.

The situation symbolized by "in the meantime" is indeed analogous to the origins of many religious orders. Bernard Lee, S.M., a process theologian and a scholar/participant in small Christian communities, cites Johannes Metz's work on the religious life, *Followers of Christ*, to substantiate his own notion that "charismatic figures . . . are more apt to make an appearance in troubled times." According to Lee, Metz "makes the same comment about the origin of religious orders. . . . These are historical times when pain is deeper, aspirations more acute, when a settled world's values are upended, in short when an old world is dissolving and a new world is in the making."[2]

John Padberg's article on those periods that give rise to new models of

1

religious life underscores Lee and Metz's analysis. Lawrence Cada, S.M., et al., in their book *Shaping the Coming Age of Religious Life*, developed periodizations; Cada portrays the period 1800 to the present as the era of the teaching orders.[3] Founders of these teaching congregations were responding to the new world that was derived from the French Revolution and characterized by public education, democratic aspirations, and the precipitous decline in Christian culture. It was in 1800, after a decade of revolutions had culminated in Napoleon's emphasis on order and a reconciliation with the church, that affected Father William J. Chaminade's (1761–1850) return to Bordeaux, where he soon founded a sodality of lay men and women representing all social classes and dedicated to the rechristianization of France. Within the sodality of Bordeaux a specialized group, "the state," developed into the nucleus of both the Daughters of Mary and the Society of Mary, the Marianists, separately founded in 1816 and 1817. Chaminade had experienced a world out of joint and perceived a new form of religious life, a community of brothers, some of whom became priests and dressed not in the traditional garb but in a suit on the model of middle-class Frenchmen. He envisioned the Society as committed to a permanent mission, and the elementary schools and a few secondary schools became the predominant form of missionary endeavor to effect the rechristianization of France under the banner of Mary Immaculate.

The prologue of this book explores the charisms and contexts of the Society during the life of Chaminade. With a relatively long advent season before the birth of the Marianists, Chaminade represents the Marian expectation of the Nazareth experience as he integrated the Society with a positive sense of God's design, with the commitment to prayer and to the apostolate of religious and secular education in the schools. Just as Chaminade's Bordeaux Sodality broke from tradition by including men and women of all classes, so the Society of Mary included priests, teaching and working brothers on a relatively egalitarian principle of "union without confusion." All Marianists begin their life in community as brothers; only later do some become Marianist priests to serve as chaplains for the community, the schools, and as retreat masters. This synthesis was derived from the spirituality and apostolate of the lay sodalist.

In accord with the prologue, all subsequent chapters are organized by a principal theme or topic. Chapter 2, the foundations of the mission in the United States by the Alsatian Father Leo Meyer was in response to German-American pastors in Cincinnati. Determined to establish a motherhouse, a novitiate, and a school supported by a farm, Meyer was very successful, but he never achieved the trust of his confreres, many pastors, and occasionally his bishop.

The next chapter, on national expansion, charts parish schools and Marianist-owned boarding schools from Cincinnati to Texas and on to Hawaii in the west and to the east as far as Baltimore. Though there were sporadic conflicts with ecclesial authorities, the Marianists moved beyond a thorough German-American identity, as San Antonio and Honolulu communities were founded on the French connection. This chapter concludes with the Marianists' participation in the Catholic Education Exhibit at the Columbian Exposition in Chicago in 1893.

With Marianist religious culture as the organizing theme of chapter 4, the thesis of the book emerges. There are periods of fragmentation and integration between the religious exercises and the teaching ministry, that is, between the monastic and the apostolic. With the emphasis on the unity of prayer life and the graced life in the new apostolic age of Christian renewal manifested in the Bordeaux Sodality and the Society of Mary, Chaminade proffered a positive synthesis of the two strands of Marianist life.

Chaminade's two successors, Georges J. Caillet (1846–1868) and Jean J. Chevaux (1868–1875) fragmented the internal spirituality from the exterior ministry by their rigorist mentality; only by restraining the human tendencies to evil could the Marianist teachers enter the exterior world of the schools. Joseph Simler, the "second founder" (1876–1905) achieved a doctorate in theology (including that of St. Thomas Aquinas) from the Sorbonne, revived the sodality, wrote a biography of the founder, and articulated an incarnational spirituality that integrated the monastic and the apostolic. Fragmented under the rigorists and integrated by a Thomist theologian, the monastic-apostolic relationship runs through the history of the Marianists and is countered not only by those leaders who synthesize the two but also by the positive anthropology revealed in the Marianist manual of pedagogy. Hence, the teaching ministry is a source of spirituality; indeed it is the sole source during those periods when the monastic routine was without the infusion of a Christian humanism.

The prevalent theme of Americanization in chapter 5 is represented by the Marianists' participation in the NCEA (National Catholic Education Association) and by the first Irish-American provincial, Bernard O'Reilly, who reflected an American activism, which the traditional German-speaking leaders of the province perceived as a deviation from the interior life. From that time until the Second Vatican Council the prevailing ideology rigidly fragmented the monastic from the apostolic.

The tensions between the modern high school and Marianist traditions, the dominant theme of chapter 6, was exacerbated by provincials who articulated a rigorist mentality. In opposition was Father William Ferree, who explicitly unified the apostolic and the monastic. He appropriated Chaminade's lay sodality spirituality and applied it to the school apostolate, stressing the graced unity of the Marianist way of life. Ferree influenced a generation of leaders in the Marianist sodality movement as well as in provincial administration during the 1960s. The modern high school was imbued with activism that was, as chapter 6 clearly illustrates, antithetical to the rigidity of the monastic routine.

The subsequent chapter highlights change and continuity in society, church, and the Marianists during the 1950s. The growth of the Society was evident in the missionary activity in Latin America, Africa, and Korea, as well as the formation of the Pacific Province. The racial integration of the St. Louis Province, continuous modernization of the University of Dayton and St. Mary's University, and the foundation of Chaminade College in Honolulu represent the transitions presaging the changes of the 1960s.

The Second Vatican Council, the evolution of the 1960s, and the developments in the academy form the context for the Marianist experience of profound changes in governance, spirituality, and ministry. The principles of collegiality, subsidiarity, and personal responsibility, blended with an incarnational spirituality, a general Christocentric humanism, and a "pilgrim people of God" ecclesiology, profoundly influenced religious life; these trends were incorporated into the Marianist spirit and the constitutional developments during this period. New lifestyles, team provincial government, and the movement toward nonschool apostolates represented a pluralism that generated a traditionalist reaction in the New York Province (established in 1961); polarization culminated in the formation of the Meribah Province centered in the community at Chaminade High School in Mineola, Long Island. Hence, the title of this chapter is "Renewal, Reform, and Reaction."

During the last two decades, the time frame of the epilogue, the emphasis is on those Marianists who articulated the intersection of past and present; my point of view and methodology shift from that of the historian to the journalist. With decreasing numbers, Marianists are experiencing a consensus that they are "Living in the Meantime" or "Between the Times." The epilogue concludes with a reflection on the ways the devotion to Mary relates to the historical self-understanding of the Society of Mary. Elizabeth Johnson's metaphor for the contemporary experience of religious life, the advent season of anticipation of the birth of new forms of religious life, is congenial to the Marianists, men of the Magnificat situated in their advent season, fragmented between times but generally integrated in a Christocentric humanism permeating governance, spirituality, and ministry.

CHAPTER ONE

Prologue:
William Joseph Chaminade
and the French Origins
1761–1850

❧ I ❧

THE SOCIETY OF MARY, UNLIKE OTHER APOSTOLIC CONGREGATIONS founded in the nineteenth century, grew out of a lay sodality; in this sense it was a "first order" that developed within a "third order." The Marianists are composed of brothers and priests who have dwelled over the past 180 years in a virtually unique state of social equality. Founded by William Joseph Chaminade in 1817, seventeen years after the first meeting of the Bordeaux Sodality, the Society of Mary was consciously dedicated to the rechristianization of France under the banner of Mary Immaculate.

The life of Chaminade (1761–1850) spanned the dramatic periods of the *ancien régime*, the Enlightenment, the French Revolution, the Napoleonic era, the romantic movement, the restoration of the monarchy, the political revolutions of 1830 and 1848, as well as the Industrial Revolution, symbolized by the introduction of the steam engine. Committed to a regimen of mental prayer and personal austerity even from his early teens, Chaminade was influenced by the French school of spirituality, by the Jesuit ideals of his older brother, Jean Baptiste, by Marian devotionalism, and by the charism of the Congregation of St. Charles at the seminary in Mussidan near his hometown of Périgueux. These influences sustained him during the culture war with the forces of dechristianization, a war that was fought not only on the field of ideology but in an actual theater of war in which most priests were considered enemies of the ascending republicanism.

The dialectic of traditional Catholicism and French secularism, despite the concordat between Napoleon and Pius VII, was the dominant force that shaped the ecclesial, the spiritual, and the political identities of religious activists: Gallicans and ultramontanists, accommodationists and preservationists, liberals and conservatives. Infused with a consciousness of their similarities to the apostolic age, the new religious congregations tended to be missionary in their drive to catechize a generation bereft of even a rudimentary knowledge of the creed and cult of Catholicity. Because the republican ideology was associated with "demonic" forces aimed at the dissolution of the sacred mysteries of the faith, the leaders of these congregations, including Chaminade, tended to construct a monastic-like cloister to defend a style of spirituality that blended warm affective devotion to Mary, the communion of saints, and to the Blessed Sacrament against the aggressive secularism of the larger culture.

But the apostolic-missionary activism broke out of the cloister with a view to ministering to young people, a ministry that for many Marianists provided alternative sources of spiritual energy dependent on religious, social, and political contexts. Though the story line of this journey from an idealistic youth to a founder of an international congregation has appeared as an inevitable development, the present author, struggling against the perception of events through the distorted lens of hindsight, is struck by Chaminade's deep sense of mission combined both with his Catholic pragmatism and a paradoxical openness to the civic culture of France.[1]

⊰ II ⊱

WILLIAM JOSEPH CHAMINADE, THE NEXT TO LAST OF FIFTEEN children, six of whom survived to adulthood, was born on April 8, 1761. Four boys entered the religious life or the diocesan priesthood: Jean Baptiste, the Jesuits; Blaise, the Recollects of St. Francis; Louis and William were ordained priests for their seminary's Congregation of St. Charles in 1785. William's father, Blaise, a man of modest means, ran a dry-goods shop in Périgueux. Catherine, his mother, had an enormous influence upon William. His first biographer remarked: "From her he received his gentleness, his affability, his moderation, his great prudence, and above all, his religious education." Besides instructing him in the creed, she imbued in him a strong devotion to Mary, "the soul of his holiness."[2]

At the suggestion of Jean Baptiste, who upon the suppression of the Jesuits had become ordained and had attained a teaching position in St. Charles College at Mussidan, Louis and, two years later, William entered this college to undertake classical studies. Located some ten miles south of the see city of Périgueux, Mussidan was a small town with the college on its periphery. Founded in 1744 by the bishop, Mussidan College also became a *petit-séminaire*, or minor seminary, under the direction of a community of diocesan priests, the Congregation of St. Charles, founded specifically for staffing this one institution. St. Sulpice in Paris, the premier seminary in France, was founded by Jean Jacques Olier as the principal locus of his society of diocesan priests dedicated to renewal of the priesthood and reform of the parish—hence the origin of the name Sulpicians. This Congregation of St. Charles at Mussidan, perhaps modeled on the Sulpicians or the Congregation of the Mission of St. Vincent de Paul (Vincentians), countered the prevailing trends of the times associated with departures from poverty within the religious orders and with the deistic intellectual climate.

Jean Baptiste was a strong role model for his younger brothers, both of whom committed themselves to study for ordination and became aspirants in the Congregation of St. Charles. After completing their Latin studies, they were assigned teaching duties as they pursued advanced training in the sciences and philosophy and later theology. Upon ordination, William and Louis became full members of the diocesan congregation. William was fifteen when he first began teaching, and he assisted his brother, Jean Baptiste, as business manager of the college. When Jean Baptiste became rector of the college, William succeeded to the position of business manager. According to the most recent biography of William Joseph Chaminade, it is certain that from 1783 to 1785 Louis attended Laon seminary in Paris, conducted by the Sulpicians, perhaps accompanied by William.[3] Here they would be instructed in scripture, liturgy, and homiletics. Jacques-André Emery, who became superior general of the Sulpicians in 1782, soon initiated a series of reforms to restore more strict adherence to the rule among seminarians and Sulpician directors, particularly at St. Sulpice in Paris.[4] Though William Chaminade frequently cited the writings of Olier, he did not actually imbibe the Olierian streams of the French school of spirituality until much later, when new editions of Olier's work were published in 1828.

William Joseph returned to Mussidan as a priest. He was primarily responsible for spiritual direction and teaching as well as being bursar of the college/seminary. He was now a full member of the Community of St. Charles with pastoral ministry at the local hospital and at Notre Dame du Roc with its notable pietà, which featured the crucified dead Jesus as well as Jesus as a young boy.[5] William's growth in spirituality began at Mussidan. With Jean Baptiste's permission, William Joseph made private vows of poverty, chastity, and obedience shortly after his first reception of communion. During this period he was enrolled in the Confraternity of the Rosary and the Confraternity of the Eucharist at the chapel of Notre Dame du Roc.[6]

His decision to enter the seminary had prompted him to enter the Congregation of St. Charles; as a "young ecclesiastic" he was, according to the constitution "to pay special honor to the divine childhood and hidden life of Jesus," a notion that may be traced back to Olier's metaphor that the seminary was the Nazareth experience for preordained ecclesiastics. Upon ordination William Joseph became a member of the second class, instructed "to honor in a special way the active life of Jesus." Mussidan closed before William could enter the third class, priests about thirty-six years old, who until they died were "to pay particular honor to the suffering life and death of our Savior."[7]

These classes emphasized three states of prayer experience of Jesus' life that are analogous to the "states" that permeate the French school of spirituality of Cardinal Bérulle, Charles de Condren, and Jean J. Olier. For example, in his description of Olier's dependence on the direction of Condren, Henri Bremond wrote that the founder of the Sulpicians absorbed his mentor's "essential doctrine of our duty of self-effacement, of sacrificing and annihilating self, in order to give place to the spirit of God. . . . In some manner, and despite himself, he had become familiar with nothingness, the *state* of childhood, the victim *state*. . . ."[8]

The Congregation of St. Charles in Mussidan promoted the notion of "state" as accessible to the neophyte, an illustration of the influences of the ideals of Olier as he incorporated them into the states of the seminary and priesthood, a popular rendering of the *esprit ecclésiastique*. The constitution of the Congregation of St. Charles also reflected Ignatian spirituality, particularly with its emphasis on "purity of intention." Marian devotion was evident in the rule directing each member "to recite every day the Little Office of the Immaculate Conception," a practice that was later incorporated in Chaminade's rules governing the Bordeaux Sodality. Despite its austerity, this rule underscored a relatively positive anthropology: frequent communion, "the Guidance of the Holy Spirit," and "to prefer, as much as possible, to avoid sin from a motive of pure love for the greater glory of God."[9]

Mussidan's spirituality was therefore grounded in a moderate asceticism and an affective devotion to Mary Immaculate and the Sacred Heart—all opposed to the spirituality of the Jansenists. (Blaise Chaminade was deeply ascetical, known for self-flagellation—that is, "taking the discipline"—and wearing a hair shirt.)[10] The small diocesan Congregation of St. Charles and the college/seminary were consciously in opposition to the prevailing trend among some religious houses to develop a cosmopolitan, even secular, tone.

After the Revolution, Chaminade would manifest severe disdain toward the Enlightenment, an ideology that he perceived as dedicated to the displacement of the supernatural with the natural law, and the displacement of faith's mysteries with science and the cult of reason. We do not know, however, his precise views of the principal writers of the Enlightenment, such as Montesquieu, Diderot, Voltaire, and Rousseau, as their work gained popularity before and during his time as a student of theology. Their general attack upon superstition, intolerance, and the hypocritical character of Catholic belief and practice no doubt alarmed Chaminade. Since he was living the so-called hidden life in the seminary before and after ordination and since he was aware of the lax ways of many ecclesiastics, perhaps he was not unsympathetic with the general criticism of the privileges of the First Estate—particularly its vast wealth, which frequently served aristocratic lifestyles rather than the corporal and spiritual works of mercy. John McManners, a scholar of Catholicism and the French Revolution, stated that

> the essential unifying conclusion of the Enlightenment . . . was the rejection of the idea of original sin. . . . Everyone agreed that man had an inalienable right to be happy here on earth. . . . For once Rousseau was at one with Voltaire. Reason [Voltaire] and sentiment [Rousseau] those contrasting inspirations of the age, conspired to proclaim that he was good in his nature and will to seek his own destiny. Enlightened self-interest was the well-spring of moral conduct, and toleration was the first of all virtues. These beliefs constituted the Enlightenment's new *doctrine* of humanity."[11]

Recent historical studies, including that of McManners, tend to agree that despite the later success of the dechristianization movement, the parish clergy on the eve of the Revolution were leading rather edifying lives. According to Ralph Gibson, the immediate pre-Revolution priest "was, on the whole, chaste, resident, and conscientious. Priests cut themselves off from the profane society and devoted themselves to propagating, in the pulpit, the confessional, a very particular model of Christianity." Gibson notes that the priests in most of France tended to be of "urban and/or elite origins," while their "model of Catholicism" was for the most part in opposition to "popular religion."[12] To cope with the recurring crises and tragedies of life—famine, disease, floods, and other manifestations of nature's capricious behavior—peasants had constructed an elaborate folk Christianity to achieve a sense of meaning and compensation within a context otherwise devoid of understanding.

Since the Council of Trent, the church had been struggling to channel the streams of popular religion within the "legitimate" boundaries of ecclesial life, that is, separate from the profane folk customs such as frolicking and dancing on special feast days and in memory of miraculous events associated with a shrine or a spring. As a member of the Congregation of St. Charles, imbued with the renewal of seminary life, William Joseph Chaminade would not have condoned these folk customs, but, nevertheless, he was ardently attached to popular religious expressions such as the shrine of Our Lady of Verdelais in the vicinity of La Réole. In later life he indicated his intention to make a pilgrimage to the shrine to pray for the recovery of the archbishop of Bordeaux, who was suffering an illness.[13] Even after the foundation of the Society of Mary, Chaminade desired to assume responsibility for his rural sanctuary.[14] It is notable that the reformed clergy, hostile to popular religion, were in opposition to "rural chapels, often the locus of spontaneous popular devotions."[15]

Also at Mussidan his experience in mental prayer on occasion entailed prostration before the statue of Notre Dame du Roc in the chapel under the direction of his congregation. This unique rendering of the Sorrowful Mother captivated him and remained a strong strand of his Marian devotion. Though it is difficult to discern the anthropological basis for these devotions of a young student, they do appear to be illustrative of traditional notions of popular religion perhaps moved beyond that context to a more sophisticated sphere of *haute spiritualité* in his personal prayer life. In any event, his spiritual formation did not easily fit into the general model of the "seminary-trained, urban, and bourgeois clergy" who on the eve of the French Revolution tended to be hostile toward popular religion. Indeed, elements of that religion appear to have been permanently etched into his *devotional* if not *theological* worldview.

❧ III ❧

WHEN KING LOUIS XVI CONVOKED THE ESTATES GENERAL IN JANUARY of 1789 with the intention of solving an increasingly distressing deficit and thereby forestall bankruptcy, he unintentionally fostered a climate of expectations among many clergy of the First Estate, located in those dioceses, primarily in the southeast, who were eager for reforms to reverse their downward economic mobility and to guarantee a more equitable system of representation in church and government. Even before 1789 these clergy struggled against several abuses, such as tithes going solely to bishops and abbots, and a system that allowed a nonresident ecclesiastic to collect revenue that never filtered down to the local pastors, or the inequitable imposition of the *décimes*, or church taxes, that ultimately went to the king's coffers. Many curés were also in solidarity with the reforms promoted by leaders of the Third Estate, such as an end to the privileges of the nobility, equality under the law, and, to accomplish these reforms, the convocation of a national assembly based on the abolition of the estates. In a sense the majority of the clergy and of the Third Estate were allies against the dominant forces in the *ancien régime*, the nobility and the episcopacy. The political and social discourse, derived from the philosophies of the Enlightenment, was reflected in many of the lists of grievances, the *cahiers*, that contributed to the heady atmosphere in May when the Estates General convened for the first time in 175 years.[16] A revolutionary dynamic had almost immediately charged the atmosphere by the end of June, and the Third Estate, joined by the lower clergy, successfully demanded that a national assembly be established, but against the wishes of many nobles and bishops, particularly the archbishop of Paris. The dynamic entailed a continuous movement to the left motivated by fear of repressive activity from the forces of privilege. This fear prompted the fall of the Bastille, the successful demand that the nobility and the church relinquish all their feudal privileges, the creation of popular assemblies and militia in the towns, and a revolutionary municipal government supportive of leftward politics and of rabid anticlericalism.

The dynamic of fear and reaction to the high price of bread led to a march on Versailles in October with the result that the king, consistently reluctant to "follow the crowd" through this period, was forced to move to Paris, and the National Assembly followed. The assembly faced the burden of solving the fiscal crisis; it had abolished the tithe and had indicated its commitment to paying salaries and administering church properties; on November 2, 1789, the assembly voted to nationalize the church and to assume responsibility for public charities, hitherto a principal role of the church.[17]

The rationale for this measure went beyond the resolution of the fiscal crisis: a clergy dependent on state salaries would seem to guarantee a sense of loyalty to the revolutionary government or at least be less likely to join the ranks of a counterrevolutionary movement; those who purchased the property—actually the bourgeois and the most prosperous peasant class— would be solidly tied to the revolution. This financial need and practical politics blended in the legislation against monasteries, except the teaching and nursing congregations. The so-called enlightened despots, such as Emperor Joseph of Austria, also operating under the principles of utility, seized the lands of the "idle" monks and nuns, the contemplative and mendicant religious orders. The French Constituent Assembly encouraged the monks to retire from their way of life by offering pensions and by transferring the monks to central locations. Monastic vows were henceforth to be prohibited. Characterized by impassioned argumentation, this antimonastic legislation, passed in February 1790, resulted in many monks choosing to leave, while the congregations of nuns remained, apparently for religious reasons, but also because of the lowly status of single women in French society. This hostility to monasticism represented in many of the *cahiers* of the lower clergy did not alienate them, but when the assembly (April 1790) voted against a measure affirming the unity of church and state, the clerical deputies nearly unanimously decried this vote as "national apostasy." The assembly's rationale was that it would be contrary to liberty and conscience for the state to protect religious belief.[18]

The Civil Constitution of the Clergy, passed on July 12, 1790, was based on the principle of "careers open to talents," assured election of curés and bishops by the voting citizens, that is, active citizens who paid taxes to the equivalent of three days' salary. Protestants and Jews could actually vote for pastors and bishops, and clergy could elect their vicars or regional administrators. The redesign of dioceses occurred in accord with the redesign of the map of France from traditional provinces to the modern departments. Bishops were to receive a salary of 12,000 *livres* annually, metropolitans 20,000, the archbishop of Paris 50,000 *livres*; curés received salaries ranging from 1,200 to 6,000 *livres* annually. The constitution was in the Gallican tradition but infused with revolutionary principles. Obviously the election of bishops and priests by groups of lay electors, though based on the apostolic era by some theorists, was the most controversial section of the constitution. Though there were negotiations between the king's representatives and those of Pope Pius VI to achieve a *modus vivendi* with the constitution, the assembly acted independently; it decided that all public officials, including the bishops and priests, must take an oath of fidelity to the constitution. As generally expected, the pope soon condemned the constitution, making it a matter of orthodox standing in the church for a bishop or priest to refuse to sign the oath. John McManners captures the profound impact of this imposition of the oath: "This marked the end of national unity and the beginning of the civil war. For the first time popular forces were made available to the opponents of the Revolution: the emigration [of nobles, bishops and soon the Royal Family] suddenly acquired a conscience . . . thus creating a refuge for every grievance."[19]

Only seven bishops took the oath, but over 50 percent of the curés did. Scholars advance several reasons for this strong show of support: the significance of geographic region relative to the practice of the faith; patriotic loyalty; material self-interest (salary and pension); political realism, the lack of strong episcopal leadership; and other religious, social, and economic reasons. The priests who rejected the oath, that is, the nonjuring or refractory clergy, resisted for various reasons, most of which were related to region and to their type of piety and ecclesiology; some moderate ultramontanists perceived the papacy as central to the faith while they saw France as the center of Catholic culture. A faction of the Jesuits (actually disbanded by royal decree in 1762) and most Jansenists, ardent Gallicanists, alienated by the papacy's long-standing opposition to their self-proclaimed role as almost a church within the church, took the oath; but the Sulpicians, moderately Gallican with an acknowledgment of the papacy's central role, were unanimously opposed to the oath, and their more than twenty seminaries were "strongholds of resistance."[20]

William Joseph Chaminade, a spiritual director in the Congregation of St. Charles in Mussidan and a priest at the chapel of Notre Dame du Roc and treasurer of St. Charles Seminary, was well known among the businessmen of the town as well as the clergy. The *cahiers* composed by the Third Estate in Mussidan were strongly Gallican but were blended with a reform spirit regarding the wealth of the church vis-à-vis the needs of the poor, the abuses of monasticism, and the end of taxation for the support of the papacy. Chaminade participated in the discussions that culminated in the composition of these *cahiers*, and this marks him as a priest at least sympathetic to the needs of the people rather than the privileges of the First Estate. We do not know his specific views on the eve of the Revolution, but he was on the side of the dissident faction that voted for two deputies, rather than their own bishop; the latter upon hearing this news stormed out of the meeting of the First Estate. Henceforth, Chaminade was a ready participant in the reform movement of 1789.[21] By the time the Constituent Assembly had enacted the Civil Constitution of the Clergy, Jean Baptiste Chaminade had died (January 24, 1790). By this time, however, William Joseph had become a dominant presence at St. Charles Seminary, and in response to the requirement to take an oath to the constitution Chaminade strongly opposed it. Though opposed to the constitution that made the church dependent on the "general will," without the requirement to take the oath, Chaminade may have followed a strategy governed by realism in anticipation of a probable accommodation between the papacy and the constitutional monarchy. Indeed, prior to the November enactment of the oath, Chaminade was supportive of the *Exposition of Principles on the Constitution* by Archbishop Boisgelin of Aix, which "summarized the case against the constitution in moderate language and appealed for an eleventh-hour compromise. Let the assembly suspend the execution until the Pope speaks."[22] However, the biographies of Chaminade cite the *Exposition* as if it were not a moderate statement but rather one that provided the ground for Chaminade to proclaim "Here I stand." When the oath was required, there was no room for compromise, and Chaminade did immediately and publicly refuse the oath. Though branded a nonjurist priest, he was not summarily declared an enemy of the nation even after he wrote an anti-constitutional pamphlet in the fall of 1790.[23]

Though refractory priests could not legally hold office, the Chaminades were allowed to remain at the seminary with salaries until replacements could be found. Encouraged by an old priest friend in Bordeaux, William purchased three acres of land called Saint Laurent, located on the outskirts of the city.[24] In response to the capture of the fleeing royal family in June 1791—partially as the rationale to gather troops to restore the unity of crown and altar and later in response to war with Austria and Prussia—the revolutionary government was continuously expanding the lists of those suspected of being traitors to the nation. The nonjuring clergy were viewed as co-conspirators with the *émigrés* allied with foreign enemies of France. By an act of the new National Assembly (May 1792) a refractory priest could be forced into exile by any twenty citizens listed on the voters' roles. The king, who would not sign this act, was a month later seized by a crowd who invaded the Tuilleries; when Prussia entered the war, any nonjuring priest was subject to deportation. The September massacres of 1792 were ignited by an impassioned group of Parisians—radicalized by fear of conspiracies and of the advancing Prussian army—who slaughtered a group of twenty nonjuring priests in one day. At the end of three days 220 priests and three bishops were among the 1,400 people killed. Canonized by Pope John Paul II in 1996, these 223 September priest-martyrs, according to McManners, once they refused the oath "as they were entitled to do, . . . were trapped in a monstrous procession of events; they had become smeared with the suspicions of treachery which they had no means of refuting."[25]

By this time Blaise and Louis Chaminade were compelled to go into exile—the former to the Papal States, the latter to Bilbao, Spain. William Chaminade, who had moved his parents into his home, Saint Laurent, was able to openly engage in pastoral ministry until the Jacobins had consolidated their power. Between the spring of 1793 and 1797 he was one of a handful of underground priests in Bordeaux. During the Reign of Terror as many as 2,000 priests were executed while 30,000 to 48,000 emigrated. In those areas such as the Vendée, where the civil war was intensely religious, the executions were most extensive.

Chaminade personally witnessed the growing dechristianization of France. There was the creation of a new secular calendar that deleted Sundays and feast days, configured on a ten-day week, ten months of the year. The Jacobin Republic of Virtue was based on a newly fabricated religion of the revolution with its own feast days, saints, liturgies to honor the pre-Christian era of the Roman republic and the heroes of the revolution. There were Festivals of Reason and binges of iconoclastic behavior; chapels and churches were seized for political cults and organizations. Various motives impelled the dechristianizers, ranging from the conviction that the church was determined to crush the Revolution to the general cult of a vaguely deistic nature.

John McManners described the psychology of dechristianization—"like the execution of the King, sacrilege was to be a gesture of defiance, a symbol of the determination to destroy the old world, a deliberate decision to press on beyond the point of no return, a final commitment to the oath 'to live free or die.'"[26] Though there was some relief from persecution with the Thermidorian reaction of August 1794, the conflict revived in 1797, and Chaminade's name turned up on a list that compelled him to go into exile in Saragossa, Spain, where he met his brother Louis. There is evidence that at Saragossa, where there is a famous statue of Our Lady of the Pillar, Chaminade experienced a sense of his mission to establish a new religious community in honor of Mary. Actually he may have first had the idea at Mussidan.

Bernard Dariès, whom Chaminade met again in Spain, had been considerably influenced by the Chaminade brothers at Mussidan. Vincent R. Vasey, S.M., described Dariès' Mariology as similar to Chaminade's and as primarily "Biblical, based particularly on the two pillars of the proto-gospel of Genesis and the Apocalypse's version of a woman clothed in the sun. From this conception of Mary emerges a woman victorious over the devil, the woman who crushes his head after a fierce struggle but only in the last days." Whether his plan was influenced by William Chaminade or he influenced the founder, Dariès, while in Spain, "elaborated a plan for a Society of Mary [in 1793], a name suggested by the Society of Jesus."[27] According to its stated purpose, the company or Society of Mary would have a three-part program: education, the praise of Mary, and the promotion of devotion to the Immaculate Conception. Though an attempt to found this community in Toledo failed to take root, there appears to be a connection between this statement and Chaminade's plan. Because Chaminade, at age twenty-two taught the twelve-year-old Dariès at Mussidan, one may surmise that Chaminade conveyed this charism to his impressionable student. It is interesting to note that two priests who later became founders of religious congregations in nineteenth-century France were influenced by Dariès. Louis

Marie Baudoin, founder of the Sons of Mary Immaculate, knew him in Spain; and Blessed Marcellin Champagnat, founder of the Marist Brothers, certainly knew of Dariès, as his correspondence includes a letter about Dariès' Society of Mary.[28]

<h1 style="text-align:center">⚜ IV ⚜</h1>

NAPOLEON BONAPARTE'S COUP D'ÉTAT RESULTED IN HIS APPOINTMENT as First Consul in October 1799, an event justified by a Jacobin threat to destabilize France during the war and the need for extraordinary measures to protect the nation. This ended the decade of Revolution and marked the beginning of the Napoleonic era. The nonjuring priests were welcomed back to France as a sign of a reconciliation which was formalized by the Concordat of 1801. This Concordat ended the schismatic constitutional church, provided freedom for Catholics to practice their religion and stated that "the Catholic Apostolic Roman Church is the religion of the great majority of French citizens."[29] All existing bishops were to resign, thereby terminating the constitutional church and the former Gallican Church as well; the state had the right to nominate bishops and was to pay salaries of bishops and priests. The pope also accepted the legitimacy of the transfer of ownership of formerly ecclesiastical property, while the clergy were to take a simple oath of allegiance. Napoleon successfully put an end to the religious conflict, which he considered divisive; a unified clergy would provide the religious and moral leadership so necessary in a society based on the inequities of wealth, power, and influence. Indeed, he explicitly perceived the role of religion as a force of social control: "If God wills it so, there have to be both poor and rich in the world, but afterwards and for all eternity things will be different."[30]

The immediate occasion of Chaminade's return was a decree by Napoleon of October 20, 1800, permitting nonjuring priests to return to France. About six weeks after Chaminade returned to Bordeaux he founded his Sodality of the Immaculate Conception. At Chaminade's request Archbishop de la Tour du Pin Montauban of Auch secured from the Congregation for the Propagation of the Faith (*Propaganda Fide*) Chaminade's appointment as Missionary Apostolic. At this time he was also appointed temporary administrator of the diocese of Bazas, south of Bordeaux.[31]

As a result of the Revolution, a generation of young people had been deprived of religious education, particularly catechism classes in preparation for First Communion and Confirmation: "A whole age cohort grew up almost without a Catholic culture."[32] As mentioned earlier, Chaminade

perceived the challenges of his era in light of an apostolic age, the establishment of a new network of ad hoc communities of faith that would lead
to a reintegration of religion and culture. The sodality was in the vanguard
of this movement to rechristianize France "from below."

In his constitution for the Society of Jesus, Ignatius Loyola set forth the
guiding principles "for an apostolate of an elite to the masses." From 1540,
when the first sodality was formed, to 1584, when Pope Gregory III recognized all existing sodalities to be united with the *Prima Primaria* sodality
in Rome, several such associations of the laity had been formed to engender
piety, to deepen the faith through reading, to engage in various forms of
ministry among the needy, and to promote devotion to Our Lady of the
Annunciation, later extended to other Marian titles. During a year of theological study in Bordeaux in the early 1780s, Chaminade had been introduced to sodalities that had been maintained after the suppression of the
Jesuits in 1762: the Student's Sodality at the Church of Ste. Colombe under
Father Lacroix and other sodalities that were nurtured by the Carmelites
and the Capuchins. Hence, Chaminade's vision of the sodality, derived from
his personal experiences in Bordeaux, was refined in the caldron of dechristianization.

In contrast to the Jesuit sodalities, each of which was composed of a
socially homogeneous group, Chaminade's sodality, in accord with the egalitarian aspirations of the age, was open to all classes at all stages of religious
understanding. According to a register of original members there were six
priests, nine teachers, fourteen salesmen, nine tailors, six merchants, three
coopers, two shoemakers, two bakers, a painter, a surgeon, an architect, a
saddler, a wig maker, and a butcher. However, since each of the men had
been a member of one of the disbanded sodalities, this was a highly trained
group of "disciples."[33] Essential to the sodality of Chaminade was its missionary activity; it was to be a "permanent mission comparable to the apostolic community in Jerusalem of St. Luke's account in the Acts of the
Apostles."[34] Chaminade described the missionary character of the sodality:

> In this age and in this period of renewal, religion demands something more of
> its adherents. It would have everyone work together, spurring on the zeal of its
> ministers and, under their guidance, striving to restore it. This is the spirit that
> is being inculcated in the new Sodalities. Each sodalist is a permanent mis-
> sionary and each sodality is an ongoing mission.

Adolf M. Windisch, S.M., quoted three reflections of Chaminade that con-
stitute a succinct description of the ecclesiology and spirituality of the
sodality.

What is a Sodality? It is a society of fervent Christians who, in imitation of the Christians of the early Church, try by means of their frequent meetings to have but one heart and spirit so as to form a single family not only as children of God, brothers of Jesus Christ and members of His Mystical Body, but also as children of Mary by means of a special consecration to her service and by an open profession of faith in the doctrine of her Immaculate Conception.

What is the nature of the Sodality? If there is question of a general definition, I would say the *genus proximus* is a society of free Catholics, of every age, of both sexes, and of every condition of life, who are dispersed throughout society, etc.; the *differentia prima* is to have the habitual exercise of the devotion to the Blessed Virgin in order to reach the final end of all Christian society.

The immediate end is the habitual exercise of a true and solid devotion to the Blessed Virgin . . . . The accomplishment of the obligations of this devotion leads to Jesus Christ, and Jesus Christ to God, the Sovereign Happiness, Who is the final end of the Sodality as for any other religious society.[35]

To evangelize "from below" meant that sodalists were to instruct those initially open to the faith, particularly those in the workplace and in the neighborhoods. The Men's Sodality was followed by the Young Ladies' Sodality on the feast of the Annunciation, March 25, 1802. They met independently and had a separate rule, but both were expected to adopt a routine prayer life and receive communion twice a month. Each had various offices with particular responsibilities and had several groups according to vocation in life. Chaminade held a monthly conference for the men and women's sodalities that included Mass, Benediction, recreation, and instruction on scripture, moral theology, church history, and Mariology. In 1803 married women, as well as unmarried women over thirty years of age and widows, formed a separate sodality, the Ladies of Retreat, because of their monthly retreat. In that same year the Married Men's Sodality was founded. Both groups were devoted to Mary and dedicated to promoting the younger sodalists and were to engage in visiting the sick and burying the dead. The men were specifically directed to visit hospitals and prisons. Because of the dominance of tradition, married women were limited to the sphere of the home as wives and mothers.[36]

Rules governing these sodalities and other groups involved in the Bordeaux Sodality under Chaminade's direction were revised with an emphasis on widespread participation through an elaborate set of offices at each level of the various groups. Of particular importance was the office of Prefect. Candidates were like the "ancient catechumenate, probationers [enrolled] not into a special elite corps but into a Christian community. The various officers were never singled out by particular calling but rather their leadership was because of experience in the community."[37]

The archbishop of Bordeaux, who had heartily supported and juridically recognized Chaminade's sodality, granted permission for it to move from its place on the Rue Saint Siméon to the new central gathering place, the Chapel of the Madeleine, which became an official oratory within the scope of four parishes. The archbishop appointed Chaminade an honorary canon of the cathedral and rector of the oratory. Apart from a few conflicts with pastors in the archdiocese, principally on the issue of the sodalists' responsibility to the Madeleine rather than to their parishes, the movement continued to flourish.[38]

As mentioned earlier, the monthly meetings of the sodalists entailed an extensive instruction. The sodality belonged to its members; at the meetings

> they sang; they listened to talks, debates, dissertations; they made known their difficulties and freely asked for explanations. Usually the sodalists did the talking; the Director [Chaminade] read all the manuscripts. He did not tolerate improvisation, but did not interfere in the meetings except to complete, reply, solve a difficult problem or conclude a debate by an appropriate exhortation. He let the young people have the satisfaction of considering the evening their work. . . . All of these meetings, no matter what their dominant character, helped to create and keep an *esprit de corps* which aided the members in the practice of Christian life by freeing them from the [inhibitions of] human respect.[39]

During his underground ministry in Bordeaux (September 1792–May 1795) Chaminade met Marie Thérèse de Lamourous and became her spiritual director from 1795 until her death in 1836. Born of a noble family in Barsac and nurtured on scripture, Thomas à Kempis, and the lives of the saints, Marie Thérèse Lamourous pursued a high spirituality blended with various ministries, particularly to the education of youth and to the imprisoned priests in Bordeaux. Chaminade corresponded with her from Spain and seemed to have been deeply affected by her strong desire for living in God's will. He wrote to her how each of them should attempt to fight their natural inclinations in order to "transcend to divine love, and interest in God alone."[40] Upon his return from Spain, Chaminade secured Lamourous's help to start the women's section of the Sodality and become its first president. Soon a situation arose that entailed Lamourous's discernment, with the encouragement of Chaminade, to enter a self-styled religious life and take charge of a recently established home for young women of the streets or who were pregnant and unmarried. With the House of the Good Shepherd suppressed, there was a desperate need for such a facility, which was called the Miséricorde. Chaminade was appointed superior of the home that opened in 1801. After several financial crises, it finally achieved stability a few years later and thrived with over three hundred "penitents."[41] Chaminade's devotion to Mary was manifested also in his spiritual devotion to several such Marys and Marthas in his own experience.

As Chaminade's Bordeaux Sodality expanded and subdivided and accepted other groups outside the city as affiliated sodalities, the director became a notable figure on the religious scene. Napoleon's government was conscious of the potential danger associated with the development of religious zeal among large groups led by former nonjuring clergy with tendencies toward loyalty to the Bourbon dynasty. As early as 1802 the police reported on the right-wing sentiments of the sodality of Bordeaux:

> The Sodality dedicated to the cult of Mary under the direction of Chaminade increased its numbers of faithful each day. Frequent conferences take place there and they exhume in an outrageous manner the memories of Voltaire, d'Alembert, Diderot and those they dub *philosophes*.[42]

The conflict between Napoleon and Pope Pius VII reverberated in the relationship between the police and the Bordeaux Sodality. On June 11, 1809, Napoleon posted decrees in Rome that he was annexing the Papal States, making Rome an imperial free city, and placing the pope on an annual salary. That same day Pius replied with a bull excommunicating all those who have "committed acts of violence against the ecclesiastical communities and against the temporal rights of the Church and the Holy See. . . ."[43] Three days later Napoleon himself was excommunicated. With the unrealistic intention of preventing this bull of excommunication from being published in France, Napoleon and his government proceeded to prosecute anyone violating this policy. Jean Baptiste Hyacinthe Lafon, a member and a former prefect of the Bordeaux Sodality, and his associates of the Paris sodality printed copies of the bull of excommunication and distributed them widely in September 1809. Because of the suspicion that the Bordeaux Sodality was behind this activity, Napoleon explicitly ordered his police to investigate the matter, which led to the proscription of the sodality as "a veritable hotbed of fanatics."[44]

There is some histographical confusion with the early-nineteenth-century sodalities. The French word for sodality, which historians have seldom translated, is *congrégation*. The date of the Paris sodality's origin is February 1801, when six students under the leadership of a former Jesuit, Jean Baptiste Bourdier-Delpuits, were formed according to the promises associated with the traditional Jesuit sodality dedicated to the Virgin Mary. Recent scholars date the royalist character of the Paris *Congrégation after* the fall of Napoleon. They also emphasize its principal identity as an association of laymen that engaged in good works and as a vital force in the religious revival of France.

One of these scholars, G. de Bertier, notes that the Congrégation spawned other sodalities such as the Bordeaux group of William Chaminade, without making any distinctions between the two. According to tradition, the Bordeaux Sodality met first on December 8, 1800, but we know promises were made on February 2, 1801, without any causal connection with events in Paris. During Napoleon's first exile, the Bordeaux Sodality was revived amid a display of impassioned welcome of the Royal Family. Charles S. Phillips, who does not mention the Bordeaux Sodality, refers to the *Congrégation* as originally a traditional Jesuit group which by 1804 had attracted leading members of the nobility, thus revealing the symbiosis of ultramontanism and ultra-royalism.[45] Adrien Dansette refers to the Congrégation as originating with the Jesuits. Though he does not mention Chaminade's Bordeaux group, he describes its distinctive marks even to mentioning one of its special ministries, "the education of chimney sweeps."[46] He too identifies it as less political and more religious. There is no doubt that Chaminade and many sodalists were enthusiastic royalists; only the monarchy could guarantee the safety of the altar.

During the period from 1810 to 1814 sodalists dwelled in anonymity, but they became an underground apostolic community. Chaminade explicitly discussed the development over the years of individual sodalists who felt called to live more fully the Christian life by taking temporarily one or more of the vows associated with the religious life: obedience, chastity, and a spirit of poverty.

As director, Chaminade guided these individuals and referred to them as living in a "State," that is, "the State of religious living in the world." In response to a letter from Adèle de Batz de Trenquelléon, a young woman from Agen desirous of beginning a group of women religious engaged in apostolic works in the world, Chaminade asked her to join the Bordeaux Sodality and referred to those members in "the Religious State" who professed temporary vows. Though political events precluded moving to Bordeaux, Adèle's group lived according to the principles of the "State." Three years later (1816) Chaminade and Trenquelléon founded the Daughters of Mary in Agen, based on a constitution composed by Chaminade that placed the group in a cloister with solemn vows. In 1836 a Third Order Regular that was engaged in an active ministry was attached to the Daughters.[47] Shortly after Adèle's initial letter, the sodality was restored to full legal status with the return of the Bourbon dynasty. During Napoleon's one hundred days, however, the sodality's monarchist loyalties led to its suppression.

From its origins those called to the Religious State within the sodality were not to distinguish themselves publicly from the other sodalists, but their zeal made them noticeable.[48] According to Chaminade's first biographer, Joseph Simler, S.M., a group of fifteen within the "State" (ca. early 1815) united their efforts for their own "satisfaction" and the mission among the people of Bordeaux. They became a "religious community" within the sodality by daily reception of communion, meditation, examination of "prevision" and of conscience. "Each one of us assumes the obligation to form one student in the true spirit of Christianity." They professed only a three-month vow of obedience to the director, Father Chaminade, and submitted their way of life for his approval.[49]

It appears that the director of the sodality had long considered the foundation of a religious community within the sodality. On May 1, 1817, Jean Baptiste Lalanne, a young seminarian twenty-one years of age and a sodalist for seven years, successfully sought Chaminade's consent to join him as a director of the sodality. The founder considered this event to be a sign that Providence was affirming a "plan I have been pursuing for twenty years," a new religious community. He told Lalanne, "The religious life is to Christianity what Christianity is to humanity. It is just as imperishable in the Church as the Church is imperishable to the world. We can not hope to reestablish Christianity without institutions permitting men to practice the evangelical counsels."[50] On October 2, 1817, five sodalists—Jean Baptiste Lalanne, a teacher and soon to be a priest; Jean Baptiste Collineau, a future student for the priesthood; two businessmen, Dominique Clouzet and Louis Daguzan; and Auguste Perrière, a teacher—committed themselves to the religious life under the direction of Chaminade. Though the founder postponed the profession of vows, this is one of the principal foundation dates of the Society of Mary. (The Society has been entitled "Marianists" since 1946, to distinguish it from the Society of Mary, the Marists, founded in Lyons in 1816 by Jean Claude Colin. Other Marian congregations founded in the early nineteenth century are the Oblates of Mary Immaculate founded by Bishop Eugène de Mazenod, the Little Brothers of Mary (Marists) founded by Marcellin Champagnat, and the Sons of Mary Immaculate founded by Louis Baudouin.)[51]

After they had adopted a provisional rule, the first five members professed temporary vows in the sacristy of the Madeleine Chapel on December 11, 1817. During the first solemn retreat of the Society of Mary, these five members professed perpetual vows publicly before the community. Two sodalists had joined the five, Jean Baptiste Bidon and Antoine Cantau, both of whom were coopers of the artisan class; they made three-year vows.

Hence, from these origins the Marianists included priests—Lalanne had been ordained—and teaching and working brothers. After their vow ceremonies, they returned to their professions or trades and continued to attend meetings of the sodality. On that notable May 1, 1817, when Lalanne joined the founder, the latter said that "it would be difficult . . . [and] inopportune . . . to revive older [religious] institutes and to give them the forms that they had before the Revolution." Chaminade was convinced that "one can be a religious under a secular appearance." He concluded that professing the three vows was the essence of their religious association. Hence, he shared with Lalanne his intention "to leave the association without a title, without a habit and without a special civil status."[52]

The first constitution was approved by Archbishop Charles d'Aviau in December 1818; the association had an official name, the Institute of Mary, the constitutional title of the Society of Mary. In 1825 there was civil incorporation of aspects of the rule, but the Marianists have never adopted a traditional religious habit; they have remained "secular in appearance"—no small matter in a culture greatly influenced by an anticlerical animus; it could be interpreted also as an expression of the egalitarian aspirations of the age.

Lalanne's provisional constitution, though not extant, was intended to be a refinement of the community's dual character as composed of a distinctive group of religious bound together by vows, and as sodalists living in the world. Chaminade's 1818 Constitution, written by Brother David Monier, was derived from the one Chaminade composed for the Daughters of Mary in 1816. It opened with "The Object" of the Institute, which enumerated three points entailed in uniting and consecrating oneself to God; the first of these, of course, was the profession of vows as a means of "seeking perfection," a formulaic statement of all religious congregations. The second point reflects the permanent-mission character of the Society "to persuade those who live in the world to lead a Christian life." The third point underscored the fact that their lives were to be in the world as well, but they must "strengthen and defend themselves against the contagion of the world to which their position exposes them." With what appears to have been Chaminade's characteristic tendency to balance a negative comment—contagion of the world—with a positive statement of faith and hope, he stated that the vocation to the Society is "a severe test" but through "the intercession of Mary whose children they are, . . . the Spirit of God . . . will never abandon them."[53]

This statement evidences a distinctive Mariological development, particularly the fourth vow of stability, by which each Marianist was committed "to constituting himself permanently and irrevocably in the state of a servant of Mary . . . [by] a devotedness to the Blessed Virgin with the filial design of spreading her knowledge and call."[54] Included in filial devotion to Mary Immaculate was the intention to transform oneself into full participation in the Body of Christ. The Marianist men wear a ring (Daughters of Mary have worn one since their origins in the "State" in Agen) to symbolize the permanence of the filial bond, one patterned after Christ's filial piety.

"The Means" by which Chaminade's Institute was to achieve the stipulated end was through the establishment of three offices, implicitly entrusted to the superior, but actually divided into elected officials on the general level and with appointed officers on the local level. The superior "was entrusted principally with carrying out in moral and religious matters the three offices . . . Zeal, Instruction and Temporalities."[55] Analogous to Christ's life of prayer, teaching, and work, manifested in the sodality offices of prayer, instruction, and works, the offices were headed by three elected officials who with the superior general, the founder during his lifetime unless he resigned, formed the council, while on the local level these three offices were appointed. Though these offices have evolved in accord with principles of adaptation and renewal, there are still three offices in the late 1990s: religious life, education, and temporalities.

The director of zeal was charged with "encouraging the perfect practice of the counsels" or vows, which entails a *haute spiritualité* associated with a particular path: preparation, purification, and consummation. Analogous to the traditional path of spirituality—the purgative, the illuminative, and the unitive—Chaminade's three groups of virtues entailed a journey from preparation, that is, the separation from the world to gain self-control by mortification, through purification, a direct cleansing of one's repeated failures and malicious intentions, to consummation, "a self-abnegation" characterized by "humility, modesty and complete renunciation of the world, . . . [and] a conformity of Christ and Mary."[56]

Though Chaminade was not yet conversant with the corpus of Jean Jacques Olier's writings, the latter composed a tripartite formula for mental prayer that presaged Chaminade's system aimed at apostolic action: "Adoration, Communion, and Cooperation; Jesus before our eyes, Jesus in our hearts, and Jesus in our hands."[57] The application of the method was to be a continuous repetitive process for beginners to the more adept. It was accessible to all Marianists and was intended not only to strengthen one's separation from the world's contagion but actually to prepare one to negotiate in the world from a position of strength and to make one more conscious of the spiritual basis of community. Recall that Chaminade professed private vows at age fourteen and had been engaged in refining the meaning of the evangelical counsels within the continuous dialectical tension with the dechristianization process—the contagion of the world—for many years.

The head of zeal was charged with responsibility for liturgy, for the religious material culture, for elevating the moral climate, and for promoting the cloister and activities of the members of the community. The 1818 Constitution was composed before the congregation had its own school, but the head of instruction was in charge of preparing each member "in such a way that he can explain simply to the people of the world the advantages and the necessity of a Christian life." To form members of the permanent mission entailed imparting "the maxims and practices of religion," imbuing a sense of Christian morality, and "developing in time the signs of their vocation." The "elite" among the head of instruction's students were to be particularly formed as "teachers for the kind of schools that have been accepted." He was also responsible for instruction in the "humanities" in accord with the wishes of the civil and ecclesiastical authorities.[58] The head of instruction was additionally charged to relate to those outside the Institute by "reuniting in Sodalities under the auspices of Mary the various persons in whom the spirit of religion has been awakened or has not been destroyed by the world."[59] When the Marianists assumed responsibilities for boarding schools, free schools, and normal schools, the duties of the head of instruction obviously expanded and related to the various civil and ecclesiastical agencies responsible for elementary and secondary education.

The responsibilities of the head of temporalities were not stipulated in detail in Chaminade's first constitution, but the 1839 document did assign to the head of temporalities the duty to provide for all the material and economic needs of the community from room and board to property and buildings. He would also establish those works of charity to the sick and the poor that were extensions of the congregation.[60]

Chaminade remarked that the members "should take part in the various works within the measure of their capacity and their means." For example, the priests within the community should participate only in those activities that are "in accord with their holy ministry. However, everyone should embrace his work with joy as the debt of sin, as a debt to the community, and as a debt to charity." The heads of zeal and instruction were to work with the head of temporalities "when the responsibility of the works of charity are equally divided." Chaminade concluded this section with the remark that the superior "is the center and the bond of the three offices: to him belongs Zeal, Instruction, and the soul of the Temporalities."[61]

The mixed character of the Society was not spelled out in this primitive constitution. In explaining the 1839 Constitution, the founder stated that the priests should occupy the principal offices of the Society: superior general, provincials, the offices of zeal and instruction, novice master, directors (or superiors) of larger institutions, preachers of retreats and parish missions, and directors of the sodalities. Teaching brothers could occupy the office of temporalities; free public schools were exclusively brothers' schools, while they could teach in other types of school. In short Chaminade said, "The priests were the light and salt of society."[62] However they have always remained a minority of the membership. (In the nineteenth century about 10 percent were priests, while in the twentieth century they were around 10 to 15 percent, except after 1970, when the number of priests rose to 30 percent.) From the time of the mid-nineteenth century (1858) the provincial office of head of instruction was filled by a teaching brother. By custom, at the local level a priest could be under a brother's authority as director of a school, but the brother had no responsibility for the priest's pastoral duties.[63] As late as 1865, there were nearly one thousand Marianists, but only forty were priests. One brother had considered separating secondary-school teaching brothers from those in primary education, because the former were more "cultured." But Chaminade stated in the Constitution of 1839: "The only difference between our teaching Brothers is in the assignment they are given." The working brothers were assigned to all the houses but, like the teaching brothers, they had a separate novitiate and in the local houses formed their own communities. Chaminade frequently referred to the principle "union without confusion," as the governing maxim for the Society.[64] According to Vincent Vasey, S.M., Chaminade, the royalist, was not accommodating to the age when he united the three groups into one society. "He saw his foundations as the Church in miniature, a reflection of the Church's own authority or universality." Since the church is the "continuation on earth of Christ, His Mystical Body . . . so the Society [of Mary] was to include all persons."[65] In a letter to the archbishop of Besançon, Chaminade explained the union without confusion:

> The three classes in the Society of Mary form really one body, such as the children of St. Benedict were for a number of centuries. The children of Mary take pleasure in regarding the great St. Benedict as specially sent by God to people Europe with numerous colonies of true religious. All three in the same spirit have the same end. But in consideration of the needs of the present age and of religion they run towards the eternal crown by different ways, that is by employing different means, according to their age, condition, and talents; all have in view their own sanctification and the salvation of their neighbor. These different classes of the Society form three distinct corporations. It is the same

body; they are linked together in the same works; they collaborate under the same head, as different members of the body obey one soul in the various functions they carry out.

Each member of the Society should keep himself in peace as to the rank that is assigned him, convinced that in the body all the members cannot be in the same place, but that all are equally necessary for the body and that the excellence of each member is to fulfill well the function that is confided to him by God, whatever it happens to be. If because of the need of time and circumstances and talents a religious teacher is named the superior of an establishment, the priest, Head of Zeal of this house, doubtless should give the superior marks of respect and deference in what concerns the order of the house and the maintenance of school regularity. But the priest does not depend on the superior in the exercise of his functions, neither in what concerns time nor modality. If the superior would find some abuse or disorder, he will refer the matter to the Superior General.[66]

The social composition of the Society derived from this document may be as close to the three Estates of the *ancien régime* as it was to the ideals of the French Revolution. Perhaps the significance of the mixed character was its relationship to the spirit of equality under the law, a departure from the old regime and in accord with a major result of the French Revolution. Hence, the mixed character of the Society did indeed represent the aspirations of the age.

In accord with traditional principles of governance of religious orders and with the centralized character of the French state, which achieved further rationalization by Napoleon's rule and subsequent governments, the Society of Mary's authority was centralized in the office of superior general, "the head, the shoulder and the bond of the whole Society . . . all who are united to him and are under his obedience." He appoints all the superiors except the three officers, his assistants, who form the council and are elected. He assigns, removes, sends, and recalls the religious at a time and place of his desire. Processed in council were all serious business arrangements—buying and selling property, relations with the Holy See, and the French civil authorities, publishing the superior general's own writings, and "the exclusion of persons already excluded." If the council disagrees with the superior general on these matters, the council's decision stands.[67]

The Constitutions were sent to Rome for the pope's approval. Chaminade was delighted with the news that Pope Gregory XVI said that the Daughters of Mary and the Society of Mary "are worthy of every commendation."[68] The pope, however, did not specify approval of the constitution but rather issued a decree of praise. Chaminade misunderstood the communique as he stated that "our constitutions . . . have [been] liberally praised and approved

. . . by the Holy See."[69] Shortly after receiving news of the papacy's praise for the Marianists, Chaminade wrote a letter to the retreat masters Georges Caillet, Jean Baptiste Fontaine, and Jules César Perrodin. Noting that the "vicar of our Lord Jesus Christ" had encouraged the Society to "instill the spirit of our constitution and works" Chaminade set the theme of the letter by quoting St. Paul's dictum, *"The letter kills but the spirit quickens."*[70]

Since the retreat masters were amid preparations to direct annual retreats for Marianist communities, Chaminade focused on those areas that the Society had in common with other religious orders, the areas that distinguish "the Society of Mary and the Institute of our Daughters of Mary from other religious orders," and the areas of general teaching ministry, which are "special and uniquely Marianist." The common area among the orders is the profession of the three principal vows; the path to "Christian perfection" is based on the model of Jesus Christ, "who was poor, chaste, and obedient." Hence, members of all orders "oblige themselves with exalted holiness of vows to poverty, virginal chastity, and evangelical obedience." The founder warned against the enslavement to the letter of the vows by circumscribing "what is strictly necessary, from what is fitting. . . . With the letter as their guide, they tell us they have measured the full extent of this duty."[71]

In contrast, those "who strive with all their hearts to practice the spirit of these vows act in a way altogether different; they strive constantly to become more poor, more like true disciples of Jesus Christ, and more like Jesus Christ himself, who declared poverty blessed and who even made it Divine in His adorable person. Oh, how happy they are. . . . The poverty of Jesus Christ is indeed a treasure."[72]

It was not coincidental that Chaminade focused on poverty rather than chastity or obedience. As a student of the history of religious communities, Chaminade concluded that the spirit of poverty "draws down the blessings and love of God," while the "love of riches" tends to destroy communities. He perceives the violation of the spirit of poverty within the context of recent history. "You can say in all truth that the origin and cause of the Revolution in France came of the immense properties which a great number of religious possessed, against their vow of poverty."[73] Besides this historical perspective as a basis for his emphasis on poverty, there was the practical consideration that derived from the penchant among Marianists, such as Jean Baptiste Lalanne, to imprudently raise expenditures with little considerations of the Society's indebtedness.

As will be explored later in this chapter, conflicts over finances, indebtedness, and rapid expansion entailed severe battles over authority between local directors and Chaminade. Convinced that the hand of God had been directing him as founder, Chaminade considered these conflicts in the contexts of the relationship between evangelical poverty and faith in the providential character of the foundation and development of the Marianists.

The Marianist vow of stability "is certainly the distinguishing feature and family character of both of our orders. We are in a special manner the auxiliaries and instruments of the Blessed Virgin in the great work of moral reform, of support and spread of the faith and, by that fact, the sanctification of our neighbor." Because Mary Immaculate has traditionally been portrayed as crushing the serpent, she is understood as reducing all heresies, "bit by bit . . . , to the silence of oblivion."[74] Chaminade considered religious indifference as the dominant heresy of the era but against this trend toward "universal apostasy, Mary's power stands undiminished. We firmly believe she will overcome this heresy . . . because she is today, as she always has been, the incomparable Woman, the Promised Woman."[75]

Though other religious orders have cultivated a strong devotion to Mary, the vow of stability set the Marianists apart: "What I consider as being the specifying characteristic of our order, and what appears to me as being without precedent among known foundations is . . . that we embrace the religious life in Mary's name and for her glory." As auxiliaries of Mary, these two communities are entrusted "with the ingenuity and inventiveness of her almost boundless charity and we make a vow to serve her faithfully until the end of our days." In contrast to Rousseau's Social Contract, which portrayed humanity "born free but, forever in chains," Chaminade proffered what he called "a sacred . . . contract," whereby the Marianist family, allied with Mary, can liberate humanity from its chains of religious indifference.[76]

In tandem with this liberation theme was the Marianists' commitment to "teaching the Christian way of life . . . as the object of a special vow." The Brothers of the Christian Schools, commonly called Christian Brothers, professed a vow of "teaching children gratuitously," which implied catechesis. The Jesuits took a "vow of teaching children." But neither the Jesuits' vow nor that of the Christian Brothers is as specific as the Marianist "special mission," which was symbolized by the Marianists' continuous commitment to Mary's words at Cana: "Do whatever He tells you." The response was the Marianist mission "to perform all the works of Zeal and Mercy for our neighbors. Consequently under the general letter of teaching the Christian way of life, we accept all possible means [not just teaching] of preserving or curing our neighbor from the infection of evil [leading to indifference], and in this spirit, make it the object of a *special vow*."[77] This vow was removed at the request of the Vatican during the approval process of the order after Chaminade's death because vows were understood to be commitments of a spiritual path of perfection. The founder perceived "teaching the Christian way of life" as inherently evangelical, as permeated with the life of Christ in mission, and as in a filial relation with Mary and in the three evangelical vows.[78]

The "making of Christians" was so essential to the ministry of the Family of Mary that the retreat masters were told to remind the members that they "were missionaries of Mary," and that they should not "descend from the high state of apostles in order to degrade themselves to the base level of workers in the educational factories of our times." Chaminade's reaction to the increasingly irreligious educational practices was consistent with his general view of the anti-Christian bases of modernity. Included in this apostolate were the working brothers, who "through their labors, zeal, and prayers . . . spread the reign of Jesus and Mary in souls. Their part is really so beautiful! New Josephs, they are charged with assisting and sustaining the children of the holy family in their arduous ministry."[79] Ever conscious of his role in representing the spirit of the foundation, Chaminade composed his letter to the retreat masters as an epistle on the distinctive marks of the family of Mary's ministry within the context of rechristianization in the new apostolic age. Many of the sodality's works for the poor were adopted by the Marianists. The Sodality of Chimney-Sweeps, first assembled at the Madeleine, was approved by the government in 1819 and joined with the Sodality of Deferred First Communions in 1821. The sodality's Christian doctrine to the sick in the hospitals and the care of juvenile prisoners and an orphanage at Besançon were all principally dedicated, like the schools, to forming new Christians.

The 1839 Constitutions underscored Chaminade's openness to any ministry related to its missionary character, one that was based on understanding the signs of the times. "The Society of Mary does not exclude any kind of enterprise." However, the chapter "On Christian Education" entailed a commitment to "all the means by which religion may be inculcated in the mind and heart of men . . . to train them from the tender years of childhood to the most advanced age, in the fervent and faithful practices of a Christian life."[80] The Constitution stipulated the types of schools run by the Society of Mary: "Free Primary Schools, Higher Schools, normal schools, and arts and trades schools." Also listed as works were "Sodalities, Retreats, and Missions."[81]

The Bordeaux Sodality had a strong educational dimension: instruction in the faith, organized lectures, conferences on specific topics, and the proliferation of catechism classes for young aspirants to the Sodality. Several sodalists were teachers, including Louis Arnaud Lafargue and Guillaume Darbignac, two men who left middle-class careers to teach the poor. Impressed with their religious commitment, Chaminade formed these men according to the rule of Jean Baptiste de la Salle, founder of the Brothers of the Christian Schools dedicated to teaching the poor. They were one of the largest of the teaching orders in France, with one thousand brothers and 121 schools enrolling about thirty-six thousand students in 1792.[82] When this order was reestablished, Chaminade contacted the superior about his aspirants to the community. Two Christian Brothers were sent to Bordeaux to join them, and the archbishop appointed Chaminade the community's ecclesiastical superior. When the community grew, the director of the sodality provided his home of Saint Laurent as the first post-Revolution novitiate in France where Chaminade continued as the spiritual director. Ultimately the brothers were transferred to their headquarters in Toulouse.[83]

Three of the original seven Marianists were teachers at a private secondary school under the direction of Jean Baptiste Estebenet. Under Napoleon, secondary schools came under the University of France, the central body of twenty-six councilors headed by a grand master. This task was implemented on the district level (there were twenty-seven districts) by a superintendent assisted by a staff of inspectors. With a monopoly on secondary education in France, no school could be opened without the approval of the university nor could one teach in the schools without having been authorized by the grand master. Religious orders were permitted to open colleges with a six-year curriculum, but the final seventh year had to be at a *lycée*, a state secondary school with a seven-year curriculum. Responsibility for primary schools devolved upon the communes, which were to authorize the clergy to run these schools; without their services such schools would have been "almost totally inefficient."[84] When two sodalists of Bordeaux offered to finance a secondary school, Chaminade agreed; and after receiving authorization by the university, it opened in 1818. Eventually the Marianists took over Estebenet's school, and though he had been a sodalist, he later joined the Jesuits. To have acquired the best secondary school in Bordeaux (i.e., Estebenet's school) was a considerable achievement.

While presiding over a retreat for the Daughters of Mary in Agen, the bishop urged Chaminade to establish a primary school in his see city, some seventy-five miles southeast of Bordeaux. He was told that the townspeople had refused to admit the Christian Brothers (popularly known as "Ignorantins" because of their habit and their association with the *ancien régime*). Since the Marianists dressed in a modest, middle-class attire, they did not offend the prevailing anticlerical sensibilities. Convinced of the need to respond vigorously to religious indifference, as well as to the plight of the poor, the Marianists began a school at Agen that became so successful it attracted favorable comment from the liberal press which dissipated any rumor of religious fanaticism among the Marianists. The reports of the *Journal du Lot-et-Garonne* noted that the Marianists were dedicated "to the sublime ideal of the moral reformation of France by beginning with the generation not perverted."[85] Limited to the indigent, the quality education at this free school at Agen soon attracted middle-class parents who had their pastors provide them with certificates of indigence. The Marianists expanded their primary and secondary education to a large estate Villeneuve-Sur-Lot, a small town near Agen in the South and to St. Remy in the Franche-Comté in northeastern France. Next to Bordeaux in importance, St. Remy represented the wide-ranging ministries of the Society: a secondary school, a normal school, an agricultural and professional school, sodalities and a retreat center for lay teachers.[86]

The Marianists entered Alsace through the mediation of Brother Rothéa, a Marianist from Alsace and an instructor of catechetical pedagogy; he approached Father Ignatius Mertian, founder of the Brothers of the Christian Instruction. Ultimately these latter brothers responded to the request of the pastor in Colmar, and soon Brother Rotheá was assigned to the primary school. After two years the Brothers of the Christian Instruction disbanded; four brothers joined the Marianists, who assumed responsibility for two schools in Alsace; and by 1850 there were twelve schools in Alsace. From there the reputation of the Society spread to Fribourg, Switzerland, in the 1830s and, in response to a request from Bishop von Ketteler of Mainz, they took charge of a new central school in 1851. When Chaminade died in 1850 there were 62 schools and 470 Marianists (20 priests and 450 brothers, including 157 working brothers).[87]

The diversity of the Marianist ministries was in accord with Chaminade's notion of the universality of the Society of Mary. Engaged in all phases of education, Marianists were committed to any activity that would vitalize the Christian mission. Students represented all classes; the wealthy would be attracted to private boarding schools; the middle classes to Marianists' business-education; and pre-professional groups to the traditional classical curriculum; the artisan-class and peasant families cherished the Society's emphasis on elementary education, moral formation, and improvement in social behavior. From Chaminade's point of view, each of these types of schools was the equivalent of the sodality that guided the graduates through adulthood into mature Christianity.[88]

The universality of the new Society was in the context of rechristianizing a nation that had been so affected by the *philosophes* of the Age of Reason. Because that "spirit of philosophy" had been perceived to have been all pervasive, reaching "the smallest hamlets, . . . all ages, all classes, and ingeniously using all kinds of means," the Society of Mary must "engage in different types of works in which we form, or cause to be formed, men who can meet this danger effectively." Despite his opposition to political ideologies, Chaminade demonstrated a sense of political realism in his pursuit of legal approval for the Society of Mary, the Daughters of Mary, and their subsidiary institutions. Hence, as noted earlier, he submitted civil statutes for state approval of the Society of Mary as a charitable association to train teachers for free public education with divisions for arts and crafts. Foundational to Marianist education was the ecclesial commitment to form Christians and to elevate the general moral life of students and the community, the latter a goal in accord with sentiments of the bourgeoisie.[89]

Marianist pedagogical training articulated in the publication of a manual beginning in 1851, the year after the founder's death, may be traced to the thought of Chaminade and Lalanne. As early as 1822 the founder stated: "What ought to fill us with joy is that our call to the ministry of teaching is a real apostolate which ought to induce us to labor in courage and patience, with unbounded confidence in Jesus and Mary."[90] He particularly emphasized patience: "We should draw the people and in a special manner the young generation, by all possible means, by kindness, amiability and patience."[91]

In the 1839 Constitution there is a reference to the importance "to review methods . . . at regular intervals . . . to improve them by introducing certain practices warranted by the best teachers." At each of these intervals it was necessary to achieve "unity of method" so necessary for "the future success of all of our establishments."[92] Two privately circulated works of pedagogy, 1824 and 1831, were commonly referred to as the "old method" and "the method." By the early nineteenth century there were three principal methods of teaching: the individual, the simultaneous, and the mutual. The first entailed the teacher instructing each student on the basis of an assigned reading, writing, or math problem. The simultaneous, developed by the Christian Brothers in the seventeenth century, featured the teacher instructing all students in one class—a noticeable improvement over the individual method, but one that required some division of classes on ability and consequently several teachers in one school. Since towns could not afford to hire several teachers, the mutual, or monitorial, method, founded by Lancaster, and also

Bell, became popular. Based on training the best students to be monitors to instruct a group of students, the mutual method assigned the teacher as an overseer of the entire system.

The Marianists adopted the system that Lalanne called "mixed"; Chaminade explained that it borrowed something from all models—the individual, the simultaneous, and the mutual. It was simultaneous in general instruction and included several classes in a school according to the number of students enrolled. In large classes monitors would be in charge of sections but would themselves be taught in simultaneous classes. However, when the monitors were responsible for their groups, the teacher could pursue the individual method.[93] Apparently, there were political issues within the Society that entailed disputes over the propriety of specific methods.

The 1839 Constitutions stipulated that the educational ministries entailed "the teaching of worldly knowledge" combined "with the subjects of religion." Though priests were expected to fulfill the Society's responsibility for "teaching Christian doctrine," the fundamentals of faith, practice, and piety were entrusted to brothers; in religion classes the simultaneous method prevailed with particular emphasis on history, scripture, and familiar examples for easy explanation of religious topics. As early as 1830 Chaminade saw the need for a course in religion in the normal schools and for the Brothers' Scholasticate: "Our Brothers generally make no distinction between the teaching of catechism and the teaching of piety; yet it seems to me the distinction has its purpose." He wished to supplement the religion course with one in "apologetics. . . . There is not enough attention paid to the signs of the times in which we live, the pretended age of enlightenment, when everyone sets himself up as a philosopher but talks most unphilosophically on matters of religion." Hence, teachers should be trained "as philosophers and logicians . . . and be acquainted with all the sources of human certitude . . . [because] we are in an age when everyone even the peasant and the maid-servant is given to reasoning, and it matters not how preposterously."[94]

The major books on apologetics recommended by Chaminade were *The Principles of Sound Philosophy Harmonized with Those of Religion*, and *The Philosophy of Religions* by the author of *The Theory of Intelligent Beings*. These works were by François Para du Phanjas, a physicist, mathematician, and philosopher at the Jesuit College at Besançon. With the suppression of the Society of Jesus in France (1764), he was granted a pension by the archbishop of Paris and a member of the royal family. Though he took the oath to the Constitution of the Clergy in 1791, he retracted it upon the pope's condemnation of the Constitution; he died in Paris in 1797 at the age of seventy-three. Chaminade may have become familiar with him through the recommendation of his brother Jean Baptiste, also a former Jesuit of southern France and of the same generation as Para du Phanjas. His apologetical works were "marked by ingenuity in answering questions and the judicious use of . . . erudition . . . , [and] proved to be very useful to the apologists of the succeeding generation."[95] Chaminade admired the *Theory of Intelligent Beings*, because it presented "three treatises embracing all that one should know of the proofs of religion." This philosophical approach to combat the philosophers on their own ground but with the rhetorical armaments grounded on religious certitude, was Chaminade's response to "the signs of the times."[96]

William Chaminade's participation in the politics of the Restoration Period was limited to his association with other royalists in Bordeaux, particularly prior to the one hundred days of Napoleon's imperial government. Because of Chaminade's deep involvement in the Sodality of Bordeaux, he had neither the time nor the personal inclination to become very involved in national movements such as the *Missions de France*.

The *Missions de France* were organized by Abbé Rauzan, a marginal member of the Bordeaux Sodality and four years older than his friend Chaminade. The chaplain of the Tuilleries revered the mission strategies of the Redemptorists of Alphonsus Liguori and the Passionists of St. Paul of the Cross, "as though nothing had happened in the intervening quarter of a century." Dansette described their activity during the period from 1815 to 1830: "They held missions in more than 1,500 centres, evangelizing a hundred and thirty of the main towns." Missions would go on for several weeks, "highlighted by spectacular events such as sermons preached in the cemeteries and mass confessions." There were "ceremonies of reparation to the crucifix for sacrileges committed during the Terror and to the memories of Louis XVI, Louis XVII [and] the august Marie Antoinette." Dansette succinctly describes the missionaries' exploitation of the Reign of Terror. "They preached a strange, violent and menacing form of Catholicism, a kind of eternal conflict between a vengeful God and a Satan present in many guises from whom it was possible to escape through a salutary fear of hell fire and an automatic accomplishment of religious duties."[97] Joseph Simler noted the friendship between Rauzan and Chaminade and concluded: "Although they were gifted with different talents, they engaged in similar activities, were animated by the same passions for the regeneration of France, and professed the same devotion to the Immaculate Virgin."[98]

Essential to the religious rhetoric of rechristianization is the dramatic Manichean struggle between the forces of Christian illumination and demonic darkness, the nobility of crown and altar, the deceptions of natural liberty, and Mary Immaculate's crushing the serpent-head of dechristianization. Chaminade's call for a permanent mission of evangelization did incorporate these dichotomies, but his effort to achieve rechristianization through the sodality and the Society of Mary was not articulated in apocalyptical language; it tended to be expressed in Christian, humanistic terms such as kindness, gentleness, and compassion and in the theological imagery of the body of Christ. His instructions to leaders within the various groups of the sodality are replete with references to inspire among the youth of Bordeaux ties of "family, friendship, and society" and to "welcome new candidates with the greatest affability and ease." "Young men," Chaminade said, "are in general very appreciative of acts of kindness and friendship." In the public meetings of the sodality special effort should be made to "make the newcomers feel at home."[99]

Though he admired the Missionaries of France, Chaminade preferred sustained religious education to temporary injections of zeal. Chaminade's own religious conversion occurred within the community of Mussidan, where he seems to have experienced a welcome to pursue a deep relationship, manifested no doubt in fear and anxiety but also grounded in a positive sense of the accessibility of grace embodied in community, mental prayer, and Marian devotion. These characteristics were united with an activist apostolate and an evangelical missionary zeal in his post-Mussidan experience in the sodality, and with additional intensity they were adapted to the Family of Mary.

Chaminade's understanding of the signs of the times in the political terms of the restoration of the Bourbon dynasty in Louis XVIII rested on the unity of crown and altar, the principles that had thrived during the seventeenth century, the height of the dynasty's power, and the prominence of the French school of spirituality. It was a time when religion was on the offensive, associated with the revocation of the Edict of Nantes, which had granted toleration of Protestants in specific areas of France, and the papacy's condemnation of Jansenism. The fall of the monarchy in 1792 conjured up images of dechristianization within the dialectical tension of revolution and religion. Religion had been deeply rooted in French life, which, in a real sense, had a religious dimension, while religion had a political dimension whether it was the monarchy, the empire, or the republic.

Chaminade eagerly embraced the cause of legitimacy. Though Louis XVIII had accepted the principle of constitutional monarchy, he came under the influence of a coalition of religious and political forces of the right—the ultras—which achieved dominance in the Chamber of Deputies and in the ministry of Louis XVIII's successor, his brother Charles X, in 1824. The latter was crowned in Reims cathedral with all the trappings of divine-right monarchy, and followed suit politically by curbing constitutional freedoms and at times ruling by decree. By 1830 a liberal backlash had gained popular sentiment in Paris and the barricades were erected. In July, Charles was deposed and Louis Philippe of the House of Orleans, wrapped in the tricolor of the Revolution, became king. The revolutionary movement that rapidly led to the July or bourgeois monarchy was infused with a strong sense of retaliation against those notables identified as proponents of the aggressive Catholic policies of Charles X.[100] Upon hearing of the abdication of the last of the Bourbon monarchs, Chaminade lamented: "So he has yielded."[101] Indeed, the founder's hope for the success of his "apostolic plans" hinged on Charles X and his impassioned culture war against liberalism. Because of his royalist sentiments Chaminade was on the liberals' list of suspects; his directorship of the Bordeaux Sodality (Congregation) was identified with the Carlist-Paris Sodality. Therefore it was perceived as a citadel of right-wing Catholicism. The founder's associates in the revival of French Catholicism were viewed as enemies of liberty.[102]

During this polarization between royalists and liberals in the revolutionary period, Bordeaux experienced demonstrations by Carlists that engendered rock-throwing outrages by the liberals against what were perceived as symbols of oppression, among which were the Madeleine Chapel and Saint Laurent, the Marianists' houses of formation for priests and brothers respectively. A newspaper reported on a police raid of the homes of leading Carlists. The police searched Chaminade's home and seized only four medals, perhaps associating them with the conspiratorial *Congrégation* of the Blessed Virgin.[103]

In a letter to a royalist activist, Chaminade claimed to be guided by the principle "never to resist an established government. I have kept this resolution through many a revolution, busying myself through my ministry and with service to neighbor." In accord with this principle and in accord with his retiring personality, he explained his dissociation from the politics of resistance. "Both my conscience and my religion make it a duty for me to submit to established authority and never contrive its overthrow. Had I received word of a plot as you describe, I would have opposed it without hesitation."[104]

The Bordeaux Sodality was proscribed and was not revived until 1834. As cautionary measures Chaminade closed the novitiates in Bordeaux. The founder wrote to Lalanne: "We are living in an entirely new world. . . . The France in which I live is almost a strange country to me. I hardly know what to do or say. I have resolved to let events happen and not to provoke them. My only tactic is to have daily recourse to the Blessed Virgin."[105] Implicit in this "tactical" dependence on Mary was a retaliation against the politics of liberalism so deeply stained by the forces of anti-Catholicism, those violent demonstrations such as the rioting that led to the destruction of the dwelling of the archbishop of Paris.

Catherine Labouré, a young novice at the Paris convent of the Daughters of Charity, had experienced several apparitions of Mary during the years 1830–1831. At Mary's alleged request, a medal was designed. David Blackbourne reports on the political motif of Catherine Labouré's description of Mary: "The Virgin appeared in the blue and white, the colours of royalist France fused with the emblems of innocence and purity." Her reported concern with "evil times fitted the prevailing mood of the faithful, and the miraculous medal requested by the vision and struck in 1832 clearly had the status of a talisman. Within four years, fifteen million medals had been made; by 1842 the figure was one hundred million."[106]

The Miraculous Medal was designed in honor of the Immaculate Conception in the iconography frequently described by Chaminade; it depicts Mary standing on the globe with the serpent's head crushed by her foot. "O Mary, conceived without Original Sin, pray for us who have recourse to thee," is the inscription around the Virgin, whose hands beam rays of light. On the reverse side are the hearts of Mary and Jesus, the one suffering from a sword piercing through it and the other from a crown of thorns.[107] This depiction functioned well for Chaminade's mission in the new apostolic age; his favorite antiphon and responsory was "Rejoice, O Virgin Mary, because thou has destroyed all heresies." As his latest biographer remarked, "He envisioned associations under Mary's protection to combat impiety, rationalism and Protestantism."[108] The more the political world became contaminated by liberalism, the more significant was the fourth vow to serve the Immaculate Mary. The four medals seized by the police in 1830 were in honor of the Immaculate Conception with the inscription, "Mary was conceived without sin."[109] The police referred to the medals as "rallying symbols" of the Carlist movement, a perception that may be explained by the identity of the *Congrégation de la Vierge* with royalist conspiracies dating back to the Napoleonic period.[110]

Lalanne's strategy during the 1830 revolution took a direction in stark contrast to that of Chaminade. In a December 22, 1830, address at St. Remy entitled "Religious Education Considered as the Surest Guarantee of Public Liberty," based on Montesquieu's *Spirit of the Laws*, Lalanne argued that a government of the people, unlike a monarchy or despotism, depends on the prevalence of virtue in society; since liberty is dependent on virtue, without Christian education as the guarantee of the vitality of virtue the government of France will certainly fall.

Lalanne was attracted to the liberal Catholic movement associated with the journal *L'Avenir* and with its leaders: Félicité de Lamennais, Henri Lacordaire, and Charles Montalembert. Lalanne viewed the movement as a symbol of the revitalization of the role of religion in the new era of liberty in France, and he envisioned the Marianists as the vanguard of the movement.[111] In his response to Lalanne, Chaminade understood the younger priest's "idea as a bold one, worthy of a stout heart seeking only the good of religion and justice. Knowing your character, I am not surprised at your suggestion; however, you may find before the end of the year that it is untimely." The founder doubted Lalanne's perception that titles for religion were congenial with the liberals' policy; Chaminade had no confidence that "the doctrines of the day" could be reconciled "with the teaching of religious virtues." Since the founder's royalist sympathies had led to a police search of his home, he was guided by the principle: "Make no change, no innovation, nothing that may put us in the spotlight. . . . Each one must go about his work in silent prayer."[112]

Lalanne was undeterred; he joined the "General Agency for Defense of Religious Liberty," whose membership included the liberal editors of *L'Avenir*. To support the cause for the freedom of Catholics to form secondary schools, Lalanne's principal area of interest in the Society of Mary, he published a polemical pamphlet, *Defense of the Liberty of Education Against the Argument of the Government* (1839). This Catholic "party," headed by Montalembert and subsequently aided by Félix Dupanloup, later bishop of Orléans, did not achieve its goal until the Falloux law was passed allowing Catholics freedom to open secondary schools.

However, this was only after middle-class leaders had suppressed the working-class demonstration during the bloody "June Days" of 1848, and were eager to form a coalition with the Catholic leaders. As a result of the Falloux law (1850), the Council General of Public Education reopened the University of France. The new council was composed of eight members of the university council, four bishops, two Protestant ministers, and six other members. There was no recognition of the rights of Catholics, but private schools maintained by institutions or individuals were recognized by the government. Their teachers were required to pass tests of "character and capacity." School inspectors of secondary schools were not responsible for instruction or curriculum but were limited to evaluating the conditions of "morality, hygiene and health"; they were also to see that classroom teaching was not subverting "morality, the constitution or the laws."[113]

The Falloux Law, named after the Minister of Education, represents an achievement for the forces of the Catholic intellectual renewal, but by this time Lamennais had been excommunicated; Lacordaire, the Dominican friar, had achieved national stature as an orator in his famous Lenten sermons at Notre Dame; and Montalembert would eventually be associated with the call of a "free church in a free society" at the First Congress at Malines, a principle condemned by Pius IX in the Syllabus of Errors (1864).

Lalanne would become rector of the Stanislas College in Paris, an institution celebrated for its students who achieved distinction in French life and thought. Chaminade tolerated Lalanne's political activity in the early 1830s, but by the time of Chaminade's Constitutions of 1839 Lalanne was on leave from the Society of Mary, not because of ideological conflict but because of the financial crisis that he himself had helped create.

During the post-1830 revolution period of 1831–1834, Chaminade was a "refugee in Agen."[114] He soon encountered not only the adverse effects of the revolution of 1830 but a series of disturbing experiences within the Society, each of which entailed severe financial crises and challenges to the founder's authority. He had an abiding trust in a providential solution to increasing indebtedness, but he became doubtful when expenditures appeared to him to be the result of imprudence and disobedience to his directives. Sentiment in opposition to Chaminade's cautious indecisiveness was manifested as early as the mid-1820s. When he circulated a draft of the Constitutions in the late 1820s, several members expressed their discontent with the centralization of authority in the person of the superior-founder. Three of the original seven members, Fathers Lalanne and Collineau and Brother Auguste, were particularly critical of the Constitutions. For a brief period Lalanne was convinced of Chaminade's inability to rule, and considered himself to be the rightful superior general; he called for Chaminade's retirement, though he expressed his deep sense of regret at the administrative intransigence. Auguste and Collineau did leave the community in the spring of 1832; the former because his desire to establish middle schools was frustrated and the latter because he wished to limit his ministry to directing sodalities.[115]

Archbishop Jean de Cheverus of Bordeaux (1826–1836), who had been a missionary in Maine, bishop of Boston, and bishop of Montauban, generously dispensed Collineau and Auguste from their vows and even appointed Collineau honorary canon.[116] Since this was a title held by Chaminade, the appointment appears to have been at best an oblique attack on Chaminade. Cheverus, like Chaminade, identified the progress of Christianity in France with the monarchy and indeed was appointed to the Chamber of Peers and was named a Councilor of State and a Commander of the Order of the Holy Ghost by Charles X. In accord with his expansive policy in Boston, Cheverus established good relations with Protestants and Jews in Bordeaux and was committed to following the policies of his predecessor and close associate of Chaminade, Archbishop d'Aviau. He was also reluctant to "establish new institutions" without extensive consideration of "people, places and circumstances involved."[117] Since he did not follow his predecessor's commitment to the Society of Mary, it appears as if a spirit of suspicion prevailed in his views on the viability of Chaminade's community. André Jean Marie Hamon, S.S., rector of the Sulpician seminary in Bordeaux and a close confidante, as well the biographer of Cheverus, explicitly stated that he was not well disposed to religious. Georges J. Caillet, Chaminade's successor as superior general, considered Hamon the principal opponent of the Society. "Fathers Carbon and Hamon were always unfavorable to the Marianists. Both men were Sulpicians and superiors of the seminary at Bordeaux."[118]

Affected by the departure of the two Marianists, the founder was severely grieved when Cheverus supported Auguste's claim that the Marianists should return the fourteen thousand francs he had presented upon his entrance into the Society. Since Auguste had contracted debts to the amount of twenty thousand francs at St. Mary's Institute in Bordeaux, much of which Chaminade considered imprudent, Cheverus's decision appeared particularly harsh. To keep peace he deferred to the archbishop's decision, but Chaminade's agreement became the basis of litigation that led to a profound crisis in the Society. Lalanne replaced Auguste at the Institute; Lalanne eventually decided (in 1835) to move the boarding school to Layrac near Agen. He had the support of the council, but Chaminade was absent at the time. Lalanne had relied on what he considered sound sources for funds for his new school, but they were not forthcoming. Nevertheless, he was undaunted and vigorously pursued renovations of the mansion on the property. Vincent R. Vasey, S.M., described the dramatic conflict between the founder and his first companion in the foundation of the Society of Mary.

> As Father Chaminade had foreseen, he witnessed the financial ruin of Layrac and the dire consequences for the Society. The two, master and disciple, came to the parting of the ways. Lalanne threatened schism, which of course he denied having any intention of creating. Father Chaminade menaced the separation of Layrac from the Society of Mary. Finally, the two agreed that Lalanne would take on all liability for Layrac, that he was temporarily relieved of the

obligation of his vow of poverty, and that he was completely though temporarily cut off from the Society. Lalanne had the intention of saving both the Institution of Layrac and himself, and of coming back to the Society with a great new institution.[119]

Three years later (1839) when Chaminade wrote the significant letter to the retreat masters in which he elaborated on the Society's distinctive characteristic, he urged them to live in the spirit of the rule rather than devising ways to live only by the letter of the rule. As mentioned earlier, his focus on the vow of poverty was easily understood considering the severe indebtedness he had been attempting to resolve over the years, a condition brought on by those who departed from the spirit of Chaminade's foundation. At this time the founder was approaching his seventy-ninth birthday.

With Auguste bringing suit against the Marianists, the founder was advised by a lawyer who had represented the Marianists for years to separate himself legally from the Society. Since he did not have the council's permission to enter into an agreement to pay Auguste, Chaminade could not protect the Society's treasury by pleading that the 1833 agreement was illegal, whereas the council could testify to that effect. Regardless of the fact that Auguste's claim was considered unjust, the council could in conscience deny the legal validity of Chaminade's signature to the 1833 settlement because the founder had made the settlement without the council's authorization. Three years later the decision favored Auguste, but by this time the financial crisis had been entirely eclipsed by a long drawn-out battle between Chaminade and the council, particularly Georges Caillet and Narcisse Roussel, a priest whose sexual involvement with young boys led to his departure from the Society and a period of self-imposed penance.

This tragic conflict of authority consumes fifty pages of Vincent R. Vasey's biography.[120] It originates with Chaminade's separation from the Society, which he considered a legal interim period and not a spiritual withdrawal but which the council considered not merely a temporary measure but a resignation that would lead to the election of a new superior general, Caillet. Until Vasey's research, many historians and members of the Society had accepted Caillet's point of view; Chaminade's age had rendered him incompetent and placed him on the shadowy periphery of the Society.

With degrees in canon law and American jurisprudence, Vasey has mounted an enormous amount of evidence in support of Chaminade's clearly stated position: he had no intention of "resigning" but was legally separating himself until the case was terminated and he would return as superior general. Vasey's collection of documents reveals a conspiracy against the founder that after 1844 became overt and elicited Chaminade's impassioned response based on conscience and the providential character of his role as founder. The council retaliated with charges of Chaminade's irresponsibility, calumny, incompetence, and abuses of authority. It did not permit him to examine the documentary evidence in the case against him, that is, the correspondence between the archbishop of Bordeaux and Rome seeking authorization to exclude Chaminade from a position of authority. In his "legal defense" of Chaminade, Vasey severely damaged the credibility and character of one of his principal opponents on the council, Narcisse Roussel, whom he describes as generally deceitful and particularly a "pederast." Vasey indicted Caillet for covering up Roussel's sexual abuse, and he noted that from Caillet's point of view "the conduct of Chaminade was more dangerous than Roussel's phallus fixation."[121] Caillet attempted to gain control of Chaminade's estate and to isolate him from the community. Though there is evidence of a poll taken among the membership resulting in an overwhelming vote of confidence in the founder, Caillet quashed it before it was made public. The council prevailed; Caillet was elected superior general, and Chaminade spent his remaining years struggling for legitimacy as superior.

The polarization between Chaminade and Caillet never achieved a resolution. As founder, Chaminade obviously considered his authority grounded in God's will and manifested in the Family of Mary. Caillet perceived him to be outside the Society; even when Chaminade attempted reconciliation if the council would rid itself of "its accursed mistrusts," Caillet rejected him unless he would apply to reenter the Society and submit himself to the council "in both temporal and spiritual orders." Shortly after, writing to Caillet on January 22, 1850, "It is with increased confidence, my son, that I embrace you as father," Chaminade died.[122]

Vasey developed a solid case, one that was officially recognized by the Vatican Congregation of Causes, as William Joseph Chaminade was declared venerable. Vasey interpreted the charism of the founder as grounded in faith and prudence. He quoted Chaminade's letter to the archbishop of Bordeaux, Ferdinand Donnet:

> The Christian, the religious, and with all the more reason a member of the Society of Mary, is in a supernatural state, and doubtless he is obliged to guide himself by reason, but reason illuminated by the far superior light of faith. Reason is only a small flame which God has placed in man when he created him in order to make him in his image and likeness, and with the help of conscience. However, faith is an actual and immediate participation in the supreme intellect; for this reason the Holy Spirit said, "My thoughts are not your thoughts (Isaiah 55.8)."[123]

By way of concluding this prologue, it is appropriate to explore the charisms of Chaminade within the contexts of religion and French culture in the years from 1780 through the 1840s. Paul Tillich's understanding of this context in general is well known: "Religion is the substance of culture; culture is the form of religion."[124] Nowhere is this aphorism so dramatically rendered as in France. For example, in French literary history from Pascal to the Catholic revival associated with Claudel and Mauriac, the religious substance was clearly evident in these cultural forms.

Political manifestations tend to be almost operatic in their religious flare: Cardinal Richelieu and Cardinal Mazarin as prime ministers to the Bourbon monarchs; Père Joseph, the gray eminence, engaged in "shuttle diplomacy" among the great powers of seventeenth-century Europe; in the next century the *ancien régime,* perceived as riddled with superstitions of religion by the proponents of natural laws. William Joseph Chaminade's religious formation at Mussidan reflects a distinctive phase in French religious culture. The Community of St. Charles responsible for the *collège* was consciously in opposition to the laxity among many religious orders. Chaminade's immersion in spirituality that was blended with a popular devotion to Mary was affected by the French school of spirituality represented by Jean Jacques Olier, founder of the Sulpicians. From Olier, Chaminade was committed to high spirituality symbolized by his understanding of the Mystical Body of Christ.

Chaminade's formation within these contexts shaped his own religious self-understanding, one that achieved a clear definition in the cultural wars of the French Revolution; in opposition to the reason and nature cults manifested in dechristianization, Chaminade sharpened his own role in the battle to restore religion in French culture. He returned to Bordeaux and founded the Sodality, which represented a synthesis derived from Chaminade's faith in Mary's victory over heresy and the *philosophes* present in the cults of dechristianization. The Sodality represented the new cultural forms for the advance of religion in society, an organized corps of lay and religious apostles dedicated to Christianity in the new apostolic age under Mary's banner. Chaminade's return to France as Missionary Apostolic is symbolic of his ultramontanism; only the papacy could bring order out of the chaos of revolution. Hence, Chaminade was never reconciled to the Napoleonic regime, which was inherently Erastian, and was deeply alienated when the emperor became the pope's jailer.

The restoration of the Bourbon dynasty, 1815–1830, coincided with the foundation of the Society of Mary. Derived from a local sodality, it included priests and lay brothers, a synthesis of a religious community adapting to the signs of the times. The Marianists assumed new religious forms, not only in their mixed society but in the promotion of commercial education, crafts, agricultural programs, and special curricula for teachers in normal schools: all were cultural forms infused with the substance of religion, while the permanent mission of evangelization was the basis of all Marianist ministries.

The expansion of the spheres of faith was the unifying principle of Chaminade's religious vision. There is a romantic quality to this perception; faith provides unity in a world of diversity, universality in a culture immersed in particularity. The romantic poets personify the impulses of nature or the heart's intuitive grasp of the mysterious indwelling in all spheres of existence. Chaminade's spirituality emphasized the heart as the affective source of divine wisdom and of the circulation of grace.

As servants of Mary Immaculate, Marianists "form themselves in the womb of her maternal tenderness to be like Jesus Christ as this adorable Son formed himself to our likeness in her womb, that is to tend to live the life of Jesus Christ under the auspices and guidance of Mary."[125] This unifying principle of faith animated Chaminade to the end of his life. Though Chaminade was isolated and on the periphery of the Society, his spirit, not that of Caillet, was imbued into the 62 houses and 469 members in the Society of Mary. Just thirty-three years old when the founder died, the Society of Mary had achieved a significant presence in its various education ministries. This particular representation of the cultural forms of religion was derived from Chaminade's determination to bring together brothers and priests dedicated to a permanent mission of a new Christian community. His self-understanding as founder, which became well perceived in the conflict with Caillet, was articulated within the sphere of God's providence; his rhetoric was in accord with the romantic idiom of the day manifested in the intuitive portrayal of the Society of Mary enlarging the spheres of faith in a new apostolic age, and in the service of the new Eve crushing the serpent of the new heresies, and representing the vitality of the new Adam in the Body of Christ.

This faith-based romanticism energized Chaminade's practical determination to overcome enemies from without and within. Though he perceived the world in terms of the ideals of crown and altar, there were no other religious communities of the time that did not wear religious garb, nor was there a religious institution in which a brother was superior of a local community that included a priest. The new religious culture that was initiated with the sodality and already in the Family of Mary represents the distinctive gifts of Chaminade: a faith-based romanticism grounded in realism, formed by multivalent experiences in the dramatic struggles of religion in a hostile world.

CHAPTER TWO

Leo Meyer, Marianist Missionary, and the Foundation of the American Province

❧ I ❧

WITH LEADERSHIP AS ITS ORGANIZING PRINCIPLE, THIS CHAPTER traces the life of Leo Meyer, the Alsatian Marianist priest who consciously cultivated his missionary drive to transplant the Society of Mary in the fertile land of the United States. The ground had been prepared by the German-American immigrants whose national parishes were in desperate need of religious women and men to staff their schools' separate classes for girls and boys. The call for Marianists originated on the Cincinnati point of what would become known as "the German triangle," including also Milwaukee and St. Louis.[1] Meyer had prepared himself to respond to this call with a deep sense of the design of providence in his prospective missionary endeavors. Indeed, he sought a sign from God that his Marianist life would culminate in a mission to the so-called New World, and when such a sign was evident he was already attuned to the need for German-speaking missionaries.

Leo Meyer shared the Restorationist mentality of William Joseph Chaminade, but Meyer's sense of the cultural crises generated by the French Revolution was expressed in an asceticism akin to monastic separatism from the contagion of secular society. Hence, when he responded to the call for brothers to teach in German-American schools in Cincinnati, he gravitated to a rural setting suitable for the American motherhouse. Like the German-American Catholics who developed a separatist and preservationist parish life to assure the prevalence of language, custom, and piety—traditions that presumably guaranteed "passing on the Faith"—Meyer envisioned separating the Marianists from the contamination of the world in a monastic

46

setting. He nurtured a deep devotion to the Holy Family, comparable to the old-world devotionalism of John N. Neumann, bishop of Philadelphia, a mentality that promoted a family of saints as models of the faith in a hostile climate infected by anti-Catholicism, the dominance of Protestantism and the license of materialism.[2]

The chapter's focus on the leadership of Meyer precludes consideration of the several schools staffed by the Marianists in San Antonio and Cleveland, foundations that will be considered in chapter 3. Animating Meyer's leadership was the spirit of Chaminade as he too perceived the mission in terms of God's design. However, Meyer's abrasive personality and his missionary strategies were distinctive traits that set him apart and greatly influenced the Marianist mission in the United States.

◄ II ►

THE SOCIETY OF MARY INITIATED ITS FIRST AMERICAN FOUNDATION in 1849, when it took charge of the boys' school at Holy Trinity Parish in Cincinnati. Leo Meyer soon purchased land in Dayton, where a school, a novitiate, and later a provincial headquarters were built. However, contacts between the United States and the first Marianists in France began as early as 1816, when Louis William DuBourg, bishop of New Orleans, with residence in St. Louis, visited Bordeaux to recruit seminarians and priests for his far-flung diocese. Born in Saint Domingue (1766) (the French colony that would become the country of Haiti) to a family from Bordeaux, DuBourg had known Chaminade since they were students together there in the College of Guyenne, and it is possible they met again in the persecuted church in Bordeaux during the dominance of the Jacobins. DuBourg later joined the Sulpicians, was president of Georgetown College, and founder of St. Mary's College on the grounds of Baltimore's first seminary, St. Mary's, in 1791.[3]

During his 1816 visit, DuBourg attended a meeting of Chaminade's Bordeaux Sodality, and by the time of his return visit on May 22, 1817, John Lalanne and Chaminade had formed the nucleus of the Society of Mary.[4] Among DuBourg's Bordeaux recruits were Hercules Brassac, a close friend of Lalanne, and Pierre Des Mouliens; both were, if not sodalists, close to the sodality and were subsequently ordained priests for the Archdiocese of New Orleans/St. Louis. One of Brassac's letters to Lalanne originated from St. Louis County, where some eighty years later, the Marianists would found Chaminade College, a well-known school in the Archdiocese of St. Louis. After his tenure in the United States, DuBourg was named bishop of the see of Montauban in 1826, an area where two small schools run by the Society were located. He became archbishop of Besançon in 1833, just a few months before he died. St. Remy, however, one of the most prestigious of the Marianist foundations—a normal school, elementary, secondary, and agricultural schools—was located in DuBourg's archdiocese. Chaminade was unable to visit his childhood friend but expressed his gratitude for the archbishop's "tokens of esteem and interest"[5] in the Society of Mary.

Another American-Marianist connection occurred in 1839, when C. J. Richard-Bôle, a Besançon priest of the Diocese of St. Louis (established as a separate diocese in 1833), wrote to Chaminade about his Arkansas mission and informed the founder that he had heard news that the Society of Mary had become "sufficiently numerous" for him to ask Chaminade to send several members to join two missionaries to "establish the reign of Jesus Christ in the New World." He explained in detail the Arkansas mission, including the price of land, and particularly the need for schools because "it is in this way the population will be won over." Chaminade responded by stating, "I do not believe that the moment fixed by Divine Providence has come for us to go to the conquest of souls in the New World." He was particularly concerned with the problems entailed in "maintaining what we hold in France. . . . I am very sure that a certain number would leave with pleasure for the mission proposed. But we are not prepared for it, and I regret it."[6]

Among those Marianists who would "leave with pleasure" to serve in the United States, none was more determined then Leo Meyer, a priest of the Diocese of Strasbourg prior to joining the Society of Mary in 1837. Born in 1800 in the Alsatian town of Eguisheim in the vicinity of Colmar, Leo Meyer had expressed an early interest in the priesthood, no doubt inspired by stories of his parents' protection of refugee priests during the period of violent anticlericalism associated with the Reign of Terror. He entered the seminary in Strasbourg after the Restoration of the Bourbon monarchy. As a young seminarian Leo Meyer revealed a tendency to be single-minded in pursuit of a particular cause when he surreptitiously abandoned his theological studies and entered the monastery of La Trappe in the vicinity of Mortagne. Because of his parents' refusal to give their consent, he had to return to the seminary and was ordained a diocesan priest in 1823. With a physical appearance to match his strong will—he was six feet two inches tall and weighed over three hundred pounds—Meyer appears to have been determined to enter the religious life. Since his bishop had planned to appoint him chaplain to the Catholic queen of Sweden, Meyer must have possessed the qualities so necessary for such a delicate position: sophistication and diplomatic ease. Because Leo's brother, Louis, died shortly before he was scheduled to be ordained, the bishop, in deference to the Meyer family, appointed Leo to the chaplaincy of a large hospital in Strasbourg that allowed him to be near his parents during their time of loss and grief.[7] With a spirituality rooted in the need for the rigors of community life, Leo Meyer appears to have been open and receptive to a providential sign that would affirm and validate his need to become a religious. Though apparent in hindsight, this reliance on a sign was clearly evident in his report of an unusual experience with a woman in the hospital. "On the 2nd of July, 1827, a very devout person who was being favored with extraordinary graces" visited him in the hospital. The "ecstatic woman" of 1827 may have been Apollone Fitsinger, a "stigmatic" since 1824 and popular among the clergy of Strasbourg.[8] She said, "I came to carry out a commission on the part of the Blessed Virgin. She told me that you should remain faithful to her and that in two months you shall be relieved of your position as chaplain so that you can follow your vocation. Finally she [i.e., the Blessed Virgin] told me that you will be obliged to cross the seas."[9]

Shortly after this experience the bishop allowed him to pursue his vocation to the religious life. On his way to enter the Jesuit novitiate in Fribourg, Switzerland, he accompanied his brother, Benedict, to the Marianist College of St. Remy in eastern France, just west of Alsace. Upon realizing that he had left behind the papers required to enter the Jesuits, Meyer remained at St. Remy for their arrival from Strasbourg. While there he met a close priest-friend, Charles Rothéa of a prominent and wealthy Alsatian family. Meyer perceived his stay at St. Remy as another sign: that he should enter the Society of Mary rather than the Society of Jesus. By the end of 1827 he was in the novitiate at the Madeleine in Bordeaux, where he formed a deep filial relationship with Chaminade, who appointed him to such responsible positions as chaplain at St. Remy, novice master at Courtefortaine in the Diocese of Saint Claude, and subsequently novice master at Ebersmunster in his home province of Alsace. Hence, his experience was a model for aspiring religious in large "monastic" institutions, where ironically he nurtured his vocation to the frontier missions in the United States.[10]

He did not know of C. J. Richard-Bôle's letters and Chaminade's response, but he did receive encouragement in 1846 that the Marianists were seriously considering a mission in the Diocese of St. Louis.[11] Meyer had expressed a strong interest in an American foundation. He attempted to convince his provincial, Father Jean J. Chevaux, to give him permission to join a colony established by the Bavarian baron G. H. Schroeder in Marienstadt, Pennsylvania, just north of Harrisburg. With great enthusiasm for a colony dedicated to Mary along with promises of land and buildings for a Marianist novitiate in this colony of German-speaking Catholics, Meyer wrote several letters to Chevaux over a period of more than a year.[12] He told Chevaux that, according to a prophecy made by an "ecstatic" woman in 1827, he was destined for the religious life and would "have to cross the seas." Meyer explained to his superior, "This is the time for . . . [the prophecy] to be fulfilled. I am telling you this so that you may weigh and examine all the circumstances."[13]

In a letter to Chevaux composed on July 14, Bastille Day, 1848, shortly after the revolution of that year, Meyer reported his encounter with another "ecstatic person," whom he later identified as the mystic of Niederbronn.[14] Though he did not mention her name, the woman was Elizabeth Eppinger (1814–1867), who, according to an article in the *New Catholic Encyclopedia*, began a period of visions, revelations, and ecstasies in 1846. As her fame spread, she became known as the "Ecstatic of Niederbronn." Later she founded a religious community, the Daughters of the Divine Redeemer, with a ministry to care for the sick-poor in their homes and for other works among the impoverished.[15] To substantiate her credibility, Meyer wrote to Chevaux: "She has already foretold what would happen on February 2 [the revolution of 1848] three weeks ahead of time; and on May 8 she stated what would happen" during the June days. Meyer visited Eppinger on July 11, and upon entering her home her pastor and spiritual director "told me that she was very anxious to see me." Meyer had indirectly communicated with her seeking her prayers for the "teaching Brothers and their Superior," apparently referring to the Caillet–Chaminade conflict. "The Lord had already forewarned her a half-hour before, of my arrival." After she admonished him for having neglected "his meditation on the sufferings of Jesus Christ" she told him that the Marianists would "go to America." She said that "the Lord would soon call [Chaminade] to Himself . . . the chief cause of the division between him and others . . . [Caillet et al. was] a very special predilection that this good aged man has for one or the other." Perhaps this was a reference to Chaminade's partiality toward Lalanne or even Meyer himself. Meyer reported on the next day's communication: "She began by speaking of the immense and extraordinary designs that God had for the Society of Mary, which was destined to contribute to the conversion of a great number of souls—that not only did the Lord consent to a mission to America, but also to other countries of the world. She mentioned my personal mission to America." The ecstatic was quite particular about the Caillet–Chaminade conflict:

> Although he [i.e., Chaminade] can no longer govern, the Lord wishes that the Superior General [i.e., Caillet] obey him, and he ought to take care, moreover, [not] to treat him harshly, as he has done. . . . From there she went on to the

Steward General [i.e., head of temporalities, Brother Clouzet]. She told me with an expression of annoyance, that he is in danger if he does not open his heart to grace, and that it was this withdrawal from grace, which was the reason for the total lack of union and peace in the house where he lived.[16]

Meyer, who had indicated his support for Chaminade prior to the 1845 chapter that elected Caillet, was well known as one of the founder's "most cherished disciples."[17] As early as 1840 Chaminade urged Meyer to "try to understand that it is the usual order of God's Providence that the founder and the co-founder of his great works should suffer very much and that their groans, their bloody sweat, should be like dew which falls upon the seed that they sow and makes it sprout." Amid the conflict in the Society of Mary, Elizabeth Eppinger "urged . . . [Meyer] to work for restoring peace and union" between Chaminade and "the other Brothers."[18]

With characteristic candor, Leo Meyer wrote to William Chaminade about the discord between him and Caillet and how such scandal appeared to him as worse than the "Society's annihilation." He expressed his own commitment to reestablishing peace and concord through his correspondence with the founder and the new superior general. Meyer told Chaminade about his meeting with the "mystic" at Niederbronn:

> Everybody is convinced that she has special gifts from heaven. . . . She told me in the interest of her Divine Spouse that you would die soon and that the reason for the disunion [within the Society of Mary] came from a particular affection for one of your children. . . . She charged me to work with all my power to establish peace and concord between you and your children.[19]

Rather than distract Chaminade from the cause of unity with his concerns to be missioned to the United States, Meyer sought out Chevaux, his provincial, for permission to pursue Schroeder's request for him to join the colony of Marienstadt, particularly now that Eppinger had confirmed his own understanding of God's will. "As a result of this, I am begging you to send me to America, as Moses of old sent Joshua and Caleb into the Promised Land to investigate the country."[20] Without evidence of Chevaux's responses to Meyer's impassioned pleas, it is nevertheless quite clear that the general council was at best cautionary. The Redemptorists of Liège and the Sisters of Notre Dame of Paris did emigrate to Marienstadt but were soon disillusioned.[21]

Meyer's dependency on a sign of God's plan for Marianist missions and for his own role in those endeavors was based on the providential turn of events in 1827 that led to his vocation as a Marianist. Chaminade's perception of the central purpose of the Society of Mary, derived from his notion of a new apostolic era dedicated to rechristianization of France, was basic to Meyer's self-understanding of the Marianist charism to dwell in permanent mission. The Alsatian Marianist seems to have projected this charism on the heroic character of foreign missionaries. The teaching brothers were perceived as engaging in the evangelical efforts to lay the church's foundation in the "New World." Reaching maturity as a priest in the 1820s during a period when Catholic thinkers were focusing on the reintegration of religion and culture, Meyer seems to have absorbed this ethos. In 1848, when the revolutionary tide of political liberalism, social radicalism, anticlericalism, and nationalism had inundated various urban centers in western Europe, even Pope Pius IX was forced to take refuge outside of Rome. A crisis mentality permeated conservative Catholicism; only severe penance, heroic missionary asceticism, and a general commitment to reparation could appease God's anger with worldly blasphemies. In accord with these notions of rigorism, Leo Meyer fastened on Elizabeth Eppinger's warning of God's anger and the need for reparation, the call to asceticism, and meditation on the sufferings of Jesus Christ as the means by which to achieve an opening to grace. Since Meyer's vigorous pursuit of an American mission was explicitly expressed to Chevaux as devoid of any wish "to escape the vengeance of the Lord," he seems to have restrained any tendency to romanticize the life of the missionary. Later he wrote that only by chastisement will "God attain His end" of extending his mercy to France caught in the revolutionary tide. "I do not think we should devise all kinds of means to escape the all-powerful hand that is chastising; we have to accept it, if not with pleasure, then at least with resignation."[22] Of course, an American mission was within God's providence.

The first episcopal request for Marianists in the United States originated with the first bishop of Buffalo, John Timon, who was a French Lazarist ordained in the United States. Writing to C. J. Richard-Bôle, who had become a "vicar general,"—that is, priest-agent, acting on behalf of American bishops in need of priests and religious communities in the particular dioceses—Timon elaborated on the needs of his diocese amid a period of accelerated immigration. Dated December 25, 1848, this letter included the following statistics: "Six years ago there were in my diocese only 17 priests and as many poor churches, and there were only six residences for the priests; now we have about 71 priests, over 100 churches, and 38 houses to lodge them in."[23] The number of Catholics rose from three hundred to five thousand.

Timon's depiction of public schools in the following apocalyptical rhetoric may have been familiar to the French Marianists, who, though they taught in tax-supported schools, were critical of their secular character. Thus Timon remarked:

> The public schools are a powerful instrument of the devil to hamper the work of God. We are taxed for these schools in which nearly all the teachers, men and women, and absolutely all the officials are Protestants and infidels; in which the spirit is eminently infidel or anti-Catholic. . . . Having paid our taxes for these schools which ruin our children, we tax ourselves a second time for free Catholic schools.

He underscored the need for religious communities to staff these schools and to encourage vocations among their students. Timon particularly sought brothers who could "care for our poor schools and orphan boys."[24] Since some of these brothers would need to "know English," this project did not have immediate appeal to the Marianists, particularly Leo Meyer, who spoke only French and German. Eventually it was his command of German that led Meyer and others to respond favorably to the call from Cincinnati.

In late 1848 the assistant pastor of Holy Trinity Church, the first German-American parish in Cincinnati, knowing of the Marianists, sought the assistance of Francis X. Weninger, S.J., to recruit the brothers to teach the boys at the parochial school. Weninger, an Austrian priest who was an assistant pastor at St. Philomena's church in Cincinnati, wrote to his friend, Sigwart Mueller, to act as an emissary. In a letter to Caillet, Bishop John B. Purcell supported the need for teaching brothers at Holy Trinity and the two other German-speaking parishes. Mueller had written to Caillet and later to Meyer; on April 28, 1849, Caillet assigned Leo Meyer to be superior of the mission in Cincinnati. In his letter to Meyer, he explained that the intervention of Weninger and Purcell had convinced him of the desirability of the mission. The superior general told Meyer that he made this appointment because Meyer had demonstrated such "devotedness to the Society of Mary and zeal . . . for the mission."[25] A month after his assignment, Meyer, accompanied by Charles Schultz, a twenty-seven-year-old working brother from Baden who had been temporarily professed for only two years, sailed from Le Havre and landed in New York on July 4. Meyer and Schultz met some Christian Brothers on board the ship who were also bound for Cincinnati in response to the same request of Weninger and Purcell, but they decided to appeal to their superior before going on to Cincinnati. They were eventually assigned to St. Louis.[26] Since the 1850 *Catholic Directory* referred to the Marianists as "Christian Brothers of Bordeaux, founded by Father Chaminade [*sic*]" even Purcell appears to have been confused about their identity.[27] However, Leo Meyer's self-understanding as a missionary was secure; hence, as he embarked on this phase in God's plan for the Marianists, he perceived his role as transplanting traditional faith in pluralist American soil.

⊀ III ⊁

LOCATED ON THE OHIO RIVER AND IN A NATURAL BASIN SURROUNDED BY hills, Cincinnati was the fifth largest U.S. city in 1850, with a population of 115,000. The entire state of Ohio and the Michigan Territory comprised the boundaries of the Diocese of Cincinnati when it was erected in 1821 with Bishop Edward Fenwick, O.P., as the first ordinary. German immigrants, who had suffered economic and social deprivation in their homeland, were attracted to the expanding economy of Cincinnati and the fertile land of Ohio. By 1840, 31 percent of Cincinnati's population of forty-six thousand were Germans. About 75 percent of these Germans were Catholic. Because Germans identified their language as the medium of their faith, Fenwick recruited a German-speaking priest for the increasing number of German Catholics, and in 1834 the first German-American parish, Holy Trinity, was established.[28]

Fenwick's successor was John B. Purcell. Born in County Cork, Ireland, in 1800, the young Purcell emigrated to Maryland in 1818, attended Mount St. Mary's College and Seminary from 1820 to 1824, and completed his theology at St. Sulpice in Paris in 1826. Returning to Mount St. Mary's as teacher and later president, he was appointed to Cincinnati shortly after Fenwick had died in the first wave of cholera.[29]

Purcell was a reluctant pragmatist on the issue of German-American national parishes, which, unlike the traditional territorial parishes, were based on ethnicity; between 1834 and 1861 ten such parishes were established. Purcell ordained three German-speaking priests for his diocese in 1833–1834, each of whom achieved significance within Cincinnati and beyond. Henry Juncker at the age of twenty-three was the first acting pastor of Holy Trinity; he subsequently moved to Dayton and later became first bishop of Alton, Illinois. John Martin Henni of Switzerland was the first permanent pastor of Holy Trinity, founder of the German Catholic newspaper *Warheitsfreund* and first bishop of Milwaukee.[30] Martin Kundig was an indefatigably activist priest in Detroit and Milwaukee; he founded the Catholic Female Benevolent Society in 1833 in Detroit during the first cholera epidemic. This society took charge of the Poor House, and Kundig was for a time head of the Poor House for Wayne County. He later joined John Henni in Milwaukee.[31]

Purcell only gradually recognized the need for Germans to manage their own ecclesial affairs, including lay participation in parish governance. Though aware of the abuses of the trustee system from the episcopal point of view, Purcell nevertheless provided for self-government of the German parishes by allowing them to elect six wardens, men who were active parishioners, at least thirty years old, but whose authority was limited to temporal affairs. Since wardens were not allowed in Irish-American parishes, this was an accommodation to German custom. He also appointed a German vicar general responsible for advising him on the needs of their national parishes; John M. Henni was his first appointment to that post, followed by John Ferneding, pastor of St. Paul's in the "over the Rhine" area of Cincinnati.[32] The vitality of German-American Catholic culture was in the parish complex of church and school, buttressed by German devotional and recreational societies in a church dominated by Irish-American prelates. Colman Barry summed up the principal motivating forces in the construction of this preservationist German parish culture. "But since the Irish and English Catholics had no language problems of their own, the German immigrants felt their new co-religionists could not properly understand the close bond which existed in the German soul between the practice of the faith and these traditional customs." Francis X. Weninger, the Austrian Jesuit missionary so instrumental in urging the Marianists to send teaching brothers to staff the German-American schools, extolled the principle "Language saves the Faith."[33]

Two German mission societies founded to fund German-American institutions were the *Leopoldine Stiftung* (Austria, 1829) and the *Ludwig Missionverein* (Bavaria, 1838). Modeled on the Society for the Propagation of the Faith, founded in Lyons, France, in the 1820s, the German societies were also dedicated to preserving German customs through their support of schools, seminaries, hospitals, and other charitable institutions. Purcell successfully appealed to them for funds and, though there was some controversy over lay control and other issues related to recruitment of priests and religious, he was grateful for the widespread support of the German national parishes.[34] Leo Meyer, so eager to be missionary to the "New World" developed a thoroughly "old world" German-speaking community at the motherhouse in Dayton.

The Marianists taught in the schools of five of the ten German-American parishes during the foundation period 1849–1862: Holy Trinity, St. Mary's,

St. Philomena's, St. Paul's, and St. Joseph's. Because of quarrels between brothers and pastors, the Marianist school that represented the longest commitment (over sixty years) was St. Mary's, 1858–1922.

When Meyer and Schultz arrived in Cincinnati on July 16, the city was in the throes of a cholera epidemic. Purcell almost immediately assigned him to assist Henry Juncker, pastor of Emmanuel Church in Dayton sixty miles northeast of Cincinnati. Within the first few days in Cincinnati, however, Meyer was confronted with a meeting of the German priests who were disappointed that the Marianists sent a priest and a young brother rather than teaching brothers to staff their schools. In an August 2 letter to Purcell, Meyer reported on that meeting and on his explanation as stated in a letter to Weninger. "I replied that I had not come to make new arrangements, that I was sent by the Superior General only to consolidate the arrangements taken and agreed upon . . . and that certainly [Caillet] will not fail his pledged word . . . to send the subjects promised for the Church of the Most Holy Trinity."[35] Indeed, a week later Meyer wrote to Chevaux for four brothers, who could easily learn English and who would live in one community but teach in two schools. As he promised the pastors of Holy Trinity and St. Paul's brothers by the end of October, he urged immediate attention to the request. Contrary to the report of problems with the German priests, he referred to how "devoted" the bishop and clergy were "to the work of the Brothers who can speak English."[36]

Meyer was even more enthusiastic about the prospect of purchasing seventy-five acres (later it came to 125 acres) of farming land in the vicinity of Dayton from a wealthy Catholic:

> The gentleman's name is Stuart and he is a descendant of the Royal Family of England. The property is a twenty-minute walk from the Catholic church in Dayton . . . . If the Blessed Virgin arranges every thing, as we have every reason to think that she will, this property will become the St. Remy of America.[37]

As a former novice master in Alsace, Meyer named those brothers suitable to the demands of missionary life. In accord with the American superior's request, the general council sent Brother Andrew Edel (1804–1891), an instructor in horticulture at St. Remy; Brother Maximin Zehler (1827–1892), a primary school teacher in Alsace; Brother John B. Stintzi (1821–1900), also a primary school teacher; Brother Damian Litz (1822–1903), born in Baden, volunteered when Brother Auguste Klein was unavailable to embark on a missionary course. A tailor who became a fine school teacher, Litz excelled in several spheres during his long life in the United States. Though Meyer had promised the pastors of Holy Trinity and St. Paul's that brothers would be available in October 1849, it was not until the first week in December that they arrived in Cincinnati.

In his centennial history of the Marianists in the United States, John Garvin describes each of these pioneer brothers: Edel was a "quiet, unobtrusive man. . . . A better man to contemplate than to meet, more interesting to speak *about* than to speak to."[38] Maximin Zehler "was a man of heart more than of mind. . . . Brother Zehler's sympathy with human kind [*sic*], and his genial, open-minded nature made him excellent company; he was a good listener as well."[39] Brother Stintzi was a master teacher, a disciplinarian effective as well "in transmitting knowledge. . . . Pedagogy was his favorite study . . . [and] he was a man of keen intellect and of the most practical turn of mind . . . a man more of mind than of heart. . . . He needed little sympathy and he craved none." However, he also had a "courtly presence and bearing but was an affable conversationalist, quite interested in politics and topical affairs of the day."[40] Damian Litz was, according to Garvin, "a pioneer among pioneers; his versatility, his enterprise, his energy and his almost nervous activity and his remarkable power of adaptation, made him especially useful in founding new houses." He achieved national fame as an entertaining, philosophical writer in the German-American press, but as a teacher he "talked too much and explained too much."[41] Since each of these brothers achieved significance in the province, their roles will be explained in a later chapter as well.

Meyer had been told that the brothers would each receive an annual salary of six hundred dollars, but when they began teaching the salary had been reduced to four hundred dollars on the basis that St. Paul's only paid four hundred dollars to the lay teachers. Since Holy Trinity paid for the brothers' living expenses, Meyer expected St. Paul's to pay six hundred dollars. The pastor of St. Paul's, the German vicar general, Ferneding, responded, as noted by Meyer in a letter to Chevaux, "If different arrangements can't be made, they would try to engage lay teachers. I took them at their word and left."[42] Though he may have actually left "in a huff," Meyer was now free to bring those brothers to Dayton, but in the process he no doubt alienated the vicar general. Hence, Meyer appointed Stintzi and Litz to Holy Trinity and brought Edel and Zehler to Dayton to assume roles in the prospective school on the Stuart property.

Meyer signed the mortgages for 125 acres at twelve thousand dollars with a 6 percent annual interest. The first payment, due on March 19, 1850, the feast day of St. Joseph, was deferred with the hope of funds from Bordeaux and other sources entirely unknown to Meyer at the time. Though semiannual payments were made with some regularity, rebuilding after a fire of

1855 and other crises delayed payments; the debt was not liquidated until two years after the ten-year agreement. In honor of the Holy Family, Meyer named the property "Nazareth," as if it were Mary's motherhouse for those brothers and priests committed by a fourth vow to Mary Immaculate.[43]

At the request of Bishop Purcell, who became archbishop in 1850, the school at Nazareth was to open as a boarding school. Since none of the Marianists spoke fluent English, Purcell assigned a young Irish priest to teach English, but he lasted only a few months; according to Meyer he had a "flighty and irresponsible character." Moreover, he was not a very effective teacher; it would be "easier to train a young man for such work, especially children who breathe the [free] air of America."[44] With three more brothers due to arrive in Cincinnati in the summer of 1850 for his "agricultural colony," Meyer announced in a prospectus the opening of St. Mary's School for boys for September 1 of that year. Meyer sent the prospectus to Purcell for his approval, which was returned with only the insertion "none but Catholic boys are admitted."[45] Because Purcell considered the two Catholic academies in Cincinnati that included Protestants as a mixed blessing, he insisted that St. Mary's be totally Catholic. The following prospectus was published in five issues of the *Cincinnati Telegraph*, the diocesan newspaper edited by Edward J. Purcell, the bishop's brother.

ST. MARY'S SCHOOL FOR BOYS
IN DAYTON

The course of instruction will embrace: Reading,
Writing, English, French and German Grammars,
Arithmetic, Practical Geometry and Mensuration,
Book-keeping, History, Geography, Drawing, Vocal
Music, Botany, Agriculture and Horticulture.

——TERMS——

Per quarter for board and tuition (payable in
advance)......................................$18.00
Day-school for externs: Tuition per quarter....$3.00
The postage of letters, books, stationery, doctor's
bills, washing and bedding form extra charges, or
may be furnished by parents.
The Scholastic year will open the first Tuesday
of September and will be finished the last Tuesday
in July, and none but Catholic boys are admitted.

Address:

Rev. Leo Meyer
Dayton,
Montgomery Co., Ohio.[46]

The Metropolitan Catholic Almanac and Laity's Directories (hereafter referred to as the *Catholic Directory*) of 1851 through 1854 did not include *St. Mary's* in its Cincinnati "Institutions" section; rather it was listed alone between "Pay and Free Schools" and "Religion and Pious Societies" (i.e., lay societies). In the directories for these years they were referred to as follows:

CHRISTIAN BROTHERS OF THE SOCIETY OF MARY,
Cincinnati, Ohio.

> This society, founded by Rev. Wm. Jos. Chaminade, honorary canon of the Metropolitan church of Bordeaux, and approved by his Holiness Gregory XVI, April 23d, 1839, was recently established in Cincinnati, to be employed in the German schools in that city. Their Superior in this country is Rev. J. Meyer, who is assisted by Rev. Aug. Rollinet. The novitiate is in Nazareth, near Dayton, on a fertile and extensive farm.[47]

In that same directory, 1853, the reference to Holy Trinity School listed the "Christian Brothers" as responsible for the boys' school.[48] The 1855 *Catholic Directory* later listed the "Brothers of St. Mary's Society" at Holy Trinity, St. Paul's, and St. Mary's, and the brief general note on the Marianists' foundation in the archdiocese is entitled "Christian Brothers of the Society of St. Mary's."[49] Finally, in the 1856 directory there is a full listing of the "St. Mary's Boarding School." It begins with a reference to "the Brothers of Mary" but then repeats the inaccuracy, "sometimes called Christian Brothers." Only two lines of the nine-line listing refer to the school, that is, costs and the admission limited to Catholic boys. The remaining remarks describe the community, including extraneous facts such as that one priest "attends a parish with a lay-brother, who teaches the children, and one student in theology."[50] Throughout Meyer's administration there was no accurate reference to Brothers of Mary or Marianists; unlike all other communities of women and men religious, the directories did not include S.M. after the priests' names; not one brother's name was listed in the directories during Meyer's term.

The Holy Cross Brothers, who taught at the Cathedral School, an Irish-American community, were consistently designated properly with C.S.S. and C.S.C. as well. The Congregation of the Holy Cross, which originally included sisters, brothers, and priests, was upon its approval from Rome in 1856 separated into three communities. The Holy Cross priests, wrote the provincial, Edward Sorin, "are especially consecrated to the Sacred Heart of Jesus—they are exclusively dedicated to missions and education."[51] Like the Marianists, the Congregation of the Holy Cross was founded in France and included teaching and working brothers. Unlike the Society of Mary, the Holy Cross community ultimately formed a separate brothers' province. While the congregation never achieved the predominance of brothers in positions of authority in parochial and higher education, the University of Notre Dame had been chartered in 1844 and was thriving (actually as an academy) in 1860 with nineteen faculty members, including some brothers. The Marianists' boys' school was not chartered to give diplomas until 1878; it was a relatively small institution, averaging about forty students enrolled with two or three teachers on the faculty.[52]

Leo Meyer's institutional achievements during the first year were considerable: the Marianists were staffing Holy Trinity and would soon be in charge of the boys' classes in St. Mary's and St. Paul's; Nazareth included a school, a novitiate, and a farm on the outskirts of a town that promised continuous growth and prosperity. By the end of 1851, however, Meyer had experienced severe problems with Archbishop Purcell, Father Juncker, and Superior General Caillet. On February 16, 1851, Meyer concluded a letter to Chevaux with a remark that harked back to the providential sign that prompted his mission to the United States: "You would not believe what difficulties I have gone through since I am in America and I do not think it is over yet. The devil is enraged to see the Society of Mary in this country, and if I had not seen the ecstatic of Niederbronn, it is ten to one that I would have returned to France. But thank God I have not been prostrate five minutes, not even one minute."[53]

The difficulties with the German pastors continued, particularly on the questions of salaries for the brothers and the control over the schools. Meyer wrote to Chevaux, "These gentlemen, [the pastors] like many others, think religious live on air and fine weather."[54] The relationship between Juncker and Meyer reached crisis proportions during the period 1850–1851.

The Juncker–Meyer relationship began amicably; the pastor relied on the Marianist superior to assist him and told Meyer that in the event he would leave the parish he wished to see the Marianists responsible for the Emmanuel congregation. But Juncker had a change of heart; Meyer wrote to Chevaux that as a result of the archbishop's influence "Father Juncker has taken all measures to sever all my relations with the parish." In anticipation of Purcell's prospective visit to Bordeaux, Meyer explained to Chevaux, "The archbishop is a holy prelate, pious and zealous, and the only thing to say about him is that he is too good; he's afraid of offending or displeasing, and has an extraordinary sensitive character for whoever speaks to him is right. . . . The good prelate is to be pitied, real missionaries are rare."[55]

After this display of condescension toward Purcell, Meyer cited preposterous statistics on the mass apostasy of Catholics in the United States.

Though German-Americans later in the century tried to substantiate their opposition to religious pluralism by citing inflated numbers of losses to the faith, Meyer's numbers were outlandish: "Since 1816, six million have lost the Faith, and have embraced heresy; one million heretics embraced the Catholic Faith; if you could only see the zeal of all those various sects; in the little city of Dayton there are 27 different churches." As if to blame the Catholics' loss of faith on the religious apathy of American Catholics, he cited as typical conduct priests rushing through classes to prepare students for First Communion in three weeks culminating with confession on Friday and communion the following Sunday. Meyer reported on the brothers' attempt to struggle against these alleged shortcomings and then told Chevaux of his forced isolation from any pastoral involvement, "and there I was, between four walls, with formal orders not to bother anything."[56]

Meyer's warning about the need to pity Purcell arrived after the archbishop had visited with Caillet in Bordeaux; the principal purpose of the visit appears to have been to convince Caillet to remove Meyer from the office of superior. Chevaux reported on Purcell's visit. Though the archbishop seemed to have been well satisfied with the brothers and "well disposed in favor of the Society of Mary," he was critical of "your position in America . . . you have not understood the spirit of the country; that as a result you have not been sufficiently appreciated; he [Purcell] fears that you will have trouble in regaining the esteem that the people ought to have for you; he finds you hold too much to your own ideas, and that there has not been sufficient prudence in some of your proceedings, etc."[57]

Leo Meyer did not hesitate to be outspoken in his correspondence with authorities in France and no doubt followed suit in his relations with the clergy in the archdiocese. In his later letters, however, he openly defended his own restraint, noted the lack of popular support of Juncker's decision to exclude and criticize him, and blamed much of the antagonism toward himself on clerical jealousy. Chevaux's letters on Purcell's visit included a commentary on Caillet's views on Meyer's recent decision to raise funds for the construction of a chapel at Nazareth. Purcell led him to believe that he had been in competition with Juncker's Emmanuel parish. "We find that you have meddled too much . . . [and] that you were against Canon Law by admitting outsiders to your chapel without [Juncker's] express permission, . . . that you wanted to erect one altar against another." He urged Meyer to proceed with "great circumspection and prudence . . . [in order not] to arouse the susceptibilities of the clergy of the county."[58]

In response to the strong letter of admonition, Meyer told Chevaux that he heard Purcell "returned very little satisfied from his interview with good

Father Caillet," who was reportedly "not very well disposed toward America." Though Purcell was in Dayton, he did not visit Nazareth but rather "sent a little boy to me to call on him at the pastor's [Juncker's] house." The interview included a charge that Meyer had heard a woman's confession near the sanctuary because there was no confessional; "Father Juncker told me that the woman's confession was null and invalid" precisely because there was no confessional. Not to let Juncker have the last word when recounting this story to Purcell, Meyer pleaded innocence since he had known Juncker "confessing women in his room while I was living with him." Meyer's imprudent remark elicited Purcell and Juncker's criticism; they "look upon my answer as an accusation, and fell upon me in good style." The Marianist superior told Chevaux, "It is useless and impossible to tell you how they framed me," but he had proceeded to attempt the impossible. He accused Juncker of several anti-Marianist tactics to the point of urging parishioners not to support St. Mary's School and not to send their sons to join the novitiate. Meyer concluded his remarks with expressions of a clear conscience, which allowed him "to bear the sequel to all of this."[59] In a December 1851 letter to Meyer, Chevaux once again admonished him "to be cautious of your words with the ecclesiastical authorities. Always manifest respect and submission." Word had reached the general council in Bordeaux that "Purcell is good, excellent—but the Irish are extremely jealous of their authority."[60]

The council, concerned that ownership of Nazareth prevented the Marianists from moving its central novitiate location to another diocese more favorable toward the Marianists—such as John Martin Henni's Diocese of Milwaukee—urged Meyer to consider selling the property but "not at a loss." In a letter composed about four weeks after Chevaux's, Caillet was even more emphatic about selling Nazareth. He wrote: "What you should desire is to sell Nazareth, which you bought inconsiderately, without consulting us, without knowing too well how to raise the money to pay for it." Considering all the opposition emanating from Juncker and Purcell, Meyer's was hardly a favorable position. Caillet reflected Chevaux's report and urged him to consider Henni's diocese, where an invitation for Marianist missionaries had been made.[61]

Without notifying Meyer, Caillet wrote to Purcell about the possibility of Meyer's departure from Cincinnati because he did not wish to remain where "his ministry and work are not appreciated" and because "a German bishop [sic; Henni was from Switzerland] would like to invite him to his diocese." The superior general assured the archbishop of Cincinnati that the teaching brothers would remain as "they are well seen by your grace."[62] In a letter to Chevaux, Meyer responded to Caillet's letter but did not include any mention of selling Nazareth or moving to Milwaukee. He defended the purchase of the Stuart property; he had received no negative comment from the head of temporalities nor from Caillet, and was compelled by circumstances to buy the land prior to a meeting of the general council.[63] The sale of Nazareth never surfaced again. To pay the debt Meyer interpreted the vow of poverty with an emphasis on strong asceticism. Such views were in accord with Meyer's perceptions of the "American way of life," which appear to have been jaundiced soon after his arrival. Not only did the putative millions lose their faith, but "America as a country is . . . unhealthy with regard to religious vocations." With apparent reference to laws against physical abuse of children in the home, but without understanding their origins, Meyer wrote to Chevaux: "There are laws in favor of children, which tie the hands of parents as soon as the children are weaned. Then also children can earn money easily, when they are only ten years old. Parents can hold on to their children only by caresses and promises." The superior of Nazareth followed a well-established tradition among Catholics who blamed American materialism and abundance for the lack of religious vocations. "You can easily see that this sensual life and this abundance of earthly goods will not allow religious vocations to germinate. . . . Alas, how many priests suffer shipwreck." In contrast, the Marianists were committed to their ascetical life: "By following the rule, we are like Trappists in France." According to Meyer, the Jesuits and Redemptorists and others "have adopted the customs of America."[64]

Brother Edel was the first of many brothers to write letters to Caillet critical of Meyer's leadership. Referring to the general need for more teaching brothers expressed by the pastors of Cincinnati, he noted that

> there is a wall between them and Father Meyer; they have absolutely no desire of entering into any undertaking with him; they hate him; we feel bad about it but they are not in the wrong. Father Meyer is irascible, rash, mysterious, and ambiguous in all he says or does. He tries to rule everybody with his heart that is cold and lacking love. I would prefer to see him back in France. I will however add that he is a good financial manager, but put another priest in his place.

Edel indicated Meyer's suspicion of his imminent removal and closed his letter with deep wishes "that they could make peace among themselves."[65]

Evidence of Purcell's growing appreciation of Nazareth, particularly St. Mary's School, surfaced as early as 1853, when the school reached an enrollment of twenty boarding students and more than thirty day students.

Father Juncker also experienced another change of heart; in 1853 two brothers were assigned to teach the boys at Emmanuel School, but the arrangement lasted only one year because of the pastor's interference in the pedagogical process. There is no evident sign of the German pastors' reconciliation with Meyer, except for the fact that the brother of the vicar general of the German-American community, Henry Ferneding, became a generous benefactor of Nazareth.[66]

Another sign of the permanence of the Marianist presence in the archdiocese was the positive response to Father Ferneding's proposal that they take charge of St. Aloysius Orphanage in February 1854, with Brother Stintzi as director and two teachers at Holy Trinity in residence to escort the boys to their school each day. The need for orphanages was made considerably evident in the wake of the cholera epidemics. In 1837 John Martin Henni, the pastor of Holy Trinity, founded the German Orphan Society, which in 1854 numbered more than sixteen hundred members, each of whom contributed three dollars to the annual fund; in 1854 there were sixty-seven orphans. The Sisters of Charity ran the orphanage until 1846, when the authorities in Emmitsburg prohibited the care of orphan boys. Laymen assumed control until around 1849, when the Order of St. Joseph took charge. According to Meyer, they were removed when a priest and a brother had been "condemned to a fine of 15 dollars each for having so mistreated two children in correcting them, as to leave physical marks."[67]

Meyer could hardly refuse the proposal "to take over the education of orphans" after "the archbishop, the Vicar General and the other priests demand[ed] insistently." Such confidence in the Marianists convinced Meyer that the "dispositions of Divine Providence are so evident" that he had to accept the work immediately rather than wait to receive permission from the general council. In light of other recent positive experiences, the Marianist superior reminded the superior general in Bordeaux: "You have already noticed that things have taken a new turn this year, the trials are over, the Blessed Virgin has triumphed."[68] Owing to financial considerations, problems with caring for orphans, and personnel problems, the Marianists departed from the orphanage in November 1855. In contrast to Meyer's adverse experiences with German pastors, this contract was terminated with relatively little acrimony.[69] With foundations expanding beyond Dayton and Cincinnati, the general council appointed Leo Meyer as the first superior-provincial of the Province of America, March 10, 1855. Also in that year John Lalanne, who had become director of the Stanislas College in Paris, the most prestigious secondary school in the city, reentered the Society, which meant that the college would belong to the Marianists; soon the general council would move from Bordeaux to Paris.[70]

The year 1855 was a turning point; the nation suffered a severe depression and high inflation, and Meyer was unable to pay the semiannual premium on the debt. Finally a fire destroyed the central house at Nazareth, including the boys' dormitory, classrooms, and several rooms of the Marianists. Even before the fire, the problem of the debt had serious repercussions; Meyer was so preoccupied with the farming economy that he imposed a quasi-monastic asceticism on the school. Damian Litz reported to Chevaux on the status of the school and the community: the boarding students and the brothers at "the so-called college sleep on straw." The students do the maintenance work, "sweep the classrooms, etc. Often food is set before them which you would hardly give a beggar. Several have run away because of the bad meals. . . . We have acquired the reputation of uncleanliness, for avarice, for trickery." He told Chevaux that Meyer had no sense of order; he was "always changing things, indeed he was spoiling our mission. . . . [This] is the consensus of opinion of all the brothers."[71] Litz was pleading for relief from Meyer's maladministration and for some direct communication from Caillet, as if a true account of the situation would never be achieved as long as the correspondence was limited to Meyer's point of view.

In a letter to Caillet a few months after the fire, Meyer reported on the withdrawal of young aspirants to the society who were not really "inclined to become religious . . . and so we can assent that the fire purified Nazareth." He noted the ideas of Brothers Litz and Heitz, "under the inspiration of Brother Stintzi" who "thought we ought to get out of our obscure condition and assume American ways." Apparently Meyer was referring to deviations from his rigidity. "Nothing was right anymore as I was holding them back by the debt we owed Stuart and the interest that had to be paid." Rather than drink the brew from the plants grown on the property "they need Chinese tea and bought $33.00 worth at one time." As if to further impugn their motive, he told Caillet about renovations at one of the cottages in order to rent it to a woman and her two daughters; "in that regard precautions are to be taken in this country." Meyer was aware of Litz's strategy to convince Paris to recall him to France; while Meyer was sick, he wrote to Caillet that Litz had "even requested a certificate from the doctor that a change of climate would be good for my health."[72]

Despite the revival of the school and the reduction of the debt through the sale of property, internal criticism of Meyer continued. Brother Stintzi wrote to Caillet seeking "the recall to France of our worthy Provincial and

Superior, Father Meyer." The rationale for this request was threefold: (1) "The good and progress of the society in this country demand it; (2) The future of Nazareth depends upon it; and (3) the care of the premature old age of the superior, Father Meyer, seems of itself to demand it." Vocations would have been doubled had Meyer been recalled eight years ago, wrote Stintzi. Indeed, the only vocations had originated outside the diocese. Purcell was temporarily supportive of Meyer in 1853, but the following year his attitude "became worse." Neither German nor English priests visit Meyer; "this is doubtless because they have orders to have no relations with our house." Though Meyer had attempted to appease the pastor of Emmanuel, "the scandal" of their conflict persisted. The brothers were highly respected, while the archdiocesan clergy, "Have nothing to do with Father Meyer."[73]

The second point, the future of Nazareth, was considered in light of the general disorder, symbolized by the inability to keep novices, and by Meyer's direction of the farm, "without, so to speak, going out of his room." Stintzi complained that he was without time for peaceful communal or mental prayer: "I am even obliged to make the spiritual exercises while supervising study periods. . . . This continual tension of mind engenders a certain lethargy in the spiritual life." Stintzi's commentary on premature deterioration of the provincial focused on his continuous ill health; "having been accustomed to wine since his childhood, and now having been deprived of it for ten years, his stomach is in a very weakened condition. . . . He suffers especially in the nervous system, the stomach having a bad influence on his brain. His corpulence is also a great inconvenience to him especially during the excessive heat of summer." He was generally so weak that he was unable to give a "short conference to the brothers." Stintzi concluded: "At the age of 60 years, the Reverend Superior, Father Meyer, is more worn out than other aged men at 75."[74]

There are no extant responses from Caillet to these letters of Litz and Stintzi. Apparently the general council, particularly Caillet, gave priority to Meyer's financial acumen over and above his ability to win the confidence of his community, the archbishop, and the German-American clergy. Hence, it was not until Meyer had made the final payment to Stuart in 1862 when news came of the imminent arrival of an official visitor. Upon receiving news of the appointment of Father John Courtès, Meyer wrote to Caillet without indicating any regret at what appeared to be a tacit recall and appointment of Courtès as the second superior of the Province of America. Since Courtès did not know German and English, Meyer advised him to rely upon Brothers Zehler and Nickels, particularly the latter, as interpreters.[75]

In his memoirs George Meyer, appointed provincial in 1896, points out that Bishop Amadeus Rappe, the French-born bishop of Cleveland, sided with an anti-Meyer faction and, during a visit to Bordeaux in 1861–1862 told Caillet to recall the provincial. Indeed, Rappe was planning to open a Cleveland "province" of the Marianists. Since John Courtès accompanied Rappe on his return voyage to the United States, he was obviously influenced by his anti-Meyer sentiments.[76] Stopping off in Cleveland before traveling to Cincinnati, Courtès reported to Caillet of his conversations with Litz, Stintzi, and Rappe. "Everyone agrees . . . any arrangement or compromise with Father Meyer as superior is impossible; and each has a thousand incidents to convince me of this."[77] After presiding over a chapter meeting, Courtès concluded that Meyer must be replaced; it is apparent that Courtès was acting provincial while he was visitor.

In the thirteen years of Meyer's administration, the Marianists had taken charge of twenty-one schools, twelve of which were viable in 1862. That year there were sixty-five brothers in the United States, twenty of whom had been missioned from France. The majority of the others were recruited from the German-American community. As Meyer told Bishop Henni in 1855: "Nazareth is perhaps the only institution in America in which the prayers are said and the instructions are given in German and I surely would not like to introduce any changes in this respect. Furthermore, there must be a German Teachers Seminary, and besides this, one for the French and another for the Irish."[78]

Nearly obsessed with reducing the debt of Nazareth and bitter with what he considered the general administration's abandonment of its responsibility to financially assist him in this effort, Meyer perceived the novitiate and the school as subservient to the interests of the motherhouse, "The St. Remy of America." For example, there were some twenty postulants between the years 1857 amd 1861. Brother Edward Gorman, who was among that group, recalled the requirement to work on the farm with only a "few months for education in the winter." In such austere conditions, of these young teenage boys "only three persevered."[79]

As noted earlier, Brother Edel considered Meyer to have been a cold-hearted person. Garvin's views corroborate Edel's: "His modesty and reserve were almost excessive. He was indifferent to food and drink; even in sickness he would not allow anyone to touch him. . . . He was averse to show of any kind, and pushed his repugnance almost to unreasonable limits." According to Garvin, Meyer's first impulses were "neighborly charity," but such impulses became exhausted in his frustrations with Juncker and other clergymen; consequently, "Father Meyer suffered in silence, and seemed really happy to be able to suffer."[80] While today such behavior would be considered passive-aggressive, it corresponds to his generally ascetical self-understanding. Though he appointed Stintzi head of temporalities and Zehler head of instruction, it was apparent to everyone in Nazareth that Meyer still possessed the power.

Leo Meyer accepted his recall to France with characteristic resignation; his only request was that two young postulants be allowed to accompany him to France, where they could complete their education in the Marianist tradition. One of the postulants was John B. Kim, who spent three years with Meyer at the novitiate in Kembs, Alsace, and at age eighteen made his profession as a Brother of Mary the year before Leo Meyer died. After completing his education at St. Remy, he taught there and later at a state normal school in Switzerland. Though Kim's historical significance will be explored in a later chapter, his academic experience was initiated by the austere yet paternalistic Leo Meyer. The other American postulant, Thomas Cleary, died in 1869, shortly after his return from France.[81]

The thoroughly German-speaking character of the American Province—prayers and conferences were in German—precluded John Courtès' easy adaptation. He received little help from the other priest of the community, Francis Louis Mauclerc, who had been engaged principally in parish ministry in Texas, Ohio, and Wisconsin. Brother Maximin Zehler was alarmed by the rumors of the appointment of Mauclerc to replace Meyer: "He is not at all competent to direct a religious community at least in America where it is so difficult to guide the minds of men," Zehler told the members of the general council of the remark of one brother about Mauclerc. "He has the fickleness of the Frenchman, and the coarseness of the German."[82] Since Meyer allowed Zehler free rein to run the school at Nazareth, he did not wish to see Meyer leave. Apparently he considered Meyer's departure a threat to stability because there was no other priest who could continue the Marianist mission in the United States. Hence, Zehler did not look favorably upon Meyer's successor. Courtès only served as provincial for two years, during which time the society achieved legal incorporation in Ohio and the novitiate received canonical approval.

Economic and social dislocation and poor communication with the distant community in San Antonio were characteristic of Marianist life during the Civil War. John Nepomucene Reinbolt, the third provincial, served the community in that position for twenty-two years, longer than any other provincial in the history of the Marianists in the United States. As will be explained in a later chapter, Reinbolt presided over the national expansion of the Society with missions as far to the east as New York City, as far west as Hawaii, as far north as Winnipeg, while in the southwest the Marianist presence had been established as early as 1852. The Society was thriving in the United States, but there was constant conflict between the Marianist and American identities, symbolized by the requirement that novices learn German.

CHAPTER THREE

National Expansion
1852–1900

⚹ I ⚹

THE FOUNDATION OF THE MARIANISTS IN THE ARCHDIOCESE OF Cincinnati under Leo Meyer represents the development of two educational models: the parish school and the independent private academy that evolved into a college. The latter provided a boarding component and was supported by middle-class families, a factor that augmented finances necessary for the continuous expansion of the campus. This private-academy model was replicated principally in San Antonio, Honolulu, and St. Louis. As will be explored later, the curriculum of such schools included primary and secondary-level courses with a strong emphasis on the humanities, mathematics, and science. A few commercial, practical, and laboratory sciences were added as the institution discerned the need to directly prepare its graduates for both a career and for further professional education. The colleges were owned by the Society and were free from outside interference until the rise of the standardization movement in the twentieth century, concurrent with the centralization of Catholic education in the diocese, symbolized by a superintendent of all Catholic schools.

Marianist parish schools during the nineteenth century, particularly in the Midwest and Northeast, tended to be in German national parishes, mostly those staffed by Redemptorists. However, the first part of this chapter focuses on Cleveland, San Antonio, and Honolulu, foundations that were of French origin. Governing the conditions of Marianist French and German schools was a contract between the provincial and the pastor that stipulated a salary and living conditions of the brothers. Salaries ranged

70

between three hundred and four hundred dollars per year. Each community was provided with a house, food, a cook, and a housekeeper.

During the first forty years of Marianist education, no brother was more significant than Brother Stintzi. He was honored by the "Stintzi" alumni at his golden anniversary celebration. Well known for his energetic pedagogy, strict discipline, and a concerned human touch, Stintzi was appointed Inspector of Primary Education of the American Province in 1869, a position created by the general chapter in 1858. Except for the combined primary and secondary schools in Dayton, San Antonio, and Honolulu, the Marianist parish schools were limited to the primary level during Stintzi's tenure, 1869–1886. Brothers composed the faculty and the brother director of the community was principal of the school.

Conflicts between pastors and the directors of communities were not uncommon; the transfer of a popular brother or the assignment of a brother unable to maintain discipline frequently triggered criticism from the parish house or rectory. Similarly, pastors who were perceived as domineering in their attempt to control the school alienated the brothers. The School Sisters of Notre Dame, founded by Mother Theresa (Karolina) Gerhardinger in Bavaria in 1834, usually taught the girls' classes in the Redemptorist parish schools.[1] Because the boys in the first three grades were viewed as too young for male teachers, the brothers usually taught boys from the fourth through the higher grades. There were some parishes, however, where the brothers were responsible for the entire boys' school. Since the sisters were not normally provided with a housekeeper and a cook and because their salaries were less than the brothers, by the 1920s it was common for pastors to turn over the entire school to the sisters. However, single-sex education prevailed in some German parishes, such as St. James in Baltimore, after the Second World War. By this time the dominant model was the new form of secondary education developed at the end of the nineteenth century, the high school, not infrequently initiated within the parishes. In the twentieth century some institutes and colleges, such as in Dayton, San Antonio, and Honolulu, evolved into institutions of higher education: University of Dayton, St. Mary's University, and Chaminade University, respectively.

Inherent in American pluralist society was the "disestablishment" of the Protestant churches and the shift to the public school as the channel through which the main goals of the nation's common values were transmitted. Discipline, morality, citizenship, and respect for authority and property dominated the classroom. Though these schools were to be free from sectarian influences, they were also grounded on biblical prayers and public readings of the King James Bible.

The Catholic reaction among bishops within the immigrant church of the 1840s, particularly Bishops John Hughes of New York and Francis P. Kenrick of Philadelphia, entailed requesting that school authorities allow Catholic students to be excused from Bible lessons or recitations. When, in deference to the Catholic position, the New York school board removed scripture from the classroom, Hughes cunningly decried the godless character of public education and thus gained support for Catholic schools. Philadelphia's board of education acceded to Kenrick's request, but some public-school defenders of tradition, generally alienated by Catholic immigrants competing for their jobs and by the Catholic attitude toward scripture, and also stimulated by anti-Catholic rhetoric from the pulpit and the press, engaged in riotous fights in Catholic neighborhoods and torched a few of their churches. Anti-Catholic and nativist hostility entered a quiescent phase for a few years only to gather momentum in the 1850s when the Know-Nothing party aimed at excluding Catholics from public office, indeed public life. John Hughes's response to the school issue may be considered paradigmatic of the general development of a separate Catholic subculture steeped in a revival of Counter-Reformation piety: emphasis on the papacy as the unifying principle in the struggle; promotion of indulgences with particular stress on Marian and Sacred Heart devotions; popularity of Benediction and public processions and ceremonies. Schools, hospitals, and orphanages represented the good works of the institutional church. Besieged by anti-Catholicism and nativism, immigrants were encouraged to identify with the church practices such as fasting and abstinence. However, the devotions to Mary and the saints and to Christ in the Eucharist during the Forty Hours of exposition of the Host not only set Catholics apart as "the other" but also exuded an affective warmth that elicited interest among some "unchurched" citizens.[2]

Rooted in a community besieged by anti-Catholicism, these devotions were widespread among many German-American parishes influenced by the Redemptorists, particularly Bishop John N. Neumann of Philadelphia.[3] The parish missions, preached by Redemptorists, Jesuits, Paulists, and Passionists, promoted these styles of devotionalism and spirituality foundational to the Catholic subculture. These parish missions, which Jay P. Dolan has referred to as "Catholic Revivalism," were aimed at conversion to a regular practice of the faith: confession, communion, temperance, and other works. Catholic revivalists, notes Dolan, aimed "to move sinners to repentance and conversion, and they aimed their sermons at the heart seeking to elicit an emotion-filled response that was ratified by a confession of sin."[4] Though doctrinal statements were laced into their sermons, preachers tended to subordinate them to the "appeal to the heart." Dolan considers Francis X. Weninger, the Jesuit who was instrumental in bringing the Marianists to Cincinnati, "unquestionably the most dramatic performer of his day. . . . The *pièce de résistance* of a Weninger mission . . . was the erection of the mission cross. . . . Thirty to fifty feet in height, inscribed with the names of Jesus, Mary and the word *mission* and the date, along with the inscription, 'He who perseveres to the end will be saved,' the cross stood as a continual reminder of the mission." On one occasion there were four thousand participants in a procession through the town that culminated in the erection of the cross. Later the sermon delivered at the foot of the cross was followed by papal blessing. Weninger proudly commented, "It was a novel scene for America, a famous one for our holy religion."[5]

Weninger was one of the few priests with a particular ministry to African-Americans. In Cincinnati he initiated the Peter Claver Society and was instrumental in the foundation of the first black parish, St. Ann's. It was through his efforts that an annual collection for Indians and Negroes was endorsed by the Third Plenary Council of Baltimore in 1884.[6] Perhaps his most controversial mission was preached to a congregation of slaves in New Orleans in 1852.[7] Weninger also preached a mission in Texas in 1859, including San Antonio,[8] where the Marianists had charge of St. Mary's Institute. He played a vital role in the Diocese of Cleveland, where the brothers staffed St. Patrick's School, their first experience in an Irish-American parish.

❧ II ❧

THOUGH THE MARIANISTS ENTERED THE DIOCESE OF GALVESTON IN 1852, just three years after the foundation in Cincinnati, their initial presence in Cleveland in 1856 was also a historical departure, since it was in the first English-speaking parish school. The French-born bishop, Louis Amadeus Rappe, who had met Brothers Stintzi and Heitz while visiting Louisville, Ohio, in early 1856, successfully urged them to teach at St. Patrick's.[9] With the permission of Leo Meyer, the two brothers arrived in Cleveland in September to take over the school, which had been staffed by lay teachers. The French bishop and the Marianists in Cleveland had a close association. Stintzi's anti-Meyer activity was complemented by Rappe's own efforts when the bishop wrote to Caillet on the crisis of confidence in Meyer's authority. As mentioned in the previous chapter, Rappe went so far as to propose the establishment of a Cleveland Province of the Society of Mary. In a letter to Caillet dated December 11, 1860, Rappe wrote that "it would be highly desirable to have one novitiate for the Germans and another for the Irish or Americans. Your Society has lost many candidates because of mixing [nationalities]." The Dayton novitiate would be for the Germans; the Cleveland, for English-speaking aspirants. Rappe would also arrange for a boarding school on the Dayton model.[10] In two subsequent letters Rappe persistently argued for a Cleveland novitiate on the basis of Meyer's incompetency. Since the latter was replaced by Joseph Courtès, the bishop's plan was deemed unrealistic. He told Caillet, however, that he would not accede to the superior general's requirement of a three-hundred-dollar annual salary for each brother. He told him two hundred was sufficient, particularly with the economic impact of the Civil War.[11]

Amadeus Rappe had been recruited by Purcell and was assigned to the missions in Toledo; in 1846 he was ordained bishop of Cleveland, which experienced phenomenal growth; in 1870 the Catholic population reached nearly one hundred thousand, most of whom were German and Irish. According to notions of authority etched in French political and religious traditions for two centuries, Rappe imposed uniformity in his diocese. Initially opposed to ethnic particularism in the form of national parishes and foreign language in the classrooms, Rappe only reluctantly accommodated the German-speaking Catholic parishioners, who, led by an ardent nationalist clergy, formed pockets of resistance to their bishop's policies. Because Rappe was strongly authoritarian in dealing with his clergy, such as assigning troublemakers to other parishes as an undisguised rebuke, he alienated the Irish as well as the German priests. Francis X. Weninger was instrumental in garnering support for the proliferation of German parishes, one of which was established without the prior approval of the bishop. Shortly after Rappe accepted this *fait accompli*, that is, St. Joseph's, he retaliated against the Jesuit by withdrawing approval for Weninger's mission at the parish because at the eleventh hour he decided to administer the sacrament of confirmation at St. Joseph's. During Rappe's sermon that evening several irate pro-Weninger congregants interrupted with shouts of "Martin Luther" and later even threatened violence.[12]

With preference for multilingual priests who could be assigned to one of several parishes, Rappe favored French priests and religious from Alsace and Lorraine—hence his immediate attraction to the Marianists, particularly Stintzi, the first Marianist to have a command of English. Of course Rappe's promotion of "Americanism" was perceived by his enemies as a mask for his own French nationalism. Rappe was considered an arbitrary administrator, insensitive to ethnicity and to priests' rights, and his style of leadership generated overt dissent in the form of letters to Rome. Eventually rumor of the bishop's solicitation of women in the confessional intensified the anti-Rappe sentiment, and in 1870, while in Rome for Vatican Council I, he was asked to resign. This is merely a sketch of a considerably complex situation, one that entailed an extensive network of priest advocates, including Eugene M. O'Callaghan, who published in the *Freeman's Journal* under the pseudonym *Jus*.[13] Perhaps this polarized situation did not directly affect the brothers at St. Patrick's, but eventually it did as O'Callaghan dismissed the brothers when he became pastor in 1878. Though they returned shortly after O'Callaghan became pastor of St. Colman's in 1882, there is no doubt they were associated with the pro-Rappe forces. Also, by 1863 they were teaching at three other parishes in Cleveland: the Cathedral School, St. Mary's, and St. Peter's. The latter was a German-American parish, where the brothers could have been privy to the controversies that led to Rappe's resignation. Perhaps Rappe even confided in the brothers. As John Garvin noted, "The friendship of the saintly bishop for the brothers, and his interest in their community was so great as to become at times almost embarrassing."[14]

When Brothers Stintzi and Heitz opened St. Patrick's School, they lived in a house provided by the bishop but without any furnishings. The pastor, Father Conlan, announced the arrival of the brothers to the parish congregation. He reportedly said, "The brothers have at last arrived; but they are poor, having made a vow of poverty. They are dwelling in a house in which everything is wanting. They have not a stool to sit upon [which was literally true]. Now although you are poor yourselves, every family can spare something be it ever so little—a spoon, a fork, a table knife, a bowl and plate, a saucer, etc., etc. . . . Anything will be accepted with thankfulness." That evening "a shower" of a variety of articles for the house arrived. On the opening day of school in 1856 there were ten students ranging in age from eight to eighteen.[15] Soon the school was enlarged and later a new school opened. In 1875 there were fifteen Marianist brothers teaching in four schools in Cleveland; this represented the most extensive Marianist parish-school endeavor in that period. At St. Patrick's there were three brothers, each of whom was responsible for three classes in one room; this required some form of the monitor plan to augment the individual and class-wide recitation. The Marianists have maintained a school in Cleveland for nearly 150 years.

Stintzi had a significant influence during his tenure as Inspector (1869–1886); he set high standards for the teacher training of scholastics at the normal school attached to the motherhouse in Dayton and attempted to improve the effectiveness of parish schools throughout the province. Even after his retirement in 1886 he spent ten years as an administrator of parish schools in Cleveland, Rochester, New York, and Dayton. In 1896 he finally retired after fifty years experience in Marianist education.[16]

❧ III ❧

FIVE YEARS BEFORE BISHOP RAPPE RECRUITED THE MARIANISTS IN
Ohio, J. M. Odin, C.M., of Galveston successfully negotiated with Georges
Joseph Caillet in Bordeaux a commitment to assign Marianists to the foundation of a school for boys to complement the school for girls run by the
Ursuline sisters in San Antonio. Odin arranged to pay the travel expenses of
the teaching brothers and to fund the school and living quarters. The agreement between Odin and Caillet also included recognition of the "teaching
method of the Society of Mary," which as mentioned in a previous chapter
was a blend of the individual and the simultaneous methods, with the distinctive feature of student monitors to instruct specific groups in the classroom.[17]

The general ignorance of the geographical character of the United States
was particularly evident in Jean Chevaux's letter to Leo Meyer in which he
reported on Caillet's agreement to send four brothers to San Antonio, "a city
situated near the Rocky Mountains." Chevaux told Meyer of the need for
one Cincinnati brother to be assigned to the new community; Brothers Edel,
Zehler, and Litz were recommended.[18] Since Edel taught botany, agriculture, and horticulture and was not very valuable to the faculty of St. Mary's
School, he was sent to be director of the pioneer community in San Antonio, an old Tejano settlement that had recently become an American frontier town with a population of about three thousand. In March 1852 he met
the other three members of the community: Brothers John Baptist Laignoux
and Nicholas Koenig, and a seminarian, Xavier Mauclerc. Temporarily stay-
ing with Claude Mary Dubuis, pastor of San Fernando parish, who later succeeded Odin as bishop, the brothers opened their school in a renovated shop
on Military Plaza on August 25, 1852. Since Mauclerc stayed in Galveston
to complete his theological studies under the bishop's direction, the fourth
teacher was a layman, Timothy O'Neil. Rapid enrollment required a large
facility; Edel designed a simple rectangular structure—sixty feet in length,
twenty-five feet in width—on ground purchased by Odin with the financial
aid of John Twohig, the first of his many gifts to the Marianists in San Antonio. St. Mary's Institute opened in its new location on the east bank of the
San Antonio River in March 1853. Many new buildings were added over the
years as St. Mary's grew to over four hundred students by 1890.[19]

Odin was born in Hauteville, France, in 1800; while attending the Sulpician seminary St. Irenaeus in Lyons, he was drawn to missionary life in the
United States by the example of his parish priest, Antoine Blanc, later his
metropolitan archbishop in New Orleans, and Bishop Louis William

DuBourg, whom he followed to New Orleans, finally completing his theology at the seminary outside St. Louis, St. Mary-of-the-Barrens in Perryville, Missouri. Prior to ordination in May 1823, Odin joined the Congregation of the Mission of St. Vincent de Paul, referred to as Vincentians or Lazarists in reference to their Paris motherhouse on the Rue Saint Lazare. After teaching at the seminary, he was assigned to the Texas mission in 1840, the year Pope Gregory XVI placed San Antonio under the authority of the archbishop of New Orleans, just four years after the establishment of the Republic of Texas. Odin was vice prefect of Texas; his Vincentian confrere, Jean Timon, later bishop of Buffalo who invited Meyer to his diocese, was the prefect apostolic of the state. Appointed first vicar apostolic of Texas, Odin was consecrated a bishop by Archbishop Blanc in New Orleans. During the next decade, interrupted by the American "defense" of Texas against the Mexican troops, which led to the republic's incorporation into the United States on July 4, 1845, Odin founded parishes and fostered the immigration of clergy. Appointed bishop of Galveston in 1847, the year Timon was named bishop of Buffalo, Odin soon recruited the Ursuline sisters for his rapidly growing diocese.[20]

According to the 1855 *Catholic Almanac and Laity's Directory*, the Galveston diocese encompassed all of Texas and included twenty-eight churches and thirty-five priests. The Catholic population was not listed. There were five schools for boys and three academies for "young ladies."[21] In the Cincinnati archdiocese there were 109 churches, 104 priests, thirty schools, eight female academies, and two colleges (i.e., boys' and young men's academies) for a Catholic population numbering some 110,000.[22] In 1855 there were nearly 120 students including many boarders and seven brothers at St. Mary's Institute San Antonio;[23] at the Dayton "St. Mary's Boarding School," there were only forty-two students and about the same number of faculty as at the San Antonio school. Irish-born and America-educated, Purcell and the French missionary bishop Odin had a common concern for the ethnic diversity of their parish communities. St. Mary's Institute was initially intended primarily for the Hispanic population who formed the vast majority of San Antonio's Catholic community, while totaling about eight thousand of the forty thousand Catholics in the state in 1850. In a letter to the Lazarists' superior general, Odin commented on the need for the brothers' school. "The city of San Antonio is crowded with children totally ignorant. Only a good school could regenerate the poor Mexican population."[24]

In 1859, Odin provided the Society with Mission Concepción and its farm to provide revenues for the new school. Of the three brothers assigned to San Antonio, however, only Brother Laignoux knew Spanish well enough to teach the Hispanic students. Brother Koenig was limited to French the first few years, while Brother Edel could teach in English. Hence, for a period St. Mary's was considered the French school. In September 1852 Edel was pleading for dictionaries in Spanish-French and English-French as well as several texts in Spanish for math, composition, and reading. There were continuous requests for both teaching and working brothers. Though there was an obvious commitment to respond to Spanish-speaking students, from its origins the school had an open-enrollment policy, related not only to ethnicity but also to religion. Unlike St. Mary's School in Dayton, the San Antonio school welcomed non-Catholic students.[25]

The open-enrollment policy for students of all ethnic groups reflected the changing demography of the city. The rapidly increasing flow of Anglo-American and European (particularly German) immigrants into San Antonio during the republic and early statehood period reduced the Hispanic residents to a minority, which was not reversed until 1970. The economic and social status of Hispanics shifted from that of insider to outsider. Timothy Matovina notes: "In the economic realm, after Texas statehood citizens of Mexican heritage became a working underclass and lost most of their land holdings."[26] Brother Joseph W. Schmitz, professionally trained historian of the Society of Mary in Texas, analyzed the motivation behind this policy:

> Bishop Odin had wanted the school to take care of Mexican children in particular. The Mexican population in 1852, however, was but little responsive to elevating influences, and if the school were to thrive and become more than an obscure mission serving a shifting population, it would have to draw its clientele from the city generally. The brothers sensed this and insisted from the very beginning that all comers be admitted.[27]

Though it was unlikely four French brothers could limit their student body to entirely Spanish-speaking students, the fact that several Hispanics did attend indicates that the population was not entirely "shiftless." For example, in 1860 Leo Meyer assigned Brother Nicholas Bohn, a working brother, to San Antonio. Edel, always in need of more teachers, placed him with the younger students. "Bohn at once took a liking to the Mexican children and became a most successful teacher, before long handling the largest class in the school."[28]

Anti-Mexican sentiment was most intense among the forces of anti-Catholicism and nativism. English-speaking Protestants perceived their growing hegemony in Texas as another illustration of God's design in the advance of Christian (i.e., Protestant) America. As one editorial writer stated in 1851, Texas statehood happened "thanks to the Almighty Being who has so powerfully wrought in our favor." Nativism blended with anti-Catholicism when Protestant ascendancy was associated with victory over the "Mexican dominions" in terms of the spread of the Savior's power of the gospel "[and] beginning of the downfall of the anti-Christ."[29]

Nativism and anti-Catholicism of the Know-Nothing party identified the evils of slavery with the tyrannical character of Roman Catholicism. Slave ownership and priestcraft were symbolic of the demonic forces undermining Protestant culture. Hence, the Know-Nothings depended on a coalition of nativists, abolitionists, and prohibitionists. Eventually the anti-slavery groups became alienated by nativist rioting and drifted into the Republican party in 1856. Nevertheless, nativism and anti-Catholicism of the Know-Nothing party continued to be active in Texas. Indeed, the party managed to garner support from those alienated by Mexicans and by the Polish and German immigrants. Sam Houston temporarily positioned himself with the party because he was convinced that Catholics held a "foreign allegiance" to Rome. He said that the Know-Nothings did not aim "to put down Catholics, but to prevent Catholics from putting down Protestants." Texas Catholics and Democrats struggled against the Know-Nothing party. José Antonio Navarro, a Texas patriot and politician, asserted: "The Texas-Mexicans are Catholics and may be proud of their fathers; they will defend themselves against such infamous aggression."[30] Nativist hostility toward Mexicans in Texas was manifested in the so-called Cart War, when Anglos attacked the carts of a freight company that allegedly hired only Tejano drivers. Nearly seventy of them were killed after the Know-Nothing vigilance committee gained support for these violent assaults. Anti-Mexican sentiment intensified as escaped slaves were frequently provided with assistance in their pursuit of safety in Mexico. With slavery basic to a significant portion of the Texas economy, this Tejano "underground pathway" exacerbated this anti-Mexican-American sentiment.

Just as the Ursuline convent in Charlestown, Massachusetts, was set in flames by nativist rioters, so the Know-Nothings supported investigations into the alleged prison conditions of all convents. There were manifestations of this "anti-nunnery" sentiment toward the Ursuline convent in San Antonio, and there was even an investigation of its moral propriety. The Civil War brought an end to the Know-Nothing movement in Texas, but because prominent Catholics were involved in the "peculiar institution" of slavery, because of the strong fear of being accused of Catholic political disloyalty, and because Catholic political ideology tended to follow general trends in society, the vast majority of southern bishops, their priests, and laity, including the Brothers of Mary in San Antonio, supported the Confederacy.[31]

Bishop Odin owned a few slaves at his home in Galveston, and the Vincentians in Perryville owned slaves. As Archbishop of New Orleans, Odin held a very conservative line. After the Union forces had captured the city and the French pastor of St. Rose's parish, Claude Maistre, who led a congregation composed principally of free people of color, praised the "Emancipation Proclamation," Odin was so critical of his stance that he removed him from the parish. In the postwar years Odin, unlike other southern bishops, did not pursue a vigorous catechetical program for the freed black people in his archdiocese.[32] His successor in Galveston, Claude Marie Dubuis, a close friend of the Marianists, was supportive of the Confederacy. More concerned with the effect of hostilities upon the people of his diocese, he pursued a policy of pragmatic realism relatively free from ideology.[33]

⋈ IV ⋊

THE STAFFING PROBLEMS OF THE MARIANISTS IN TEXAS AND THEIR remoteness from Dayton were persistent factors that plagued Brother Edel. When Dubuis was pastor of San Fernando parish, he occasionally provided some financial aid. In 1854 Edel purchased ninety acres of land from Bishop Odin, which created a significant debt, but Edel mentioned to Caillet: "Father Dubuis gave me at once 100 piasters to defray initial expenses."[34] The farm was to reduce food expenditures of the school only if the general administration would assign working brothers to the San Antonio community. Four years later Odin gave the Marianists "a fine fertile piece of land situated about 1/2 leagues from town on the banks of the river and watered by an irrigation canal." Odin told Caillet that he had been offered the equivalent of "62,500 francs for it. On this plot of land are found the ruins of Mission Concepción with its beautiful and solid stone church built by Indian converts." Odin projected a restoration of the church and the hope that it would attract pilgrims to the cherished sanctuary. Odin planned a manual or trade school on the property "where we could educate the orphans of the surrounding county."[35]

Though Odin had intended to present this gift of ninety acres of land to St. Mary's, it seems to have been precipitated by Leo Meyer's intentions to close the school. Edel had written to Caillet to that effect twice, September 1857 and December 1858. D. Clouzet, head of temporalities in Bordeaux, told Meyer "that the establishment in San Antonio has a future; it is in your province, try to support it as much as possible."[36] Because of his health problems and his almost compulsive concern about Nazareth, Meyer had never attempted to visit San Antonio. There had always been conflicts in the community. Brother Laignoux considered Edel too demanding of his time, but too lax in not abiding by the rule regarding meat at the evening meal and other minor matters of "indiscretion." Brother Koenig was continuously bothered by the climate, while all the brothers agreed that Father Mauclerc asserted his authority as a priest above the brothers and refused to teach at the school. Koenig and Laignoux were transferred to Dayton in 1858, but as early as 1854 Brothers Charles Francis and Elegius Beyrer (later ordained a priest) had been assigned to San Antonio.[37] Since Meyer never visited San Antonio, Edel made the trip to Dayton in the spring of 1858 with the intention of recruiting brothers for the Texas mission. However, he left without a confrere. Apparently Caillet and Meyer held Edel responsible for the conflict in San Antonio. Caillet considered Edel's trip to have been excessively expensive, but the visit with Meyer would allow the provincial "to have long and repeated chats with him [Edel] about the union of the brothers in San Antonio."[38]

Later that year, October 1858, the superior general reported to the provincial of the general council's reaction to the many "surprises [at Meyer's] facility with which you open new places and close down the old ones. . . . We don't understand how that can happen with advantage for the Society and for the welfare of the work undertaken." Caillet urged Meyer to engage in "mature reflection" before deciding on a new foundation and "more constancy in sustaining what has begun." Perhaps he had received news of Meyer's June 12, 1858, letter to Odin, in which Meyer stated, "I frankly acknowledge that I was thinking of suppressing the establishment of San Antonio." In a letter to Caillet, December 17, 1858, Meyer informed him that he had written to Bishop Odin: "I directed him to make certain arrangements: Among other things I mentioned that it would be desirable that the brothers' school be reserved for Catholic students only, as the mixture of non-Catholics was not good, that the Society have charge of Catholic children only, and in this case two brothers sufficed, to whom a fixed salary should be paid; that the farm [purchased in 1854] be eased out and the revenue be employed for the school." With experience limited to the German parishes in the Archdiocese of Cincinnati and St. Mary's School in Dayton, Meyer, in characteristically authoritative style, imposed such severe conditions upon the school that Odin and Edel were led to consider Meyer's letter as tantamount to closure.[39] Hence, Odin proposed that title to the property of St. Mary's School and Mission Concepción be in the name of the Society of Mary, so that none of the bishop's successors could say, "Gentlemen, you may retire, I no longer need your services." On the other hand, if the Society decided to leave San Antonio, all properties would revert back to the diocese. The title was signed and became a legal document in 1859.[40]

Brother Beyrer, who was studying for the priesthood, shared Leo Meyer's disillusionment with American religious pluralism, particularly when faced with the interfaith character of St. Mary's, San Antonio. Writing at the end of the Civil War, Beyrer described conditions at the school: "One-third of the boarding students are between 12 and 18. Being Protestants they frequently are the cause of our Catholic children becoming corrupted," since these Protestants attended religious exercises with the Catholic boys "and even during Divine Office they make others laugh so that they worry us greatly." He considered the thoroughly Catholic enrollment of Dayton so fortunate as the "northern brothers are not obliged to contend with such large and mature Protestant boys who are pure infidels."[41]

The vast majority of Marianist schools in France were primary schools, while in the United States they were, unlike the public community schools, parish schools. Without a viable public school system in Texas until the 1870s, Protestants had a choice among private schools. Characteristic of Catholic schools in general, St. Mary's projected an image of academic and social discipline and integrity that attracted Protestants. Dependent upon the tuition, board, and other fees from the families of boarding students, St. Mary's also waived tuition for more than a few students.[42] In an 1854 Texas school law, private schools that provided gratuitous tuition could be partially supported by the public school fund, a law that obviously benefited Catholic schools. A law of 1875 stated that "private academies on receiving and teaching such pupils as required secondary training, have been allowed compensation out of the school fund."[43] St. Mary's benefited from these funds, which by 1914 went exclusively to public schools.

After the Civil War, Edel traveled to Dayton and Paris to place before the general council a set of requests that entailed the assignment of more brothers and a priest to the expansion of the Society in Texas and to the establishment of a province in the state to obviate the need for reliance on the distant authority in Dayton. He returned with the news from the provincial, John Nepomucene Reinbolt, of the imminent closure of the San Antonio school. However, Edel successfully urged Reinbolt to visit the school, which led to a strong commitment to St. Mary's. In his March 1, 1866, report to Caillet, Reinbolt concluded that, since the bishop and the brothers had been so committed to the school, "it would be great cowardice to quit such a painful post." Reinbolt noted the absence of any previous provincial visitation, and the separation due to four years of war had a significant impact.

> I found the brothers in costume (uniform clothing) that resembled but faintly one or the other piece of clothing worn by the Brothers of Mary. The community had neither conference nor council sessions of any kind. There was a gradual non-observance of the common regimen and regular time table. . . . There was but little, if any, direction [by Edel] whether material, professional, or spiritual.[44]

Reinbolt therefore transferred Edel to Mission Concepción, where he could thrive as an enthusiastic agronomist, and appointed Brother Charles Francis as director.

Edel had never really achieved a secure sense of his authority, had difficulty implementing his decisions, and had been on occasion impatient with students; during two or three situations he had employed corporal punishment. After three years devoted to improving the land at Mission Concepción, Edel was transferred to Dayton. He soon returned to his rustic home in the woods, where he pursued his penchant for gardening on a remote portion of the farm attached to the motherhouse.[45]

His replacement at St. Mary's, San Antonio, Brother Charles Francis, possessed a personal style of leadership and an academic professionalism that were quite distinctive. Unlike Edel, Charles Francis asserted authority, was trained in the three principal areas of the school—classics, science, and mathematics—and spoke Spanish and English to complement his native French. Edel was pragmatic when it came to imposing the rules governing meals and seems to have been rather sentimental. In contrast, Charles Francis was distant, given to a calculated mentality apparent in his businesslike approach to conducting the school. As enrollment of boarders and day students continued to expand, the new director/principal led an ambitious building program, which in 1870 would provide for a student body of over four hundred, while the Marianist faculty had increased to thirteen. As a result of another building program in the late 1870s, St. Mary's, which had changed from an academy to a college, was recognized as one of the preeminent institutions of its kind in the southwest.[46]

During the administration of Charles Francis and his successor, there was an increasing enrollment of Mexican students. By the 1870s these students, many of whom knew some English, challenged the administration's adaptability to integrate them into the social and academic life of the school. Though the teachers were encouraged to learn Spanish during the summers, few took the time to do so. Because many of the Mexican students were deficient in English and were required to take on part-time labor in the fields and orchards—which for many entailed migrant labor with the family—scheduling classes became a serious problem. Perhaps the anti-Mexican sentiment so prevalent among the majority of San Antonio's population was reflected in the student body of St. Mary's, despite whatever counteracting influences the brothers may have had. These factors, combined with the requirement that the Mexican students attend religious-education classes at San Fernando parish run by the Spanish Claretians, led to a tentative solution: the formation of a separate class composed only of Mexican students. Because this "school within a school" seems to have created more problems than it solved, the administration, in tandem with the pastor of San Fernando, decided to establish a parish boys' school staffed by the Society of Mary. Though the school experienced chronic absenteeism during the fall harvest period, and though it would be a few years before a suitable school building was provided, San Fernando parish school had an enrollment of nearly four hundred students.[47] By this time San Antonio had become a diocese (1874), and it was Bishop John C. Neraz, successor to the first ordinary, Anthony Dominic Pellecer (1874–1880), who supported the new San Fernando School.[48] In 1892, the diocese had a population of sixty-five thousand; San Fernando's boy's school had an enrollment of 160; there were eighty-five students at the parochial school for girls run by the Sisters of Charity of the Incarnate Word, a French community founded in Lyons for the Diocese of Galveston. This comparatively small school may be explained by the open enrollment of the sisters' academy in San Antonio. The other parish schools in the diocese were coeducational.[49]

At the San Fernando school, English prevailed in the classroom, but a knowledge of Spanish was essential. Brother Joseph Schwaab, who had been strongly inclined to teach the Mexican students at St. Mary's, was the principal of the Cathedral School. To foster Spanish he successfully implemented the recitation of community prayers in Spanish among the brothers and priests at St. Mary's. In accord with the pattern in German and other ethnic parochial schools, religion classes at San Fernando's were conducted in Spanish, and the school closed on those parish feast days that had been observed for over a century at the church built in 1755. Indeed, its character as the Mexican cathedral was developed during the late nineteenth century when it was noted that in San Fernando there was "a wooden figure of a Mexican representing Christ," which Timothy M. Matovina notes "reminded San Fernando congregants that the divine image was not reflected exclusively in Anglo-American newcomers, but also in Mexicans who suffered the agony of military conquest."[50]

In a letter to the superior general in March 1899, Brother John B. Kim, the inspector of the American Province, provided several reasons why the San Fernando School "is far from satisfactory." The teachers placed blame for the decline in enrollment and the "very poor" quality of the classes on the pastor: "They tell me he never comes to visit the school and that he never speaks of it in church." According to Kim, the Spanish Claretian pastor was known to be "most affable towards the brothers and never refused them anything he could grant." It appears that the Marianist faculty may have been scapegoating the pastor. Kim listed several reasons for the decline in enrollment: "Most of the Mexicans are very poor and cannot pay tuition; they lead a nomadic life and sometimes live far from the school; the school is located in one of the worst sections of the city which explains why we receive very few children of the better families."[51]

The director of the community, and therefore the principal of the school, Brother Joseph Schwaab, well known for his commitment to the ministry of Mexican students, had been in office for fourteen years. In his history of the Marianists in Texas, Brother Schmitz noted that Schwaab's "close-cut hair suggested a Prussian Field Marshal, which by temperament he might well have been. Like many stern men, he demanded docility from those over whom he had authority. . . . Although his paternalism was appreciated by children not capable of thinking for themselves, it was not particularly acceptable when applied to his equals who had ideas of their own." He appears to have been compulsive about class and religious discipline; he composed a list of seventy-four "enumerated observations on what the brothers should and should not do in the classroom and in the community."

Kim wrote that Schwaab wished to be relieved of his position of director of the community, composed only of two other brothers: "he said he needs a rest [and] that his nerves are so weakened . . . . he makes on me the impression of a man that may soon lose his mind. But it may be that this state is only passing."[52] In any event, the small faculty for a school of 160 boys was a severe challenge, particularly when there was a wide cultural gap between students and faculty. Nevertheless, San Fernando's school remained with the Marianists until 1927, when, as an economic measure, it became coeducational under the Incarnate Word Sisters.[53]

⚜ V ⚜

ST. MARY'S COLLEGE HAD EXPERIENCED OVERCROWDING, PARTICULARLY with 85 boarders and 330 "day schoolers" in 1892.[54] To relieve this situation a new boarding college had been proposed for many years, but finally in 1892 the central administration assigned the American provincial and the inspector of schools, L. Beck and J. B. Kim respectively, to make an on-site evaluation of the proposed property on the western periphery beyond the city limits. San Antonio's population had grown to fifty thousand, and that affected the expansion of the commercial district in the vicinity of St. Mary's downtown campus. It became quite evident that adequate space for boarding students required a second campus in the metropolitan area; seventy-five acres of West Heights was approved for the development of what was named St. Louis College. In preparation for the school's opening in September 1894, a prospectus composed in English, Spanish, and German described the environment as "sufficiently distant from the city for quiet undisturbed application to study . . . furnishing ample space for outdoor exercise."[55] In the 1898 *Catholic Directory*, St. Louis College listed "21 Brothers of Mary, Bro. John Wolf, director, Rev. Jos. Weckesser, chaplain, 70 boarders, 12 day-schoolers."[56] St. Mary's listed only "10 Brothers of Mary" for the "290 day-schoolers." A boarding school obviously required a widely diversified faculty, and the environment attracted some Marianists in semi-retirement, such as Brothers Damian Litz and Charles Francis. St. Mary's downtown location was vital for the Catholic population of the surrounding parishes. The *Catholic Directory* noted that its "day-schoolers are children of the different parishes, English, German, Mexican, and Polish."

❈ VI ❧

SINCE THEIR ORIGINS, THE MARIANISTS HAD BEEN COMMITTED TO flexibility in the development of their principal educational ministry, including orphanages. The college model developed in Dayton and San Antonio embraced the boarding-school feature and the combination of primary and secondary education for students ranging in age from about eight to eighteen. Though enrollment represented various social classes and ethnic groups, the limited number of poor students was dependent on free tuition provided by the Marianists. These various ethnic groups did not include African-Americans until the mid-twentieth century.

The courses at St. Mary's Institute in San Antonio during the early years embraced "Moral and religious instruction; English and Spanish (with lessons in French and German to such who desire same); physics; chemistry; astronomy; bookkeeping; history; geography; penmanship; drawing; vocal and instrumental music."[57] Under Father Francis Feith's administration, enrollment reached over three hundred students in the 1880s and required separate classes with distinctive course offerings. The "high class" was established for those teenage boys ready to move on to an independent career or to attend some form of higher education or professional training. Their courses included "natural philosophy, grammar, history, algebra, geometry, trigonometry, physiology and bookkeeping." The lower grades reversed the order of primary school with seventh to first, roughly equivalent to second through ninth grade, with courses in religion, literature, science, mathematics, music, penmanship, and drawing.[58] It was not until 1908 that St. Louis College, later called St. Mary's University, adopted modern academic structures, a development that will be fully explored in a later chapter.

In general, the San Antonio experience is a significant and distinctive chapter in the history of the Marianists. Though it was always considered on the fringe of the American Province, there was a certain flavor to the Texas story: pragmatic adaptability, an easy openness to the culture, a less than competitive spirit with non-Catholic neighbors, and a generally good relationship with bishops and other religious that revealed a mutuality of interests in "taming" the frontier. The latter required, in contrast to frontier roughness, a "civilizing" mission to bring culture, elegance, and the principles of morality, manners, and civility to the students.

❖ VII ❖

IN SEPTEMBER 1883 THE MARIANISTS TOOK CHARGE OF ST. LOUIS College in Honolulu, Oahu, one of the larger of the seven major islands settled by the Polynesians in the fifth century. In the early nineteenth century (1810) the islands were unified by King Kamehameha, with the support of Europeans. After his death, his son and successor, Liholiho, and two of his widows destroyed much of the traditional religion, which had discriminated against women. In 1820, Protestant missionaries from Massachusetts, the last state to disestablish religion around 1820, arrived in Honolulu, and soon the unity of church and state had been tacitly achieved. Hence, from its origins, education was headed up by Congregationalist missionaries from Boston, who determined its religious ethos.[59]

Catholic missionaries assigned to the islands by *Propaganda Fide* were priests and brothers of the Congregation of the Sacred Hearts of Jesus and Mary, the Picpus Fathers, founded by Pierre Coudrin in 1800. Arriving in 1827 under the direction of the superior, Alexis Bachelot, SS.CC., six missionaries represented the official foundation of the church in the islands. However, the anti-Catholicism of the Protestant missionaries, so characteristic of Massachusetts during this period, dominated the king's policy, and within three years the priests were expelled, but, as if "priestcraft" was perceived as *the* problem, the brothers were allowed to remain. Persecution of Catholics continued to the extent that for refusing to attend the required Protestant services, they were imprisoned. With the support of the French government, priests were allowed to return in 1839: a representative to the king's court read a proclamation demanding that Catholics be granted freedom of religion on a par with those rights held by the Protestants. A refusal of this proclamation would lead to war. The Picpus Fathers returned in 1840; three years later Louis Maigret, SS.CC., was appointed first bishop of Honolulu. In addition, in 1840 King Kamehameha III, in council with the chiefs of the islands, passed the first constitution of the Hawaiian Islands.[60]

According to the comprehensive school law of that year, the government took charge of Protestant and Catholic schools and thereby transformed them to public schools. Since the Protestant missionary board had virtually composed the law, their dominance was ensured by several factors, most significantly that the Protestants controlled all authority in awarding teacher certificates. The king later changed the law to provide for two independent religious school systems under state control.[61]

Even after Protestantism was once again proclaimed the state religion in 1846, there was recognition of "freedom of conscience for all." The parents of each school district selected the school agent, and later the school's trustees were to reflect the religious character of the school. Hence, the government was committed to impartiality in the development of its school system. Private secondary education was subsidized because of its general public utility. When St. Louis College came under the direction of the Marianists in 1883, it received a ten-thousand-dollar subsidy, while twenty-five hundred dollars in government scholarships was awarded biennially until the islands were annexed by the United States in 1898, a process that ended the government's control of Catholic and Protestant education.

The Sacred Heart priest who recruited the Marianists to Hawaii was Leonor Fouesnel, SS.CC., described by one historian of Catholicism in the islands as "a patriarch-like figure, with long hair and a long beard."[62] Prior to being sent on a recruiting mission to France and the United States in 1883 by Bishop Herman Koeckemann, SS.CC., Fouesnel had been pastor of St. Anthony Church (1855–1882) in Wailuku on the island of Maui. He was vice-provincial of the Sacred Heart community in 1883 and served as provincial from 1891 to 1898. Fouesnel visited the Marianist superior general, Joseph Simler, in Paris in early 1883, followed by a letter to John Reinbolt. As a result, five brothers were assigned to teach at St. Louis College, and three brothers were appointed to take charge of the boys' classes at St.

Anthony's parish in Wailuku, where Fouesnel had been pastor for twenty-seven years.[63]

Brother Bertram Bellinghausen, director of the community at St. Louis College, recorded the events on the brothers' arrival in Honolulu, September 3, 1883:

> We were taken to the only church (Our Lady of Peace) in hacks [i.e., horse-drawn "taxis"] and the bishop, Mgr. Herman Koeckemann, received us in full Pontificals. Rev. F. Damien Deveuster of the Leper Settlement-Molokai, said mass after which we were taken to the college through the Chinese quarter, Beretania St., the only approach.[64]

With a population of around twenty-three thousand, Honolulu was a cosmopolitan city with Chinese, Japanese, Portuguese, and Americans complementing the native Hawaiians, both full and part Polynesians. The majority of the Americans traced their heritage to Protestant missionaries, and toward the end of the nineteenth century they dominated the economy and were making a significant mark in politics. The Protestant Mission Board, which had initiated a successful christianization, were political leaders; but they had also introduced diseases to the island to such an extent that only 10 percent of the population of Hawaii was native in 1920. In the same year the census reported that the large Japanese population had grown to 43 percent of the total population.[65]

St. Louis College had been founded in 1880 by William J. Larkin, a priest with pastoral experience in Australia and New Zealand. That year there were 4,078 Hawaiian students enrolled in 159 Hawaiian schools and 3,086 students enrolled in English schools. After a successful fund-raising effort, Larkin opened the College of St. Louis, a Hawaiian commercial and business academy. The name St. Louis was in honor of Bishop Louis Maigret's patron saint. Because Larkin was involved in politics, both Hawaiian and ecclesiastical, and because a new building that he had designed collapsed with one fatality, Larkin was forced to leave the islands in 1881. The Fathers of the Mission, the title of the Priests of the Sacred Hearts congregation associated with the mission in Hawaii, assumed control of the college with lay teachers until the following year, when the Brothers of Mary arrived. However, priests of the Mission, accountable to the bishop, remained as principals of the college, a source of periodic conflict for several years.[66]

St. Louis College was an immediate success; by the end of the first year there were 245 students, 45 of whom were boarders. As enrollment increased by almost one hundred the next year, the motherhouse responded by sending four more brothers to Honolulu. By the end of the school year the brothers at St. Anthony's in Wailuku on the island of Maui taught 105 students in a three-classroom building. A third school, St. Mary's School for Boys, opened in Hilo, located on the island of Hawaii. Beginning in 1885, the brothers' school in Hilo, a town of about four thousand, featured a practical curriculum, in contrast to the heavily academic training at St. Louis College and St. Anthony's parish school. Courses in business, art, speech, and drama dominated the instruction at St. Mary's. St. Louis College featured a curriculum similar to the traditional Marianist academic courses: a superior class and a commercial class that was secondary, with a grammar course representing both late primary and secondary; the second class and intermediate were primary school classes and were listed as tuition courses of instruction. The "free school" was assigned to brothers, but there was no curriculum listed in the annals.[67]

Extracurricular activity was principally in music and drama. Brother Bertram, who had been one of the first brothers to attend post-secondary school at the Collège Stanislas in Paris, was an accomplished violinist and organized an annual music festival. In 1895 "Brother Bertram took the proceeds from a concert, $358, to Queen Kapiolani [*sic*] for her poor people," recorded the annalist.[68] The Hawaiian traditional love of music affected the popularity of St. Louis's program; Brother Francis Marx was bandmaster at St. Louis from 1887 to 1934, and on one occasion joined the Royal Hawaiian Band.

In a relatively brief period of time, the Marianists had achieved prominence in the educational order of Hawaii. Anti-Catholicism was occasionally injected into the conflict between public and religious schools, contentions common in the American Protective Association (A.P.A.) movement. Dr. C. M. Hyde, a Protestant minister in Hawaii, was critical of all independent schools, including St. Louis, because their instruction was "mediocre" and their leadership was incompetent. Hyde, driven by his anti-Catholic animus, was severely critical of Father Damien of Molokai. He condemned Father Damien as a "coarse, dirty man, headstrong and bigoted [who] . . . was not a pure man in his relations with women."[69] Robert Louis Stevenson, who had visited Molokai, was deeply impressed with Damien of Molokai (recently beatified). In his novel *Dr. Jekyll and Mr Hyde*, Stevenson portrayed his demonic possession as symbolic of Dr. C. M. Hyde's anti-Damien bias and his anti-Catholic animus.[70]

Such external threats were rare, but there was internal division at St. Louis College. Just as the Marianists reflected the anti-Mexican sentiment in San Antonio, the brothers in Hawaii discriminated against the Hawaiians at St. Louis College, Honolulu; they established separate dormitories for the

Hawaiians and for "whites." For example, the annalist for the St. Louis community remarked on September 4, 1900: "Enlarged dormitory of the whites. It had been lined and painted in 1898 and accommodated all the whites. Since there were but two dormitories that of the Kanakas remained unlined." The multiethnic character of this college was the most diversified of the Marianists' schools. "This year [1905] the record of St. Louis College shows an enrollment of 630 scholars, of whom 275 are Portuguese, 70 Kanakas, 135 part Hawaiian, 16 English, 33 American, 24 Germans, 58 Chinese, 8 Japanese, 1 Frenchman, 3 Spaniards, 6 Scandinavians, and 12 Italians."[71]

Brother Bertram, besides being an excellent teacher of the natural sciences, was, as mentioned earlier, a violinist and skillfully led the school's music program. His leadership as an educator, musician, and religious earned him the admiration of King Kalakaua, who was a well-known raconteur, world traveler, and political reformer, particularly under the influence of the descendants of the American Protestant missionaries, the dominant sugar planters. When the king died in 1891, his sister, Queen Liliuokalani, was an opponent of the planters and an ardent advocate of the ascendancy of native Hawaiians in opposition to the foreign domination under her brother's administration. Indeed, she dismissed the ministers supportive of the sugar planters and attempted to impose a constitution reflecting her goals of native rule. But she was unsuccessful. With the support of 150 American Marines under direction of John L. Stevens, the U.S. Counselor, a virtual coup d'état took place. The queen was imprisoned, and a provisional government under Sanford Ballard Dole (of Dole pineapple fame) was established in 1893. Rationalized as a protective measure during the Spanish-American War, the Hawaiian Republic was annexed by the United States in 1898. During this period the Marianists leaned toward the monarchy but accepted what appears, in hindsight, to have been an inexorable drive toward American annexation.[72] All but one of the Marianists voted in the general election of November 6, 1900. The predominance of the American Protestant planters, however, seems to have alienated the Marianists. For example, the annals for November 28, 1900, read "Hawaiian Independence. Gov. holiday. The Idea!! *We* had class."[73]

As superior of the community but not principal of the college, Brother Bertram experienced frustration at the bishop's appointment of the principal, since admissions were out of the brothers' hands. The principal's policies were often decided by financial needs or for reasons other than academic standards.[74] On one occasion, the anonymous annalist—but actually Brother Bertram—stated that the new principal had admitted an unqualified student "without consulting anybody—as usual . . . . He wants to show his power as 'boss' and there's no redress for us except a new contract."[75]

A resolution to the conflict finally occurred in 1893 after the American provincial, Father Landelin Beck, visited Hawaii, and, at the direction of the general administration in Paris, negotiated new contracts for the three schools—Honolulu, Hilo, and Wailuku—with Bishop Gulstan Ropert, SS.CC. In 1893 Brother Bertram became principal, with responsibility for keeping the financial records and admissions. The bishop, however, retained ultimate control in these areas. As Beck reported to his provincial council,

> Mgr. positively refuses to leave to the director [i.e., Bertram] the power to admit and send off pupils, and to keep the accounts. He will consent to our desires only in case we would decide upon withdrawing the brothers; and then his Lordship would say that violence was done to him. Father Provincial assured his Lordship that he may admit children whenever he would think it proper and that quarterly statements would be submitted to his consideration.[76]

Though the bishop considered a Marianist administrator to be contrary to the good of the mission of Hawaii, he seemed to respond favorably to Beck's promise to appoint a director who would merit the bishop's trust. In any event, new contracts were signed that brought Marianists into the governance of their schools.

The appointment of Libert Boeynaems, SS.CC., as bishop was a severe blow to the Marianist community at St. Louis College. The annalist noted that the bishop "is no friend of the Brothers. He has never lifted a finger for them the many years he was in Wailuku nor of the school there (I mean the boys' school). The late bishop's friendship for the bros. galled him and he expressed himself antagonistic to them on several occasions. . . . I tried him with *facts* to prove my assertions and he could not answer."[77]

A Bertram–Boeynaems conflict ensued that was exacerbated by Brother Thomas Neuberger, who acted as director while Bertram was away on business. Without informing Bertram, Neuberger was engaged in an extensive correspondence with the provincial, George Meyer, about Bertram's ineffectiveness in dealing with the bishop. Bertram discovered this effort to undermine his authority and told Meyer that Neuberger was actually responsible for the bishop's "distance" from him. By this time, however, Boeynaems had notified Meyer of his decision to seek the director's removal from the college. As early as July 1903 Bertram noted that he "feared that Brother Thomas N. had been deliberately *disloyal* in order to curry favor with Rev. Libert."[78] Though he was transferred to St. Mary's in San Antonio in June of 1905, he received an emotional farewell message from students at St. Louis, where he left a significant mark on the history of the Marianists in Hawaii.

❧ VIII ❧

WHEN BROTHER BERTRAM AND SEVEN OTHER MARIANISTS WERE traveling from Dayton to Honolulu in the spring of 1883 they spent a week in San Francisco, where they were hosted by the Dominicans and the Christian Brothers. In their visit with Archbishop Joseph S. Alemany, "his grace spoke with us for about half an hour and told us, among other things, how much he wished to have some of our Brothers in California."[79] Though the Marianists seriously considered Alemany's request, it was the need to provide a California base for the Dayton–Honolulu connection that became the operative principle in the foundations on the West Coast.

Among the various requests from pastors and bishops, two propositions from parishes in the west were accepted: St. Mary's School in Marysville, located in the Diocese of Grass Valley, a mining town in northern California, and a school in Stockton. Bishop Eugene O'Connell (1861–1884) had received the majority of his twenty-one priests (in 1881) from Ireland. Soon after the brothers had arrived in Marysville, the new bishop, Patrick Manogue, a former miner himself, moved his see to Sacramento. When Brothers John Kautz, John Holtman, and Bernard Leimkuehler arrived at St. Mary's in Marysville, they were shocked to discover that the German church, Immaculate Conception, had merged with St. Joseph's and that Father Louis Bucholzer had been relieved of his duties and was waiting further assignment in San Francisco. The bishop requested they stay with Bucholzer and later assigned them to teach at St. Mary's Cathedral School under the rector of the parish, J. J. Callan. Though the parishioners were supportive of the boys' school—there were one hundred boys enrolled in 1885—Callan was never fully in favor of the Marianist community, which numbered five brothers in 1885.[80] Because of Callan's negative attitude, John Reinbolt removed the community from Marysville, and later they were assigned to St. Joseph's School in San Francisco.[81]

The school in Stockton in the Archdiocese of San Francisco opened after the brothers received a very warm reception from the pastor of St. Mary's, William O'Connor. Brother George Albert was director; James Hans, Anthony Hoffman, John Rost, and Joseph Sauerbier composed the faculty.

Listed in the *Catholic Directory* as St. Patrick's College in Stockton with 150 students, this school thrived, but the brothers lived without indoor plumbing until the late 1890s.[82]

The pastor of St. Joseph's in San Francisco, Patrick Scanlon, influenced by Archbishop Patrick Riordan, invited the Marianists to staff his school in 1885. As noted earlier, the removal of the community from Marysville allowed the provincial council to respond favorably to Scanlon's request. Located in a thriving business and residential area, St. Joseph's School enrolled four hundred boys the first year. The brothers encountered several disciplinary problems during the early days; their students, reflecting the "yellow peril" scare of the era, would taunt the Chinese immigrants on their way home from school. In response to this problem, brothers accompanied groups of older boys to their homes, a measure that appears to have resolved the problem. St. Joseph's School reached a peak of five hundred students with a faculty of nine brothers by 1902. Brother George Sauer, who became a noted educator as the provincial inspector of schools, was principal during the period.[83]

A third Marianist parish school, St. Joseph's, was opened in San Jose in 1898. The Jesuits staffed the parish and were very supportive of the four relatively young brothers assigned to the school. Located in a small town surrounded by a large agricultural area, primarily fruit-growing, the parish school experienced fluctuating enrollment until early September after the harvest, when boys were free from laboring in the fields. According to the 1902 *Catholic Directory*, five brothers were assigned to St. Joseph's Academy in San Jose with an enrollment of 148, while the girls' school enrolled 260 students with seven Sisters of Notre Dame on the faculty. The Stockton school, St. Mary's College, had 165 students and four brothers.[84]

The Marianists had established a permanent presence in California, which could have developed even more extensively had there been a determined effort to expand, but the provincial council appears to have been ambivalent regarding its schools in California. During the first few years the council went on record as desiring a congenial location for Marianists en route from Dayton to Honolulu. During the mid-1880s there had been some discussion of establishing a house of formation presumably with a scholasticate. The council had approved annual retreats in California, usually Stockton, to obviate the need for expensive travel to Dayton each year. In contrast to San Antonio and Honolulu, the Marianists in California did not develop a boarding school. Located in parochial schools in a large metropolitan district, the Marianists in San Francisco represented the core experiences of the Marianists in the United States in cities such as Cincinnati, Dayton, Cleveland,

Pittsburgh, Brooklyn, New York City, Rochester, and Baltimore. However, because they were teaching on the western rim of the province remote from the motherhouse, and because, as in Honolulu and San Antonio, they were not identified with German-American culture, they were on the periphery rather than at the center of the nineteenth-century tradition. To staff the schools in California the Marianists were dependent on a steady flow of young boys from the German-speaking parishes in the East. Among the parishes those in Baltimore stood out as a vital source of vocations.

⊀ IX ⊁

IN 1792 THE FIRST GERMAN CATHOLICS MET IN BALTIMORE IN THE HOME of a John Brown, where they attended "for the first time, their Divine Service, in their own language. . . . On Wednesdays and Fridays, in Lent, will be sung the Psalm *Miserere*, accompanied with a sermon in the German language delivered by the Reverend John Baptist Clouse."[85] Clouse or Causse, was without faculties to celebrate the liturgy or administer the sacraments, because Bishop John Carroll had "suspended him in 1791 for insolence and insubordination." The recently appointed ordinary of the first diocese in the United States was concerned with providing a priest for the German community, but because Causse apparently had celebrated mass in the vernacular in direct opposition to tradition, Carroll announced the excommunication of the German priest and all who followed him.[86]

Problems with German priests continued to haunt Carroll. He was compelled to excommunicate two Philadelphia priests, William Elling and John Goetz, because of their roles in the movement toward the vernacular. Though he had appointed a German Franciscan, Frederick C. Reuter, for the German community in Baltimore, there were several conflicts with him, one of which entailed a visit to Rome requiring Carroll to show respect for German Catholicism, and to allow Reuter to publish a German catechism. Reuter and the trustees of St. John's German parish were sources of continuous conflict with Carroll, who, according to his commitment to American principles of self-government, held moderately liberal views on the trustee system. Several years after Carroll's death and after several pastors, St. John's became a relatively quiescent German-speaking parish community.[87] There were no trustee conflicts in the German Protestant congregations because they had dwelled under a more flexible system of governance and they could adapt more easily to the Americanization process.[88]

In his history of the Archdiocese of Baltimore, Thomas Spalding noted two dominant styles of episcopal leadership: the Maryland tradition, which was cosmopolitan, respectful of religious pluralism, of the separation of church and state, and of the republican ethos; the other tradition, Catholic separatism, was characterized by a protective canopy for German and other immigrants subjected to the forces of anti-Catholicism and nativism. Arch-bishops John Carroll, Ambrose Maréchal, James Whitfield, and later James Gibbons, represented the Maryland tradition; Samuel Eccleston, Francis P. Kenrick, and Martin John Spalding cultivated Catholic separatism. Eccle-ston welcomed the Redemptorists to care for the Germans, whereas it was during Spalding's administration that the Marianists staffed the schools in these parishes.[89]

The Redemptorists, or the Congregation of the Most Holy Redeemer, founded in 1737 by St. Alphonsus Liguori, settled in Baltimore in 1840, when Archbishop Samuel Eccleston asked the congregation to take charge of St. John's parish, the oldest German parish in the archdiocese. Joseph Prost, the superior of the Redemptorists in America, immediately assumed responsibility for the parish. Having established parishes in Rochester and Pittsburgh, Baltimore's St. John's was soon razed and replaced by St. Alphonsus Church, on the property on the old St. John's. This became *the* German parish in the central part of the city, just a few blocks from the Cathedral of the Immaculate Conception.[90] However, while the church was under construction, Eccleston offered the congregation St. James parish, located on Eager Street in "Old Town," on the east side of Jones Falls. It was originally an English-speaking parish, but, when the new St. Vincent's church was built for that community in 1840–1841, principally Irish-Americans, St. James became a German national parish. It was not until 1844 that St. Alphonsus, built with funds from the Leopoldine Soci-ety, opened as one of the architectural gems of Baltimore. Four years later, the Redemptorist house at St. James was given to the School Sisters of Notre Dame (S.S.N.D.), their first house in the United States.[91]

With the growth of St. James, the other German parish, St. Michael the Archangel, was founded in the Fells Point area, a busy port village later incorporated into Baltimore. This was the third Redemptorist German parish, opened in 1850, five years after a parish school had been built. Hence, the Redemptorists, who numbered ten priests, including St. John Neumann, later (1852) bishop of Philadelphia, were responsible for the pastoral care of the Baltimore German-American community, which num-bered about twenty thousand. However, the schools in the three German-American parishes enrolled only a total of six hundred male students.[92]

Though the first Marianist-Redemptorist association was in 1859 at St. Philomena's parish in Pittsburgh (1859–1883), the Brothers of Mary staffed the three Baltimore parishes, St. Michael's (1870–1943), St. James (1873–1941), and St. Alphonsus (1872–1879). Of the forty schools opened during Reinbolt's twenty-two-year provincialate nearly one-half were in Redemptorist parishes. Because these schools were governed by a uniform system, brothers who transferred from one school to another tended to adapt more readily to a familiar rectory-school arrangement. More importantly, they shared a strong preference for the language that fostered solidarity among parishioners, brothers, and Redemptorist priests. Since no other German religious order had such an extensive network of parishes, the Redemptorists and Marianists formed a cultural association that persisted in many parishes until the mid-twentieth century.[93] However, at St. Alphonsus a conflict ensued principally because of the German language issue. A comparative study of St. James and St. Alphonsus schools illustrates the Marianist and German styles of education during this crucial period in the history of the Society.

With a Catholic population of two hundred thousand and a school population of fifteen thousand in eighty-four parochial schools in 1880, the Baltimore archdiocese was a thriving center of Catholicity. Enrollment in the Marianist schools numbered nearly one thousand students, and by the 1890s over sixty of their students had entered the Marianist novitiate. Damian Litz, director at St. Michael's parish—who during the 1870s gained national notoriety through the pages of the archconservative German-Catholic newspaper published in Baltimore, *Die Katholische Volkszeitung*—was the most significant recruiter of aspirants to the Society among the Baltimore Marianists.

Though the *Catholic Directory* persistently listed secular teachers at St. James School (a new church opened in 1870 to accommodate five thousand to six thousand parishioners) throughout the 1870s, the annals of the community noted that the contract between the Marianist provincial and the Redemptorist rector was signed on March 18, 1873. Referring to the teachers as "professors," not an uncommon title among Marianists, five brothers taught 440 students. Hence, the use of monitors was essential for effective teaching. The significant school events were principally related to the devotional and liturgical rhythm of the year—Forty Hours devotion of the eucharistic adoration, All Souls Day, Advent, Christmas, Lent, Easter, First Communion, and Confirmation. There were the annual fairs, "pec nics, [*sic*]" and in the late 1880s the brothers held public examination of the students at the end of the school year. This was a Marianist tradition which included awards for scholarship, improvement, and conduct. The record listed the visitation of the provincial and the brother inspector of schools, and various bits of news about the Society of Mary.[94] Unlike women religious, the brothers employed a cook, and this freed them to pursue the religious and educational routines in their house.

In 1878 there was concern that the Redemptorists were slighting the brothers when the School Sisters of Notre Dame, who taught at the three Redemptorist parishes, took charge of the first- and second-grade boys. Sometime during the early 1880s the younger boys returned to the classrooms in the boys' school.[95] Five years later, 1883, "a rumor spread in the congregation that after vacation [in July] the services of the Brothers will be dispensed with, that two seculars [i.e., lay teachers] were to take the high classes [14+ year olds] and the rest be taught by sisters." This rumor caused "great uproar in the [St. James] congregation."[96] After a delegation of Marianists, led by Damian Litz, interviewed the pastor, the rumor was dispelled. The following year a change of rectors occurred, which was advantageous to the Marianists, as the successor "was a friend of the Brothers."[97] As will be noted later, the Redemptorist rector at St. Alphonsus requested the brothers to leave the school in 1879, an act that helped start the rumor. Though the sisters did not take over the boys' classes at St. Alphonsus, the School Sisters of Notre Dame did have charge of the entire school at St. Mary's German parish in Washington, D.C., in 1881.[98]

In the earlier days the summer vacation did not commence until the middle of July, with half-day classes in the summer months. Toward the end of the 1890s the calendar was crowded with social activities, "entertainment" by literary societies, and other parish and archdiocesan events, such as a parade to greet Archbishop James Gibbons on his return from Rome after becoming a cardinal. In 1889 there was another parade of forty thousand to celebrate the centennial of the appointment of John Carroll as bishop; this was also the occasion of the first lay congress in the United States. Each year St. James School concluded with examinations by the pastor or his assistant, and with the principal religious event of the year, First Communion.

The annalists rarely provided more than a chronological list of the major events, with no editorial comment or even a hint of contents of meetings, examinations, visitations, or instructions for First Communion. One exception occurred in 1883, when the annalist recorded "Ascension Day was made memorable here this year. J. Waellisch, teacher of the third class, left this P.M. for his native city of Pittsburgh to seek his fortune in another state of life."[99] Three weeks later "this example of apostasy was followed" when another brother from Pittsburgh left the community. "The Lord have mercy on the renegades."[100] Though several brothers left the community during this period, these events were generally not recorded in the annals. Since brothers entered teaching at an early age and were subjected to large classes with little formal training or supervision, there was a tendency to question one's vocation. Provincials' reports during this period testify to this problem and urged the directors of the communities to actively nurture the younger brothers in their ministry.

Of the four brothers assigned to the first Marianist community to staff St. Alphonsus School in 1872, two were fifteen years of age, one was nineteen, and the director, Brother Edward Gorman, noted that he spent "part of his time with the younger Brothers who never taught school before."[101] The Marianists had replaced the Christian Brothers. The annals, apparently composed by Edward Gorman, frequently referred to the concerted effort to ban all forms of corporal punishment, with explicit references to abuses by the former teachers at the school. "From what I was told by the priests and the boys that our predecessors ruled with the ferrule [i.e., a rodlike instrument identified with the discipline of the Christian Brothers] and I'm sorry to say without regard to the age of the children and the rules of moderation."[102]

At first, the students at St. Alphonsus "were afraid of the Brothers because they had no cassock and resembled laymen."[103] After they were disabused of this misunderstanding, the students gradually came under the authority of the brothers, who were told not to engage in any corporal punishment. The brothers discussed this problem with the provincial of the Redemptorists. Because the Christian Brothers had enforced strong discipline, including the use of corporal punishment, it took some time before the Brothers of Mary could gain control. According to the annalist, the boys were disorderly "because we did not use the ferrule and because they were so glad that their former teachers did not return. A strange rejoicing indeed."[104]

Relations between the Marianist faculty and the Redemptorist rector were more than cordial; there were several positive comments relating to salaries, living conditions, and the various visits by the priests of the parish. A severe fire destroyed the brothers' house and the school, but they and the students adapted well to the crisis. The brothers had so salutary an impact on the students that several students entered the Society each year.[105]

Brother Edward Gorman, director/principal during the first six years, was transferred to St. Michael's School in Baltimore, but since the remaining annals were in his hand it appears as if he composed them long after events occurred. His replacement as director, Brother Joseph Martin, became acutely ill soon after school opened in 1878 and eventually returned to Dayton, where he died.[106] In a paragraph entitled "Signs of a Storm," Gorman noted that "on one occasion, having business at the priests' house, I heard the school status was in a bad condition."[107] What he meant by "bad" entailed criticism of the brothers' pedagogical ability and lack of discipline. Gorman then proceeded to arrange for an outside examiner, the director of the Christian Brothers, to assess the quality of education in each of the classes. In anticipation of this unprecedented event, Edward Gorman prepared each of the teachers, pointing out their strengths and weaknesses. Obviously, he was quite confident: "I invited the [examiner] . . . in order to show that the pupils were able to answer a stranger as well as their teacher and also to show that there was no humbug in our work."

After the examination the rector "acknowledged" the quality of the faculty's classes but "found occasion to run down the third class [5th and 6th graders] his remark being out of place and not strictly true." Gorman recorded that the rector, Father Andrew Ziegler, was also critical of another class, not based on his direct experience but rather on information provided by "one of our high officials," who out of "imprudence" told the rector "more than was strictly necessary." The next remark recorded in the annals related to the dismissal of the brothers from St. Alphonsus School. Gorman concluded, "We all felt very sorry for what had happened, as St. Alphonsus School and parish are dear to us. Many of our friends showed their sympathy for us in different ways, but they could not help what was decreed."[108] In contrast to the Marianist annals, those of the Redemptorists reveal a different story. There was a financial problem related to the brothers' laxity in collecting tuition; they were criticized for being overgenerous with families unable to pay, while the Redemptorists called for greater strictness. Eventually a committee was established to deal with the situation on a case-by-case basis.

The annalist, the rector, Father Andrew Ziegler, referred to the Marianists as the "brothers of the Blessed Virgin Mary founded in Alsace [*sic*] by William Chaminade." Ziegler's principal criticism of the school was that the students "were so ignorant of the German language that they do not understand what is said to them." Since the priests taught catechism in German, this was a severe criticism, particularly as the language was considered *the* medium of faith. He also complained of the rapid turnover in the faculty, and of the brothers' teaching and poor discipline as the bases for dismissing the brothers from the school. There were "other reasons I prefer not to talk about." "However, it must be understood," he wrote "about their morality there has been no complaint."[109] Perhaps there was a personality conflict between Edward Gorman and Andrew Ziegler, Irish-American and German-American, brother director/principal and Father Rector, that may have prompted Ziegler not to record this in the annals. In any event, the Christian Brothers returned to St. Alphonsus School.

A chronicle of events at St. Alphonsus, composed by a former teacher there, Brother Julius of Mary, in 1920, provides the point of view of a Christian Brother on the crucial years 1872–1879. In contrast to Gorman's account of the causal role of corporal punishment in the dismissal of the Christian Brothers, Brother Julius stated that they left because "a little misunderstanding occurred between the Rev. Fathers and Brother Candidian, the Director of Calvert Hall." He referred to the "Marist Brothers [sic] of Dayton . . . [who] enjoyed a good reputation. . . . These Brothers, especially Brother O'Gorman [sic] were very kind to us." The Marianists at St. Alphonsus as well as at St. James's and St. Michael's sent many of their graduates to Calvert Hall. Brother Julius of Mary concluded that after reconciliation between the Redemptorists and the Christian Brothers had been achieved in 1879, they were "invited back" and "they maintained their old traditions: zeal, activity, devotions."[110]

In each of these three accounts, composed sometime after the fact, a defensive apologetical tone prevails, particularly on the events of 1879 as recorded by Ziegler and Gorman. Julius of Mary's account of 1872 and 1879 minimized the degree of conflict. Though there is some ambiguity, Gorman's twenty-seven-page narrative in the form of annals noted the Redemptorist-Marianist consensus on the causes for dismissal of the Christian Brothers and concluded with an attempt by the Marianists to reach a reconciliation with Ziegler in 1879. Amid the ambiguity, one can only conclude that, first, the Marianists had certainly alienated the Redemptorist rector, who then sought the return of the Christian Brothers, and that, second, throughout this period there was no conflict between the Marianists and the Christian Brothers.

The Marianist annals of St. Alphonsus School end on one page, and on the following page there is the notation "St. Martin's Archives."[111] In the three-page introduction, Edward Gorman provided a description of events not as they happened but once again after some time had elapsed. The Marianist provincial approached Archbishop James Gibbons for permission to establish a private independent academy to be located on Broadway Street between St. James's and St. Michael's schools that would appeal to parents with means to send their boys to a private school. The *Catholic Directory* listed the Male Literary Institutions in Baltimore in 1880: three Jesuit colleges (Georgetown, Gonzaga, and Loyola); three run by the Christian Brothers (Calvert Hall, Rock Hill, and St. Matthew's Institute); one by the

Xaverian Brothers (Mount St. Joseph) and one by diocesan priests (Mount St. Mary's College).[112]

Since the Redemptorists staffed the parishes that would feed the prospective academy, Gibbons asked the provincial, Father Reinbolt, to consult them. After the provincial of the Redemptorists expressed his opposition to the plan, it was apparent to Gorman and later to Gibbons that the main reason for their negative response was resentment that many students from the Redemptorist parishes had been drawn to enter the Marianists rather than the Redemptorists.[113] Indeed, according to Gorman, more than fifty boys from Baltimore joined the Marianists between 1870 and 1880. Gorman simply stated: "The Redemptorists opposed the academy because we would have gathered the brightest and richest peoples of their congregations and might just get those candidates they wanted for Ilchester," the C.SS.R. house of formation in Maryland.[114] In their interview with Gibbons, the Redemptorist authorities led him to believe that the principal issue was a conflict of authority between the Marianist brothers and Redemptorist priests.[115]

As an alternative to an independent academy in east Baltimore, Gibbons suggested the boys' school at St. Martin's parish, located in an Irish-American neighborhood in west Baltimore, and pointed to the advantage of a fixed-sum income in contrast to the tuition-dependent income of the proposed academy in the German neighborhood. The provincial and the pastor agreed, and a contract was negotiated. Brother Edward Gorman, who had visited with the pastor of St. Martin's, John S. Foley, while at St. Alphonsus School, was to be director of the new school. There had been attempts to establish parish schools run by lay teachers, but they had never achieved permanence. The brothers' school drew from several parishes; the annals referred to the school as an academy, but the *Catholic Directory* listed it as a parochial school. The girls' school was staffed by the Daughters of Charity.[116]

Upon the opening of the school in 1880, there were only forty-seven boys. A year later the enrollment was 120, drawn from fourteen parishes. Gorman noted that such a diversified group required "some time before we had the whole amalgamated. Corporeal punishment was not resorted to, in fact, banished from the school; in a short time everything was working smoothly."[117] In 1888, John Foley was appointed bishop of Detroit. He had been close to Cardinal Gibbons and was aligned with the progressive wing of the American hierarchy, which at this time was in opposition to the attempt to establish a German-American prelature, symbolic of the ethnic separatism that resulted from the perception that the Irish-American bishops were persistently biased against the German-speaking parishes. Gibbons, ever the realist in his own archdiocese, supported national parishes, but on the national level was in opposition to the movement to establish such a separatist ecclesiastical stronghold as a prelature. The Americanist sentiment of Archbishop Gibbons was clearly revealed in a letter to Joseph Simler, dated October 17, 1881. This letter was one of fifty-six letters included in a large packet of documents which Simler submitted to the Vatican in 1881 in order to substantiate the case for papal approbation of the Marianists. Rather than refer to the Marianists at St. James or St. Michael, German-American schools, he cited the "American" school: "The Brothers of the Society of Mary have recently assumed charge at the school for boys attached to St. Martin's church in this city. I cheerfully testify that since their advent among us they have given eminent satisfaction to the Pastor by their ability as teachers, their piety and discipline and devotions to the training of youth."[118]

In a history of St. Martin's parish (1895) there were sections on "St. Martin's Male Academy" and "St. Martin's Female Academy." Given the emphasis on the education of males over females, the boys' school received more attention with references to particular brothers, such as Edward Gorman, a description of the "high class" curriculum and a list of male graduates and their professions.[119] Those students who remained in school after they had made their First Communion around the age of thirteen were introduced to a broad curriculum, the equivalent of early secondary education: "Christian Doctrine, arithmetic, both mental and written, algebra, geometry, reading, spelling, etymology, grammar, composition, history, hygiene, physics, writing, book-keeping, both theoretical and practical, the latter taught by the commercial system, civil government, type-writing, Pitman's system of short-hand." The female academy offered a comparable curriculum in "the advanced grades" except that it did not include type-writing and etymology but did provide courses not offered in the boys' school: "literature, physiology, mental philosophy, drawing, palm and ornamental penmanship."[120]

Included in the introduction to the male academy was a statement on the nature of a Catholic education. The statement opens with praise of the "enlightenment and progressiveness" that characterized contemporary America, but then criticized the prevailing "doubt and infidelity." The investigations of true science "lead to enlightenment and the pretension to false sciences leads to infidelity." It was incumbent upon the church to struggle against infidelity, which was considered synonymous with "irreligious education as well as heresy." Hence, "the Catholic school is an indispensable adjunct to a parish."[121]

An explicit nod to Catholic domesticity with the idyllic picture of true motherhood opened the reflection on the school's Catholic ethos and commitment to catechesis: "The faith of the child in his tender years, can nowhere be better protected and nurtured than under the almost divine love of the Christian mother." To confirm that faith "by the teachings of a good school" is crucial, as the young Catholic can only successfully confront "the storms and temptations of the world" with a faith that will "ripen into the beauty of a well-ordered Christian life." In short, the parish school "is the nursery of the church, and also its strong rampart."[122]

It was shortly before this statement was published that Catholic schools throughout the country were mobilized for display of both American patriotism and loyalty to Catholic education as the defender of religious values foundational to the good of the republic. The occasion was the quadricentennial of the landing of Christopher Columbus, October 12, 1892.

Baltimore's celebration reflected the interfaith tendencies of Cardinal James Gibbons; the festivities were "under the management of Catholics but they are receiving aid and cooperation of Italian societies and a number of Protestants, who are quite enthusiastic," wrote a reporter in *The Catholic News* of the District of Columbia.[123] The school children were included in the parade, which featured floats from many of the parishes. St. Martin's float, like most parishes both German-American and Irish-American, depicted a scene from Columbus's voyage. The New York parade was a grand march of thirty-six thousand parochial school students. A reporter for the *Catholic Herald* noted that this "demonstration" should symbolize the cross of double taxation of parents who send their children to Catholic schools and still pay taxes for public schools. The parade, stated the reporter, should "open the eyes of our rulers of the injustice done to Catholics in the matter of education, and lead them to make an equitable provision for those schools."[124]

Such parades functioned as displays of power, legitimacy, and advocacy. Assertions of the positive contribution of Catholicity to the moral fibre of the nation were frequently expressed in the public Catholicism of the era. The competitive dimension of these parades represented religious pluralism in action, underscoring the unwritten code that no one denomination should ever be allowed to gain hegemonic ascendancy.[125] Of course, the general Protestant–Catholic tensions over education periodically broke out with new waves of immigration. The American Protective Association (A.P.A.), founded in Clinton, Iowa, in 1887, revived the old Know-Nothing animus, and once again portrayed the public schoolhouse as a shrine of republican virtue while the Catholic schools were considered antithetical to democracy.[126]

As an illustration of a Catholic appropriation of Columbus, an editorial in the *Connecticut Catholic* noted that the quadricentennial parades were out to dispel any "lingering doubt that to be a foreigner was a menace to American institutions and to be a Catholic was a menace to free will." It then asserted the basis of Catholic citizenship: "Catholics are an integral part of the American population, and they are not here by sufferance. They are here by right of discovery and by right of colonization. They had a share in the glory of American freedom, for it was Catholics who first planted the banner of equal rights and free conscience in America."[127] While the latter remark was reflective of the popular civic rendering of Lord Baltimore's commitment to religious toleration and Maryland's colonial legislature's codification of that principle, it was invoked in opposition to "A.P.A.ism" as a legitimation of the Catholic school as fostering the continuity of religious liberty. As will be noted in the next chapter, the school issue not only underlined divisions in society in general, but it was a divisive factor among Catholics as well. However, the Columbus Day parades and participation in the Catholic Education Exhibit at the World's Columbian Exposition in Chicago, which opened in early 1893, represented a broad consensus within the Catholic community.

This display of Catholic education included exhibits from the schools in twenty dioceses and from the principal teaching orders; besides those included in the dioceses, the Brothers of Mary, under the direction of the provincial inspector of schools, Brother Kim, sponsored five such exhibits, which was not an insignificant number. The Benedictines and the Brothers of the Sacred Heart had one and two exhibits respectively, but the Brothers of the Christian Schools in the United States sponsored thirteen exhibits. Only the Christian Brothers and the Jesuits were present on stage with notable prelates, priests, and laity. Indeed, on "Catholic Education Day" at the Exposition, Brother Maurelian, F.S.C., was the secretary and manager of the Catholic Education Society. The Marianist provincial, Father George Meyer (listed as Rev. Bro.), was acknowledged as one of the more than one thousand sisters, brothers, and priests whose names were obtained for the published volume commemorating the event.[128]

The collective exhibit of the Brothers of Mary highlighted the multi-ethnic "college" contexts in San Antonio and Honolulu, the cosmopolitan character of the California experience, and the predominantly German-American schools in Cincinnati, Cleveland, Rochester, Baltimore, and

Chicago. Dayton, with its college and normal school, was prominent in displaying a rich curriculum, including intricate science, engineering, and mathematical exhibits. The Marianists', like many displays representing dioceses and religious communities, abounded in examples of penmanship and various types of patterned drawings. The schools of the Brothers of Mary in the German-American parishes conveyed the traditional status of language as the medium of faith with many displays of compositions in German.[129] The *Catholic Mirror* of Baltimore, May 15, 1893, featured a front-page article entitled "Our Educational Exhibit," which praised the premier see's excellence in various fields of academic endeavor. Among the descriptions of parish-school exhibits, which excluded St. Alphonsus, St. Michael, and many others, those of St. Martin's Boys Academy and St. James Male School were included in the account. The Irish-American editor published an extended piece on St. Martin's prefaced by the remark: "Between five and six hundred of the parents and friends of the boys visited the display." For many parishioners to make such a trip to Chicago clearly underscores the strongly middle-class character of St. Martin's. A serious tone, almost reverential, was quite evident in how the men "took special interest in twenty sets of bookkeeping laid out for inspection. Each boy had written out business transactions for three months in the day-book, journalized, and then posted them in a ledger, closing out each month and making out the balance sheet." After a nod to the typewriting and the map-drawing skills of the boys, the article concluded with a brief notation on the boy's academy: its founder was Bishop Foley of Detroit, and its current pastor was T. J. Broyderick. "The Brothers of Mary have charge of the school, of which Bro. Edward [Gorman] is the director."[130]

In contrast, the description of the exhibit of the St. James Male School merely listed the contents as a "creditable display" of the school "conducted by the Brothers of Mary." Besides art, penmanship, and bookkeeping there were compositions in "German and English."[131]

The newspaper portrayal of the class and ethnic distinctions between these two academies is striking. St. James parish included middle-class families, but it appears that they were not as affluent as their counterparts in St. Martin's. What is evident is the absence of any remarks on the religious dimension of the boys' education, as if that was so well grounded in the parish identity as to require no mention. There was no defensive tone or explicitly contentious remark on how Catholic schools contributed to the civic culture of the nation. At the World's Columbian Exposition, however, particularly on Catholic Education Day, the speeches stressed the religious and moral gifts of Catholic education to the life and thought of American enlightenment and progress.

From the opening welcome by Archbishop P. A. Feehan of Chicago to the last remark by Bishop John Lancaster Spalding of Peoria, president of the Catholic Education Exhibit and director of ceremonies on the occasion, there were many tributes to the convergence of Catholic education and American patriotism. John Lancaster Spalding, who would soon contract with the Marianists to staff his new academy, Spalding Institute, was *the* intellectual among the active bishops. Only Spalding expressed his deep admiration for the laity. The achievement of the Catholic school system "does not exist through the power of the priesthood alone, it exists because the great heart of the people beats God-ward." He complimented the "hundreds of thousands of young women who go forth from happy homes, turning away from worldly love and domestic bliss; go believing that it is a God-like thing to rear children for heaven, even as it is a holy thing to bring them forth to be citizens and patriots on earth."[132] This identification of a religious vocation of the laity and that of women religious with the vitality of the school to instill piety, morality, and civic virtue reveals an integration of spirituality and social activism that is at the core of the Americanist understanding of the young republic.

This lengthy exploration of the national expansion of the Marianists from the Know-Nothing era to the rise of the A.P.A. in the 1890s, culminating in the Catholic Education Exhibit of 1893, reveals a pattern etched into its American identity. The dominance of the local and regional character, even when it emerges in a national exhibit, is merely the aggregate of the work of individual schools. Parish schools, academies, and colleges shaped by disparate contexts were unified by spiritual formation, including teacher-training at the motherhouse in Dayton. Though Marianists did not articulate a Spalding-like understanding of the spirit of their education, the foundational story of the Society reveals the perception of the Marianist schools moving God-ward.

CHAPTER FOUR

Marianist Religious Culture

❧ I ❧

THE RELIGIOUS CULTURE OF THE MARIANISTS HAS BEEN TRADITIONALLY developed in the formation years of the postulate, novitiate, and scholasticate, those centers where the prospective brothers and priests pass through their "initiation rites" or their "rites of passage" that place them on a journey as a member of a teaching congregation.

Ideally these were nurturing experiences and processes of socialization into the Family of Mary as priests, teachers, and workers committed to an active apostolate anchored in monastic routine. The annual retreat at the motherhouse in Dayton was an opportunity to unite the disparate small communities into the larger family intended to vitalize their identity as Marianists, and at the same time it offered individual brothers and priests an interview with the provincial, who, with his council, would either reassign or transfer the teachers for another year.

The strongly centralized character of the community, with the superior general and the general council authorized to appoint provincials and their councils, imbued the office of superior general, the "Good Father," with spiritual and moral charisms derived from the foundation period when William J. Chaminade articulated the initial vision. Since the founder was relegated to the periphery during his later years, his successors, Georges Joseph Caillet (1845–1868) and Jean Joseph Chevaux (1865–1875), who were not deeply opposed to the marginalization of Chaminade, nevertheless invoked the founder's spirituality and moral vision. According to Joseph Simler, Chevaux's successor, Caillet was a "pious and charitable" priest, while Chevaux revealed a rigoristic piety with a quiet asceticism.

This chapter will attempt to capture the French-American cross-currents with particular focus on three areas: the leadership of Joseph Simler (1876–1905) in governance, spirituality, and ministry; the tension within the religious culture of the Marianists symbolized by the relatively rigorist tradition of Simler's predecessors and many of the provisions of the Constitutions of 1891, and the relatively positive character of *Manual of Christian Pedagogy* (1899) in promoting that religious culture in the communities and schools. The tension between the monastic and the apostolic is related to the tension between nature and grace, mission and prayer life. The chapter will conclude with the foundation of two Marianist high schools, Spalding Institute, a diocesan academy in Peoria, and SS. Peter and Paul parish high school in the heart of the German-American community in St. Louis.

❈ II ❦

IN ONE OF WILLIAM JOSEPH CHAMINADE'S LAST LETTERS TO GEORGES Joseph Caillet (November 29, 1849), the founder asserted his role as the "spiritual father" of Caillet and more importantly "father of your authority and of the Constitutions." Chaminade admitted that he himself was also "dependent on Caillet" because he received his authority "from God and from the church." As founder, Chaminade maintained his role as mediator of Caillet's authority just as his parents were mediators of God's creative process in the physical realm. Hence, Chaminade reminded Caillet "that the Society should . . . be guided by my advice."[1]

The vision of Chaminade, defined in the Constitutions of 1839, which codified the mixed lay-clerical character of the Society, envisaged brothers in positions of authority as directors of primary schools, by which they became *ex officio* delegates to general chapters. The absence of a traditional religious habit and the lay-clerical mix set the Marianists apart from all other teaching congregations. The fourth vow of stability, one of filial fidelity to Mary, and the commitment to a diversified education ministry blended with these other features to compose the so-called primitive spirit animating the Society of Mary.

This charism, grounded particularly in the Constitutions of 1839, developed during the life of Chaminade, allowed the brothers to dominate the general chapter, as delegates were apportioned on a one-to-five ratio, with the vast majority of the Society composed of brothers. In addition, teaching brothers ran the primary schools and were on faculties of the few secondary schools. The 1839 Constitutions, however, had not been formally approved by the papacy; Gregory XVI had only issued a decree of praise of both the

Society of Mary and the Daughters of Mary.[2] While the Society of Mary was expanding in the Midwest, the Northeast, and in Texas, the superiors general were seeking papal approval for the Society.

In 1855, prior to his initial visit to Rome for Pius IX's official approbation, Georges Joseph Caillet wished to seek reelection of himself as superior general and of his three assistants. The previous general chapter, actually the only one convened, had been in 1845, when Caillet was elected for a ten-year term. Rather than call a chapter meeting as prescribed by the Constitutions, Caillet sought a yes-or-no vote, or a plebiscite, so recently invoked by President Napoleon Bonaparte in seeking the title Emperor Napoleon III. Though Caillet and his assistants received more than the required two-thirds vote, the forces of dissent, led by two Alsatian brothers, demanded a general chapter on the grounds that Caillet was attempting to rule by fiat. Three years later the accusations moved Caillet to reluctantly call a general chapter for 1858. But immediate response in 1855 prompted comments on the utterly disloyal and indeed diabolical voices of dissent: "The enemy of our salvation" had overwhelmed those "who are not sufficiently diffident of their own lights. He [i.e., the devil] makes them so attached to their own opinions that they forget the duties imposed by humanity, religious obedience and Christian charity."[3] Though it was probably his fear of opening the wounds of the Chaminade–Caillet conflict that prompted him to seek a plebiscite, the invocation of the demonic suggested a divine mandate for Caillet's authority. This was also the basis for rigorism; human rights are subsumed in the superior's authority.

The 1858 chapter, however, actually confirmed the plebiscite by an overwhelming vote. It also approved minor changes in the constitution. Symbolic of the significance of the new Marianist institutions in Paris, Collège Stanislas and St. Mary's Institute, the general administration moved from Bordeaux to Paris in 1861, but it assigned a priest to continue the promotion of the sodalities in Bordeaux. Soon the Province of Paris was founded. With evidence of a substantive vote of confidence, Caillet announced preparations for a visit to Rome (1864) in a climate of high expectations of papal approbation of a revised constitution. Pope Pius IX's deep devotion to Mary, symbolized by the declaration of the dogma of the Immaculate Conception in 1854, had contributed to Caillet's hope that the Society of Mary would receive a warm welcome in Rome.[4] The general chapter of 1864, the year of the papal encyclical *Quanta Cura*, which included an appendix entitled "The Syllabus of Errors," worked out the final revisions of the 1839 Constitutions, which, along with testimonials from over thirty bishops, formed the documentation of the case for approbation.[5] While the American Civil

War was nearing its dénouement, with Brother Edel and other directors calling for more brothers missioned to the United States, Caillet traveled to
Rome.

After three months in the Holy See, the second superior general returned
with a favorable response to the revised constitutions, but the Roman
authorities would not make a final decision until the Society made revisions in accord with forty "animadversions": a strict construction would
interpret the meaning of this term "animadversion" as censorious criticism, while a loose construction would interpret it as merely strong suggestions for improvement. Though thirty-six of the forty animadversions
called for changes that did not require lengthy consideration, the remaining
four demanded deliberation by a general chapter. While in Rome, Caillet
received permission to place in effect new constitutional directives that
substantially altered the composition of the chapter: local houses met in
what were referred to as "domestic colleges" to vote on representatives to a
provincial college; each province was allowed eight delegates. According to
the former constitutions, directors of each of the communities were delegates to the chapter: in 1864 there were 122 capitulants, while at the 1865
chapter, under the new constitutions, there were only 44 capitulants. The
first animadversion was the most radical: "It will be absolutely necessary to
see to it that in the future the number of priests be increased in the pious
institute in such a way that at least the superior of every house in the four
provinces be a priest."[6] This created such a furor that the elections resulted
in an overwhelming vote for brothers who were opposed to such a drastic
change, for it was tantamount to dissolving the primary schools because it
would require the recruitment and training of hundreds of priests, literally
dissolving the mixed composition in favor of a clerical society. Jean
Lalanne, the director of Stanislas and an impassioned opponent of clerical
superiors, was one of the chapter's two representatives sent to Rome to seek
a modification of this animadversion. They returned with the approval of a
proposed change: only those communities with twelve members were
required to be directed by priests, and only with the approval of the local
ordinary. Eventually Rome also decided that priests must occupy the principal offices: superior general, head of zeal, provincials, master of novices,
and superiors of secondary schools; brothers could be elected to the general
council as heads of primary instruction and temporalities, and were
approved as directors of primary schools. An official visitor was appointed
by the Vatican Congregation of Bishops and Regulars; Cardinal Césaire
Mathieu of Besançon, who had known Chaminade, presided over the chapter. This appointment was apparently required because of the continuously

acrimonious discontent, often accompanied by letters to the Holy See critical of what was perceived as the eventual clericalization of the Society. This represents the persistent need to carry on a vigorous campaign to preserve the proper mix envisioned by Chaminade.[7]

On the fiftieth anniversary of the Society's foundation (1867), despite the crisis of the previous year, Caillet distributed copies of the new constitutions, and he recommitted the community to the five characteristics of the Society of Mary: "A true body of religious in all the fervor of the primitive [apostolic] times. . . . A mixed body, that is made up of priests and lay members." Caillet's third characteristic enumerated "education of youth of the middle class" as the first on the list of ministries, which appeared to considerably reduce emphasis upon their free public elementary schools for all classes. However, Caillet also listed missions, retreats, and the formation of sodalities as characteristic ministries. Foundational to the Marianists was their aversion to any religious habit that would only feed the prejudices of anticlerical enemies. The final characteristic was that the Society was placed "under the protection of the Blessed Virgin, being, as it were, her property."[8] Whereas Chaminade portrayed these characteristics in terms of vital relationships, particularly among the Society and between the members and Mary and Jesus, Caillet's imagery appears less organic and more mechanistic or juridical, that is, class, status, and property. The following year, the chapter (November 19, 1868), presided over by the Cardinal Visitor, elected Jean Joseph Chevaux superior general. Father Joseph Simler was elected head of instruction, while Father de Lagarde, who would succeed Lalanne as director of Stanislas, was elected head of zeal. Brother Girandet was elected head of primary instruction, and Brother Fontaine was reelected head of temporalities, positions that had traditionally been filled by brothers.[9]

Superiors general communicated with the members through their circular letters, most of which were spiritual and moral exhortations that reveal the distinctive spirituality of each "Good Father" in relation to "My dear children," frequently abbreviated, M. D. Ch. These were authoritative letters aimed at energizing the Society of Mary with zeal, monastic observance, and severe asceticism based on the negative views of humanity in the grip of a godless society. For example, Georges J. Caillet's circular no. 71 (June 25, 1863) was a lengthy series of guidelines for an effective and proper annual retreat. He wrote of "Grace operating in us," and urged a "desert place of recollection." However, he added: "[In] our relations with seculars, occasioned by our functions, we may have sufficiently noted how God is offended, and how much the important affair of salvation is generally neglected." However, "the grace of the retreat is a double-edged sword issu-

ing from the mouth of the Son of Man, curing some and killing others."
Caillet explained that it is a "decisive grace; it is an occasion for all those
who endeavor to turn *a profit* [my emphasis] this precious pledge of divine
mercy; but by a just judgment of God, it blinds, hardens and makes worse
those . . . who do not profit by this wholesome visit of the Lord." He stressed
the presence of the devil to instruct the retreatants for the need for atone-
ment. Parts 2 and 3 of this circular stressed the need for fidelity to superiors,
to the rule, and in general to the spiritual and moral imperatives. Because the
religious has a high calling, based on a suppression of human urges, there was
an implication of the inherent incompatibility of nature and the graces of the
"state of a religious." This was actually in accord with Chaminade's 1839
Constitutions, which included a warning against the diabolical contagion of
the secular world. In this perspective, authority and a well-regulated interior
life were crucial to reconciling this incompatibility.[10]

Jean J. Chevaux's rigorism went beyond the level delineated by Caillet. In
his circular no. 16, May 15, 1872, Chevaux succinctly summarized a theology of grace congenial with that of the Jansenists:

> Death of nature is the essential condition of a life of grace. . . . Death of the old
> man, crucifixion of the flesh, interior and exterior mortification, self-renunciation,
> renouncement of all terrestrial objects, flight and contempt for the world, inces-
> sant struggle against thousands of enemies, persecutions, trials, penances, aus-
> terities, sufferings, privations, labors, pains, humiliations, lastly, self-sacrifice,
> continual martyrdom, perpetual holocaust, behold an incomplete series of well-
> known terms of the Christian language to express, in a varied manner, and from
> different points of view that death whose necessity St. Paul proclaims in his epis-
> tle. . . .
>
> There is a perpetual war between nature and grace, allow nature to live, and
> the life of grace will be extinguished in you, put nature to death and you will
> possess the life of grace. . . . This immolation of nature is the first condition of
> the spiritual life.[11]

Chevaux, an Alsatian, carried a heavy cross when, in the wake of the
Franco-Prussian War, Alsace and Lorraine were incorporated into the German empire in 1870. There were thirty-two houses in Alsace with a total of
three hundred Marianists who were educating nearly nine thousand students. At first, the only effect of annexation was the prohibition of teaching
French. There were other impositions such as placing religious under the
laws governing conscription into military service and forced exile, if one
wished to remain French. However, the May laws (1872), which formed the
basis of the *Kulturkampf,* the culture war against Catholicism, ultimately
meant the exclusion of all teaching congregations (1874), including the

Society of Mary. Later a school and a novitiate were opened on the border, but the Alsatians, so dominant in the American Province, were spread throughout the French schools, and some joined their confreres in the United States. Chevaux died in December 1875, a year after the death of Caillet.[12]

Chevaux's successor, Joseph Simler, represented a second-generation leadership in the Society. He is frequently referred to as the second founder. From the late 1860s he had been responsible for guiding various phases of the constitutions-revision process through the chapters and had related these concerns to the visitors appointed by the Sacred Congregation of Bishops and Regulars. As superior general he personally represented the Society in the process of papal approbation of the constitutions. Throughout this lengthy period of twenty-five years (1866–1891) there were several episodes of dissension related to the fear of a Vatican-imposed clericalization, which severely obstructed the approbation process. A few brothers were alienated by the polarization in the Society and wrote to Rome requesting that the Society be divided on lay-clerical lines; some priests retaliated against this open dissent by the brothers and concluded that a mixed community was impossible to hold together with a sense of equipoise.[13]

As early as 1866, Joseph Simler responded to Father Perrodin, who was one of those priests who concluded that a mixed society could not be maintained. Simler stated his belief "that the mixture of laymen and clerics is a source of difficulty, a source of jealousy and discord, in short, a permanent reason for suspicions and fears badly formed." However, he considered it "quite easy to remedy this situation," by articulating clear roles and responsibilities for members of each group so that they may sense their indispensability to each other. In chapter meetings delegates must be evenly distributed between brothers and priests to foster cooperation and to achieve consensus, a condition that should be achieved in the general council as well. He concluded this very long letter by drawing an analogy between the growth and development of a religious congregation as a moral person to the development of an individual person. The Society of Mary is like "a young man who is facing himself for the first time. Memories of his childhood weigh upon him and almost make him blush. He resists the yoke he bears. For time does not pass fast enough. He is ardent, rash, violent, presumptuous, thoughtless . . . a simple remark will make him sullen. He defies the whole world because he thinks himself wiser and he does so because he lacks experience . . . under the reign of reason all will be put in order." He urged Perrodin not to "despair of our Society, for she is young and a defect it is correcting day by day." Obstructing this maturation process, however, was the tendency among some members to blame all problems on

the mixed composition of ecclesiastics and lay members: The lack of members, the limited capacity of some, the lack of religious fervor of others, the inferiority of several establishments, the Society itself too poorly developed, too poorly underdeveloped, too little known, etc., etc.—all this and much more are the result, the inevitable consequence of the mixture of clerics and lay members.[14]

Unlike Caillet, Simler did not demonize dissenters, but rather considered them within the sphere of loyal opposition. In the end, Simler's faith in the maturation of the Society prevailed. Through his efforts approbation of the constitutions was achieved in 1891. The Vatican Congregation preferred some procedural changes, such as election rather than appointment of provincials, but Simler successfully appealed the case for centralization of authority on the precedent of the Redemptorists, a position the Vatican had approved. There was a provisional problem with the vow of stability to Mary and its symbol of a ring to be worn on the ring finger of the right hand. The Society reserved the vow for those at least ten years professed; the Vatican wished to place it much earlier, during the profession ceremony of final vows—poverty, chastity and obedience—and made the ring ceremony dependent on the approval of the local ordinary. The mixed composition was firmly lodged in the approved constitutions.[15] These many years of negotiations and internal conflicts culminated in an equipoise symbolic of the balanced intelligence of Joseph Simler. Just as second-generation immigrants tended to revive the spirit of the Old World, Simler consciously cultivated the positive spirit of the foundation period. He may be perceived as a superior general who, in the terminology of Max Weber, routinized the charism of the founder. Because he immersed himself in the original documents pertaining to the life of the founder in preparation for a scholarly biography of William Joseph Chaminade, he also revitalized the charism of the founder. It was during the siege of Paris in 1870 that he took the time to do initial biographical research, which, after the 1891 approbation of the constitutions, became the basis of the book.[16]

In contrast to Georges Joseph Caillet's stringent spirituality and the rigorism of Jean Chevaux, Joseph Simler was a Christian humanist grounded in a positive anthropology and clearly manifested in an incarnational spirituality. Simler drew upon his experience as a "Doctor of the Sorbonne"; his 1869 dissertation for a doctorate was entitled, *Sommes de Théologie*.[17] These summaries of theology represent a synthesis of the principal schools of theology, but the humanist tradition left its mark on his 1878 treatise entitled "Filial Piety in Christian Life," which was in the form of a circular letter of 122 pages.[18] Since the only theologian cited in this work is Thomas Aquinas, and since Simler occasionally draws upon his principles of analogy, a Thomistic humanism derived from a direct reading of the texts rather than those of the neo-Thomistic scholars appears evident in this lengthy reflection on piety.[19] With an abundance of scripture citations, frequent syllogistic reasoning of the scholastics, as well as metaphors drawn from his own intuition, Simler's writing reveals an eclectic theological background grounded in the sources rather than in the writings of the manualists.

After tracing the Latin origins of "piety," Simler concluded that it was a "natural inclination" manifested in

> acts of charity, benevolence, of justice, of obedience, of respect, of love, of assistance, but everywhere piety is at the bottom of these acts, because they all aim at drawing closer between fathers, mothers, children, brothers, sisters and relations these bonds of respect, love and mutual dependence which God has established as a reciprocal support and protection for the conservation of families and societies.

He quoted Cicero: "I see that you render justice to what I call my piety toward you."[20]

Proffering a positive anthropology, Simler states that "grace supports the good qualities and noble inclinations of nature, it fertilizes and verifies them; it elevates our thoughts and our vows towards a superior order . . . under its influence our natural virtues become supernatural." He noted that the gifts of the Holy Spirit transform the natural virtues to theological virtues in a life of grace. "The supernatural virtues of piety," wrote Simler, "cause us to love God, the angels, the saints, man, i.e., all the members of the divine family, because it is according to order." Throughout the remaining 110 pages he nuanced these themes in light of the Incarnation (which "alone explains, corrects, sums up and ennobles all that God has made outside of himself"), Mary ("The Masterpiece of Piety"), and Providence. The positive ground, so characteristic of his experiences as a consensus maker, permeates the spirit of piety in the religious life, so those committed to poverty, chastity, and obedience are perceived as fully participating in the life of Christ; with grace perfecting nature, the vowed life is not understood as at war with the body.[21]

All of Joseph Simler's circulars, including his extensive instructions on topics such as piety and the "distinguishing features" of the Marianists were published in translation in the United States. Since Simler was completing his biography of Chaminade during the 1890s, much of this material found its way into that work. However, chapter 3 of the 225-page circular on the Society's distinctive "features" is entitled, "Zeal eminently maternal." Chaminade's commitment to a universal vision, to exclude no ministry if it appears to be God's will, was understood to be congenial with Mary's universal motherhood.[22] Maternal zeal responds to all the concerns of her children. Marianists should adopt Mary's maternal zeal of meekness and benevolence. The former "supposes an invincible patience, a profound humility, control of one's passions, mortification of inordinate appetites . . . , continual watchfulness, prudence and discretion, justice blended with mercy and benevolence." Since one can only achieve meekness through struggle, it is not to be considered characteristic of a "soft and timid" (i.e., womanly) person; rather "it is a manly virtue" not that of a "cold soul." Because this maternal zeal is manly, it represents a determined commitment to the humble and hidden life illustrative of Mary's life as handmaid of the Lord and her hidden life in Nazareth; her humble loyalty to her Son on the cross.[23] The emphasis on maternal zeal reveals the ambiguities of gender of the period but to even proffer the model of maternity as a model for men's spirituality was a departure from the stereotypical male interpretation and is certainly in accord with Simler's Christian humanism, as well as with the strong oral tradition still evident in the 1990s embodied in the popular remark, "The Marianists have an androgynous character."

❧ III ❧

AS A YOUNG ASPIRANT TO THE RELIGIOUS LIFE, JOSEPH SIMLER WISHED to be a missionary. He was influenced by the *Annales de la Propagation de la Foi*, published in Lyons and featuring articles on mission work that the Lyons society had sponsored. When he joined the Society of Mary he had hoped to be sent to follow Leo Meyer. When he did finally arrive in the United States in 1874 as an assistant general, he was quite open to the nation's ethnic diversity. At St. Mary's Institute in Dayton he initiated a young boys' sodality, the Holy Angels' Sodality, and for the older boys, the Sodality of the Immaculate Conception. Since the Society was founded on the feast of the Holy Guardian Angels, Simler's historical sensibility made its mark in the choice of names. He had a particular devotion to Guardian Angels: "Have not our function toward our neighbor and toward the children a happy analogy with those of the Guardian Angels?"[24]

The minutes of the first meeting of the Sodality of the Holy Angels include this notice: "On the 18th of April 1875 Rev. Joseph Simler, 2nd Assistant of the Superior General of the Society of Mary, paying a visit to the American Province of his Society, established, while residing at St. Mary's Institute, Dayton, Ohio, the Sodality of the Holy Angels."[25] This appears to be the first Marianist sodality formed in the United States. William Dwyer, sixteen years of age, was elected first president of the sodality. He reflected on the role of the sodalists on the day he assumed office, April 29, 1875. This distinctive religious address is worthy of a full report:

> Allow me to profit on this occasion by making a few remarks concerning us all. You are aware of the title by which our dear sodality is known, and you also know the very obligations this title imposes upon us. If we were bound to live well before, we are still more now since we have become members, and taken Angels as patterns, as models. We are bound to give each other good example by striving to excel in every virtue and respect for those who have not the happiness of being members, we are required not merely to edify them as good Catholic boys, submissive and grateful pupils, and loving playmates, but should in a special manner pray for them that they may see the advantages we enjoy and strive earnestly to be participants in the same. Let us well understand that the greater the number of good members the more numerous will be the graces showered upon us by the Almighty when addressed by united and fervent prayer. If two or three assemble in his name having him in their midst to listen and grant what may fifty, sixty or even a greater number expect. On this occasion, I would also like to remind you of the gratitude we owe Rev. Father Simler who established this sodality in our midst, and thus united us in a particular manner with each other. Let us prove this gratitude by unreserved submission to our Spiritual Director Bro. Zehler [president of St. Mary's Institute], who even alone has done sufficient to insure our life long gratitude.
>
> Let us also remember them, together with our teachers in our daily prayers that God may protect them and prosper them. The different regulations relating to our exterior conduct will be made known to you by and by, and I have full assurance that you need only be acquainted with them in order to observe them faithfully. In conclusion let us place ourselves and our good resolutions under the patronage of our good Mother and let us beg of her to be a special guide that living here united we may assist each other to merit the happiness for which we were created and which we mutually wish each other.
>
> Wm. Dwyer[26]

With about twenty members enrolled, this sodality was treated to a remarkable exhortation by the president that was explicitly non-elitist, yet self-consciously communal in the call for mutual support. With a sensitivity that God was present in their gathering, Dwyer manifested a devotion to the holy angels as viable models for their Christian life together. For a young boy to preside with such sophistication was perhaps not all that uncommon; indeed temporary professed brothers not much older than Dwyer were teaching in elementary schools, such as St. Alphonsus, Baltimore, in the mid 1870s. Later minutes reveal that several sodalists did enter the Marianists, certainly one of the implicit intentions in establishing a sodality.[27] Ideally, sodalists were proactive young apostles, but dependent upon the Marianist chaplain, the spirit could develop with rigorism or humanism.

Eight counselors were elected and with officers, president and secretary, met independently between regular Sunday meetings. Since it was not uncommon to make one's First Communion around the age of fourteen, some members of the Holy Angels Sodality engaged in that rite of passage during the year. For example, on May 5, 1876, "Father Feith" [Brother Zehler's successor as spiritual director] told the members to say the following prayer for those who were making their First Holy Communion, "Holy Mother of Communion pray for us."[28] The next day the council met so that "each officer and counsellor should take charge of a certain number of boy's [sic] and should watch them carefully." Later that week the council met to decide how to celebrate St. Aloysius's feast day since he was the patron saint of young boys. They decided to go to communion six Sundays "and that we should pray for the Pope, and that the more we go to communion the better for us. We should also ask St. Aloysius to tell us our vocation and we should say every day a little prayer for the Holy Father, the Pope, and should watch the boys that we have under our care."[29] Since there were no other references to the leadership's responsibility for watching particular boys' behavior, it appears this practice was discarded.

The Sodality of the Immaculate Conception for the older boys was directed by Joseph Weckesser. Apart from a few perfunctory remarks by the president or treasurer, the director normally provided a strongly moral message such as the need for "reparation for the sins committed before and during Lent, referring to balls and immoral dances."[30] For two meetings the director narrated the story of Catherine Labouré, D.C., particularly the dreams she had of three hearts:

> the natural heart of St. Paul [St. Vincent de Paul]. The second [heart] showed his great love for the societies which he had founded [i.e., the Society of the Mission—The Lazarists—and the Daughters of Charity]. The black heart [the third vision] signified his sorrow for the misfortune of France . . . shortly before the Revolution [of 1830].[31]

As mentioned in chapter 1, the anti-republican, Restorationist mentality prevailed among most religious communities in 1830, and appears evident in the above narrative.

❧ IV ❧

THE RELIGIOUS FORMATION OF THE MARIANISTS BEGAN IN THE postulate, where young aspirants were assigned to secondary school courses that included about two years of classes, until the establishment of a full high school curriculum around 1900.[32] This was followed by a novitiate, which included courses on the history and the rule of the Society as well as on education as a basis for teacher training in the subsequent years in the scholasticate. Throughout the nineteenth and early twentieth centuries the temporary professed brothers spent usually two years completing the theoretical training in pedagogy for elementary education.

During Simler's 1875 visitation he introduced the practice of allowing some young brothers to study in France, with experiences at the Collège Stanislas. Though this was generally applauded by those who evaluated this project as a departure from the stringent financial concerns of provincial administrations, it appears that Simler was more concerned with providing an opportunity to imbibe the primitive spirit of the Society in France than with initiating study for advanced degrees. For example, Brother William Wohlleben was one of the early American brothers to study for a Ph.D. (1904–1908) in Europe. He enrolled at the University of Fribourg in Switzerland, where the Marianist seminarians studied for the priesthood under the Dominicans. Wohlleben remarked:

> two years . . . was the customary limit for sending brothers to Paris to our Collège Stanislas which was not of a university standing. They went to school then for about a year and a half. By the time they were there for half a year, they got a pretty good introduction in French. . . . By the time they were proficient they had to go home without a college degree or anything of that sort. It was merely to get them over into Stanislas and live under the same roof as the General Administrators to get the spirit.[33]

Continuing education after the scholasticate was a persistent problem throughout the late nineteenth and early twentieth century. The brother director/principal of the local Marianist school was urged to be immediately concerned with the "newcomer," the neophyte teacher. Jean Chevaux's circular on this topic included an admonition. "He [the director] should work with the programmes and time-tables for the house in general and for each class in particular, containing the proper details. . . . At the arrival of a new teacher, the director hands him the text of the time-table, of the disciplinary system, of the programmes, of the method and all the regulations adopted and observed in the house, and, if necessary, explain them to him."[34] The brother director was instructed to sponsor pedagogical conferences during the year, while summer-vacation courses of study were instituted and papers were submitted prior to the annual retreat at the motherhouse in Dayton. This became more routine as education became more organized under diocesan school superintendents and the Marianist inspectors of schools. In the 1920s degree programs were offered during the summers at Dayton, and later some brothers attended the Catholic University of America, where the Marianists had a house of studies.[35]

For continuing education and religious formation young brothers were dependent on directors, inspectors, and provincials, who also introduced them to the general rules of effective behavior for teachers. In his 1881 "Supplement to the Instructions Given in the Retreat of 1879," John N. Reinbolt, provincial, noted that the retreat is "the most proper time for developing good manners, polite and correct language, friendly corrections in both, all of which cannot take place in the time of silence and study." The principal topic of this "Supplement," however, was the many complaints of the brothers' poor teaching that had been sent by priests to directors, to the inspector, and to Reinbolt himself. "Complaints have become so numerous and of so serious a nature, that if we do not immediately remedy the prevailing evils, the reputation of our dear Society will be greatly endangered."[36]

The provincial cited several letters, one which criticized a brothers' school for its total absence of a positive spirit; "it is best characterized as a lazy, morose, dragging and sleepy concern." Reinbolt concluded that the spirit reflected the brothers' apathy. One complaint was a general one. "The very little English grammar is below criticism, unpardonably bad, an unintelligible, disconnected babble." Reinbolt withheld the criticism of catechesis; however, he did say, "The knowledge of the pupils is generally too limited." He concluded, "No middle class should be found where the commandments of God and of the Church have not been given thoroughly and explained. It is impossible for the priest to do all before the first communion, what the teacher ought to have done in the course of years." (The average age of First Communion during this period was around thirteen.)

A long complaint related to the general incivility of their students: "They are awkward and ill-bred in their carriage, manners, gait and language." He was particularly distressed by the general lack of respect toward priests. Another priest noted that the brothers had manifested "a dangerous spirit of independence" which could "prove fatal to the very existence of the schools." Rather than deal with specific ethnic, pedagogical, and professional problems at the root of these complaints, the provincial found "the fault in the absence of a truly religious spirit, in too great a tendency to ease and comfort, in a certain fear of hard labor and fatigue." He described the ideal spirit as essentially one of "humility, of obedience, of devotedness and of self-denial." Hence, he called for religious renewal, prayer for "our . . . efforts for the Glory of God, for the salvation of souls, and for the honor of our dear Society." Only with a "renovation of zeal" would the brothers satisfy "the just demands of priests and parents."[37]

During the late 1870s and early 1880s the number of recruits reached 130 in the postulate program. According to one brother, who was a postulant during this period, this was a time of "storm and stress . . . when a fanatic reformer suppressed our games, removed our library, abolished or curtailed recreations, and punished slight infractions of the rule of silence and the like with a lack of sleep or incarceration in the filthiest imaginable hole infinitely worse than a vile dog kennel." This rare example of documented views from below was composed by Mathias Leimkuhler, who attended St. Alphonsus School in Baltimore and who had spent twenty-six years as a brother before leaving the Society rather abruptly in March 1907. He admitted that "deep down in my heart I have always chafed under the exigencies of what is called the spirit of the Society." That is what led him to recall the origin of his alienation during his experience as a postulant. "The fear of losing one's vocation with the direful consequences both here and hereafter drawn in the most lurid colors kept most of us where we were, despite brutalizing injustice and degrading oppression. Such an experience sears a man's character for life." Finally aware that this trauma had resulted in his inability to respect himself within the Society, Leimkuhler left alone and quietly rather than as a "mutineer"—as he was aware of "the worth of the work done by the Society."[38]

In a commentary attached to this letter dated October 1944, Brother Robert Holzmer explained the context of the years 1879–1881. The director of the postulants who so alienated Leimkuhler was Brother Joseph Sennety. Holzmer did not attempt to fully justify Sennety's behavior, but he did state that the superior was reacting to a "rough element" and to impose conduct "upon the mob may well be excused for resorting to drastic methods more suited to a reform school than to a decent boarding school, let alone a religious house." Holzmer also noted that Sennety was "subjected to outbursts of temper." He also distrusted Leimkuhler's motives: "He must have been hard up for a grievance" to go back twenty-six years for the source of his departure from the Society. Indeed, he concluded that Leimkuhler "was not too honest in exploiting" the experience of the era of storm and stress.[39] In any event, during the period when Reinbolt was quoting the many complaints of the brothers' incivility, poor teaching skills, and generally poor religious spirit, the postulancy was under a brother who was at best "resorting to drastic methods suited to a reform school."

Such conditions defiled the ideals of an interior asceticism associated with the structured routine of prayer and study in the clearly defined monastic enclosures as stated in the Constitutions of 1839 and 1891. While these rather stringent directives were intended to separate the religious from the pervasive temptations of the secular world, the section dealing with "the salvation of souls," that is, the Marianist ministry of education, evokes a less negative assessment of the human condition. Prefaced by the formula on the commitment to the salvation of souls entitled "On Christian Education," both constitutions refer to the two ways for "saving souls: to preserve them from contagion of the world and *to heal* them if they had been contaminated by it."[40] When dealing with the "poorest and youngest children," the brothers were to preserve them from the evils of the world: it follows that the teacher should "with the solicitude and kindness of Jesus and Mary, be committed to healing those whom error and vice have corrupted in a more advanced age or in a higher state of life." The Marianist teacher should maintain study within a climate of "order, silence" and respect for the rules, but "he perseveres in the depth of his heart an unalterable calm and a wise tendency toward indulgence." The directive, "He is careful not to reject as bad what is not absolutely good," is a tacit warning not to err on the side of rigorism as if God's grace is absent in those students who are not behaving at the level of absolute goodness.[41]

Of course, religious education is not limited to catechesis but permeates the school. The teachers were to adapt their methods of teaching according to "the progress of human society and be adapted to its needs and its wishes." The superior general and the head of instruction were to meet regularly to discuss improvements in methodology based on the "experiences of the most capable teachers." Not to adapt would mean to "limit to a very short time the services and the existence" of the Society of Mary.[42]

The constitutional provisions related to Christian education represent elements of development, adaptation, and struggle but were grounded in the division between teaching and the rigors of the religious exercises. Teaching was not articulated as a source of grace for the brothers' growth as religious; because of the brothers' pursuit of their commitment to a life of perfection, their lives as religious were indirect sources of spiritual growth for students. However, teaching was certainly considered an occasion of grace in the lengthy *Manual of Christian Pedagogy for the Use of The Brothers of the Society of Mary*, composed in the 1850s by Father J. B.

Fontaine and published in France in 1857.[43] Translated from the French and only slightly adapted for the American Marianists, this manual was published in the United States in 1899 and later marketed among Catholic teachers, both lay and religious. The distinctive character of the manual is its elaborate treatment of the positive human capacities basic to the students' physical, intellectual, moral, and spiritual development. Another distinctive mark is the thread of psychology woven into the pattern of the text; hence, the child is not a *tabula rasa,* nor imbued with tendencies toward mischief, but rather is portrayed with complex qualities. Marianist teachers were to continue the nurturing tasks of the parents "in their education, formation and development of the bodily organs as well as the moral life of the soul. Hence, the teacher will have to consider himself as the father rather than the master of his pupils." Not only does education promote a family-minded, neighborly, patriotic, and religious student, but it will also "promote the happiness of the Christian teacher."[44]

In the chapter on physical education there are directives based on the child's need for play and gymnastics, hints for meeting the needs of nutrition, and "the fundamental rules of hygiene." Because the so-called passions of the heart, such as "hatred, envy, anger, fear, shame, etc.," greatly influence physical health, controlling such passions is related not only to moral education but to physical development as well. To set the tone and the example, the teacher must be a model of self-control and introduce the pupils to lives of the saints as examples of "subduing" the passions.[45]

In the section on "education of the intellect" the teacher should capture the attention of the students by making his lessons "interesting"; they must be "a treat for the mind," and the teacher must educate with "a will and with pleasure." To develop a keen sense of judgment he must expose biases and prejudices; to strengthen memory the gradual introduction of memorization is encouraged; to cultivate the imagination the teacher should be inventive, artful, and "warm the hearts" of the students by citing the wonderful events of scripture, of the lives of the saints, and of fables and parables. The teacher should introduce an "endless variety of subjects" and represent ideas with analogies, comparisons, and connections.[46]

Since education had been advancing throughout the nineteenth century without corresponding progress in general happiness, the "supreme need for the times is virtue. . . . It is ever safe to say that science without religion is more dangerous than useful, for, as sad experience proves, science which is not guided by virtue often becomes the tool of passion and renders it more ingenious and skillful in producing evil." This lengthy treatment of moral education entails cultivating the positive inclinations of the heart, among which are "an instinctive desire, a necessity of loving God"; the love of self through preservation and defense; "the natural disposition of kindness" toward one's neighbor; and "to love the good" by helping students "discern good from evil."[47]

The author wrote on the "culture of the heart," whose "object . . . is to direct the exercise of love and hatred." The teacher is instructed to be "filled with indulgence, tenderness, and compassion for the hearts he is to model." The excessive love of the body or "concupiscence of the flesh," has four preferences. The first is sensualism, the concentration of all energies "upon the gratification of sensual desires." The second preference reveals the traditional gender bias of the period that defined "masculinity" as a virtue and "effeminacy" as a vice: "Effeminacy, which enervates the body, leaves it without energy, without courage against temptation and without power of endurance in hardships or pain." The third, intemperance and profligacy make the person "a slave of vilest passions." While the fourth also relates to "effeminacy"—a "total degradation of manhood with a loss of honor and self-respect." There is also a warning about "concupiscence of the eyes," by which the person tends to focus on those objects that lead to the above four evils of the flesh. Of course pride in all its manifestations such as "insubordination to established authority" must be countered, like all the above tendencies and preferences, by good example and through the positive influence of religion by cultivating piety, reading scripture, and prayer.[48]

The chapter on love and hatred, "the center towards which all other passions converge" is based on a relatively positive assessment of humanity; though original sin had perverted love and hatred, the aim of Christian education is "to restore them as far as possible to their original function." The Marianist teacher should avoid discussions of God as the "pure spirit, infinite almighty . . . and saving Lord . . . ," as such descriptions may instill in the child "awe and admiration, but not love." To elaborate on God as the ruler and judge who "commands obedience under pain of eternal damnation . . . may fill the heart with fear but not love." In contrast, the Marianist teacher was to present God as a "tender father who loves them dearly, who provides for their temporal and eternal welfare and who is continually with them by day and by night. What child could refuse to love such a God." The rhetorical basis for the love of Jesus should not be a "dry explanation" of the catechism but "the enthusiastic language of the heart." Jesus should be portrayed as "friend, consoler, a guide, a companion on the voyage of life" and as sacramental food for the "passage from time to eternity." The Holy Spirit is "the Comforter" who from baptism "sanctifies the soul . . . who dwells in the heart to keep it pure and holy, who inspires it with love of virtue and hatred of sin," and who "will make [the person] a saint in heaven." The teacher's motto throughout his life must be "God is love."[49]

The manual commissions the "Brother of Mary" to be a model of devotion to Mary "as the most tender of Mothers." Students should "invoke her with confidence and to place all their filial confidence in her." As a result Mary will "save them from the shipwreck in the tempest of the passion and will guide them on the paths of fair love of which she is the mother."[50] The weaknesses of self-love are manifested in learning. Riches, honor, distinction and pleasure should be transformed from an elitist selfish disposition to a balanced sense of understanding grounded in humility. The insatiable love of riches should be counteracted by the poverty of Jesus, who "called the poor blessed." To acquire wealth as a means rather than as an end in itself is of course justified. Honors based on a "natural sentiment" of emulation may be encouraged in the schools of the Society of Mary as long as it is opposed to "proud ambition, jealousy, or envy." Though Georges Joseph Caillet had remarked that the Society's commitment was to the education of the middle class—which has been portrayed as almost intrinsically driven to climb the social and economic ladder—the manual of pedagogy calls upon the teacher to "combat this tendency . . . admonish his pupils against pride and presumption and inspire them with a love for the station in life in which Providence has placed them." This rather countercultural and anticapitalist sentiment was preceded by a brief comment on how the drive for improved status has meant the "exodus from country to town, the desertion of farms and congestion of our centers of population to the detriment of agriculture and to the menace for public peace." In so many words, the author noted that these factors result in the frustration of unfulfilled expectations that lead to "revolutionary schemes." If the capitalist spirit is to seek wealth as an end in itself, the manual is anticapitalist. Realism prevailed, however, as the Marianist schools must "be abreast of the times," which may entail a "concession of principle," with the caveat that students must be prepared to "strictly comply with wise reserve that prudence demands."[51]

In the same vein, self-love's manifestation in the pursuit of pleasure must be countered with emphasis on innocent pleasure guided by moderation, prudence, and "duty before pleasure." To achieve love of neighbor teachers must cultivate the "natural sentiments" of "Filial Piety, Gratitude, Benevolence, Compassion, and Friendship."[52] These admonitions, indeed the dicta of the entire manual, are analogues to Joseph Simler's work on piety, as well as an elaboration on the Christian cultivation of positive natural inclinations. Though both works extolled mortification, discipline, and restraint as means to attain piety and a well-ordered school, they are remarkably related in their emphases on the goodness of human aspirations and the accessibility of grace; it is likely Simler was both influenced by the *Manual* and promoted its publication in the United States. Since Simler was the assistant general for instruction for nearly ten years before he became superior general, he had the experience, the interest, the theological and philosophical background, and the opportunity to affect the promotion and development of the *Manual*. Brother John Kim, responsible for its translation and adaptation, had stressed the need for a generally affective, paternal style of teaching in his conferences as director of communities prior to becoming assistant provincial and head of instruction in the American Province and later holding that position on the general council level.

Part 2 of the *Manual of Pedagogy*, a lengthy treatise on methodology, also composed by Fontaine, was never published in the United States, but there was an 1885 English translation in manuscript form "for the use of the Scholastics of Nazareth." The work is divided into seven chapters that deal with methods and content for each of the subject areas according to the three levels within the elementary school: the lower classes, ages six to nine; middle classes, ages ten to thirteen; and the upper classes, ages thirteen and over. There is also a chapter on moral and religious education. Other chapters deal with discipline—rewards and punishments, particular regulations for classes—including prayers, and a chapter on boarding schools. In accord with the published editions of part 1, privately circulated editions of part 2 are a blend of principles and methods governing the Marianist schools.[53]

The introduction to part 2, which relates to religious instruction, aptly illuminates the general direction of the Marianist mission in the school. The first consideration in teaching religion is to emphasize that the subject matter "is not mere imaginary thought; it is a fact we relate to our scholars. . . . The simple and natural narrations of the bible cause the child great pleasure, and in our time cause religion to grow firmly in the soul, and make it a true enlightened Christian."

To underscore pleasure and enlightenment as congenial with the positive character of part 1, there is also an emphasis on sacred history, as well as "the history of religion in their dioceses," which would cultivate an interest in the vitality of the religious heritage and "cannot but strengthen in them the faith of their forefathers . . . and an attachment for their native soil." Besides learning their catechism "word for word and especially so that they will understand well the meaning," the students were introduced each week to the next Sunday's Gospel, which after several years "will not only remain graven in their minds, but also leave salutary impressions imprinted in their hearts."[54]

The Christian Brothers in the United States published an adaptation of St. Jean Baptiste de la Salle's *Instruction of Christian Schools* entitled *Management of Christian Schools*. Published in 1887, twelve years before Brother Kim's adaptation of the *Manual of Christian Pedagogy*, this work is divided into two parts: part 1, on the methodology recommended for the various subjects required in the curriculum for parish schools; and part 2, on the formation of the master or teacher and essential qualities of the teacher. The latter part is comparable to part 1 of the Marianist work, but rather than explore the psychological, intellectual, and spiritual aspects of the child's development, the understanding of which develops the qualities of a good teacher, the Christian Brothers' work is structured differently. In a paragraph on the cultivation of the heart, the Christian Brother was urged to prevent the students' "passions and vices from developing themselves . . . by inspiring them with a horror for, and an estrangement from, the occasion of sin, by opposing himself to the bad inclinations they exhibit; by leading them to love and admire Christian virtues; and in what manner they should practice them; and lastly by endeavoring to make them form good habits."

In contrast, the Marianist teacher is encouraged "to secure their [students'] confidence and win their affection. Let the teacher entertain a well-regulated affection, paternal tenderness for all that are in his charge. Let him manifest these dispositions of his heart by habitual meekness, gentleness and devotedness. . . ." The Christian Brother was also instructed to be "a kind and benevolent father." He was told to have "faith in the power of goodness and the virtues of the human heart." Meekness, blended with firmness, was extolled in the Christian Brothers' manual. Hence, there is some similarity between the two manuals. One nuanced distinction is the Marianist emphasis upon internalization of the specific paternalistic qualities. Not only was the Marianist to internalize the habitual "gentleness," but also admonitions against the use of fear were frequent reminders to Marianists that they were to use scripture and the lives of heroic saints as means to prevent students from succumbing to vice and passion.[55]

On the other hand, as mentioned earlier, the Christian Brothers' manual does not model the teachers' behavior on a thorough exploration of psychological development so essential to the Marianist work. They both emphasize manliness as a virtue and effeminacy as a vice. Whereas the Marianists were critical of effeminacy because it "enervates the body" to the degree that the student "lacks the courage" to struggle against temptations and "without the power of endurance in hardship and pain." In this sense manliness relates to "honor and self-respect."[56] The Christian Brothers' manual refers to the vice of effeminacy in the discussion of abuses of meekness when "a good master shall avoid a too ready compliance or an effeminate condescension." If the Christian Brother is "not constant" in applying necessary firmness, or when he "looks upon something as too light or indifferent, what in reality is a considerable evil, he is guilty of effeminate condescension."[57] A muscular Christianity is extolled by both manuals, but the Marianist teacher was merely warned about being effeminate in his authority, whereas it was a terribly dangerous tendency among the Christian Brothers.

Perhaps the most distinctive difference is that the Marianist manual engages the personal loving relationship of God and humanity in a strongly affective tone, while the Christian Brothers' manual is more theoretical and not as elaborate in its discussion. It would be a mistake, however, to draw the parallels in black and white; they represent varying shades of gray with distinctive tonalities.

⍟ V ⍟

SINCE THE MARIANIST COMMITMENT TO CHRISTIAN EDUCATION was at the core of the Society's identity, provincials would refer to that ministry in their reports on the area of zeal. But in the United States, the German-American context was prevalent. In his 1899 report to the membership of the American Province, Father George Meyer, a German- and French-speaking Alsatian, like his predecessors Leo Meyer and John Reinbolt, underscored the importance of catechesis in the schools. He noted one significant development:

> In the German [American] schools the teachers have to contend with extraordinary difficulties, which arise from the fact that the great majority of the children no longer understand the German language. To explain the catechism in German is to explain it in an unknown language, and yet the Rev. Pastors want German catechism. In the lower grades, the children recite the letter of the catechism.[58]

Because the pastors paid the salaries of the teachers on the assumption that they would foster German as the language of the faith, and because lay religion teachers appeared to have been more successful than the Brothers,

Meyer urged them to consider solutions to this problem with patience. He noted that when the Brothers taught catechism in English in the higher grades "the knowledge of our holy religion is carefully imparted to the pupils."[59]

A year later (1900) Meyer returned to this topic. Besides reiterating the perennial problem of teaching catechism in German he traced the source of the problem to the parents: if they do not "speak German with the children at home, this language will become a dead language and the children will be obliged to study it as now advanced pupils study Latin and Greek in a classical course." He noted that pastors admitted the problem but, perhaps influenced by the *Pastoralblatt*, a periodical for the German-speaking clergy, were determined not to introduce the English catechism. Many assistant pastors presented their explanations of the catechism in English, while in some schools, said Meyer, "the children have German catechism with a corresponding English translation."[60]

Brother Damian Litz, a native of Baden, was the Marianist most closely identified with the German-American community. He had served in more schools than any of the first-generation missionaries in the United States: Cincinnati, Cleveland, rural missions in the dioceses of Milwaukee, Dayton, New Orleans, Rochester, Baltimore, and New York. He was identified with the monitor system, as he was frequently in charge of a large class and found the method the only viable means of teaching. During the visitation of Joseph Simler in 1875 he had successfully interested him in establishing a formation program, a boarding school and a normal school for scholastics in Cedar Hill near Paterson, New Jersey. The site was a poor choice, unsuitable for farming and too costly to make into a thriving boarding school. It closed five years after its foundation.[61]

While Litz was at St. Michael's School in Baltimore, with a preponderance of parishioners from Baden, he began a thirty-year association with German-American journalism. Though he was a feature writer on various topics, it was his role as a humorist on family and parish life, under the pseudonym "Sepp," that secured him a large following. In 1870 he began writing for the *Katholische Volkszeitung*. As one scholar of the German press noted, "with his homespun, folksy, jovial manner, he [i.e., Litz] seems to have catered to the readers' taste, for his articles were admittedly the main attraction of each number."[62]

This German-American Catholic weekly was founded in 1860 by the Kruetzer brothers, Joseph and Christopher, who within a few years transformed it from a regional to a national newspaper. Its vitriolic tone, anti-Semitism, and extremely reactionary policies set it apart from other

German-American newspapers. Though it became more respectable, the editorial opinion and the topics for articles reveal a conspicuously conservative Catholicism: its ecclesiology was excessively ultramontanist; its spirituality was a baroque piety that extolled the passion of the cross as symbolic of the struggle with the anti-Christian character of liberalism, Protestantism, and the Masonic-Jewish alliance aimed at frustrating the church's restoration of Christendom. Father Peter Fresbier of St. Michael's parish in Baltimore and Francis X. Weninger, S.J., the indefatigable missionary and German-American activist, were frequent contributors to the weekly.[63] Between 1880 and his death Damian Litz contributed on almost a weekly basis. When the Kruetzer brothers died (1874 and 1878), Christopher's widow became publisher "and from that time on she was even more dependent upon the assistance and contributions of Damian Litz." Dieter Cunz, a scholar of the German experience in Baltimore, concluded: "Without him [i.e., Litz] the periodical certainly would not have been able to keep its unusually large and far-reaching circulation."[64] For Litz to have been such a major publishing force while also teaching was indeed an achievement.

German-Catholic conservatism was manifested in Litz's articles attacking the antireligious forces in public education and in Masonry, liberalism in the church, and Protestantism in society. In the struggle between the German-American preservationists and traditionalists, and the transformationist, or liberal, Catholics, Litz was clearly opposed to the Americanists—John Ireland, archbishop of St. Paul; John J. Keane, bishop of Richmond and later rector of the Catholic University of America; and Denis O'Connell, rector of the North American College in Rome. Litz was allied with the German-American archbishop of Milwaukee, Frederick Katzer; and the anti-Ireland spokesman Peter Paul Cahensly, who advocated a prelature for the German-American Catholics; and Arthur Preuss, editor of the *Fortnightly Review* published in St. Louis.[65] Besides the German drive for self-governing parishes within an Irish-dominated church, the issues that polarized the two camps were membership in secret societies, the Knights of Labor, the temperance movement, the direction of the Catholic University of America, and the legitimacy of public education; the Fairbault-Stillwater school plan, whereby Catholic sisters were hired to teach in public schools (former Catholic schools sold to the public school board); the French translation and publication of a biography of Isaac Hecker, founder of the liberal Paulists; and, in general, John Ireland's and John Keane's speeches extolling the republican ethos of the United States as a sign of God's providential design. To Litz, Preuss, and others, this Americanist movement was identified with heterodox "Catholic" liberalism in its most dangerous forms. Pope Leo XIII's January 1899 apostolic letter, *Testem Benevolentiae*, addressed to Cardinal James Gibbons, an ally of Ireland, Keane, and O'Connell, condemned Americanism —without naming an Americanist. The conservative German-Americans, allied with Michael A. Corrigan, archbishop of New York, and Bernard McQuaid, bishop of Rochester, New York, felt vindicated. Though the liberals referred to Americanism as a "phantom heresy," there were indeed Americanists who fit many of the principles condemned by Leo XIII: the church should adapt to the spirit of the times; the separation of church and state, religious liberty, and the republican ethos fostered an era of the Holy Spirit signaling the prominence of American Catholicity in the transformation of the church in the world, and the primacy of the active over the contemplative life of the monastic enclosure.[66] Litz wrote impassioned articles in opposition to Americanism. He was particularly critical of the Americanist press, even diocesan newspapers published by local bishops. In 1900 he wrote an article attacking John Phelan, the priest editor of the *Western Watchman* and his enthusiastic expressions of pro-Ireland sentiment. Litz predicted that the hierarchy would eventually suppress such liberal Catholic journalism, as well as the entire Americanist movement.[67] By this time he was in retirement in San Antonio.

Since Damian Litz was highly regarded by his confreres, his German-American Catholic conservatism represented the prevailing ethos of the majority of the German-Americans and Marianist religious culture in the United States at the turn of the century. The predominance of the German-American dimension of the American Province was manifested in 1897, when the Marianists took charge of their first high school at SS. Peter and Paul parish in St. Louis, whose pastor, Francis Goeller, had been a significant clerical voice in the German-American community. He was in the national *Priesterverein*, which boycotted the meeting of the lay Catholic Congress in Chicago in conjunction with the World's Columbian Exposition, because it represented the predominance of Archbishop John Ireland and his aggressive assimilationist strategy.[68]

Brother William Wohlleben, one of the first three brothers assigned to SS. Peter and Paul, recalled that the parish was "sort of a big German village."[69] Brother Kim had been instrumental in arranging for the Marianist presence in this large parish; his sister had been a School Sister of Notre Dame at this parish school for many years. These sisters ran the primary school; listed in the *Catholic Directory* of 1904 were thirty sisters in a school with an enrollment of 1,360, while there were six Brothers of Mary at the parish high school for boys with an enrollment of one hundred.[70] The *Catholic*

Directory of that year described the high school as featuring "Thorough Business Education." Brother Wohlleben noted that there was no classics department but that there was a well-grounded science program. He referred to the significance of Arthur Preuss, editor of the *Fortnightly Review*; the journal "treated philosophical and religious subjects, and was quite controversial."[71] Preuss, the son of a convert from Lutheranism who edited *Amerika*, was an impassioned anti-Americanist. He considered John Ireland to be at best a well-intentioned but heterodox archbishop who preached the church's adaptation to a nation entwined in Protestantism, materialism, and a bogus religious liberty that was license for vicious anti-Catholicism. To legitimate the public school was tantamount to recognizing that the godless state has the right to impose its secularism upon innocent minds and souls. The *Fortnightly Review* was published in English, and its editor promoted a gradual assimilation into American life but maintained a vigorous opposition to Americanist adaptation to the spirit of the age.[72] Consideration of the SS. Peter and Paul High School will be featured in a later chapter, but it is important to place this first Marianist parish high school within the continuity of the Society's identity with the concerns of the German-American community, which was at the origin of the mission to Cincinnati in 1849 and was the medium of its religious culture.

In 1899, two years after the opening of the St. Louis High School, Bishop John Lancaster Spalding of Peoria asked the Marianists to staff an academy, Spalding Institute, which was not to be associated with a parish but was to appeal to Catholic families throughout the diocese who wished to enroll their boys in a program of classical studies that would prepare them to enter higher education. Spalding had known Brother Kim when both were stationed in New York in the early 1870s. Though Spalding preferred the Christian Brothers, they were immersed in the so-called Latin crisis, characterized by polarization over the propriety of teaching Latin in their schools, prohibited by their founder St. Jean Baptiste de la Salle because of the fear that if his brothers learned Latin they might go on to study for the priesthood rather than remain committed to their original ministry.[73]

No doubt Brother Kim informed Spalding of the classical programs included in the curricula of St. Mary's College in Dayton and St. Mary's and St. Louis Colleges in San Antonio to illustrate the Marianist experience in teaching Latin and liberal studies in general. In any event, after Father George Meyer and Brother Kim visited with the bishop, a suitable arrangement was negotiated.

John Lancaster Spalding, considered to be the principal founder of the Catholic University of America (1889) and the strongest episcopal proponent of women's education, was sympathetic with the Americanists but departed from the Fairbault-Stillwater school plan and was not a strong opponent of German separatism. His was such a singularly critical intellect that he alone among the hierarchy joined other anti-imperialists in opposing America's role in the Spanish-American War and the aggressive foreign policy of seizing lands in the Caribbean and the Pacific. After the Marianists opened Spalding Institute, the bishop traveled to Rome, where in the Church of the Gesù he delivered a sermon that was remarkably pro-Americanist—divine providence has assigned America a prophetic role in the development of the church in the modern world—that has been perceived as particularly courageous in light of Leo XIII's recent condemnation of Americanism with a reference to principles included in Spalding's address.[74]

As mentioned earlier, the Marianist presence at Spalding Institute was in accord with trends in their Dayton and San Antonio colleges. However, because these schools originated as independent elementary and secondary schools in the 1850s, the Peoria Academy, a four-year city-wide secondary school committed to classical studies, represents a departure from Marianist tradition as well as a new phase in the history of Catholic education in the United States. There were a few German parishes in the Diocese of Peoria, but the vast majority of the students were Irish-Americans. As will be noted in a later chapter, the Marianists were asked to leave Spalding Institute by the first German-American bishop of Peoria. Just as SS. Peter and Paul High School symbolized continuity of its German base, Spalding represents the trends of professionalization and Americanization that will be framed within the developments of Marianist history in the brothers' role in the foundation of the National Catholic Education Association. In its monastic routines as promulgated by Caillet and Chevaux, Marianist religious culture was rigorous, ascetical, and remote from the putative contagion of the world. However, as the constitutions from Chaminade to Simler indicate, and as the *Manual of Pedagogy* clearly fosters, teaching was an occasion of grace. In the Marianist schools there was a stream of spirituality without which the religious life would have been parched by the arid climate of a formulaic style of life. Hence, there was a fragmentation between the monastic rigor and the graced apostolate. Simler's incarnational spirituality integrated the two. According to Simler, the Marianist sodality represented the permanent synthesis of nature and grace, the immanence and transcendence of God in the Marianist way of life.

CHAPTER FIVE

Americanization
1900–1925

❧ I ❧

THE AMERICANIZATION OF THE MARIANISTS WAS A PROCESS THAT occurred gradually but accelerated with the modernization of the Catholic school system and the subsequent need for professionalization of the teachers. The evolution of the institutions of higher education in Dayton and San Antonio meant that many brothers and priests were pursuing graduate degrees. Also entailed in Americanization were the demise of the old collegiate system and the development of the four-year high school on the public school model. Educational accreditation agencies such as the North Central and the Middle States developed criteria for evaluating schools that included faculty requirements, which obviously had an impact on the brothers. Though some Marianist parish high schools were in German ethnic neighborhoods, the majority of the high schools were consciously American; indeed, they became Americanization schools, where the boys of the immigrant families of southern and eastern Europe were religiously educated in English and were to be absorbed into a new nationality.

As mentioned in the last chapter, in the early twentieth century the Marianists had noted the decline in German-language skills among students and their families. Philip Gleason observes this general decline and cites Arthur Preuss, the conservative Catholic editor of the *Fortnightly Review*, who in 1900 noted "beneficial" trends in assimilation which, said Gleason, "required concessions to the English language if many of the old German parishes were to survive."[1] The dominance of the second generation and the rapid reduction of German immigration at the turn of the century marked a critical phase in assimilation. Conscious of a gradual adaptation to the larger cultural trends, these German-Americans were indeed Americanizing while maintaining their ethnic sense of peoplehood.[2]

In his book *The Search for Order, 1877–1920*, Robert H. Wiebe describes and analyzes economic, social, and intellectual trends toward the "regulative, hierarchial needs of an urban industrial society. Through rules with impersonal sanctions, it sought continuity and predictability in a world of endless change. It assigned far greater authority to government—in particular to a variety of flexible administrative devices—and it encouraged the centralization of authority."[3] The complex changes in these developments entailed the significance of a strong organizational impulse.

Toward the end of the nineteenth century the majority of those entering the Society of Mary were born in the United States. By 1920 the predominance of the American-born Marianists was quite evident. Indeed, the first Irish-American provincial, Bernard O'Reilly, was appointed in 1918. German-American parishes and religious congregations in the United States were compelled to shed most of their culture by the anti-German feeling of World War I, a trend that was an obvious catalyst in the Americanization process. Father O'Reilly had been appointed president of St. Mary's College in 1908, which was an early acknowledgment of this Irish-American's leadership abilities.

During the war, the American hierarchy established the National Catholic War Council, which evolved into the National Catholic Welfare Council (NCWC; in 1922 changed to National Catholic Welfare Conference) in 1919. All the bishops now met annually and were assisted by a large staff of priests and lay people. An administrative board of bishops monitored the council and set the agenda for the annual meeting. The general secretary and the dominant figure of both the council and the NCWC was the second-generation Americanist John J. Burke, C.S.P.[4]

The NCWC was the predecessor of the NCCB/USCC. Representative of the organizational impulse in American society, the NCWC was preceded by the Federation of Catholic Societies (1901), the Catholic Education Association (1903–1904), the National Association of Catholic Charities (1910) and the Catholic Hospital Association (1915). From their origins the Marianists were involved in the Catholic Education Association (later the NCEA). Because of the need for higher education, the Marianists also established a house of studies at the Catholic University of America (1916) in the nation's capital, a sign of the national consciousness of the American leadership.

The organizational impulse was manifested in the establishment of the Western Province, or St. Louis Province, in 1908. Later the Cincinnati

Province established a postulate in Beacon, New York (1922), solely for high-school candidates for the Society of Mary. Concurrent with the modernization, professionalization, and expansion of the Society in the United States, the advance of the anticlerical Radical Party in France led to the 1905 prohibition of religious congregations from running schools and colleges, a measure which prompted the general administration to move to Nivelles, Belgium. This chapter opens with this latter development and concludes with the Marianist involvement in the NCEA and the high school movement.

⊀ II ⊁

DURING THE PERIOD OF THE SECOND EMPIRE OF NAPOLEON III, the Falloux Law permitted private secondary education to compete with the lycées run by the University Council; as a result, Catholic education flourished. The Marianists ran fifteen secondary schools with a total enrollment of 2,225 students, while the Jesuits enrolled 5,074 students in fourteen schools.[5] As mentioned in chapter 4, superior general Caillet referred to the Marianist schools as serving students of middle-class families. One historian noted that the congregations sponsoring these schools tended to be ultramontanist. According to Hippolyte Taine, the late-nineteenth-century man of letters and an avowed anticlerical, the nobility promoted Catholic schools as "well arranged hot houses, with the chinks carefully stopped up to keep out modern draughts."[6] In general, the middle class viewed Catholic schools as providing the means of upward social mobility, and, through the association with sons of the nobility, the students would be introduced to proper manners and elegant styles of life. But the Marianist *Manual of Pedagogy*, considered in the last chapter, fostered a clarity of presentation and commitment to the needs of the student and to the creation of a positive religious climate in the school that ran contrary to the radicals' image of obscurantist power-based education.

The Third Republic, which had replaced the Second Empire after its defeat in the Franco-Prussian War, assumed an increasingly anticlerical character. The culture war between the church and the French Revolution had been tempered by the regime of Napoleon III (1849–1870). The French emperor had attempted to balance his loyalty to the church with his support for Italian nationalism. The latter movement drastically reduced the Papal States to include only Rome, which was seized in 1870, thereby marking the end of the temporal power of the papacy. Pius IX's 1864 encyclical *Quanta Cura*, particularly its Syllabus of Errors, listed all the evils of polit-

ical and social modernity derived from the French Revolution and fundamental to the republic of the United States. Representing another episode
in the culture wars between the forces of evil and the church, this encyclical was followed six years later by the declaration of papal infallibility at the
First Vatican Council (1869–1870). During this period, French ultramontanism gained momentum, while the latter declaration was the death knell
of Gallicanism as a viable ecclesiology.[7]

The Marianists had been moderately ultramontanist but became even
more so when the pope became the self-declared prisoner of the Vatican. At
the strong suggestion of Pope Leo XIII, the Marianists founded the Collegio
Santa Maria in Rome (ca. 1889) near the Basilica of St. John Lateran. That
same year a Marianist procurator office was also established in Rome. The
politics of anticlericalism of the Third Republic, born in 1871 after the
French defeat in the Franco-Prussian War in 1870 and the Paris Commune of
1871, focused on Catholic primary and secondary education. The Marianists
interpreted this movement as simply another phase in the persecution of
Catholic schools by a secular government, masked in the cloth of freedom.

Despite the intensity of the Marianist response to anticlericalism, the
Society did not engage in the kind of ideology of catastrophic apocalypti-
cism that was characteristic of the Assumptionist journal *La Croix*, which
perceived the advance of republicanism as a conspiracy among the Masons,
Jews, and radicals that could be defeated only by a legitimate monarchy
united with a vigorous papacy and promoted by the unity of throne and
altar.[8] The Marianists never engaged in polemics, but in his circulars Joseph
Simler did evaluate the struggle against anticlerical legislation as a contest
between the embodiments of good and evil. The first legislation in opposition to the Catholic presence in public education was in 1886; by 1891 all
male religious were prohibited from teaching in the communal schools. The
Marianists, like other congregations, continued to teach in local schools,
now owned by the laity, and of course in schools owned by the Society. This
allowed the Brothers of Mary to teach in twenty such schools by 1890. The
ralliement policy of Pope Leo XIII encouraged Catholics to support the
French Republic, but this period of "détente" was dissolved by the renewal
of government hostility partially fueled by the anti-Semitism and the anti-
republicanism of extreme right-wing Catholics. A 1901 law initiated by
Waldeck-Rousseau, president of the Council of Ministers since 1899, prohibited nonauthorized religious congregations not only from teaching but
also from any legal standing in France. The Marianists had received state
authorization in 1825 and were legally recognized in 1860. However, a 1905
interpretation of the 1901 law removed all prior authorization, which,

according to Roger Price, led to "the immediate dissolution of all teaching congregations and as a result the closure of several thousand schools. In spite of the recourse to such measures as the secularization of clerics in order to circumvent this measure, and an increased reliance on devout lay teachers, this was a major blow to Catholic education. Private (mainly Catholic) schools educated around a third of all pupils in 1886–87, but only a fifth in 1912–13."[9]

In 1902, when it appeared that the Marianists were to be dissolved, they attempted to assert their rights as an authorized congregation, but their attempt was frustrated by the Council of State. Hence, in 1903 all of the Marianist houses were legally dissolved. In the meantime Joseph Simler outlined the policy governing the Marianists in France: members had the choice of leaving France and retaining full status as religious or, remaining in France, they could sever their legal status, live the life of a religious, and teach in the schools taken over by sympathetic citizens. The Marianist exiles left for Spain, Switzerland, and Belgium. The scholasticate of Besançon and the seminarians at the Antony in Paris were transferred to the Villa St. Jean in Fribourg, Switzerland. Postulants and novices were sent to Belgium near the new motherhouse in Nivelles.[10]

Joseph Simler's response to the anticlerical laws, which he referred to as "the persecution," over the course of the years 1902–1904, was to call for a period of penance, expiation to balance acts of persecution and to view these difficult times as the opportunity to renew one's vocation as a Marianist. In November 1904, as he was conscious of the imminence of death (February 4, 1905), he wrote in his last circular, "Methought I could die confident of the future, if family spirit was maintained and strengthened among you." He encouraged them to be united in devotion to all things Marianist: "Be one with the Society. Have confidence in it; it is certainly and manifestly the work of God; by the union of your efforts it will realize the great things God has in store for it." Besides exhorting everyone to be one with authority, and the constitutions, he concluded by urging each member to be "one with Mary herself. The Society belongs to her, we belong to her; we are but her auxiliaries and instruments. She is our dearly beloved Mother. . . . In this crisis, she manifestly took up our defense; she came to our assistance, as we are all aware, by the most tender solicitude."[11]

❧ III ❧

COLLÈGE STANISLAS, THE MOST PRESTIGIOUS OF THE MARIANISTS' schools in France was a casualty of the suppression. Since the status of a collège diploma, the baccalaureate, was dependent on the accumulated scores on the national examination and acceptance at the University of Paris or one of the special institutions of higher education, such as law and architecture, Stanislas achieved national recognition. Joseph Simler resided at the collège during his years at the university as well as when he was superior general. He and other Marianists were supportive of the early efforts of one of their most significant students, Marc Sangnier, founder of the Sillon movement, which originated at meetings of students of the collège. Prior social Catholic movements, such as Albert de Mun's Association Catholique de la Jeunesse Française (1886), had attempted to "evangelize" the individual members of the elite, who were to be models of the selfless Christian for the working class, but they did not possess the charism of the Sillon.[12] Marc Sangnier was a left-wing Catholic concerned with forming alliances with the national union movement. While de Mun's association had been influential in the origins of Leo XIII's social encyclical *Rerum Novarum*, Sangnier's own enthusiastic and idealistic leadership predated the encyclical and went beyond its teaching, as the Sillon adopted the ethos of the French Revolution. For example, at a dinner on a principal feast day at Stanislas, he gave a toast to the republic. In 1898, he established a committee to promote Christian democratic principles among the people, and the journal *Le Sillon*, initiated by a friend, became the committee's official organ, which established study circles for popular education. In the hand of laymen, with chaplains limited to advisory roles, the study circle was similar to the Marianist sodality with its nonelitist character and its missionary zeal. Indeed, Sangnier's organization was unstructured; the personalist *élan*, the idealism, and the promotion of popular Christian democracy were its overriding characteristics. However, in Rome's Basilica of the Holy Apostles, Sangnier gave a sermon on the topic of Mary to a congregation composed of priests, with three cardinals and nineteen bishops in attendance.[13] The ecclesiastical popularity of Sangnier could not persist within the context of the strident polarization in church, politics, and culture. Pius X's 1907 encyclical *Pascendi Dominici Gregis*, which condemned modernism as the "heresy of all heresies," was promulgated as Sangnier's Sillon "was making its attempt to bring French Catholics into touch with democratic and social realities of the modern world."[14] The ecclesial-political climate of France was increasingly hostile to Sangnier, particularly his independence from episcopal authority.

Comparable to the condemnation of Alfred Loisy and George Tyrrel, theological modernists who were advocating a Catholic apologetic in accord with contemporary historical and philosophical movements, was the Vatican's judgment of Marc Sangnier. Though Pius X's letter to Sangnier dated August 25, 1910, urged him to place his organization under the authority of the bishop, this was a tacit condemnation, as the Sillon movement was intrinsically democratic, reformist, and autonomous. Sangnier "complied" but continued to pursue his goals in a political rather than in an ecclesial forum; as Charles Péguy remarked, "What begins as mystique ends in politique."

The tone of a substantial amount of evidence of Marianist association with Marc Sangnier can be picked up in a remark about Brother Louis Cousin, who wrote a popular life of William Chaminade to be a companion to Joseph Simler's scholarly work. In 1896 he was made inspector general of the Society. Hence, he was in Paris during the rise of Sangnier (1896–1905). Michael Schleich held that position after the death of John Kim, Cousin's successor. In 1912 Schleich wrote to George Meyer, provincial in Dayton, that the Cousin manuscript "will be published under the name of Father [Henri] Rousseau and not under that of M. Cousin for reason of [his involvement in] the Sillon; it is better that Cousin remain quiet for some years yet."[15] Guarding the "good name" of the Society, particularly related to its founder whose "cause" had been introduced in Rome, was the rationale for such duplicity. The Marianists never went on record in opposition to Marc Sangnier. While the vast majority of the French Marianists were ostensibly opposed to his ideas after 1905, they no doubt took pride in his sermon on Mary and in the cultural significance of their famous alumnus.[16]

❧ IV ❧

THE 1905 GENERAL CHAPTER ELECTED JOSEPH HISS (1848–1922) superior general. He had been head of instruction from 1881 to 1891 and of zeal from 1891 to 1905. Born in a small town in Alsace in 1848, he had been involved in leadership on the provincial and the general levels for over thirty years and had assisted Simler in his research on the life of Chaminade and on the preparation of the Constitutions of 1891; he represented the Society on several matters during the political crises in the years 1899–1903. Also elected in 1905 as inspector general, the chief assistant to the head of instruction, was Brother John Kim, the first American to serve in the general administration. From that time on, an American brother served as inspector general until 1961, when the position was restructured into the office of education. Hiss relied upon Kim for advice on the American Province, and no one knew better than he of the enormous task of administering a province that encompassed such a vast area—Honolulu to Baltimore, Winnipeg to San Antonio. Hence, Kim acted as an unofficial liaison between the general administration and the American Province.[17]

Brother Michael Schleich, who was appointed provincial inspector of instruction after John Kim's election, was a frequent correspondent with his predecessor. They had formed a sound working relationship over the years, and both were delegates to the 1905 chapter in Belgium.[18] As early as December 28, 1905, Schleich told Kim about a prospective postulate in St. Louis, "as there is an abundance of postulants in the United States. A site has almost been chosen in the western part of St. Louis."[19] The two St. Louis schools in 1906 were SS. Peter and Paul High School (1897) and St. Anthony Parish School (1901) in south St. Louis. The prospective postulate, the thirty-acre Ried Farm near the town of Ferguson, Missouri, was purchased in 1907 for fifteen thousand dollars. Since postulants were boys between the ages of thirteen and sixteen, parents in the Midwest were reluctant to allow their sons to attend a high school postulate as far east as Dayton. As early as 1874 the provincial council, aware of parents' objections, considered dividing the provinces. Such a division became a serious topic immediately after the 1905 general chapter, when Joseph Hiss met with his council and the American delegates, but a decision was postponed. During the superior general's 1907 visitation of the houses in the American Province he approved plans for building a postulate on the Ferguson site, but there was no general discussion of a western province.[20] Nevertheless, according to Michael Schleich, there had been an increasingly positive opinion of the division that another postponement would frustrate rising expectations. He also noted the benefits of having the two provinces, the increase in morale, decrease in travel for the provincial and the inspector, and the resultant time to provide more attention to the academic, intellectual, and spiritual needs of the members.[21]

John Waldron, who had been director/principal at St. Patrick's School, Cleveland, where he had attended school, was a member of the provincial council in 1908. He informed Kim that as early as 1896 he had considered the division of the province. He underscored the onerous duties of the provincial and the inspector, which "call most urgently for relief." To illustrate this point he told Kim that after three years in the position Schleich had still not visited all the schools in the province. Hence, the superiors were unable to monitor the affairs of the province, thereby alienating the brothers and allowing local directors to make decisions normally the responsibility of provincial leaders. On the other hand, the travel schedules of the provincial and inspector precluded an efficient management of province affairs at Dayton. Waldron's analysis of the authority crises in the province included the remark that there were only a few mature priests ready to assume the office of provincial of the new province. He recommended as provincial George Meyer, who had completed his previous term in 1906.[22] Joseph Weckesser was appointed that year; the two councils would then provide the younger priests with the experience to assume leadership, which would resolve the problem of the paucity of mature Marianist clergy. Several other Marianists in the United States whom Kim consulted reiterated the views of Schleich and Waldron.

Though the general council had made its decision as early as January 2, 1908, prior to this correspondence, the promulgation of the decision was dated September 27, 1908. Vatican approval, the designation of boundaries, the appointment of personnel and provincial administrations were factors related to the delay in the formal announcement. In accord with Schleich's and Waldron's suggestions to Kim, George Meyer was appointed provincial of the Eastern Province (Cincinnati) and Joseph Weckesser of the Western (St. Louis) Province; the boundary line was 87° longitude with the exception of California and Hawaii, considered missions of the Eastern Province. However, two Canadian and two Mexican schools were in the Western Province: Winnipeg (1880) and Provencher Collegiate Institute in St. Boniface, Manitoba, and Colegio Nuestra Señora de Guadalupe in Durango, and Colegio Santa Maria in Hermosillo, both of which were founded and staffed by the Midi Province of France.[23]

Brother John Waldron was appointed inspector of the St. Louis Province with administrative offices of the provincialate at the new house of formation, Villa St. Joseph in Ferguson, Missouri, where the new novitiate was also located. John Waldron was responsible for managing the province's building program as well. Indeed, for seven years (1917–1924) he was both inspector and provincial head of temporalities, or financial officer. In his acceptance letter to Joseph Hiss, Waldron indicated his "complete surprise" to know that Hiss had reports of Waldron's "negligence in the direction" of his community. He had been aware of his need for a well-regulated spiritual life but was committed to never "lower[ing] the tone of the religious body." Since his responses to the superior general's admonition consumed nearly the entire letter, Waldron was not only surprised but disturbed by the tone and content of his letter of appointment, traditionally referred to as "an obedience."[24] The views of Hiss were confirmed by Schleich, who told Kim, "Some brothers reacted negatively to the appointment of our first St. Louis Province Inspector."[25]

A student of mathematics and science at Collège Stanislas in Paris, Waldron was disappointed that he was not assigned to study for the priesthood. After his various assignments in formation and in elementary schools, he became vice president of St. Mary's Institute and had an impact on its evolution as an institution of higher education. As will be noted later, he had a significant influence in the Catholic Education Association and the Education Department of the National Catholic Welfare Council. Archbishop John Glennon of St. Louis appointed him to the board of advisors for the construction of a new seminary. He submitted a fourteen-page study suggesting changes. As pro-labor and sensitive to labor–management relations, he was respected by both. Regarding his role in the construction of Kenrick Seminary, Archbishop Glennon quipped, "There are several distinctive styles of architecture: the Gothic, the Baroque, Romanesque and Waldronesque." Hence, by the time Waldron became inspector he had gained national recognition, a status that no doubt generated both admiration and envy among his confreres.[26]

In his first inspector's report to the provincial chapter, John Waldron noted that at the eighteen schools, including the two Mexican schools, there were thirty-four hundred pupils taught by nearly one hundred brothers. The strongly local character of Marianist education was emphasized with one state school, Provencher Academy in St. Boniface, Manitoba; several small schools that included two or three years of high school, Dyersville and Dubuque, Iowa, respectively; very small schools, such as St. Mary's in Winnipeg, where four brothers taught eight grades with 165 boys. The largest parish school was St. Michael's in Chicago—sixteen brothers teaching 856 boys in eight grades and a three-year high school. St. Louis College and St. Mary's in San Antonio were experiencing considerable growth, while Spalding Institute had the most distinctively academic program. Among the eighteen schools, the Marianists had control of four in the States and two in Mexico, one "practically under its control" in Peoria; diocesan parish priests were responsible for SS. Peter and Paul in St. Louis, and schools in LaSalle, Illinois; St. Aloysius in Chicago; and the two schools in Iowa. Five religious orders were responsible for schools staffed by the Marianists: Oblates in Winnipeg; Redemptorists in St. Michael's, Chicago; the Lazarists in LaSalle, Illinois; the Franciscans in St. Anthony's, St. Louis; and the Spanish Fathers of the Immaculate Heart of Mary at St. Fernando's in San Antonio.[27]

Waldron's report underscored the bilingual character of the schools: English-French and English-German in the north (Canada, Iowa, Illinois, and Missouri), and in the south (Texas and Mexico) English-Spanish. With a strong emphasis on the need for the brothers to learn languages, Waldron was particularly critical of the acute problems in the Spanish-speaking schools in Texas and Mexico. He singled out St. Louis College in San Antonio: "When we reflect on the great missionary possibilities resulting from the return to their country of our young Mexican students after a careful training in Catholic doctrine and principles as well as in pious practices" by teachers fluent in Spanish "it is to be regretted that not one single member of the faculty, excepting the director, can speak Spanish."[28]

Influenced by statistics of decline in school attendance derived from research in public education in Missouri, Waldron announced to the chapter delegates his intention to study the province's school attendance. However, he did cite severe decline in attendance at St. Mary's College in San Antonio; of the 463 students it lost 122 during the academic year 1908–1909. "Making all allowances beyond our control this leakage of over 26% is without justification. In varying degrees the same problem exists in a number of our schools notwithstanding the efforts of directors and proctors." Waldron placed the blame on "brothers who expel boys outright, or if they do not proceed to this length they manage to drive undesirable pupils away by nagging, excessive or cruel punishment, petty persecutions and by other questionable or even forbidden means. The evil is greatest where older members covertly or openly abet and suggest such methods."[29] Though these views were obviously anecdotal and contrary to Waldron's commitment to a thorough study, they conveyed a strongly critical tone evocative of various probable reactions ranging from mildly affirmative to excessively negative and defensive. However, to openly criticize a superior would not have been tolerated. Indeed, to compose a letter to a friend with even moderate criticism of another member would have been intercepted by the house director and, at best, returned to sender.

In agreement with those who decry the decline in "respect and reverence for authority as well as for law and order" prevalent in the Society and reflected in the schools, Waldron set the blame on those brothers who do not have a deep sense of faith and therefore do not manifest reverence and "careful cultivation in all our pupils. . . . We expect reverence and respect from our pupils in the class room or from the brother in the community and yet we cultivate it with sarcasm, harsh rebuke, ridicule for mistakes of inexperience and with a general lack of sympathy."[30] In accord with the spirit of the *Manual of Christian Pedagogy* and his commitment to the progressive education goals of the CEA, Waldron pointed to the "developments of modern pedagogy, along the lines of child study and methodological work in the process of instruction." He called for pursuit of "specific aims in every lesson, chapter and branch for the cultivation of various faculties as much as for the acquisition of mere knowledge." This is an early-twentieth-century parallel to the contemporary emphasis on process in contrast to acquisition of *mere* knowledge. Waldron closed with an endorsement of "manual training," which had recently been introduced in St. Boniface, Manitoba, and which the Eastern Province had established in its scholasticate.[31]

Even before he became inspector of schools for the St. Louis Province, John Waldron had been active in the Catholic Education Association (CEA). Founded in 1904, thirty-four years after the foundation of the National Education Association, it was preceded by a conference of Catholic seminaries in 1898 and the Association of Catholic Colleges in 1899. Thomas J. Conaty, rector of the Catholic University of America and one of the leaders of the Catholic Summer School movement during the 1890s, was the principal force in these meetings, which culminated in the CEA. In the 1898 conference of seminaries he remarked, "There is a need of organization that we may realize that our different schools are not disjointed elements of a system, but that one hinges upon the other, and that all should be closely bound together in order the better to move in a solid phalanx in the interests of knowledge and religion."[32] The connections among all phases of education would redound to the benefit of the only national educational institution, Catholic University, located in the nation's capital.

The conference of Catholic colleges reflected the chaotic condition of Catholic "higher education." Colleges were predominantly a mix of the upper grades of elementary school with a prep school; some had higher degree programs. Without general standards, a bachelor's degree in 1900 represented the successful culmination of the higher courses defined by the college, such as the college of Dayton, recognized by the state of Ohio to grant such degrees. Throughout the 1890s, as the various regional accrediting agencies—the New England, Middle States, North Central, and Southern States—were founded to establish criteria for evaluating secondary schools, the lines between secondary and collegiate studies were drawn: standardization of high school courses into units and credit hours for each course in the curriculum, and the articulation of a four-year program of studies required for diploma; while colleges and universities mandated either an evaluation of the particular school's program or a college-entrance examination for admission to their institution.[33]

This articulation and correlation of secondary and collegiate education, which John Waldron was strongly advocating for elementary and secondary education, took several years to develop in the public and non-Catholic private spheres and was in a rather refined phase when the first CEA meeting was held in St. Louis in 1904, the year of the World's Fair. The annual meetings of the college and university educators from 1899 to 1903, and those of the Parish School Conference of 1902–1903, had precipitated the foundation of the CEA as the correlation between college and secondary had its parallel between secondary and elementary. Though it was strictly a voluntary association of seminaries, colleges, and schools, the members, who met according to their roles in one of the three groups, were confronting the need for standardization, modernization, and professionalization because these processes were mandated not only by accrediting agencies but also by Catholic leadership committed to progressive models of educational reform. It was left to religious communities and dioceses to devise their own particular educational plans, but the CEA developed strong moral authority.

Despite the positive forces promoting the growth and development of the CEA, it faced an enormous problem in garnering the support of bishops, superintendents of schools, religious communities, college presidents, and seminary rectors. Indeed, the organization could have disintegrated had there not been determined leaders: Monsignor Conaty, later Bishop of Los Angeles, and his successor at the Catholic University, Denis O'Connell, later bishop of Richmond; Francis W. Howard, a priest of Columbus, Ohio, and later bishop of the Diocese of Covington, Kentucky; James A. Burns, C.S.C., head of Holy Cross College at the Catholic University and later president of the University of Notre Dame; and John Waldron, the Marianist educator. The discrimination against women religious sharing leadership roles with men was clearly reflected in the CEA.[34] This was a glaring illustration of gender bias, since the majority of communities of women religious in education responded positively to the CEA and were represented through their participation in annual meetings and in the presentation of papers, most of which when they were published were not attributed to their authors by name but remained anonymous, with attributions such as by "a Sister of Mercy."

John Waldron's activity in the Parish School Department led to his election to the executive committee of that division in 1906. In 1909 he was elected to membership in the executive board of the CEA, which was the governing body responsible for electing the secretary general of the association for triennial terms; Francis W. Howard served in that capacity from 1904 to 1929. Howard and Waldron formed a close association, and for two critical periods Howard asked the Marianist to act as secretary general because the situation required the analytical, diplomatic, and tactical skills Waldron had demonstrated over the years. He also served on the advisory council—composed of bishops and priests—as the only lay religious. The council was charged with discussing the educational issues between annual meetings and acting as a liaison to the three departments of the association.[35]

Waldron's appointment to the executive committee of the NCWC

Department of Education also derived from his CEA work. The episcopal chairman of the department, Archbishop Austin Dowling of St. Paul, sought Waldron's advice on its general direction, to which the experienced Marianist educator responded with warnings that a strongly centralized department would at best stifle local initiatives and at worst destroy the local character of education. His fears were similar to the apprehension over a federalized Department of Education lodged in the Smith-Toner bill in Congress. The volunteer character of the CEA was the model for the NCWC Department of Education.[36] Timothy Walch succinctly compared the distinguishing features of each national endeavor:

> Just as the NCEA had become the voice of Catholic teachers and educators, so also did the Education Department of the National Catholic Welfare Conference become the voice of the American bishops on education. Both organizations were reflections of a national search for order on the part of the American Catholic community. Beyond this common goal the similarity ends. Whereas the NCEA was established as a national forum for educational ideas, the NCWC'S Department of Education was created to defend Catholic schools against increasing government involvement in the Catholic schools and to provide a unified voice on education for the hierarchy.[37]

Waldron's prodigious educational activities in several spheres included the area of religious publishing—the educational board of the *Catholic School Journal,* published by Bruce in Milwaukee. According to correspondence between Frank Bruce and John Waldron, the association developed into a friendship. His papers at the CEA were published, as were those of several other Marianist brothers. Waldron's 1906 CEA paper entitled "Methods in Teaching of Bible History" appeared in the *CEA Bulletin* and in abbreviated form in the *Catholic School Journal.* In the rhetoric of post–Vatican II ecclesiology, Waldron said that "Sacred History . . . is the history of the people of God." He emphasized the importance of the Bible in illuminating catechetical doctrine, without which the catechism would "run the risk of becoming an assembly of dry theological formulas incomprehensible to children." However, history was not only to make the catechism more meaningful, but the scriptural narratives would "lay the foundation of religion itself in their young minds. It would be profound ignorance of the essentials of religion not to recognize that religion is entirely historical." It is ironic that as ahistorical, neoscholastic theological manuals were prevailing in seminaries and in many colleges and universities, historical catechesis was advocated for the parish schools.[38] Central to his method of teaching the Bible was the nonliteral interpretation of specific events such as the story of the first chapters of Genesis, with particular references to the embellishment of oral tradition and the imagination of the author, who, according to the Vatican's Biblical Commission, was still denominated "Moses."[39]

Several Marianists presented papers at the CEA in support of the high school program led by James A. Burns, C.S.C., who headed the committee on the high school. In general, Waldron and others were on the liberal side of the spectrum; they advocated a clear articulation in the system of education between elementary and four-year college based on principles and standards of public education. Conservatives, particularly among the leadership of Catholic colleges, wished to preserve the collegiate-based preparatory school. "These conservatives had little use for reforms emanating from secular quarters," wrote historian Philip Gleason.[40] The plan of elementary, secondary, and collegiate education appears clear today, but the CEA, particularly the president, Francis Howard, attempted to mollify the liberals by adopting the standardization necessary for accreditation and the conservatives by advocating a program that would limit elementary to six grades and allow six or seven for attendance at the collegiate prep school. James A. Burns salvaged Howard's plan, which had garnered support, with a six-three-three program—elementary, junior high school, and senior high school. Since the high-school committee report at the first national meeting of the CEA in St. Louis, Burns had promoted the central Catholic school that would be financially supported by the parishes and staffed by several religious communities of women and men.[41]

Comprehensive high schools with two principal curricula—college prep and commercial—fulfilled several needs: state requirements that the young remain in school until age sixteen; college entrance standards; and the accreditation agencies, such as North Central, which required colleges to be four-year institutions of higher education separate from the prep schools. And as Burns noted, there were many second- and third-generation Irish- and German-American middle-class families who could afford to send their children to high school.[42]

Marianists such as Brothers John Waldron and Joseph Gallagher, principal of St. James School for Boys in San Francisco, presented papers related to the six-three-three plan at the annual meetings in 1910 and 1918 respectively.[43] Both men held to a six-year elementary program and a three-year parish junior high school. Though Waldron did not specifically support Burns's long-standing proposal for a diocesan central Catholic high school, Gallagher's plan envisioned a central diocesan senior high school. Both brothers promoted manual training particularly in junior high schools. In Gallagher's view, the senior high school should operate on a tuition-free basis with parishes taxed pro rata. Under the control of a religious community, the boys' and girls' central high schools would be under the diocesan superintendent but would retain autonomy in the selection of teachers and organizing of curriculum. The superintendent of the Catholic schools would coordinate the parish junior high schools with the central high school, particularly by developing and monitoring entrance exams. In general, Gallagher's plan envisioned a Catholic moral ethos and the predominance of religious education, but the curriculum would be the same as the public schools.

❧ V ❧

BROTHER GEORGE SAUER, WHO REPLACED MICHAEL SCHLEICH as inspector of the Cincinnati Province, when the latter replaced John Kim as inspector general in the general administration in Nivelles, Belgium, was also active in the CEA. Waldron, Sauer, and Schleich were delegates to the general chapter in Nivelles in 1910. They had been influenced by Thomas Edward Shields, who established the Department of Education at the Catholic University of America.[44] A priest-scholar (Ph.D. in biology from the Johns Hopkins University), Shields is identified with the success of the Sisters College at the University, as well as with publications in the psychology of education published by the Catholic Education Press and the *Catholic Educational Review*, both of which he founded in the early twentieth century. These publications extolled progressive notions of methodology derived from John Dewey, William James, and others.[45]

The three Marianist educators, influenced by Shields, were in the vanguard in promoting educational or pedagogical developments at the general chapter of 1910. Of course, Jean Lalanne's writings and Fontaine's *Manual of Pedagogy* had manifested a sophisticated and prescient understanding of the psychology of education; in general, European educationists tended to be more philosophical than their American counterparts. However, the chapter recommended to all Marianists, particularly to inspectors, "the study of psychology applied to the education of the child and the youth." In his circular letter on the chapter of 1910, Joseph Hiss, reelected superior general at that chapter, made a strong case for this study as basic to the teacher's commitment. He urged the Brothers of Mary to be like the "serious professional man [who] esteems the science of his profession. . . . You must be attached to this science [of education] and cultivate it as long as your ministry lasts."[46]

Each of the Marianist teachers was to discern the rich diversity among his students and to recognize "the manifestations of consciousness of each pupil, [particularly] to discern the part played by instinct, heredity, early education or surroundings, the first movement of passion, the force of habit or deliberate act of the will" in order to ascertain the proper methods for "formation, correction and encouragement of the child." Hiss was concerned with the significance of modern methodologies to enhance the Marianists' "prestige in the eyes of your competitors and of families" as well as their "influence over your pupils."[47]

Hiss expressed an extraordinary commitment to the values of the psychologist for the teacher's self-understanding:

> How will you be initiated into the realities of the inner life. . . . The psychologist alone is able to make you penetrate into this order of phenomena so different from any other, to place you face to face with yourself, to unravel with you this riddle which you scarcely perceive in the depths of your consciousness. And after having thus explored the depths of your own being, he has also rendered you capable of entering into relations with the soul of the child or youth and to discern the means of forming it well. You will thereafter be in touch with a living, acting, individual reality, instead of remaining in the domain of cold and personal abstraction.[48]

Hiss followed this reflection with an exposition of the benefits of philosophy in understanding the "moral side" of the Marianist "mission." However, in the formation of a good moral conscience "the heart comes into play as much as reason."[49] Of course, the significance of faith, the existence of supernatural revelation, and the direction of the church were basic to Hiss's advanced notions of psychology.

As an activist in the Catholic Education Association, John Waldron promoted a thorough rationalization of Marianist education with particular attention to director/principal supervision and control of the school to assure professional qualities among the faculty, such as modern methods of class preparation and teaching. He had to struggle against the dominance of local autonomy: "Almost every school is a law unto itself with programs depending upon the director and often the teachers, changing with the changes of the teacher, and modified according to the tastes or acquirements of the teacher and director."[50]

To improve the quality of professionalization a new program of education courses (referred to in the traditional terminology as pedagogy) was introduced into the provincial scholasticate, which was equivalent to a year of post-secondary education when Mount St. John in Dayton was opened in 1912. A series of examinations during the early years of teaching was based on continuous reading in cognate areas related to elementary, secondary, or collegiate curricula.

Waldron's school inspections included classroom visitations to evaluate discipline, pedagogical style, and the role of lesson plans—class journals—in effective teaching. In 1911 he reported on the directors' efforts to supervise classes. In his 1911 report, however, Waldron noted several "weaknesses" in the directors' supervision. He was particularly critical of the

> general ignorance of, or indifference to, the laws and rules which should govern the basic features of our work. Thus the coordination of courses and the correlation of cognate studies, the articulation of class programs, the relation between allotments and the contents of the programs, the problem of retarded pupils, the value and meaning of school statistics, attention to the physical condition and home influences of the child, observation and study of what is going on in the educational world, all are important factors in the success of our work, and yet except in rare instances ignorance of their existence as factors of success is in lamentable evidence.[51]

Waldron's list of essential characteristics of "our work," reflects his commitment to modernizing Marianist schools. In his book *Teachers' Manual of Primary Methods*, Thomas E. Shields remarked:

> The principle of correlation as it is now currently accepted in the field of education demands that each new thought element be related to the previous context of the mind, not along structured lines alone, but in a relationship of reciprocal activity. . . . This principle of correlation should find a threefold application in every school. It should enter the structure of the curriculum; it should govern the organization of the materials in each subject and it should find a clear embodiment in the text books used.[52]

As mentioned earlier, Waldron was acquainted with Shields and others through his participation in the CEA. To dispel the general ignorance of the modern principles of education and to foster faculty growth, Waldron persistently criticized the nonprofessional "light reading" of the brothers. In his 1911 report he warned the provincial chapter delegates "that the progress of our studies is not keeping pace with the increasing demands for . . . [improvement] which the nature of our schools are making of us." He had introduced "a kind of system and method into collateral reading which should accompany the studies of the brothers." Waldron criticized abuses, such as visiting public libraries (a privilege requiring the director's permission), and "indiscriminate reading of magazines and newspapers." He proposed reading works of a religious and pedagogical nature "to affect the blighting effects of mere secular study and reading."[53] He was gratified by the general improvement in replacing "novels and other light reading" with books on religious and monastic history. He reminded them of the Vatican's ruling prohibiting seminarians from reading magazines and newspapers. Though Waldron did not identify the ruling as a phase of the antimodernism of the era, he said that the spirit of the papal decree "should control the reading of all of us."[54] Waldron also relied on traditional principles of authority, including policy directives relevant to restrictions on free inquiry, which were so characteristic of religious life and the authoritarianism of the period.

Essential to the educational reforms were the supervision and control of the local school authority, the director. The effectiveness of the modern and Catholic character of Marianist education rested upon his shoulders. As young brothers pass through the two diplomas in religious and secular pedagogy—principles, methods, psychology, and history of education, and secular degrees in "profane studies"—local communities of teaching brothers could be adversely divided according to educational background, ability, and age. Waldron tacitly admitted this tendency but urged directors to prevent the young brothers from slipping into conformity or laxity in preparing themselves for college and university programs. "[W]ithout supervision there can be no unity of plans, no continuity of efforts, no correlation of methods and means." Basic to control and supervision of the local community was the director's ability to mold and influence "the public opinion of the community."[55] Besides the positive notion of promoting civility, harmony, and piety, there was the negative factor of vigorously opposing "the virus of discontent, carping criticism, uncharitableness and secularism. If honest disagreement is manifested with civility, open discussion should be encouraged but . . . rebuke of authority and attacks on persons' reputations should not be legitimated but suppressed."[56]

In his annual reports to the provincial chapters John Waldron articulated his philosophy of education grounded in realism. For example, in 1916 he underscored the significance of reform to assure the advance of "Catholic interests" in accord with the professional qualities of public education: "A well-organized school is not a haphazard putting together of selected parts taken from the catalogue without due regard for the purpose and aims of the branches, the needs of the school, the environment and status of the child in social and racial [i.e., ethnic] conditions."[57] He was opposed to a Catholic separatism that was triumphalist in its religious character and was reluctant to adapt to progressive movements in public education. He remarked,

Even the Catholic school can no longer remain isolated from the rest of its kind, nor, for that matter, from the workings of the public school system. It may be admitted that standardization of programs had been pushed even to excess; however, reports of school surveys, syllabi of studies prepared by specialists, plans for organized teaching worked out by the committees of educational experts, the publicity and approval given to these agencies, all combine to create a situation in the educational field that cannot be ignored, even if they put burdens on us.

The directors were urged to be committed to "scientific organization" and to adapt "modern practices" such as enabling the students to receive "proper credit for completed courses" along standardized lines. This entailed correlating the curriculum in "a sequence of studies" with regard for a "time allotment and time-table schedules" to assure quality pedagogy. Since the implementation of the new plan of studies for young brothers, in accord with these trends, was successfully encouraging them to pursue undergraduate-degree programs, they would be prepared to implement standardization.[58]

The national high school movement, which had accelerated during the first two decades of the twentieth century in Catholic education, had a significant influence upon the Marianists. In 1916, out of the 131 brothers and priests engaged in teaching in the St. Louis Province, 64 were teaching in high schools or colleges, a figure that John Waldron considered "entirely too high for the best interests of our work. It calls for more years of training for most of our candidates than we are financially able to give." As head both of instruction and temporalities Waldron would be more concerned about such cost than most inspectors. He was also concerned, however, about the moral implications of this large number involved in high school and colleges. "It forces young men into classes with students nearly of their own age, with the consequent dangers of failure, discouragement and discredit of our work." He advocated accepting more elementary schools to accommodate the young teachers, "even in the face of other strong reasons militating against the easy acceptance of new schools."[59]

Waldron was alluding to the perennial problems confronting provincials: the rate of increase of vocations was never high enough to meet the needs of bishops and pastors eager to have brothers to staff their schools. From the time of Leo Meyer (1849–1862), there was a persistent anti-American or anti-capitalist refrain to explain the lack of vocations. George Meyer, provincial of the American Province from 1896 to 1906 and of the Cincinnati Province from 1908 to 1918, stated it quite succinctly in his 1910 report to the chapter delegates in Dayton: "The commercial spirit of the age and country, often the opposition and hostility of priests, and the unwillingness of parents to make the sacrifice of their children to God, all combine to hinder this great and necessary work." Meyer told them about "a short notice of the Society and its works" that was intended to be "placed in the hands of parents, pastors and wherever it may be expected to stimulate vocations to the Society." Of course, the brothers' "zeal" was the primary source of vocations. "Experience proves that the best results are obtained just below the high class," the age of thirteen or fourteen.[60] Hence, as the provinces were shifting their resources from elementary to high schools, the concern for vocations may have prompted Waldron to draw a line at 50 percent of the brothers remaining in parish schools.

The inspector general, Michael Schleich, explicitly noted the significance of elementary schools as *the* principal source for vocations. "[In] a conversation with Father Howard in regard to our taking high schools and letting the primary to the sisters [Schleich] replied that we were willing but we needed the Primary in order to secure vocations; that when the boy reaches the H.S. he has already made up his mind and generally it is not in the direction of the religious life, that we needed a certain number of lower grades to start in the young teachers as it is easier to do so . . . [Howard] felt the force of the argument." Schleich was favorably impressed with Howard's openness: "You can reason with him and be sure of a hearing and consideration."[61]

Brother George N. Sauer, as mentioned earlier, inspector of schools for the Eastern, or Cincinnati, Province, presented a paper at the 1921 annual meeting of the NCEA, "On Vocations to the Teaching Brotherhood."[62] He cited statistics of membership of the Marianists to illustrate the continuous rise in vocations, but they were far short of serving the educational needs of the rising Catholic population:

> The Society of Mary in the United States shows the following development: In 1849 the first six members reached Cincinnati from France. In 1860 there were 50 members, in 1880, 230 members; in 1900, 340 members; in 1920, 535 members. Without doubt many of the teaching societies, at least the Sisterhoods, have far outstripped this record of progress, and still the cry goes up incessantly, almost universally from the Superiors of teaching Brotherhoods and Sisterhoods: "We are short on personnel! We need more candidates." What is the explanation of the seeming paradox.[63]

Besides the growth in Catholic population there had been a considerable increase in school population because of compulsory education laws. Sauer also cited the precipitous rise in Catholic high schools that had "drained the energies and personnel of some teaching congregations." He referred to the typical schools of "a generation ago" with overcrowded classrooms that numbered between eighty and one hundred students. In the late nineteenth century it was not uncommon for four brothers to teach the upper grades of a parish school with total enrollments of 250 to 300 boys: "but luckily public opinion today holds that 40 to 50 pupils will keep any teacher comfortably busy." Sauer noted the clearly evident progress in requirements for certification of teachers by both the states and the dioceses, requirements that demanded more years in formation. Reflecting the contemporary American tendency toward "efficient methods" Sauer urged superiors to establish "a system of recruitment which comprehends the sowing, the cultivating and harvesting of religious vocations."[64]

Sauer based the need for recruitment on a decision rendered in Rome in 1912 "[which stated that] the old theory of vocation, based on interior attraction or call, must be modified, as it is now held that the Bishops . . . [and] the superiors alone implant the vocations in the souls of the chosen ones—They do not verify the vocation in the souls of the candidates presented to them: they give it to them."[65] Sauer referred to clergy and parents as in need of encouragement through recruitment efforts. In his treatment of the third group, the religious, Sauer noted that "loyalty to the religious body" would prompt members to interest themselves in developing their congregations. "That this loyalty has ever been manifested by our Brothers is evinced by the fact that 90 percent of our present membership in America has been drawn from our own schools."[66] Traditional Marianist measures, rather than "a special or uniform method of recruitment was ever in vogue." These measures included sodalities, eucharistic leagues, spiritual reading, and the Friday afternoon recitation of the Litany of the Blessed Virgin "to beg an increase of vocations," as well as the promotion of Marianist ministry.[67]

In 1920 a recruitment committee was established "with a view of making extraordinary and more systematic efforts to get candidates." Sauer reported on the committee's distribution of promotional materials, the designation of a recruiter to visit pastors and schools run by women religious, and on the need to present the Marianist story to boys of the seventh and eighth grades. Like George Meyer, Sauer drew upon the experience of the Marianists; most boys entered the Society at age fourteen. "Happily boys are not deep logicians; they are more readily overcome by action on the heart than on the mind." Hence, it is not by means of the recruiter alone but the teacher as a model for students to enter the religious life. He reiterated the traditional refrain about the hollowness of secular popularity of "honors, money and pleasure" eclipsing the ideals of religion and morality. According to Sauer, these cultural trends adversely affected vocations to the ministry among Protestant denominations as well.[68]

Through his rather wide-angled lens he perceived the roles of gender and poor salaries as inhibiting factors: with women dominating elementary education and "teaching not remunerative . . . [or] in high repute, it is very difficult to attract young men to a teaching career, especially in the Brotherhoods."[69] Sauer's perspective also included the roles of class and gender in the Catholic community as a likely factor in the choice of vocations to teaching brotherhoods:

> May it be because Brothers are not sufficiently appreciated or esteemed even in the household of faith; because the Brotherhood is so far inferior to the priesthood that the former is not worthy of the aspirations of the ambitious and gifted; because defections from the ranks destroy confidence and thus doubly prevent development. Finally is there something, which of its nature, renders the Brotherhoods unattractive to the boy, seeing that by comparison the Sisters vastly outnumber the Brothers and that though we have several flourishing native Sisterhoods, there is up to date not a single Brotherhood that has originated in the United States?[70]

These rhetorical questions reveal Sauer's rather remarkable candor in grappling with social and ecclesial problems in motivating boys to consider teaching communities of brothers.

As a countervailing force to what he perceived as the negative factors of gender, class, and "old-world" styles of ethnicity, Sauer preferred a positive line of reasoning, grounded in an Americanist understanding and articulated in an imaginative public-relations statement.

> Words like the following if more frequently expressed, would create a higher opinion of teaching and teachers: "If there is any greater service in a democracy than the training of children I don't know what is. But unless public opinion recognized the profession of teaching as an eminently dignified and admirable profession, worthy of social as well as economic recognition, we can never attract the type of person that in a democracy we must have."[71]

Sauer was concerned with the significant financial burden of educating brothers according to the standards set by state and regional accrediting agencies. Because the formation program was aimed at the large number of candidates age fourteen and fifteen, high school and two years of college for elementary teachers and additional college years and graduate school for prospective teachers in Marianist high schools, colleges, and universities entailed a significant cost. There were 125 candidates in the Marianist novitiates and normal schools in Dayton and St. Louis. By this time each of the provinces had freestanding novitiates and normal schools located in relatively remote areas and on property of considerable acreage: Mount St. John in Dayton and Maryhurst in Kirkwood, Missouri, in the St. Louis area. Hence, with additional funds the Marianists could expand. To augment the number of candidates in proportion to the demand for teaching brothers would be beyond the resources of the Society of Mary. Scholarships and endowments, dependent on modern and systematic fund-raising measures, comparable to recruitment policies, were one solution.

Sauer concluded his paper as a spokesman for all communities of teaching brothers:

> With full confidence that God will bless their labors if they but serve Him faithfully, the teaching Brotherhoods make this appeal to all who are interested in their development in the welfare of Catholic education: "Give us men: give us means."[72]

The 1925 annual chapter of the Cincinnati Province reiterated Sauer's remarks about the low status of brothers among pastors and parents. The chapter also reflected Sauer's general proposal by particularly asking parishes to sponsor a five-thousand-dollar scholarship for a candidate to the Society.

The chapters of the Cincinnati Province reflect Sauer's criticism of the anchor of French traditionalism inhibiting vocations. In their 1919 report to the superior general, the chapter delegates went on record for the fourth consecutive year to seek permission to change the coat worn by the teaching brothers from an Edwardian length to something more modern. Not only did young brothers "refuse to go for weekly walks" out of embarrassment, but the old garb was considered an obstacle for those potential aspirants to the Society and a rationale for "defections."[73] In 1922 permission was given to wear a short coat outside the classroom and outside the community residence in accord with contemporary styles, but the vest and coat had to be buttoned. Though this was a modest measure, it at least symbolized a gradual adaption to American ways.[74] Much later, in the 1940s, the long coat was finally done away with completely and the short coat could be worn at all times.

The culture of the high school, on the ascendancy in both provinces, appears to have influenced the lifestyles of those younger brothers who had received advanced certificates to teach in the secondary schools. Since the generation came of age in the postwar period of the 1920s, characterized by the Americanization of many second- and third-generation immigrants, it was at home in the popular and intellectual culture of the period. The leadership of the Marianists expressed some anxiety about their lifestyles. As early as 1919 the chapter delegates noted "the tendency of younger

Brothers to associate more with girls of the higher grades as also with young women in general. In the numerous defections of the past year, sexual attraction was a decisive factor in the majority of cases." It was therefore necessary to suppress such behavior; in particular, "the indiscriminatory riding in automobiles with women is an abuse that cannot be too strongly condemned."[75] In 1924 the provincial, Lawrence A. Yeske, reported to the delegates about a

> tendency among younger Brothers to seek popularity with those pupils by assuming worldly airs, taking on their mannerisms of slang and ungrammatical speech and to exercise an interest in the sport world. If, along with this, jazzy music is tolerated, love songs and trashy records, and the reading of sex novels and reviews, religious life is jazzed, and vocations are jeopardized.[76]

Such an absorption of the popular culture of the 1920s has never been so clearly revealed; a generation gap had developed, another fissure running between the advances of education and the traditional description of the rule governing religious life. As Yeske states, "It is true we must be up-to-date and progressive; occasional relaxation is advisable [such as permission for listening to radio programs after night prayers]; but innovations of a worldly nature must be feared and deprecated because they seriously undermine religious discipline."[77]

Despite the incessant refrain on the continuous need for more vocations, the Cincinnati Province had 146 candidates in 1922, 96 of whom were postulants. The new postulate that opened at Beacon, New York, in 1923 was definitely needed, particularly since the vast majority of candidates continued to come from the eighth and ninth grade classes of such parish elementary schools as St. James's and St. Michael's schools in Baltimore.

The rise in vocations still could not keep up with demand particularly at West Philadelphia Catholic High School, which experienced an enormous growth in enrollment. Between 1916 and 1922 the enrollment climbed from one hundred to well over one thousand, while the number of brothers went from four to twenty-five. Cardinal Denis Dougherty had built, according to Father Yeske, "the best equipped and developed [Catholic] high school in the U.S." Because he planned to open an annex for junior high school students numbering nearly eight hundred, he required more brothers, who, according to Dougherty, should form a second community of brothers separate from the senior high school. In a letter of January 1924, Yeske reported to Dougherty of the province's commitment to the school, but he concluded: "We are loathe to increase the faculty to forty or fifty religious. If we are to maintain and increase our standard, we must give our Brothers a longer training and prepare them for degrees, as required by practically all standardized agencies." He also noted that the severe stress for a director of "a large community in a large city, under the prevailing *'Zeitgeist'* . . . [is indeed] nerve-wracking."[78] Yeske, in consultation with his council, informed Dougherty that the Marianists had fulfilled the contract by educating many more students than anyone could have expected; hence, he suggested the solution of hiring lay teachers to take the place of those additional Marianists he had requested. However, the cardinal archbishop of Philadelphia decided that the Marianists had not fulfilled their contractual obligations. The Christian Brothers assumed control of the school in 1926. According to Yeske, the Marianists left West Philadelphia Catholic High School because of "the Cardinal's refusal to raise our salary and hire more lay teachers. We could not supply more Brothers as requested. We are making little progress in providing our high school teachers with degrees."[79] However, the Marianists continued to staff a high school at St. John the Baptist parish, which they began in 1922, in the Archdiocese of Philadelphia.

Born in the vicinity of Pittsburgh in 1880, Lawrence Yeske had been appointed provincial of the Eastern Province in 1923. His experience in the Marianists was chiefly in administration at St. Mary's and at the normal school. As noted earlier he was a moderate Americanizer. Indeed, it was during his administration that St. Mary's earned the title of college. His predecessor, Bernard O'Reilly, was an extrovert and an activist given to direct promotion of the college among businessmen. O'Reilly represented an upwardly mobile Irish-American leader. He had succeeded George Meyer, the last of the German-speaking Alsatian provincials. Meyer, identified by many as a rigid traditionalist who evinced a fear of modernism, wrote to Michael Schleich at the general administration in Nivelles, Belgium. In a letter of June 1919, Meyer told Schleich of O'Reilly's "hustle and bustle" with frequent trips in his automobile or by train. According to Meyer, the recently appointed provincial seldom says mass with the provincial staff and novices at Mount St. John, but prefers the chapel at St. Mary's College. "Probably he takes time to say his breviary. As to taking time to look into himself, that is out of the question. Not surprising therefore that his spirituality is at a low ebb." He had spent such little time at Mount St. John's, only four days in a year, that, said Meyer, he leaves "the impression . . . that the air of the Mt. is too close." O'Reilly's lifestyle convinced Meyer of the thoroughly "exterior" character of the man. Though the superior of Mount St. John, Father Yeske, had often been away, "his interest in the brothers is much keener than that of Rev. Provincial. These considerations strike so forcefully, because our superiors in the past have been such exemplary models of piety and regularity."[80] Since Meyer had been provincial for twenty years, he may have had himself in mind when he referred to the edifying role models of past superiors.

Brother George Deck, head of temporalities of the province also wrote to Schleich about O'Reilly's "very active" schedule. "It is all exterior show and very little attention given to the interior."[81] Since such critical remarks of superiors were quite uncommon, Meyer's perception of O'Reilly may have had an impact upon the superior general via Schleich, whose conduits to the communities in the United States were seriously respected by the general council. Meyer was highly regarded in Nivelles as well. He had presided at the American centennial celebration in 1917 and was identified with stability, order, and disciplined piety. Because in a sense O'Reilly was the antithesis of Meyer, he was not reappointed provincial. O'Reilly's activism was centered at St. Mary's College; only two institutions were opened during his term: the postulate in Beacon, New York, and St. John the Baptist High School in Manayunk, Pennsylvania, in the metropolitan area of Philadelphia. He returned to the university in 1923, where he could apply his public relations and fund-raising skills to lay the foundation for a modern campus: residence for students (Alumni Hall), a library, and a stadium. Under his administration the college admitted women in 1928, some forty years before many Jesuit colleges and universities became coeducational. Though as provincial he represented Americanizing tendencies of the era, as president and later as regent of the university law school, O'Reilly had a significant influence on the American character of the center of Marianist higher education in Dayton.

John Waldron experienced a severe crisis in 1924, one that seems to have been developing for some time. His position as inspector and chief financial officer of the province entailed almost continuous travel. The NCEA and the NCWC tasks were stimulating for him as his expertise was frequently called upon. The symptoms of his illness, compounded by a stomach disorder, appeared at the 1924 NCEA convention in Milwaukee, where he manifested a bout of what was first perceived as an alcoholic binge, which was marked by more than a public scandal. From his own point of view he had a nervous breakdown followed by severe depression. His provincial, Father Joseph Ei, had been very supportive of Waldron during the early 1920s, when there were reports that he had been alienating many brothers. Though there is evidence of the superior general's directive to resign from the office of inspector, Waldron consistently referred to his resignation as derived from his acute nervous disorder. After spending some time in Santa Cruz, California, where the Eastern Province had recently founded a school,

Waldron spent the remainder of his life in San Antonio at St. Mary's College/University. In accordance with the traditional principles of confidentiality, there was no mention of the "motives which prompted" the superior general, Ernest J. Sorret, to remove Waldron from office.[82] In 1928 he celebrated fifty years in the Society. By 1930, John Waldron had made "a complete comeback," wrote Eugene A. Paulin, a successor to Waldron as inspector of schools in the St. Louis Province. He told Michael Schleich about St. Mary's Academy in San Antonio. "The school is now in good hands with the advent of Brother Waldron." Though the provincial council had considered Waldron "too nervous to do anything," Paulin's positive assessment prevailed. "Picture a man that has always been intensely active, and then force him to give up everything and you have a condition tantamount to solitary confinement. Everybody is surprised at his new lease on life."[83]

He remained active in the NCEA until his death in 1937. He had left a significant mark on the history of Catholic education and the Marianist experience, particularly the modernization of Marianist schools and the professionalization of their faculties through the continuous development of their normal schools.

John Kim, Michael Schleich, John Waldron, and George Sauer were inspectors of schools at the provincial and general administration levels; each of them was identified with excellence in Marianist pedagogy. Though they were progressive, open, and expansive to the trends in school culture and in fostering a positive, personalist and child-centered philosophy of education, laced with advanced psychology, their lives reflected a commitment to the austerity of the monastic-like enclosures relatively bereft of those values they promoted in education, thereby widening the fissure separating interior piety from exterior ministry.

FOUNDERS

Father William Joseph Chaminade, S.M.
(1761–1850). Founder and first Superior
General of the Society of Mary, 1817–1844

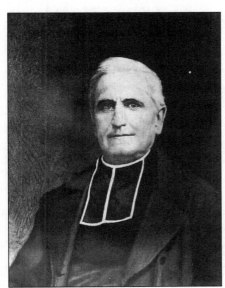

Father Joseph Simler, S.M. Fourth
Superior General and "second
founder," 1876–1905

Father Leo Meyer, S.M. Founder and
first Provincial in the United States,
1849–1862

THE PIONEERS OF 1850

Brother Andrew Edel, S.M. First Director of St. Mary's College, San Antonio, Texas, 1852–1865

Brother Damian Litz, S.M. Master teacher and longtime columnist in the *Katholische Volkszeitung*, 1850–1891

Brother John Baptist Stintzi, S.M. First Inspector of Schools in the American Province, 1869–1886

Brother Maximin Zehler, S.M. First President of St. Mary's College, Dayton, Ohio, 1858–1876

U.S. SUPERIORS GENERAL

Father Sylvester Juergens, S.M.
Eighth Superior General, 1946–1956

Father Stephen Tutas, S.M.
Tenth Superior General, 1971–1981

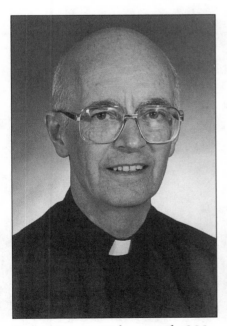

Father Quentin Hakenewerth, S.M.
Twelfth Superior General,
1991–1996

Father David Fleming, S.M.
Thirteenth Superior General,
1996–

Facade of the chapel on the campus
of the University of Dayton

St. Mary's Institute. Nazareth.
Dayton, Ohio (before the fire of 1883)

A view of Cathedral Latin School, Cleveland, Ohio

Brother Anthony Bishop, S.M., with students of Cathedral Latin School, 1946

Father William Ferree, S.M. Provincial of the Cincinnati Province, Assistant General for Education, 1955–1960, and for Apostolic Action, 1961–1965

Father Joseph M. Davis, S.M., was a brother when he served as the first Executive Director of the National Office of Black Catholics, 1970–1978

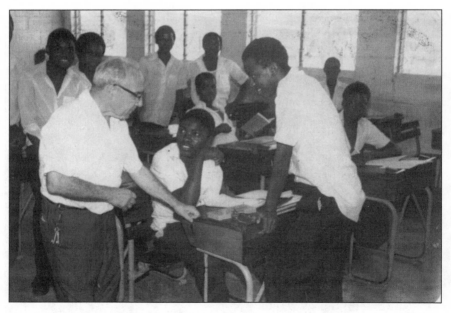

Brother George Dury, S.M., with students of Chaminade Secondary School, Karonga, Malawi, ca. 1975

ST. LOUIS PROVINCE

Members of the Sodality.
St. Louis College,
San Antonio, Texas

Brother John Waldron, S.M.
Inspector of Schools, St. Louis
Province, 1908–1924

Brother Eugene Paulin, S.M.
Inspector of Schools. St. Louis
Province, 1929–1949

Brother Vincent Gray, S.M.,
teaching at McBride High School,
St. Louis, Missouri, during the
academic year 1953–1954

Chaminade College Preparatory School, St. Louis, Missouri, 1910–.

St. Mary's University, San Antonio, Texas, 1894–.

LEFT TO RIGHT:
Brother James Jaeckle,
S.M., Brother Richard
Dix, S.M., Brother John
Totten, S.M., Brother
Edwin Johnson, S.M., at
a session of the
Provincial Chapter of
the St. Louis Province in
the 1970s

The Student Leadership and Interaction Week.
Workshop of the St. Louis Province. St.
Michael's High School, Chicago, and Chaminade
College Prep, St. Louis, ca. 1975

Father James Tobin, S.M.,
with the "ragpickers" in
the slums of Bangalore,
India, ca. 1985

THE PACIFIC PROVINCE

Brother Bertram Bellinghausen, S.M.
First Director of St. Louis College,
Honolulu, Hawaii, 1882–1905

First Marianist community at St. Mary's School in California, Marysville,
1884. Brother John Krautz, S.M., director, in center. This and other schools
in California and Hawaii were in the Cincinnati Province until the
foundation of the Pacific Province in 1948.

St. Louis campus, Honolulu, Hawaii, 1938

General Administration visit to Honolulu, 1951.
LEFT TO RIGHT: Brother James Wipfield, S.M., First Inspector of Schools of the Pacific Province; Brother Bernard Schad, S.M., General Administration; Father Walter Tredtin, S.M., First Provincial of the Pacific Province; Brother Joseph Guiot, S.M., General Administration; Brother Herman Gerber, S.M., Director of St. Louis College

Father Joseph Stefanelli, S.M.,
Provincial of the Pacific Province,
1973–1981

Riordan High School, San Francisco, California

NEW YORK PROVINCE

Chaminade-Madonna College Preparatory School
Hollywood, Florida

Foundation of the New York Province, 1961.
LEFT TO RIGHT: Brother John Darby, S.M., First Inspector of Schools of the
New York Province; Father John Dickson, S.M., First Provincial of the
New York Province; Brother John Jansen, S.M., Inspector of Schools of the
Cincinnati Province; Father James Darby, S.M., Provincial of the
Cincinnati Province

Provincials of the New York Province.
LEFT TO RIGHT: Fathers John McGrath, S.M.; Patrick Tonry, S.M.; and John Mulligan, S.M.

Colegio San José, San Juan, Puerto Rico

MERIBAH PROVINCE

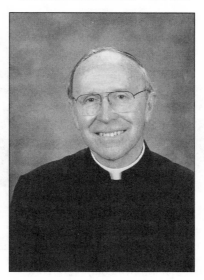

Father Philip Eichner, S.M.
Provincial, Meribah Province,
1984–1992

The dedication of Chaminade High School, Mineola, New York, 1931.
LEFT TO RIGHT: Brother Alexander Ott, S.M., Founder and First Principal; the
Reverend James Burke, Pastor of Corpus Christi Parish, Mineola, New
York; the Most Reverend Thomas Molloy, Bishop of Brooklyn; the Very
Reverend Joseph Tetzlaff, S.M., Provincial

Chaminade High School, Mineola, New York

Brother Maurice Miller, S.M., with
students of Chaminade High School,
Mineola, New York, ca. 1955

CHAPTER SIX

The Modern High School and Marianist Traditions 1920–1945

❧ I ❧

IN HIS 1912 BOOK *THE GROWTH AND DEVELOPMENT OF THE CATHOLIC School System in the United States*, James A. Burns, C.S.C., referred to the Marianists as playing a significant role in the evolution of high schools: "the Brothers engaged in elementary teaching have, nevertheless, felt the strong tide of popular sentiment for the establishment of Catholic secondary schools. The Community has been a leading part in the high school movement."[1] By 1920 there were three Marianist colleges with high school departments: St. Mary's in Dayton, St. Mary's in San Antonio, and St. Louis in San Antonio. Separate Marianist high schools numbered seventeen in 1920; that figure rose to twenty-six in 1930 and to twenty-nine in 1940. This chapter focuses on some of these Marianist high schools, which ranged from parish and diocesan high schools to those owned by the provinces, such as Chaminade College in the St. Louis area, Chaminade in Mineola (Long Island), New York, and the high school departments of the colleges.[2] As higher education developed, the high schools separated themselves and became freestanding secondary schools. Of the twenty-nine schools in 1940, nine were owned by parishes, but a few received financial support from other parishes in the vicinity and were, therefore, ad hoc regional high schools, such as St. Michael's in Chicago. The central high schools, or those built and maintained by dioceses and incorporated into systems, were prominent in the Archdioceses of St. Louis and Cincinnati. Cathedral Latin School in Cleveland was a diocesan school but not bound by a district. As will be noted later, this school was exclusively academic, with admission based on a competitive exam. Parish and diocesan district high schools offered inclusive programs, with a commercial program to appeal to students entering the job market upon graduation as well as college preparatory academic and scientific programs. All students, however, were required to attend general education classes such as those in social studies, mathematics, English, and religion; electives included public speaking, journalism, typing, and drawing. The influence of public education was paramount in the development of Catholic high schools.[3]

The Marianists' early commitment to high schools was reflected in their roles in the evolution of the NCEA. John Waldron and Bernard O'Reilly were influential in the formation of the secondary school section of that national association. Brother Eugene Paulin, who had played a significant role in the establishment of regional offices of the section, was national president in 1940 and a vice president of the general executive board for many years in the 1940s. Other brothers were chairs of the various regions, while Brother Julius Kreshel became editor of the *Catholic High School Bulletin* in 1947. Hence, James Burns's remarks on the Marianist commitment to the high school movement, which of course was intended to provide for the upward mobility of American Catholics, has been evident in several spheres.[4]

In 1937 a Committee on the Orientation of Secondary Education, whose report was published by the National Education Association, emphasized the "emotional and intellectual integration of the individual as well as social integration." The social purpose of public education occurred through a common education. The report stated:

> Integrating education being concerned with habits, skills, attitudes, emotions, and ideals is a matter of outcomes, not of curriculum organization or school administration. . . .
>
> . . . "General Education" will harm the clear-cut social purpose of making youth effective agents in organizing and guiding social and economic changes toward democratic goals. . . . Only as we keep our eyes on social goals can we evaluate curriculum outcomes in a public school.[5]

Some Catholic educators were critical of this principle of education for democracy; one priest-educator, John F. Dwyer, referred to those "schools and systems where a false theory of democracy dictates the system and makes the slowest boy [sic] of the slowest class the norm of the group's achievement."[6] Most Marianist schools, diocesan and parish high schools, did not fit Dwyer's caricature but rather absorbed the ethos governing public schools. In her recent work on twentieth-century education, Paula Fass's chapter on Catholic education in the twentieth century, "Imitation and Autonomy," aptly captures the dynamic relationship of Catholic educational adaption and religious separatism. This appears clearly evident in Marianist schools in particular as well as Catholic secondary schools in general; this is also present in the significant degree of commonality between the NEA and the NCEA.

Fass illustrates her command of the separate character of Catholic education:

> The Catholic viewpoint on education, with its strong Christocentric emphasis, roots in Thomistic rationalistic psychology, and dependence on papal pronouncements and conciliar decisions [e.g., the Third Plenary Council of Baltimore mandating attendance in Catholic schools under pain of mortal sin unless unavailable] provided a strongly conservative center of gravity for educational goals and practices. . . . Catholic schools have heavily emphasized throughout the twentieth century issues of character formation, self-discipline, the unity of training and high levels of academic proficiency.[7]

In his 1940 work *Secondary Education of the Society of Mary in America*, Edmund J. Baumeister explores a Catholic philosophy of education and cites Jacques Maritain, the Thomist philosopher, on *Freedom in the Modern World*, Pope Pius XI on *Christian Education of Youth*, canon law, the works of Chaminade, and those of Thomas Shields of Catholic University. He contrasts the notions of "Supernaturalism [i.e.,] a reasonable faith" with the naturalism and utilitarianism of John Dewey.[8] Indeed, Baumeister elucidates the Catholic and Marianist philosophy of education in opposition to that of Dewey. He points out, however, that in the Catholic tradition, philosophy provides principles with wide latitude for interpreting the practice derived from a theoretical foundation. He notes that Chaminade emphasized universality: "Many other organizations are limited by their constitutions to a special area of education. Father Chaminade positively refused to impose such a limitation upon his organization explicitly stating that universality was to be a feature of his Society and this gave a special adaptability to the variation of time and place."[9]

Further illustrations of Fass's description of Catholic education in the twentieth century are found in Baumeister. He pointed out the Christ-centered permeation of the curricula as religion was integrated into the courses: "the service of God and neighbor should dominate the whole educational program."[10] Social integration through a common education for democracy, a central principle of the 1937 "Report of the Committee on Orientation of Secondary Education," found its parallel in Baumeister's religion as the integrating principle. He cites the unity of social sciences and religion fostered in the Marianist schools, "Here barriers no longer separate economics, sociology and political science from ethics and religion. History naturally blends these with English as the instrument for binding them together in the actual process of [social and religious] integration through the [democratic] solution to life's problems."[11]

Paula Kane's cultural and religious history of Boston Catholicity, *Separatism and Subculture*, highlights the construction of religious identity in dialectical tension with American self-understanding,[12] frequently revealed in an attitude of "separate and superior." Kane cites an early witness to the aura of Catholicity in the Catholic school: "A Catholic atmosphere is what all children should breathe, both at home and in school; . . . where can they imbibe Catholicity if they attend non-Catholic schools?"[13] The intersection of American cultural values and separatism on the high school level is symbolized in extracurricular activities that were thoroughly American—for example, drama and art clubs—and religious extracurricular activities that reflect the subculture: Catholic Student Mission Crusade, living rosary, and Marianist sodalities. Pope Pius XI's encyclical of 1937, *Christian Education*, fashioned gender separatism in his warning against the dangers of coeducation in the high school.[14] Five Marianist high schools were closed between 1926 and 1943 and absorbed into coeducational schools run by women religious, usually because of the higher costs of salaries and living conditions of the men. These pragmatic reasons for ignoring the traditional ecclesiastical antipathy to coeducation represents the American Catholic drive for efficiency, which could be justified by the rationale that no European nation had developed such a vast subculture based on a vital parish life, missionary experience, and lay participation in the economic and social activities of the parishes and dioceses. This latter was exemplified by the Knights of Columbus, the Catholic Daughters of America, the Holy Name Society, and the St. Vincent de Paul Society.[15]

This chapter, which opens with an exploration of the wide-ranging experiences of Marianist high schools during the 1920s through the 1940s in the St. Louis Province from Detroit to New Orleans, and in Cleveland and Philadelphia of the Eastern Province, closes with the integration of social sciences and religion in the context of the Great Depression. This integration was present in all Marianist schools in California and Hawaii and in the mission areas of Latin America, China, and Africa, a topic that will be considered in the following chapter. Educational modernity and religious tradition, "imitation and autonomy" are appropriate dialectical themes integrating the various historical spheres of the Marianist experience in the United States, ca. 1920–1945.

✖ II ✖

IN HIS DOCTORAL DISSERTATION ON THE EARLY YEARS OF THE NATIONAL Catholic Education Association, Edgar Patrick McCarren cited a 1960 address by the education editor of *America*, Neil G. McCluskey, S.J., who "was to startle many casual observers of the educational scene when he advocated *centralization* of Catholic schools."[16] Though centralization in the form of diocesan superintendents of schools had originated some sixty years before this address, parochial education in the United States has allowed "a wide latitude of free choice on the local level."[17] The high school movement in the NCEA (then CEA) under the vigorous leadership of James Burns, C.S.C., was, as mentioned in the last chapter, also subject to local variations. In St. Louis the Catholic high school was a topic of considerable interest at the NCEA meeting there in 1904. In addition, as mentioned in the last chapter, the Marianists staffed the first parish high school at SS. Peter and Paul, the first high school in the archdiocese. Though the central-Catholic movement, specifically promoted by Burns was prevalent in many diocesan systems, the parish high school persisted because of the countervailing trends of parish autonomy and the weight of local tradition even in such highly organized diocesan systems as those of Philadelphia, Detroit, and Chicago. Parish elementary boys' schools were gradually taken over by communities of women religious, but a few were staffed by Marianists until the 1950s and 1960s. This exploration of the diversity of Marianist education focuses on critical periods of significant change, the closure of schools caused by social, educational, and economic factors, and the opening of new high schools of various configurations.

The first Marianist involvement in a central Catholic High School was in Hamilton, Ohio, in 1909. As noted in the previous chapter, the central character of the school was based on subsidies by the parishes in the district, which allowed students to attend free from the burden of tuition. The central Catholic ideal entailed accommodating students from various economic and social backgrounds, not just from upper-income families. Hence, the curriculum was divided into commercial and academic courses in the latter two years. The predominance of German-American families in Hamilton was also reflected in the curriculum, as four years of German were required up to World War I.

When the CEA met in St. Louis in 1904, Archbishop John Glennon, who, as coadjutor to John Kain become the ordinary of the archdiocese, had participated in the discussion of James A. Burns's proposal for central high schools with particular focus on episcopal leadership:

> Unless the bishop takes the lead, the priests would hardly come together of their own *proprio mota* and build a high school. . . . I am a little afraid when you get eight or ten parishes converging . . . they might discuss parochial friction rather than the high school. Still I think . . . the parish priests are coming to think of it as a common cause, and little jealousies must be laid away for the purpose of upbuilding for the great work of education.[18]

Glennon appointed Reverend Aloysius V. Garthoeffner as the first superintendent of schools with the task of establishing a system that entailed uniformity in textbooks and teachers' qualifications, as well as sponsorship of teachers' institutes. Plans for diocesan high schools included consultation with Brother Gerald Mueller, director/principal of SS. Peter and Paul High School. In 1911 Glennon approved a "project of creating one or two high school centers" in the archdiocese.[19] SS. Peter and Paul Parish High School became Kenrick High School Center in September 1911. In a *St. Louis Globe-Democrat* article on the project, Garthoeffner stated that the prospective high schools will be "free schools; we shall try to reach the ranks of pupils recruited from the poorer and middle classes. We can best reach these classes by higher education." He noted the considerable numbers of Catholic elementary school graduates who were attending public high schools and the need to recruit them to Catholic institutions. This would be far more significant than the archdiocese's charity efforts because in that area "we reach only the individual but in an educational institution [we are] helping future generations."[20] In a letter to the superintendent, Glennon urged all priests and laity to perceive the project as "part of a grand Catholic system of training; that is one faith; one Lord; one baptism . . . and that oneness should be not alone of faith but of system as well."[21] The archbishop called upon parish priests to "forget for the moment parish lives, and may never forget diocesan lives and make the sacrifices . . . that are necessary to insure the survival of that system which stands for the survival of all truth and the permanency of our civilization."[22]

To equate the progress of the Catholic school system with the advance of civilization, Glennon's vision was illustrative of the mission-to-America theme popular among Irish-American prelates eager to assert the compatibility of American and Catholic loyalties. Such sentiments were evident in his remarks that "religious education leads to a purer patriotism, a more responsible government and a happier people than any other" because it fosters a loftier ideal of life and a moral ethos of citizenship.[23] Indeed, he acknowledged his gratitude to Denis J. O'Connell, the "Americanist agent" in Rome, for support of Glennon's appointment as coadjutor to Archbishop John Kain in 1896. As rector of the Catholic University and as a principal voice of support for the CEA, O'Connell was in St. Louis for the first convention in 1904.[24] Later Glennon gladly accepted an appointment to the Board of Trustees of the Catholic University of America.[25]

Opposition to the high school system surfaced among pastors saddled with debts, among the proponents of trade schools, and by John Phelan, the priest editor of the independent Catholic weekly, the *Western Watchman*, who not uncharacteristically tagged free schools with the label of socialism.[26] Despite such opposition, Kenrick High School, run by the Marianists, and the two girls' high schools, Rosati and Kain, later combined into one institution (Rosati-Kain), opened in September 1911. Enrollment at the brothers' school continued to increase from 54 in 1911 to 328 students ten years later. The school moved three times and, because of a gift from the widow of William Cullen McBride as one half of a $250,000 donation to the archbishop on the twenty-fifth anniversary of his episcopal consecration, the student body moved once more to a new building in the north central section of the city; this school was appropriately named William Cullen McBride High School and was located on North Kingshighway Boulevard across the street from where the Christian Brothers College had stood before it burned down, a situation that necessitated moving to a site on Clayton Road, just outside the city boundary. In the 1930s the Marianists took charge of two other schools in the archdiocesan system, South Side and North Side Catholic High Schools.[27] Until Archbishop Joseph Ritter opened coeducational institutions in the late 1940s and early 1950s, the Marianists dominated boys' secondary education in the Archdiocese of St. Louis.

Chaminade College, which featured a fourth- through eighth-grade elementary school and a full secondary school, was based on the independent academy model, with roughly 250 students, half of whom were boarders. It required a considerable capital outlay; in 1925 the mortgage on Chaminade property was $100,000 of the total provincial indebtedness of $353,000. According to the treasurer's report for the St. Louis Province of that year, the account of the expenses of Maryhurst Normal School for Marianist scholastics and the other formation program, "we have only a moderate income to fall back on. It means that this income must be increased by adding to our earning Powers [sic] and by lessening where possible our expenses."[28] With the severities of the Great Depression, the St. Louis

Province had considered selling the Chaminade property to liquidate the mortgage because the province was unable to meet the monthly interest payments. (Moreover, Central Catholic High School in San Antonio was built as the depression began.) Due to the intervention of Glennon, the mortgage was restructured, thereby allowing the province to maintain Chaminade, the only school it owned other than Maryhurst Normal and St. Mary's College, San Antonio. Of course, the Marianists were exceedingly grateful for the archbishop's intervention, though, as will be noted later in this chapter, Glennon's Jim Crow Catholicism was a source of alienation among some Brothers of Mary.

❧ III ❧

ARCHBISHOP JOHN GLENNON'S AMERICANIST IDEALS WERE CLEARLY expressed in his admiration for John Lancaster Spalding. In an address in the early 1890s Glennon remarked on the bishop of Peoria's dedication to bringing "unity and strength [to] the parochial [school] system." As if to remind those listeners who promoted German particularism, Glennon praised Spalding for liberating Catholic education "from the narrow confines of race (i.e., ethnicity) or language to the broad platform of Christian education."[29] As mentioned in a previous chapter, Spalding invited the Marianists to staff an academy, Spalding Institute, in Peoria in 1899. Since 1863 the Sisters of St. Joseph of Carondelet had been sponsoring a school for girls in Peoria, the Academy of Our Lady of the Sacred Heart, but there was no Catholic secondary school for boys. Some parish elementary schools had attempted to add higher levels beyond the eighth grade but had not been successful. Bishop Spalding, peerless in his refined notions of Catholic education, established the diocesan-wide secondary school. Though he had hoped to attract the Benedictines to Peoria, their administration chose instead to establish a school in Peru, Illinois.[30] He was quite familiar with the work of the Christian Brothers, and in a letter to Daniel Hudson, C.S.C., editor of *Ave Maria*, Spalding indicated his concern about the famous order of teachers. "A decision from Rome forbids them to teach the classics. This is a severe blow at our educational interests."[31] Students from the several German and Irish parishes were the potential recruits for Spalding Institute, named for the bishop's uncle, Martin John Spalding, archbishop of Baltimore from 1863 to 1877. Located near the cathedral, the Institute was built at a cost of nearly seventy thousand dollars, financed by gifts from the priests of the diocese, from the local Knights of Columbus, and from the royalties of John Lancaster Spalding's several books.[32]

The three brothers assigned to Peoria, Gerald Mueller, Albert Hollinger, and Peter Schlitt, had little experience in secondary education. Two of the brothers were in their twenties. When Spalding discovered their ages, he remarked with humor, sarcasm, and a sense of resignation, "Well, God loves little children, and we hope his blessing will be upon you."[33] As a "Catholic High School and College for Young Men and Boys," its stated objective was "to fit students for active business life and prepare them to meet the requirements for entrance into the seminary or university."[34] Hence, the curriculum offered commercial and classical-scientific courses, programs in accord with the prevailing public high school curriculum. The Institute included a preparatory program for seventh- and eighth-grade students until 1906, when it presented itself as a "Catholic High School for Young Men."[35] After ten years of recruitment efforts, enrollment averaged a little under one hundred as late as 1910. Since the original tuition was twenty dollars for freshmen, thirty for sophomores, and forty for juniors and seniors, the Institute was not based on a central-Catholic plan, that is, a free school subsidized by the parishes. John Lancaster Spalding was his own superintendent of schools, but he did form boards of education for each of the deaneries. He was president of Spalding Institute, but it was symbolic of his deep interest rather than of any intention to interfere with the brothers' administration. Robert N. Barger, a scholar of Spalding as "Educator and Social Emissary" concluded: "Spalding Institute was the Bishop's most noted local contribution. He endowed it and acted as its president for ten years. It was one of the first central Catholic high schools. The differentiated curriculum provided an object lesson of its founder's meritocratic bias."[36] Despite the fact that it was the bishop's most significant mark upon diocesan education, the school did not enjoy an endowment; however, the differentiated education was a strong strand of the Marianist tradition harking back to its foundation in France.

John Lancaster Spalding's successor, Edmund M. Dunne, was consecrated on September 1, 1909; in November of 1910 he wrote to Father George Meyer, then provincial of the Cincinnati Province, informing him that he was "anxious to relieve the diocese of financing the Spalding Institute. . . . Offers have been made by various religious teaching orders. The Brothers of Mary however, are entitled to first consideration."[37] Dunne referred to transferring the property to the brothers and indicated his concern for the school's continuity.

Upon its establishment in 1908, the St. Louis Province took charge of Spalding Institute, with Joseph Weckesser as priest-provincial and John Waldron as inspector. Weckesser met with Dunne and brought the issue to the provincial council, but it could not reach a decision, "We were strongly for and sharply against" accepting the grant of the school, which was free of debt; but, with only fifty students in 1911, the financial responsibility entailed expenditures that would augment the indebtedness of the province.[38] The director, Brother Albert Hollinger, told Weckesser that the bishop would have immediately offered the Institute to the Benedictines of Peru, Illinois, but that the rector of the cathedral, Peter J. O'Reilly, urged him to give the Marianists first consideration.[39] Perhaps O'Reilly and other influential priests prevailed because the Marianists rejected the bishop's offer but continued to staff the Institute during the remainder of Dunne's administration until 1929. One may also surmise from the increasing enrollment figures—280 students in early 1931—that the financial burden of the diocese had been considerably reduced, if not liquidated.

Dunne's successor, Joseph Henry Schlarman, had studied in Innsbruck and was ordained near there in 1904 before pursuing a canon law degree and a Ph.D. in philosophy at the Gregorian University in Rome in 1907. Appointed chancellor of the Diocese of Belleville in late 1907, he was familiar with the Brothers of Mary at the Cathedral High School and Central Catholic High School in East St. Louis. He was consecrated bishop of Peoria in June 1930 in the early days of the Great Depression. Despite the flourishing educational programs, the extremely popular extracurricular activities, and the increasingly high enrollments, the Marianist provincial in St. Louis, Father Joseph Ei, received a telegram, dated June 27, 1933, from the chancellor of the Diocese of Peoria notifying him that the bishop "desires an interview with you" when he visits St. Louis.[40] Schlarman notified Ei of the fact that Spalding Institute had been sold to the Benedictines and, according to Brother Albert Hollinger, the director/principal, the bishop "found it eminently expedient for him to sell at the present moment." Hollinger reported on the strong groundswell of support for the Marianists among the Peoria Catholics in general and the school's parents and students particularly. He told Ei that only the bishop would profit from the sale: "The school will probably be run at a loss for the Benedictines, the pastors have been requested to help financially those students" unable to pay full tuition. Schlarman assured Hollinger of his continuing high regard for the brothers. He closed with the remark on the impact of their "ouster" from the diocese, "we feel very keenly our departure from Peoria, since we have been identified with Spalding from its very inception." It was especially distressing because the brothers had "labored painfully for thirty-four years to build up a high reputation that Spalding has achieved both scholastically and in athletic circles." The loss was compounded by the tragic irony that during a time of considerable achievement all must be sacrificed because of "the whim of a bishop who saw financial gain promised." Hollinger's final word was that the loss violated "a sense of justice."[41] Six weeks before this letter of July 23, 1933, all the evidence pointed to a continuously prospering and rewarding experience among Marianists, students, and their families.

The relationship between the bishop and the provincial became acrimonious during the process of transferring the Marianist property to St. Louis. The source of the conflict was the musical instruments that Schlarman insisted be returned to the Institute. Of course, it was not simply the conflict of interpretation of ownership but the level to which Schlarman descended. In Father Ei's last letter to Bishop Schlarman he cited Schlarman's letter of September 25, 1933. The bishop said, "Any further delay in returning these instruments will make the illegal seizure known to the public of Peoria and create a very bad impression regarding the Brothers of Mary." In response, Ei intimated that only Schlarman would be promoting the bad name and that the Marianists "having departed from Peoria . . . are not in a fair position to defend our good name." Hence, he returned the musical instruments "*under protest* [his emphasis]. We do not waive the rights to this ownership."[42]

References to the Great Depression were absent from Schlarman's rationale for selling Spalding Institute, but since many dioceses and parishes throughout the nation were suffering from the severities of economic dislocation, it must have been a factor in his decision. Provincial indebtedness obviated a positive reply to Dunne's offer to turn over the deed to the property to the St. Louis Province, a situation about which Schlarman may have known by consulting the diocesan files on the Institute. Spalding's enrollment continued to hover around 280 students during the next decade. Schlarman remained in Peoria until his death in 1952.

The St. Louis Province lost St. Francis High School in Dyersville, Iowa, and Cathedral High School in Wichita, Kansas, both of which became coeducational in order to cut costs during the Depression. Even before the crash of Black Tuesday, the loss of St. Mary's Commercial High School in Dubuque occurred, in part because of a conflict between the Marianist principal and the diocesan superintendent of schools, and in part because the diocese wished to augment enrollment in its own college, Columbia College, later named Loras College.[43] Since the brothers had been in Dyersville for twenty years and Dubuque for twenty-two years, they had established deep roots in the communities. The pastor in Dyersville attempted to support a separate boys' school, but, according to the brothers, he was unable to make the sacrifice. In Dubuque, the brothers had attempted to add a college preparatory curriculum which would have entailed adding another year to the three-year commercial course of studies. Monsignor J. J. Wolfe, superintendent of diocesan schools, who had urged the Brothers of Mary "to accept . . . a certain element of sameness [which] must pervade a system of schools," indicated his approval of a fourth year in May of 1928, which was added to the curriculum the following year.[44] However, the principal of St. Mary's appears to have been opposed to Wolfe's "many plans as to the future," which, he told Father Ei, "are better spoken than written about."[45] As if to clarify the superintendent's position, Archbishop James J. Keane, who had appointed Wolfe, had visited the brothers at St. Mary's toward the end of May 1928, a visit which Brother Paul Roesner noted "caused much gossip in this wing." A reconciliation between Wolfe and Roesner was never achieved; a year after Keane's visit he notified the provincial "that the services of the Brothers will be dispensed with at St. Mary's High School with the end of the present school year."[46]

Amid the conflicts between Wolfe and Roesner, enrollment at St. Mary's remained quite low; in 1929 there were ninety-one students, seventy-one of whom were from outside the parish. Hence, there were several layers to the Dubuque situation. Brother Gerald Mueller, the successor of John Waldron as inspector of schools, had informed Michael Schleich, the inspector general, about the crisis in Dubuque. Schleich perceived St. Mary's as "exemplifying the mounting evidence that the *parochial* high school, except for a few cases, is fast becoming a thing of the past. And it is a natural consequence of the demands made by a modern high school on the finances of the parish." However, the diocese "could well afford a central Catholic high school without bearing umbridge [*sic*] to the [Columbia] College."[47] Because of the high number of vocations from Dyersville and Dubuque, the St. Louis Province wanted to staff the Iowa schools, but as educational institutions they did not evoke as strong a sense of loss as did Spalding Institute.

In New Orleans, where the Brothers of Mary ran two elementary schools, St. Alphonsus (1878–1896) and St. Mary's (1869–1882), the Society also had two high schools, Verrina (1916–1925) in St. Stephen's parish, staffed by the Congregation of the Mission, or Vincentians, and Liguori (1915–1926) in St. Alphonsus parish under the Redemptorists. Since the brothers were dismissed from both of these schools in the mid-1920s to be replaced by women religious, the Marianist experience in New Orleans represented an early trend in parish education, the shift from single sex to coeducational schools. Though this was not unusual among elementary parish schools, it was less common in the high schools, particularly in German-American parishes. As noted in a previous chapter, St. Michael's and St. James's

parishes in Baltimore had single-sex elementary schools until after World
War II.

Liguori Boys' High School was incorporated in the Sisters of Mercy
Schools, elementary and secondary, with an enrollment in 1927 of 798 girls
and 886 boys.[48] Again, one presumes that economic considerations based on
the higher salaries and separate residence of brothers were the principal reasons for the decision. The Vincentians at St. Stephen's parish were also
motivated by the economics of the situation, but, according to the principal, Brother Francis J. Wohlleben, and the pastor, Father McCabe, the decision was precipitous, made at the end of March for a June closure. Indeed,
Wohlleben believed the financial burden could have been relieved by an
archdiocesan development fund and by neighboring parishes, which were
not allowed time to consider alternative financing.[49] Shortly after the closing, Wohlleben told his provincial, Father Louis A. Tragesser, of the many
protests and efforts to reestablish Verrina: "Closing Verrina is a different
proposition than was the closing of Liguori. There is no comparison. The
Lazarists [i.e., Vincentians] had assumed a MORAL OBLIGATION, which I
maintain, they were in DUTY bound to have performed, when they invited
the people of the outside parishes to send their boys here and were intent to
accept . . . the indirect support."[50] Bishop John Shaw was reportedly supportive of the brothers at Verrina, but he was in the process of centralizing
schools and must have perceived the brothers' mission in parish high
schools as an unnecessary expense.[51]

The Verrina Alumni Association testified to the myriad contributions of
the brothers, "We have seen these good Brothers, employed to teach school
and receiving but a mere pittance, support themselves and their order. . . .
We have seen them do painting, plumbing, carpentering, masonry, pipe-
fitting . . . and do their own housework." The association went on record in
opposition to the decision to close the school, "these eleven years of labor
of love . . . [were] thrown to the four winds."[52]

Though the Society had been asked to leave the high school in a Redemptorist parish in New Orleans, they worked with the Redemptorists in
Chicago's St. Michael's for over a century. The Marianists took over the
parish school in 1874, just three years after the great Chicago fire. Most
schools only required three or four brothers but with over six hundred boys
enrolled in 1875 seven brothers were assigned to St. Michael's, located on
Eugenie and Cleveland Streets. The parish included Germans from a wide
diversity of regions in the old country, creating almost continuous conflict
and leading to the removal of pastors incapable of placating the parishioners. With the arrival of the Redemptorists in 1860, a sense of unity pre-

vailed, as all respected the priests and brothers of this community. The growing prosperity of Chicago was reflected in the social and economic development of the German-American community of the parish.[53] The Redemptorist responsible for the parish annals in the fall of 1892 provides insight into the Americanization process.

> The month of October brings thoughts of Christopher Columbus. In these days Columbus Day had a very special meaning and this externalized itself in parades and other festivities. When one considers that so many of these people, especially in St. Michael District were foreign born—America had new ways, new languages and mannerisms and to observe their wholehearted cooperation in these civic events these people were to be admired with many of them more patriotic then some of the flag-waving individuals. . . .
>
> The St. Michael's District in the main very Catholic took an intense part in the Columbian celebration. They had a large band that would do justice to any orchestra or music hall.[54]

There was a reference to the school children but no mention of the Brothers of Mary throughout the entire volume 1874–1894. Enrollment figures were recorded; in 1892 there were 820 boys attending St. Michael's School.[55] The brothers' annals also recorded the parade and noted the school children singing "patriotic hymns" at the Lincoln Monument. The progress of school was noted; in 1899 "on account of the increase in pupils a new class was formed and to the satisfaction of parents and the success of the school a new commercial class was formed."[56] In 1902 a three-year commercial high school was opened, indicative of the need for preparation for careers beyond the trades. St. Michael's experienced some Americanization in the form of English-language drama productions and printed publications, but since the parish continued to receive immigrants from Germany there was a tendency to preserve the German language longer than in most parishes.[57] Since the high school did not add a fourth year until 1923, it appears that only with the prosperity of the 1920s was there a demand for a college preparatory program at St. Michael's. This parish high school represented developments in the archdiocese. In 1915 the editor of the archdiocesan newspaper, *New World*, made one of several pleas for parental commitment to secondary education: "This is a time Catholic parents must shut their ears to the grammar school student who would sooner go to work than to high school."[58]

When George Mundelein became archbishop in 1916, the Archdiocese of Chicago entered a new era. Born into a German-American family in New York City (1872), Mundelein was trained for the priesthood in Rome's Urban College for the Diocese of Brooklyn and ordained in 1895. He rose from chancellor, monsignor, to auxiliary bishop in a fourteen-year period. His appointment to Chicago had been attributed to the influence of Archbishop John Bonzano, apostolic delegate to the United States and his former rector at the Urban College. At forty-four years of age, Mundelein was the youngest archbishop in the American hierarchy, and in 1924 became the first cardinal in the Midwest, and head of the largest see in the United States.[59]

According to his biographer, Edward R. Kantowicz, the young archbishop represented a generation of "American-born but Roman trained bishops [who] came to power in the largest urban dioceses of the United States." Besides Mundelein, these included William Henry O'Connell of Boston, Denis Dougherty of Philadelphia, John Glennon of St. Louis, and Francis Spellman of New York, all of whom "like their counterparts in business, saw the need for more order and efficiency in their bailiwicks."[60] Thoroughly American in their administrations and fiercely loyal to the Vatican, these consolidating bishops were variations on the theme of modernity as Americans, but they were antimodernist and ultramontanist in ecclesiology. Kantowicz described Mundelein's sense of "giantism," as represented by building the largest seminary in the United States, Our Lady of the Lake, and frequently heading up the largest Peter's Pence collection in the world. More than an acquaintance of President Franklin D. Roosevelt, Mundelein enjoyed such prestige that his Illinois license plate was #1, while the governor's was #2.

Shortly after his February 1916 installation as archbishop, Mundelein appointed a board of supervisors of parochial schools, composed of three pastors representing the Irish, German, and Polish communities and charged with creating a uniform and centralized school system, the largest such system in the American church. Except for courses in religious education and reading, the curriculum was to be in English. Though there was eventually a uniform-salary schedule, pastors remained in charge of finances and controlled hiring sisters and brothers, accommodations that were contrary to the prevailing system.[61] Emblematic of the "system," the new institution was named St. Michael Central High School; over forty parishes were represented in the enrollment of boys and girls in the high school. The school was coinstitutional, not coeducational, constructed with two separate wings but with a central library, gymnasium, an auditorium site for later development and a cafeteria. There was a girls' marching band and a boys' athletic program. (Ten years later a diocesan school in St. Louis, Coyle High School, also coinstitutional, was opened in Kirkwood, an old Missouri town which by 1939 had become a suburb of the city.) On the eve of the Great Depression, the Redemptorists at St. Michael's received permission to build this new high school, dedicated by Mundelein in May 1929.[62] With a loan of $350,000, the parish debt soon became a problem in 1930. In a letter to the provincial of the St. Louis Province of the Redemptorists, E. K. Cantwell, John P. Miller, the rector, remarked that Mundelein wanted St. Alphonse parish, also run by the Redemptorists, to help pay for the building of the school: "It is the express wish of the Cardinal that St. Alphonse should help pay this as a regional high school." Miller reminded the provincial that St. Michael's parish "is by no means what it was some years ago. Our best [i.e., most affluent] people have died or moved away."[63] There was a total debt of $502,000 and further expenses for "the dwelling rooms . . . for the brothers."[64]

The provincial's response to Mundelein's proposal was enthusiastic. "I am delighted that the Cardinal made that happy remark about St. Michael's being a regional school and that St. Alphonse would be expected to shoulder the loan."[65] Eventually St. Alphonse did contribute $100,000; however, the rector did not report the payment to the people of the parish but to the diocesan education office.[66]

Amid the Depression, Catholic education experienced a severe setback after a decade of phenomenal growth, particularly on the elementary school level. Though there was a decline in the attendance at that level, enrollment at Catholic high schools was actually expanding at a high rate, principally because of rapidly increasing unemployment and the general expectation that attendance at high school was necessary for economic and social security.[67] The superintendent of schools noted a rise of one thousand high school students between 1930 and 1935. "Inability to find employment, reduced tuition rates, and the splendid spirit of generosity on the part of the sisters, brothers and priests towards boys and girls unable to pay tuition are factors which have enabled us to show an increase in attendance."[68]

The parishioners of St. Michael's experienced the full impact of the Depression. The Redemptorist rector described the situation to his provincial: "The poverty of the people is appalling. They are in need of everything. A Bolshevik indignation meeting is scheduled to bring us to time tonight."[69] According to the *Catholic Directory*, enrollments of the boys' high school rose from 233 in 1929 to 275 in 1935, but in 1930 the School Sisters of Notre Dame took control of all the elementary grades; a coeducational enrollment of 980 in 1935; seventeen sisters and five lay persons composed the faculty. Relations between the Redemptorists and Brothers of Mary were considered generally rather good.[70] In 1941 the rector reported to the provincial that such relations "during the past year had been [only] of the best; better than in other years past."[71] In 1945 the rector agreed to an increase of the brothers' salaries, but urged the provincial to notify "the Brother Superior you expect the Brothers to return to their former salary when costs of living have dropped to their normal level."[72]

St. Michael's, while not an academic jewel such as Spalding Institute, was certainly well loved by the Marianists of the St. Louis Province; over its 104-year history seventy-five former students of St. Michael's entered the Society.[73] (Reynold Hillenbrand, the rector of Our Lady of the Lake Seminary, a national figure in Catholic Action and the Liturgical Movement, was a loyal alumnus of St. Michael's elementary school.) As late as 1950 St. Michael's was listed as a German parish in the *Catholic Directory*, no doubt to distinguish it from the other four St. Michael's parishes—Slovak, Lithuanian, Polish, and Italian.[74] The persistence of ethnic identity within an archdiocese that had become Americanized and modernized in its policies and administrative practices may be explained by the immigrant roots of the city's neighborhoods.

One of the few Redemptorist parishes in an Irish neighborhood was Holy Redeemer in Detroit. Father Francis Friedel recalled that an alumnus of St. Michael's Central High School (N. L. Franzin), who had become the Redemptorist rector of Holy Redeemer, invited the brothers to open a parish high school for boys in 1915.[75] Friedel was one of the five brothers assigned to Holy Redeemer, which in its first year enrolled 230 students in seventh through the twelfth grades. Thirty Sister Servants of the Immaculate Heart of Mary (I.H.M.) of Monroe, Michigan, were in charge of the elementary and high schools for girls; they were in charge of the boys through the sixth grade and later through the eighth grade. Since their enrollment was 1,450, the faculty increased to thirty-three sisters and an additional three lay teachers.[76] Friedel recalled that of the five brothers assigned to Holy Redeemer two left the Society, a situation that must have been not uncommon since it appears to have shaped the reputation of the Detroit school among Marianists in the United States.[77] Nevertheless, a good number of Marianist vocations came from Holy Redeemer.

In 1937 Holy Redeemer was transferred to the St. Louis Province "to make boundary lines between . . . [the] Provinces accurate." Since the Cincinnati Province had recently opened Chaminade High School in Mineola on Long Island, St. John's Home, an orphanage in Brooklyn, a high school in Ponce, Puerto Rico, and a mission in eastern China, the transfer of Holy Redeemer was not considered a loss, as it would free up ten brothers for these works.[78] On the other hand, the St. Louis provincial, Father

Sylvester Juergens, persistently strapped for funds, noted in his report to the 1937 chapter that the "salary of the Brothers is one of the highest, 11 men earn $7,000 a year. The Brothers have nothing to do with athletics; the parish has a paper but not the school."[79] However, by 1940 Juergens reported that the "pastors would like to reduce our salary [to] $635, but we are holding out because of the teaching load of the Brothers."[80]

The archdiocesan school system was established at the direction of Bishop Michael James Gallagher, a prelate who, in accord with the organizational impulse, rationalized and centralized authority and built a magnificent cathedral symbolic of his militancy and triumphalism. He encouraged the broadcasts of Father Charles Coughlin, the famous radio priest, and defended him against those bishops who deplored Coughlin's exploitation of the pulpit for radical politics, which became quite anti-Semitic after Gallagher had died. The principal, Brother L. J. Meinhardt, was impressed with Coughlin but was just one of the hundreds of thousands of Catholics who fastened on every word uttered by the priest. Holy Redeemer, a working-class parish, was in a pro-Coughlin Catholic neighborhood.[81]

The Archdiocesan School Board was responsible for evaluating schools. It appears that Holy Redeemer Boys' High School had been rated rather well over the years. However, the School Rating Chart of April 30, 1940, was quite negative. Of the ten areas graded, four were average—building cleanliness, books and equipment, administrators, and courses of study—four were poor—pupil notebooks, class size, teaching, and school organization—and two were very poor—testing and pupil activity.[82] The school had achieved accreditation by the University of Michigan's Bureau of Cooperation with Educational Institutions. Though it never lost that status, there were criticisms by the visitors in 1940 and 1941. They were particularly concerned with "too much teacher, rather than pupil activity in the classrooms." The visit of 1940 also cited the general cynicism of the brothers about the futility of teaching students with a nonsupportive home environment. According to the visitor, this cynicism should be transformed into "self-appraisal" by the faculty on meeting the students' needs, interests, hobbies, and on tailoring the curriculum and extracurricular activities to be "generally more functional."[83] That year there were 451 students in the seventh through twelfth grades; 255 in the high school. Ten brothers and one layman, a coach, composed the faculty.[84] With poor ratings by both church and state authorities in general, Brother Meinhardt's term as administrator was not renewed. Known as a strongly authoritarian yet diplomatic principal, Meinhardt appears to have been at least partially responsible for these negative evaluations. He was replaced by Brother Vincent Brand in the summer of 1940.

In his 1943 Visitation Report on the Marianist community at Holy Redeemer, Sylvester Juergens was quite positive. His remarks included: "excellent . . . spirit of the community"; the "school disruption [i.e., lack of discipline], improved over last year, is very satisfactory"; and "the fine relations with the pastor and the school authorities in general is commendable."[85] Brother Brand, who also received a thoroughly positive report from the State of Michigan visitor,[86] must have been quite surprised when a year later he received news from Father Edward Malloy, the Redemptorist rector of Holy Redeemer, that as of June 14, 1944, the brothers' school would be discontinued. Malloy's letter to Sylvester Juergens, which listed five reasons for this decision, was made in consultation with Archbishop Edward Mooney, the superintendent of schools, and the provincial of the Redemptorists. Since the I.H.M. sisters' salary was one-half that of the brothers, the "cost of maintaining a separate school for the boys . . . was overtaxing Holy Redeemer Parish. With only 175 boys from the parish [125 students were from other parishes] makes the salary and other costs for sixteen Brothers an intolerable expense." According to Malloy, the seventh- and eighth-grade boys "are not sufficiently developed to be with the big boys of the higher grades and entirely excluded from the influence of the Sisters. These boys need a more delicate atmosphere than they have under present conditions."[87] Though there were other reasons, such as lower tuition, restricting the school to students from families of the parish, and the need to use the brothers' house for classroom space, Malloy's interpretation of the benefits of the sisters' refinements was the fundamental rationale for closing the boys' school.

This conclusion was derived from a meeting between Malloy and Juergens. In the memorandum of the visit, the provincial noted the pastor's admission that "it was not finances, not even the economics of the parish" that prompted the decision to close the boys' school. In his discussion with Juergens, the rector of the parish elaborated on the brothers' tolerance "of a good many things that a woman will not stand for, [such as] lounging in the seats, feet up on the desk, a lack of respect for a priest, a toughness and general lack of delicacy so evident in . . . the students." Though the brothers were not blamed for these characteristics, they were unable "to effect a change in the boys. Father Malloy thinks that the boys do not come back to the Brothers to talk things over confidentially when they are in trouble. They seem to dislike their teachers in general and lack confidence in them."

Malloy cited occasional use of corporal punishment and the severity of the principal's general attitude. "The method does not produce what is desirable, a woman's influence in a boy's manners. Despite the problems entailed in coeducation of high school students, the influence on the boys will lead to a refined way of conducting themselves."[88]

Eugene A. Paulin, the inspector of schools of the St. Louis Province, notified Michael Schleich about the brothers' dismissal from Holy Redeemer and verified the results of Juergens's personal interview with Malloy. He added that "the school is in the Ford district . . . and many parents and even boys work. In the seventh grade of 48 boys, 18 mothers were working and 17 of those seventh graders had jobs after school and on free days!" Paulin also expressed confidence in the community: it was "above average in regularity" of attending the spiritual exercises. Paulin generalized on the experience: "Our tenure in schools where we are hired is so unsafe" that he advised "owning our own schools" as soon as the province achieved financial stability. "The Christian Brothers and the Jesuits have been for the most free of such worries."[89]

Malloy's rejection of a rough masculinity or the muscular Catholicism of the brothers and his advocacy of the moral and cultural benefits of the sisters' domesticity may not be limited to his gender biases but also to a class bias, as he seemed determined to refine the manners of boys from the blue-collar workers' families, particularly during World War II, when many women were working in the factories. As the brothers were preparing to leave Holy Redeemer, Father Edward Malloy wrote to the archdiocesan superintendent of schools, Father Carroll F. Deedy, Ph.D., about the Brothers of Mary because he understood "they are trying hard to get a school in Dearborn. I know nothing of it, except a rumor here and there." Malloy told Deedy about the poor spiritual leadership of the Marianists. Indeed, he considered them to be poor role models:

> I can not recall a single time, when we had services, as Forty Hours, Men's processions in church, etc., when they even made a visit . . . not having a religious garb, they are going about mostly in shirt sleeves, sitting in the school office smoking cigarettes, and, in general, not setting the pace we expect to find in men who are supposed to be helpers in the formation of character.[90]

Malloy criticized the brothers for independence in school fund-raising drives and their attempt to sell Marianist textbooks. He lashed out at the poor discipline prevailing in their classes. Though he reiterated his contention that the "Sisters can do a better job in all cases," he then revealed what may have been the critical factor in his preference for the I.H.M. sisters: they "are perfectly submissive to authority, which is owed to you and the diocese."[91] Malloy's excessive criticism of the brothers' style of relating to students ran contrary to the experience of Vincent Gray, a high school senior at another school and the first African-American brother in the St. Louis Province. Gray recalled the warm encouragement he received from Brother Vincent Brand when he first indicated interest in joining the Society of Mary. As will be considered in the next chapter, Vincent Gray was a gentle person who could have been easily alienated by the gruff type of Marianist described by Malloy.[92]

Edward Mooney, archbishop of Detroit, was an old friend of the brothers from their time together in Cleveland and would have been supportive of a new Marianist school. There is no evidence of the brothers' attempt to remain in the Detroit area apart from the rumors referred to in this letter. Despite this poor experience with a Redemptorist in Detroit, the Marianist–Redemptorist association thrived at St. Michael's in Chicago, Most Holy Trinity in Brooklyn, and St. Michael's and St. James's elementary schools in Baltimore. However, St. Michael's in Chicago, St. Joseph's High School in Victoria, Texas, and Holy Redeemer, Detroit, were the only parish high schools in the St. Louis Province. SS. Peter and Paul Parish School closed in 1940 because of a decline in German-Americans in the area, which reduced school enrollment. As mentioned earlier, Detroit closed four years later. Except for Chaminade College in St. Louis, St. Mary's University, and Central Catholic in San Antonio, the remaining secondary schools were either parish or diocesan schools. One Canadian elementary school, St. Jean Baptiste in Manitoba, was placed under women religious.

The Provencher School in St. Boniface, Manitoba, was a thriving secondary school with an enrollment of 792 boys. Because "Americans were not welcome on the teaching staff" and because there were so few Canadian vocations to meet the needs of the school, there were thirteen lay teachers and only nine brothers. St. Anselme's in the Quebec Province was a small elementary school with a two-year secondary school of only nine students in 1940. This was the only elementary school in the province.[93]

With the vast majority of brothers involved in secondary education in urban areas, the St. Louis Province in 1939 decided to send its third- and fourth-year scholastics to Mount St. John, the formation center for the Eastern Cincinnati Province. They attended the University of Dayton to complete their undergraduate education, which was a significant development because the university had just become a coeducational institution. In 1940 there were 325 religious in the St. Louis Province; 81 in formation; 32 priests and 244 active brothers, 220 were teaching while 24 were engaged in manual work.[94] As mentioned earlier, the province's indebtedness was a severe burden; the treasurer had attempted to sell St. Mary's University to the Congregation of the Holy Cross at St. Edward's College in Austin, but its administrator, dependent on the Congregation's University of Notre Dame, was unable to get a loan during the mid-1930s; Archbishop John Glennon indirectly provided the financing and directly loaned the province the funds to meet their interest payments, thereby avoiding bankruptcy.[95]

The Cincinnati Province, which also experienced economic crises necessitating bankruptcy and reorganization, remained committed to holding on to its elementary schools. As late as 1941, the inspector of schools, Brother Bernard Schad, presented a threefold plan for improving the fourteen elementary schools in the province, which at this time included California and Hawaii: "a) preparing elementary principals, b) keeping some of our younger teachers in this field, c) direct some scholastics into the elementary program at the University of Dayton."[96] It was not until 1947, when the provincial chapter concluded that, because it is difficult to prepare scholastics for three levels of education and because "Sisters can handle grade school education," that it was decided to "keep only [those] grade schools owned by the Society."[97] The Cincinnati Province still had thirteen elementary schools in 1947. The German-American parishes in other eastern cities were determined to maintain single-sex elementary schools as long as it was feasible.

One of the most prestigious Marianist high schools, the Cathedral Latin School in Cleveland, opened in 1916 with an unusual arrangement; both brothers and diocesan priests served on the faculty. The president of the high school was Father Edward A. Mooney, later ordinary of Detroit. In 1922, after Mooney had departed the diocese for Vatican service in Japan, the diocesan consulters decided to place the school "under the scholastic control of the Brothers of Mary, subject, however, to diocesan inspection." Bishop John P. Farrelly had started the high school in the hope that it would provide several students for seminary training. Hence, he appointed priests to manage the school. The decision to turn it over to the Marianists was derived from a report to Farrelly from two bishops who had visited the school. They told him, in the words of Farrelly, "that there was a want of technical knowledge of the art of teaching in the priests, whereas the brothers gave evidence of possessing it. Again it took thirteen priests to do the work of six Brothers. . . . [The priests] were not amenable to discipline—a lot of free and easy learning, was in vogue; which was not good for them as priests."[98]

Brother Patrick Coyle, the first Marianist principal of the school, had to confront the problem of collecting the tuition funds from pastors for their students attending the diocesan high school. Though Bernard O'Reilly, provincial in 1923, asked Farrelly's successor, Bishop Joseph Schrembs, to assign that responsibility to the chancellor of the diocese, it devolved on the principal to collect tuition.[99] Brother Coyle was far ahead of his time. As the director of the religious community at Cathedral Latin he promoted not his own authority but rather that of the individual conscience of the brothers. Upon seeking funds for expenses, a brother had only to go to the director's office and take from the cash box what was needed, a drastic departure from tradition. Severely criticized by a visitor for his liberalism, Coyle eventually left the Society.[100] Joseph A. Tetzlaff replaced Coyle in September of 1924. Because admission to the school was based on a competitive exam, of the 300 students tested in 1924 only 220 were admitted. As mentioned earlier, the cost of tuition could not be borne by the families of the students, but some pastors would not bear their responsibility for paying the "implied tuition" on a pro rata basis. In 1925 Tetzlaff reported a deficit of $6,934 from the total tuition owed by the pastors.[101]

The curriculum at Cathedral Latin included academic and scientific programs which began in the junior year with enrollments comparable to the statistics of 1924.[102] Schrembs, who as a consolidating bishop of the 1920s cherished efficiency and centralization, was a prominent episcopal figure in the NCWC. He was obviously concerned about vocations to the priesthood. He inquired of Tetzlaff about the number of students enrolled in seminaries in 1925; the principal listed twenty-two at the seminary of Our Lady of the Lake, and five others who entered the religious life; one entered the Society of Mary. Since the graduating class of that year was 145, 101 of whom enrolled in colleges or universities, the figure for vocations appears quite high.[103] Hence, it seems that the loss of the priests from the faculty did not adversely affect the number of vocations. However, there appears to have been a concern about brothers teaching courses in Christian doctrine. For example, Tetzlaff responded to an inquiry about the topics included in such a course for seniors at Cathedral Latin. No doubt the bishop was pleased by the following list of topics, with its emphasis on the infallible church and its struggle with Protestantism and modernity.

1: The Schism of the West a Proof of the Divine Foundation of the Catholic Church.

2: The Protestent [sic] Reformation the Cause of the Present Day Irreligion.

3: The French Revolution the Logical Consequence of the Protestent [sic] Reformation.

4: The Temporal Power of the Pope has a Better and More Legitimate Origin and Foundation than any Royal Dynasty.

5: The infallibility of the Church and the Necessity of an Infallible Teacher, can be proved from Reason, Tradition, and the Scriptures.

6: The True Church can be recognized by the Ernest Seeker from Certain Marks Impressed upon it by its Divine Founder.

7: The Church of England cannot claim to be a Living Branch of the True Church because She can claim no Apostollic [*sic*] Succession.[104]

Though there is no corroborative evidence that this was a typical Marianist course in doctrine in the 1920s, it seems likely because of the common interprovincial formation programs.

Schrembs insisted on increasing enrollments at Cathedral Latin beyond the building's capacity. An annex was built that allowed the enrollment to exceed nine hundred students, but because of capital improvements and the cost of additional faculty, it required an increase in tuition.[105] The bishop agreed, but the Great Depression prevented the diocese from asking parents to pay more for Catholic education when they were no doubt tempted to send their sons to public schools.

During the period from 1931 to 1936 annual tuition from students averaged $36,000, while receipts from pastors went from $17,250 to $3,780.[106] During that same period the Marianists' salary reached a deficit of $8,250. Since the tuition was only fifty dollars per student, while the Jesuit high school, St. Ignatius, was one hundred, the Marianist principal sought a tuition increase for 1937–1938 to seventy dollars.[107] Though the tuition was eventually raised, problems persisted between the school and the diocese until 1953, when Bishop Edward Hoban agreed to transfer ownership of Cathedral Latin to the provincial of the Cincinnati Province. The Marianists assumed the unpaid portion of a $141,500 mortgage and 20 percent of the cost of a new residence for the Marianist faculty, and other fees totaling $9,500. Annual tuition in 1953–1954 was to be $125.[108] To own the most highly accredited and most prestigious school in the province was very significant. It guaranteed a Marianist presence in Cleveland that stretched back to the 1850s. St. Joseph's High School in Cleveland opened shortly before the Cincinnati Province assumed ownership of Cathedral Latin.

Whether it was Cathedral Latin or the relatively small parish high schools such as St. John the Baptist in Manayunk, Pennsylvania, in the area of Philadelphia, or Most Holy Trinity in Brooklyn, the modern character of these schools was manifested in a vast array of students' and parents' activities: athletics, a marching band, a school newspaper, a yearbook, literary publications, clubs dedicated to specific talents—photography, art, and languages—and societies fostering religious commitments—Catholic Student Mission Crusade and the sodality. The mothers' and fathers' clubs sponsored social and religious events appealing to students and religious as well as parents. Though elementary schools were attached to parishes with a wide range of social, athletic, ethnic, and pious societies, the brothers limited their commitment to the educational and devotional life of the students whose after-school activities were organized by the clergy assisted by parents. On the other hand, the Catholic high school was steeped in a social, religious, and athletic subculture that increasingly absorbed the time and energy of the Brothers of Mary. Provincials, particularly in the Cincinnati Province, which embraced California and Hawaii as well as the area encompassing Brooklyn, Baltimore, Pittsburgh, and Dayton, repeatedly warned the brothers of the dangers of engaging in those activities which were so intrinsic to modern high school life and simultaneously considered so threatening to the interior life of the teaching brother.

The 1928 provincial chapter of the Eastern Province made several "recommendations" for improving the atmosphere of the high schools: "Dancing is not to be sponsored by our schools. . . . Athletics are necessary but not to be over-emphasized. . . . Hazing is never to be tolerated. . . . Provincial must approve of any school paper. . . . PTAs [Parent-Teacher Associations] and card parties should not interfere with privacy and regularity of our communities." A summary of reports by the provincial offices listed two abuses related to activism: "Too much coming and going from the community; . . . dangerous contacts with outsiders at PTAs."[109] The provincial of the Eastern Province, Joseph Tetzlaff, represented the authority of the traditional religious life in its encounter with the high schools' threatening wedge of modernity, which appears to have been inexorably gaining momentum, particularly as the young brothers were products of these schools.

Tetzlaff's circular letters of the 1930s and his reports to the provincial chapter clearly convey his leadership in this struggle. In January 1931 he noted "attendance at athletic events are for the benefit of the students, not teachers. There must be some connection with the school before a Religious may attend."[110] Two weeks later he announced that among the "banned magazines are *Atlantic Monthly* and *Time* because they are unfair to the Church or offensive to Christian modesty."[111] At the 1937 provincial chapter Tetzlaff submitted these propositions: "Extra-curricular activities cause some religious to miss evening exercises. . . . Director has to be watchful over Religious being involved in Parents' organizations. . . . Many candidates are coming directly from our schools and often come with bad habits incompatible with the novitiate—how to work out this difficulty?" The intrusion of extracurricular activities was the prevalent concern: "Overburdening of young religious with extra-curricular activities should be stopped."[112]

During that 1937 provincial chapter there was a lengthy discussion of religious "defections," "a problem of such complexity and magnitude [that] would seem to lend itself . . . to an exhaustive, yet discrete [sic], study." Among the complexities were those related to "the varied duties of our professional and religious life . . . the modern trends and tendencies in multiple forms that must be faced in active life . . . ; and finally the great problem of bringing all these elements under the influence of deep supernatural motivation." The chapter delegates discussed studies on "personnel work and human relations . . . recognized as a science today should be a valuable aid to those who have responsibility directing religious." However, the chapter decided "not . . . to take any definitive action" on such an elaborate study.[113]

As late as 1945 Sylvester Juergens reported to Francis J. Jung, vicar general of the Society, that the St. Louis Province had "lost 58 men since I took office over nine years ago." He knew of no reason for these "defections" other than a "general lack of depth in our religious spirit," and perceived no remedy "other than a general reform toward the integral observance of the Rule." Juergens placed the responsibility for the problem on the "program of our high schools which has broken down the time-table of our communities so completely that you might almost compare the break-down with the effects of the war in Europe." Juergens then described the impact of the modern high school upon traditional religious life:

> The [religious] exercises are crowded into the morning and the evening each day and just performed physically, by a presence not by any attention or fervor. Meals are upset; breakfast immediately after Mass; a lunch at noon; supper at 5:30 P.M. These meals are most irregular in quality and in service. . . . The greatest difficulty is the extra-curricular works assumed by the Brothers in directing athletic teams . . . or taking care of other events like drama, oratory, debate, the school paper, etc. There is competition in these matters with other schools and the result is absence, over-work, contact with women (girls' schools in school affairs except athletics) and with the world and a general lack of religious silence and recollection. . . . Our meditations are not made; Brothers sleep so easily as they are tired from extra work and are staying up nights to read, study or just be alone. We have been fighting promptness and physical presence at exercises and we have achieved a minimum. This letter is gloomy but I suppose you want the truth. We have suffered from the ravages of over-activity and

superficiality, from worldliness and lack of generosity. Our greatest gains have all been physical I'm afraid.[114]

Father Juergens's critique of the negative impact of the modern high school, on the one hand, and the insistence on a professionalism among the brothers, on the other, reveal the paradoxical character of the Society of Mary during this period from the 1920s through the 1940s. A new generation of Marianists who attended the modern high schools and who were socialized in the Society during this period of professional and religious conflict received their bachelors' degrees at the University of Dayton, attending coeducational classes instructed by brothers, sisters, and lay professors. Severely restricted socially, the brothers' experiences were distinctive and, in contrast to those scholastics of previous generations, who began teaching upon the completion of one year of post-secondary education, these brothers tended to easily internalize the activist ethos of the contemporary high school.

The defensive attitude about the monastic routine of the religious life was clearly expressed by those in authority; but they did not perceive the religious activism of sodalities and other religious extracurricular activities as threatening; indeed they reflected a considerable interest among the brothers in the high school as recorded in the Marianist publication, the *Apostle of Mary*.

⚔ IV ⚔

HISTORIAN PHILIP GLEASON, WHO EXPLORED IN DEPTH AND BREADTH the meanings of Americanism and Americanization, deals with the 1920s as a period when Catholics were placed on the defensive, particularly because of the rise of another wave of nativism and anti-Catholicism revealed in the popularity of the Ku Klux Klan and the anti–Al Smith sentiment in 1928.[115] For example, in 1925 the National Catholic Welfare Conference developed a program for American Education Week (November 16–22) to underscore the contributions of Catholic schools to the life of the nation. In a letter to the pastors of the Archdiocese of New Orleans, the ordinary, John W. Shaw, noted the NCWC program and cited the enormous saving in tax dollars derived from an independent Catholic school system "as proof of our Americanism." He also referred to the schools' eagerness to be "examined by lawful authority . . . on the quality of our Americanism."[116] The successful passage of the initiative in the state of Oregon that had prohibited attendance at nonpublic schools resulted in the famous

Oregon Schools Case in 1925. Though the law was declared unconstitutional, the nativist sentiment of the so-called tribal twenties was a dominant feature of the educational topography.[117]

The movements of Americanism and Americanization were eclipsed by the Great Depression, Franklin D. Roosevelt's New Deal, and the threat of war in Europe.[118] The stock market crash exposed deep structural weaknesses of agriculture, industry, and finance—that is, interlocking directorates of banks and corporations—that had ramifications throughout the nation. A precipitous decrease in production and increased unemployment created grave doubt of the principles of laissez-faire capitalism and the virtues of rugged individualism. The New Deal's emphasis on the three Rs—relief, recovery, and reform—FDR's fireside chats, and the immediate, pragmatic relief projects generated some confidence from below, but it was not until World War II that confidence from above yielded increased employment. Permanent reforms such as Social Security, unions' rights to represent labor, and laws strengthening the social safety net secured the necessary loyalties to capitalism. But during the 1930s there was deep disillusionment with the economic system and its ideological bases.

Catholic responses to the Depression were quite wide-ranging: the encyclical of Pope Pius XI on the fortieth anniversary of *Rerum Novarum*, *Quadragesimo Anno*, on the *Restoration of the Christian Social Order*; the social thought of Monsignor John A. Ryan, head of the social action office of the NCWC, who had authored the bishops' statement on social reconstruction in 1919, a liberal document that presaged many measures of the New Deal; the personalist radicalism of the Catholic Worker movement of Dorothy Day and Peter Maurin; the Friendship Houses of interracial justice of Catherine de Hueck; Catholic trade unionism, and various forms of specialized Catholic Action—the Young Christian Students, the Young Christian Workers, and others—infused with the common method—observe, judge, act—and committed to restoring all things in the Mystical Body of Christ.[119]

As mentioned earlier, the Marianists experienced the fallout from the Depression in the closing of schools, in the drain on revenues and the need to restructure mortgages to pay interest on existing mortgages, and in the need to tighten the budgets of each of the Marianist houses.

The general chapter of 1933 emphasized the vow of poverty and adopted "as a guiding principle for this time of Depression . . . a serious effort . . . to reduce expenses and increase revenues." It summoned the "family spirit" to support general austerity. Hence, all prospective projects requiring capital investment would be "for the present abandoned." The general administration was to increase the reserve fund to sustain all projects already initiated and the "creation of new work." Though upholding traditional detachment from the world and warning about using the radio, viewing motion pictures, and attending plays,[120] the chapter decided "that the sociological training of the pupils is an integral part of their formation. It asks that in all our schools and colleges the social doctrine of the Church should be thoroughly taught." There were references to *Rerum Novarum* and *Quadragesimo Anno*, to the continuous need to prepare pupils for Catholic Action, "since social training is not a novelty with us." Because Chaminade's sodalities cultivated "organized activities ad extra," the Marianists should respond to the social encyclicals "with zest." Social training should be placed in the religious education of all pupils, not just the elite, should permeate many courses such as church history, and should be evident in the study of the Gospel and the liturgy; here one may "foster habits" and social action as well as instruct in theory. Teachers should engender a spirit analogous to athletics: "To learn by doing," "to work for the common good," and "collaboration" will produce "social results." The St. Vincent de Paul societies, Catholic Youth Movements, and Catholic social clubs were extolled as vital examples of Catholic Action.[121]

The Marianist most deeply associated with Catholic Action was William Ferree, ordained a priest in 1937 and during the next two years a professor of philosophy at the scholasticate at Mount St. John and the University of Dayton. In a series of articles in *Apostle of Mary*, published at Mount St. John, Ferree focused on the "Principles Governing the Roles of Sodality in Our Secondary Schools." Steeped in the writings of Chaminade, Ferree noted that the original Bordeaux Sodality was dedicated to the "complete spiritual life: instruction, rule of life, exercise of devotion, and even the Sacramental aids of the Church." In contrast, the sodality in the contemporary Marianist high school was an "extra-curricular activity" incapable of assuming the responsibility for the total spiritual life of the school.[122] Since the Society of Mary in the school was charged with integrating religion into the entire school, sodalities should consider their roles limited to those tasks not directly manifested in the high school. Even in Chaminade's time the sodality was to be the "complement" of the school; this provided the religious with the means to follow up the work of education even to "old age." Ferree cited the early "Sillon" of Marc Sangnier in France as analogous to sodalities for alumni. Dedicated to completing the sodality ideal that the school has absorbed, the directors of sodalities in Marianist high schools should, according to Ferree, "concentrate . . . [their] efforts on systematic spiritual direction, on exterior Catholic Action and on the motivation of all activities by an intense "filial love and devotion to the Blessed Virgin." To be effective, sodality activities had to be integrated "with all other spiritual activities of the school so that the whole forms one unified program."[123] As one who was a specialist in the writings of Chaminade, he perceived the school as the successor of the Madeleine Sodality of the early nineteenth century.

Ferree placed a strong emphasis on the sodality ideal in the school, which made it important for all Marianists to become like sodality directors, responsible "for the success of the school as a whole in its apostolic mission." Hence, the sodality, in Chaminade's vision, should not be an extracurricular activity, but rather it was intrinsic to the core of a Marianist school, which entails a "total reorientation" whereby the actual student in sodality is relieved of the burdens of being the only "manifestation of the ideal." This allows the sodality to pursue "an increased exterior activity in the works of the Christian apostolate." In an article in the *Nouvelle Revue Théologique*, William Joseph Chaminade was considered a precursor of Catholic Action. According to Ferree, however, his struggle for the restoration of order was political and defensive, while the modern Catholic Action of the sodality was a social and moral offensive. The leadership of the sodalists in Catholic Action was dependent on individual spiritual direction and on the personal sanctification of the individual sodalist by developing a life of filial piety to Immaculate Mary.[124]

Ferree appropriated Chaminade's description of the Bordeaux Sodality and altered it to apply to the religious scope of the Marianist high school's activities, which included the school sodality.[125] Chaminade wrote of the "intense Christian life" and secondly of "an apostolic zeal" inspired by a "filial love of the Blessed Virgin Mary."[126] Ferree's list of school activities included religion classes, retreats, weekly chapel services, vocation week, religious societies such as Holy Name, St. Vincent de Paul, and the Catholic Student Mission Crusade, as well as other extracurricular activities, athletics, drama clubs, and so on.[127] In contrast to the perennial criticism of extracurricular activities as invasive of the interior life and as representative of "the heresy of activism," Ferree's interpretation of the apostolic life of the school, inspired by the interior life, appears as a countervailing model not only of the school's embodiment of the Bordeaux Sodality ideal, which predated the foundation of the Society, but also as a model for integrating the monastic spirituality and the apostolic spirit of the Marianists within the context of the high school. The unity of the Christian life and, it seems, of the Marianist life "is a step toward a much more fundamental view of the Christian life whereby it is no longer to *unite* the two, for the simple reason that they are one already." To deal with them separately was, in Ferree's vision, "the result of confusing the mental abstraction for the concrete reality and acting accordingly"; the external and interior life "are as much one as body and soul are one human personality." Though he admitted that in the "practical field we must pretend to unite them, we must also struggle to readjust our practical efforts to unite activity and the interior life to the realization that they already are one."[128]

Joseph P. Chinnici, O.F.M., has cultivated a distinctive field in the history of spirituality, in which the thought of William Ferree gains clarity.[129] Ferree's unity of interior prayer and apostolic action is in the tradition of John Carroll, Isaac Hecker, Mother Théodore Guérin, Virgil Michel, and others. These historical figures recognized the unity of spirituality and ministry, monastic prayer and all human activity, and liturgical worship and social justice; they perceived God's presence in humanity in the affective terms of human relationships. Hence, Ferree's view of the inherent unity of the interior and apostolic life may be perceived as an antidote to the fragmentation between traditional spirituality and modern culture, but more importantly his view was based on an understanding of the foundational unity of an incarnate God, the son of Mary and brother of Mary's adopted sons, the Marianists.

There is no evidence that William Ferree was consciously applying the inherent oneness of the Christian life to the Marianist vocation; perhaps some Marianists considered his remarks truisms because they would tend to understand their interior and exterior lives as integral. There is ample evidence, however, derived from provincial chapter reports and provincial circular letters to substantiate a division between these spheres.

Ferree was a rising star on the Marianist horizon. He was encouraged to pursue graduate studies in philosophy at the Catholic University of America, with particular emphasis on social Catholicity; his master's thesis was entitled "Individual Responsibility in Social Reform" (1941), and his 1942 Ph.D. dissertation was "The Act of Social Justice." He was so highly esteemed by the provincial, Walter C. Tredtin (1938–1948), and his council that Ferree was appointed editor of *The Marianist*, the descendant of *The Apostle of Mary* (1942–1944), general manager of Marianist publications (1944–1953), and director of Mount St. John, which was, as mentioned earlier, the house of formation.[130] From my interviews with Marianists who were in formation during this period, there is a broad consensus that Ferree was articulating a new model for the Marianist way of life, which ran counter to the prevailing schism between the interior life, or the spiritual exercises, and the works of the apostolate.

He also introduced a strong intellectual strain into formation that ran counter to the anti-intellectualism of the scholasticate. He consistently structured his ideas on the documents and conceptual framework of William Joseph Chaminade. Perhaps a majority of brothers, who were thoroughly immersed in the activities of the school did not so clearly articulate the integral life, but they may have sensed teaching as an occasion of grace and perhaps in the quiet of the enclosure absorbed the full meanings of their Marianist life. Some may have easily bridged the cloister and the classroom. Joseph Simler and William Ferree, on the other hand, appear to have gone a step further; they understood the common ground of the interior and the exterior obviating the need for bridges.

Despite the support of Ferree by Tredtin, the latter was still deeply committed to drawing rigid lines of separation between the secular life of school activities and the religious life within the traditional atmosphere of docility toward authority. For example, in his report to the 1944 provincial chapter, Tredtin explicitly forbade religious to attend dances; he told directors to "suppress" all "social visits" with families "particularly those families with girls and those serving refreshments." The provincial also wished to quash anything in the communities that would undermine traditional authority: "Concerning obedience some religious want to talk to the Superior as man to man; this attitude is not inspired by faith." There was also a proposition allowing brothers "to propose names for directorship and vote on the transfer of a director upon the completion of his term." Since this process was not included in the constitutions it was "voted out."[131]

The majority of the propositions submitted to provincial chapters during the period 1920–1945 were related to traditional areas of the religious life, such as prayer schedules, recruitment efforts, and professional qualifications of the teaching brothers. Conformity to tradition within the high school culture was the prevailing concern of the delegates to the provincial chapters. Amid the democratic proposals was the recruitment "of Negro candidates" for the Province of Cincinnati. In the 1920s there was consideration of recruiting Hawaiian natives on a case-by-case basis with no immediate results. However, in response to the question of recruitment of blacks, the Cincinnati chapter of 1945 decided that "for the present we would have to refuse acceptance of them because of the nature of our S.M. works and it would hamper our work for recruitment."[132] Though the delegates did not admit to harboring racial prejudice or discrimination, they rationalized their decision on the basis that students and prospective candidates for the Society could not adapt to the presence of black brothers. Such a racist admission policy was characteristic of the vast majority of religious communities of men and women, as well as of pastors of many northern parishes and nearly all southern parishes. It was not until the late 1940s that the first black brother professed vows as a Marianist.

A democratic movement occurred in the St. Louis Province in 1946 prior to the provincial chapter. There were meetings at South Side High School in St. Louis, and two groups "met in Texas" to draw up a list of nominees for the election to the chapter.[133] Sylvester Juergens reported to Francis Jung, vicar general of the Society, that those at the meeting in St. Louis avoided "all uncharitableness" and based their proposal on a liberal interpretation of canon law "permitting preliminary meetings to evaluate the suitability of candidates." Juergens was opposed to this "caucusing" but did not prohibit such meetings.[134]

The origin of these moderate reforms in the Cincinnati and St. Louis Provinces may be traced to several experiences: the predominance of student-government models of democracy in their schools; the union of religion and social studies, the Catholic Action model—observe, judge, act; and the impact of World War II as a catalyst of Americanization. The predominance of large high school communities influenced by a new generation drawn to a cosmopolitan spirit—in contrast to the small, relatively conformist and less educated elementary-school communities—were likely to promote modest reforms within the context of traditional structures of the religious life.

During the war the European communities directly experienced conflict. Just as in the First World War, the French Marianists were conscripted into the armed services.[135] Many brothers, including the American inspector general, Michael Schleich, sought refuge in Spain. Schleich became a friend to Carlton J. Hayes, a Catholic and former professor of history at Columbia University, the U.S. ambassador to Spain, whose son was a student at a Marianist school in Saragossa. As will be explored in the next chapter, the Marianist missions were severely curtailed during the war. The American Marianist seminarians in Fribourg returned to study at St. Meinrad's Seminary in southern Indiana. St. Louis College in Honolulu, taken over for the war effort as a hospital, was the American Marianist house most directly affected by the conflict. Eventually the students of St. Louis shared the facilities of McKinley College until 1945. Many working and retired brothers helped in hospitals and on campuses in support of the armed services. Though Pius XII had urged religious orders to elect Americans as general superiors, the American provinces' inexperience of the direct burdens of war and the ascendancy of the Marianists in the United States also influenced the election of Sylvester Juergens as the first American superior general in 1946.

His election certainly represents the growing dominance of the American provinces. Of 2,215 Marianists, 866 were members of the two American provinces. Though there were many secondary schools in the other provinces, the high school was a distinctively American institution. Marianist high schools were adapted to the requirements for accreditation, which entailed modernization of the academic program, administration, extracurricular activities, and professionalization of the faculty. The schools' Catholic character was protected by the religious separation rooted in a devotional subculture, by the opposition to secularism, and by academic courses and school activities integrated by Catholicity. William Ferree proffered a vision of a united interior and exterior life that was not fully appreciated until Vatican Council II. Though many Marianists promoted Catholic Action and the sodality as unifying forces in the religious life of schools, those aspects of modern high school that promoted Marianists' interaction with students in extracurricular activities, with lay teachers, and with parents and families were perceived as breaking down the separate sphere of Marianist life that was originally intended to protect the brothers from the contagion of the world and to provide a secure atmosphere for the cultivation of the interior life and the spiritual exercises. The positive features of the teaching apostolate were still in tension with the Marianist devotional commitment; Ferree and others were promoting the unity of prayer and apostolate: ministry as spirituality.

CHAPTER SEVEN

Traditions and Transitions
1945–1960

❧ I ❧

WORLD WAR II ENDED THE DEPRESSION AND INITIATED SEVERAL social and economic changes. The general prosperity stimulated the growth of suburbs which in turn effected the decline of core urban areas. The great black migration from the South to northern cities, such as Chicago, Detroit, and Milwaukee, created a white backlash that included Catholic parishes. Some Catholic bishops, such as Joseph Ritter of Indianapolis and later of St. Louis, and Edwin O'Hara in Kansas City, desegregated Catholic schools and healthcare facilities. Jim Crow Catholicism was gradually declining in the South, but only after the Civil Rights Act of 1964 would it finally collapse. Similar transitions among the Marianists in this area were relatively early; in 1947 an African-American entered the novitiate of the St. Louis Province.[1]

Those servicemen returning from wartime duty were provided with the "G.I. Bill of Rights," which included funds for college education. Catholic colleges and universities developed into thriving centers of higher education, with enrollments increasing three- or fourfold in a matter of a few years. The University of Dayton and St. Mary's University in San Antonio went from modest institutions of about six hundred to over two thousand students, while a diversified lay faculty was recruited to keep pace. To adapt to the growing number of new students, curricular changes were introduced in business, education, law, nursing, and engineering; amidst these changes the religious tenor was still set by the traditional neo-Thomistic synthesis. Mandatory mass attendance was another traditional measure supportive of the separate Catholic subculture. However, from the mid-1950s onward

197

this and other traditions gradually gave way to respect for Christian plural-ism in a climate of freedom.

The Catholic Action model, so vigorously promoted by William Ferree in the Marianist sodalities, gained momentum in the postwar world. The social Catholicism of the Young Christian Workers, the Young Christian Students, and the Christian Family Movement was particularly vibrant in Chicago, where Bishop Bernard Sheil founded his School of Social Studies, and where Monsignor Reynold Hillenbrand fostered the Liturgical Move-ment and recognition for the rights of labor. These were joined by labor priests and Catholic interracialists such as George Higgins and Daniel Cantwell.[2]

The intertwining of tradition and change may be perceived in terms of self-identity in tension with forces outside of Catholic spheres. There was a surge of Americanism in the postwar era, a trend evident in the victorious war over the antidemocratic forces of German Nazism, Italian fascism, and Japanese militarism and imperialism. The attitude of Americanism was complemented by the *process* of Americanization that was apparent in political activism, in organizational structures, and in professional associa-tions. Marianists reflected these trends in their own academic institutes for continuing education, in the establishment of offices of public information in their schools, and the promotion of democratic education, that is, alter-native vocational education. For example, Brother Louis J. Faerber's disser-tation on high school education for the nonacademic or remedial student was dedicated to "Mary, Heavenly Shepherdess, God's Provision for Indi-vidual Differences." Brother Faerber based his argument on American democratic principles as well as on the fundamental equality of all God's children. Rather than "shunting off those pupils who fail to the public schools" the Catholic secondary school has an obligation to provide for "equality of educational opportunity" by introducing curricular changes to meet the needs of those who could not adapt to the standard sequence of academic courses.[3]

There is a general consensus among both those living in this era and later historians evaluating the period that a strong religiosity prevailed. In pub-lished essays derived from two symposia held at the University of Notre Dame in the late 1950s, Will Herberg opened his treatment with these remarks.

> Whatever may be true about the religious situation, it certainly can not be
> doubted that religion is enjoying a boom of unprecedented proportions in Amer-
> ica today. Well over 95 percent of American people identify themselves reli-
> giously, as Protestants, Catholics and Jews, an incredibly high figure by all

available standards of comparison. The proportion of Americans who are church members—that is, actually on the rolls of the churches—has nearly doubled in the past half century; in the last twenty years indeed, church membership has been increasing twice as fast as the population.[4]

Despite this growth in popular religiosity, there was still a trend toward secularism, not only in ideas but, said Herberg, "in attitudes and values as well." First adumbrated in a 1955 book *Protestant, Catholic and Jew: An Essay in Religious Sociology*, Herberg's thesis on the Americanization of religion was refined in this essay.[5] The three-religion model that replaced an immigrant religious separatism was based on a commitment to American democracy and to the American way of life. Indeed, the identification of belonging to one of the three religions gave Americans a heightened sense of citizenship and a positive assessment of their roles in society. The secularism of America was being absorbed into one's American Catholic or Jewish identity. Herberg concluded that some American Protestants, Catholics, and Jews held creedal claims in opposition to "the American way of life," but the stronger trend was in the opposite direction.[6] Regardless of the long-range value of Herberg's thesis, the Americanization process was a dominant factor in the decade prior to the Second Vatican Council and certainly was demonstrated in Marianist schools, colleges, and universities.

Will Herberg discerned the demise of immigrant separatism as early as 1955, the same year John Tracy Ellis perceived a "frequently self-imposed ghetto mentality which prevents [Catholic scholars] from intermingling as they should with their non-Catholic colleagues." There were other significant factors in Ellis's critique, including anti-Catholicism, immigrant status, and the absence of a vital center of graduate education in the diffuse and competitive system of higher education.[7] The story of the Marianists during this period reflects more the Americanization process than the ghetto mentality. As educators they were committed to democracy and to the apostolic vocation without a strong stress upon the traditional discipline of the interior life. This latter development appears to reflect the influence of William Ferree, who proffered a synthesis of the interior and the apostolic life during the 1940s and early 1950s, when he was so influential in the scholasticate at Mount St. John. Hence, there was a greater emphasis on the transitions rather than the traditions in the crucial period 1945–1960.

The following wide-ranging discussion opens with the general chapter of 1946, chaired by the first American superior general, Sylvester J. Juergens. The treatment of his visitations to the Far East and Latin America includes a brief synopsis of the American missions in these areas as well as later missionary movements in Africa. Three years after assuming office, Juergens, in consultation with the Cincinnati provincial, Walter Tredtin, established the Pacific Province, an official recognition of the distinctive Marianist presence on the western rim of the country. This chapter closes with a consideration of trends in education during the 1950s.

The working brothers, Chaminade's "Third Category of the Society of Mary," developed a "class consciousness" during the postwar world, which was expressed in their own periodical, *The Working Brother*, comparable to *The Marianist Educator*. In a sense this movement among the working brothers represents the pluralism of the community, which was augmented by gradual racial integration. The high enrollments at Dayton and St. Mary's Universities and the diversity of the curricula convey a sense of the modernization of higher education. While women religious were immersed in the Sister Formation Conference, this community of men religious was also experiencing structural changes, though the anchor of tradition was still quite evident.

◌ II ◌

IN HIS FIRST BRIEF MESSAGE TO THE SOCIETY OF MARY, SYLVESTER J. Juergens reported on the "frank spirit of fraternal love" that characterized the "post-war union" of the general chapter of 1946, which elected him the first American superior general. Meeting in Switzerland during the weeks of August 1946, in the wake of World War II and the advance of the Soviet Union into Eastern Europe, a deeply serious tone pervaded the statutes passed by the chapter. The general administration was mandated to appoint a committee to "elaborate a program" to foster the practice of personal consecration to Mary in accord with the Marianist vow of stability grounded on filial piety to Mary.[8]

In honor of the celebration of the triple centennial—arrival of the Society in the United States, the foundation of the University of Dayton, and the death of Father Chaminade—the university established the Marian Library. The chapter "heartily" approved this library, which became the largest repository of Mariana, with every conceivable media represented in the collection: printed manuscripts, records, audio and video tapes, music, museum pieces from hundreds of cultures throughout the world, and popular-art renderings of Mary from nearly every nation in the world.[9]

The codification of tradition, though with a modest nod to adaptation, included a commitment to the continuity of elementary schools. Juergens noted that the chapter was "reacting against current hostility to primary schools."[10] As provincial of the St. Louis Marianists, he had witnessed the hostility of many pastors to the costs of single-sex parochial schools. Brother Bernard Schad, elected inspector general of schools, had proposed a plan for recruiting and training scholastics for elementary education when he was inspector of the Cincinnati Province. Nevertheless, two Baltimore elementary schools closed in the 1940s and the downward trend continued irreversibly.[11]

As a vital sphere of the Society's apostolate, the chapter encouraged "the creation of projects among our graduates: study clubs, retreats, sodalities, alumni associations." Juergens captured the postwar mood of the culture: "The futility of life has been impressed on men by the horrors of war and the uncertainties of peace."[12] Such a mood was later perceived as the cause of many veterans entering seminaries and novitiates. Between 1946 and 1961 the numbers of Marianists in the United States increased by nearly 100 percent, with the majority entering after the war.[13] There were more diocesan and religious-order seminaries founded between 1945 and 1965 than were founded in the period since 1791 (the year of the foundation of the first seminary, St. Mary's Baltimore).[14]

The chapter strongly reasserted the mixed clerical-lay character of the Society. Though a prospective candidate for the priesthood may have indicated his interest upon entering the formation program (at first profession the religious was asked whether he wished to be a priest, a teaching brother, or a working brother), the process for selecting particular brothers to enter the seminary was not initiated until after some years of teaching. Those involved in the selection included the council in charge of the formation, perpetually professed brothers who had served with the candidate, the provincial council, and ultimately the superior general and his council. The initial phase of the process entailed, according to Juergens, "a delicate" discernment among various spheres of the Society.

The chapter specified the spirituality required of its candidates for priesthood. They were expected to have followed the regular exercises and to have displayed an interior commitment to the monastic routine, but more particularly, certain interior qualities, "particularly a profound spirit of faith, a great spirit of abnegation, and a good judgement which enables them to appreciate persons and things correctly." Besides the quality of self-abnegation, so characteristic of the French school of spirituality, Juergens emphasized a "family spirit." The "future Marianist priest" must cultivate "a proper religious sympathy for other members of the family," thereby obviating the development of a clerical subculture. Juergens was eloquent in expressing his "esteem, love, and devotion" for the Society of Mary—"when I consider its ideals, in other words its Constitution, as something grand, glorious, divine." His shift to the first person appears to be characteristic of the American background of the superior general. He said that the model for the future Marianist priest was: "As Christ esteemed his Apostles, a future priest must recognize the religious dignity of every Apostle of Mary." This particular quality "connotes an optimism and hidden reverence" in the future Family of Mary.[15]

The priests' first responsibility was to their local communities. They conducted retreats for students and spiritual conferences for brothers. They were encouraged to be involved in Catholic Action.[16] Some teaching brothers had received advanced graduate degrees, but doctorates were principally in the sciences. In colleges and universities, the priests dominated the faculties of theology and philosophy.

Among the statutes of the 1946 chapter, the one dealing with public relations or "Publicity for the Society and its Works" was the strongest accommodation to modernity. Since the late nineteenth century, schools, hospitals, and religious communities of sisters and brothers had been advertising in various Catholic publications, including for a time in the *Catholic Directory*. The Marianists were relatively silent about their schools or the Society. Hence, this statute represents a departure not only in the promotion of the Society, but in the mode of that promotion through a "central office of publicity" which was mandated to "stimulate, control and centralize" all public-relations initiatives.[17]

The statute on "Trends in the Field of Education" urged reflection and thorough study before "rejecting or accepting" the current methodologies "eulogized" by educationists. However, the chapter strongly endorsed the professional education of the scholastics, "up-to-date libraries, subscriptions to periodicals, reviews by any religious of outstanding books" and interprovincial visits by brothers eager and qualified to learn the method current among other Marianists.[18]

Juergens's commentary on this statute blended traditional principles of Marianist education with the "masterful encyclical of Pope Pius on 'Christian Education of Youth.'" In the spirit of adaptation "to the changing needs of human society," Juergens urged a progressive spirit among "our teaching personnel," a term that implies lay teachers as well as religious. Concerned about the development of the entire child, teachers in Marianist schools should be "animated by a professional spirit," that is, conversant with the latest research. Though the schools should nurture religious vocations and be characterized by a "professional vitality to Christian education," Juergens contrasted the religious values to what he referred to as "grades education" of the public schools. To foster education of future teachers and working brothers, "centers of professional preparedness" should be established, particularly in those nations affected by the war.[19]

In the immediate postwar era, Juergens's list of the compelling needs included restoration of social and religious stability, adaptation and consolidation to changes in education and priestly ministries, and a reiteration of traditional spirituality. With a slight opening to modernity in public relations and education, the principal focus remained on nurturing the interior life of the Society. There were no statutes on the need for programs of peace and justice, for fostering civic culture in the schools, as was so clearly demonstrated in previous chapters. Sylvester Juergens was aware that there were some brothers and priests "who had expected drastic action or less traditional treatment in certain matters" and were therefore "disappointed in the work of the Chapter." All were expected to embrace these statutes as the law and in the spirit of "faith and a general religious sense accept them as such." He invoked "Obedience and Religious Stability as unifying characteristics of all the Marianists." His final remarks were on the filial relationship and communal pledge to "advance the cause of Father Chaminade, [to] increase our recruitment and . . . to promote God's Kingdom and Glory."[20]

❊ III ❧

AFTER VISITING THE RESTORED PROVINCE OF AUSTRIA, THE AMERICAN superior general visited the war-ravished Province of Japan. In 1887 the vicar apostolic of northern Japan and later archbishop of Tokyo, Bishop Osouf, successfully sought the Marianists to enter the field of missionary activity in education.[21] Morning Star School was opened in Tokyo in 1888 with only six students, but by 1891 there were over one hundred enrolled. By 1898 there were three Marianist schools: Tokyo, Nagasaki, and Osaka— the latter, Shining Star, a school of commerce. A fourth school, St. Joseph in Yokohama (1900), was opened to foreigners and was under the French Province; the American Marianists helped staff the school, which, besides the Hawaiian mission, became the major foreign-mission effort of the American Province. Eventually the other Marianist schools became incorporated into the Japanese educational system, with authority to grant diplomas, while some Marianists were appointed to chairs of French, Latin, and English at the Imperial University. Prohibited from attending religion classes during the school day, the Catholic students compensated with classes after school. One famous convert from Morning Star School was Vice Admiral Yamamoto Shinjiro, who was the English interpreter of the prince regent, later emperor of Japan. With native vocations continuously rising, particularly in Catholic areas, Nagasaki was a significant city in the Vice Province created in 1898. Most of these schools were tragically destroyed by incendiary bombs, and in Nagasaki by the massively destructive atom bomb.[22]

In his circular letter of January 6, 1948, Sylvester Juergens described the devastating impact of the war. He successfully sought an interview with Emperor Hirohito, who had received Superior General Sorret in 1924. After Juergens had described the general situation of the eight Marianist schools, the emperor "put things compactly." "Tell the boys to work, tell the teachers to make them work for the restoration of our country along the lines of the new democracy." Juergens then provided the emperor with a "digest of our Catholic philosophy of life and the general aims of the Catholic school system. I emphasized the Catholic doctrine of a soul directly responsible to God; of the need for liberty, for the right development of the personality." Juergens told the emperor of "the Catholic and American principle that just as the school exists for the boy, so a government exists for the citizen." As Angelyn Dries, a historian of American missionary efforts, points out, this blend of American and Catholic values was emblematic of the general missionary thrust during this period.[23] According to Juergens, the emperor understood, and after further discussion on the impact of war he told Juergens that the Marianist schools should "teach morality based upon religion." In discussing the church's opposition to communism, the emperor said, "Fight Communism everywhere in the world Father, especially here in Japan."[24]

Many of the Marianists from Nagasaki, particularly the suburb Urakami, the center of the atomic blast, and their families suffered enormous losses. Seventy Japanese Marianists were drafted into the army, most of whom returned to the community. Members of the province, encouraged by Juergens, were determined to rebuild. The superior general made a direct appeal for food, clothing, and volunteer brothers and priests to aid in this renovation and renewal process. In 1953 Juergens returned to Japan, where he found the schools thriving and signs of continuous growth of Catholicism. Since 1888 twenty-five Americans had served in St. Joseph's School for foreign students in Yokohama.[25]

Juergens also visited North China, where the Marianists of the Cincinnati Province had mission schools. Li Ming, the Marianist school in Tsinan, was staffed by Austrian as well as American Marianists.[26] Angelyn Dries notes that these Marianists emphasized "the education of young boys, the future heads of households, . . . [as] the targets of evangelization."[27] The

Marianist experience in China was short-lived. Joseph McCoy, one of the American Marianists, was an enthusiastic missioner who, shortly after his return during World War II, pursued a Ph.D. in theology. His book *Advice From the Field*, derived from his dissertation, was valuable for preparing religious for missionary work.[28]

Sylvester Juergens visited one of the oldest missions of the Cincinnati Province, Colegio Ponceño in Ponce, Puerto Rico.[29] The island had become a possession of the United States as a result of the Treaty of Paris, which stipulated the separation of church and state and the influx of Protestant missionaries. According to Jaime R. Vidal, the Pentecostal churches, without a bureaucracy and unattached to any centralized foreign ecclesiastical body, "quickly acclimatized themselves in the popular class and became churches of the people, run by and for the people in a popular style." Vidal also notes that the early American bishops attempted to respond to this challenge and were most effective in retaining the elite.[30]

A group of lay teachers, headed by Maria Serra Gelabert, founded a school for boys in Ponce during the mid-1920s. With the authorization of Bishop Edwin Vincent Byrne the school flourished. When Byrne was appointed to the Diocese of San Juan he was succeeded by Aloysius Willinger, C.SS.R. A graduate of St. James School in Baltimore, the new bishop was loyal to the Marianists. The Redemptorist–Marianist association that went back to the 1860s was evident in a 1930 arrangement between Bishop Willinger and Provincial Joseph Tetzlaff.[31] With 433 members in the Cincinnati Province, 150 more than Paris, the next largest province, Tetzlaff certainly had the personnel.[32] Despite the onset of the Great Depression and the province's commitment to build Chaminade High School in Mineola, Long Island, and Chaminade High School in Santa Cruz, California, and to assume control of Trinity College in Sioux City, Iowa, Tetzlaff was drawn to Ponce particularly because the bishop assumed all the indebtedness of the school. By this time a mission consciousness had expanded throughout the American church, symbolized by the Extension Society, the Catholic Foreign Mission Society of America (Maryknoll), the Catholic Students Mission Crusade, and the American Board of Catholic Missions associated with the National Catholic Welfare Conference, the administrative arm of the bishops.[33]

The assistant director of the Social Action Committee of the NCWC, Raymond McGowan, became director of the Latin American Bureau in 1929. The latter's purpose was "to help Catholics of Latin America and the United States to know one another and to become acquainted with one another's accomplishments and experiences particularly in Catholic Action."[34] McGowan's visit to Latin America in 1931 resulted in a threefold critique: (1) The U.S. policy was patronizing toward Latin American nations. (2) North and South America had become subverted by the "false gods of secularism, nationalism, and business individualism." (3) It was necessary that U.S. and Latin American Catholics engage in cooperative programs in education and Catholic Action in order to promote the advance of Christian civilization. The rise of Protestantism in the region was an issue, but religious indifference was a more significant problem. In a 1932–1933 report on "The Church and Reconstruction in Latin America" for the NCWC and the bishops of Puerto Rico—all Americans—it is clear that the imposition of American Catholic culture, particularly with the withdrawal of Spanish clergy, was the source of problems in the islands.[35]

In September 1930 the Marianists assumed control of Colegio Ponceño de Varones in Ponce, Puerto Rico. The founder, Maria Serra Gelabert, as well as Bishop Willinger, had welcomed Brothers Adolph Eiben, Joseph Mohrhaus, and John Sauer the previous month; close to one hundred students were enrolled the first year. The Depression had disastrous effects on the Puerto Rican economy; per capita annual income was reduced from a mere $122 in 1891 (45 percent of the per capita income in the United States) to $85 in 1933. The independence movement, based on opposition to American colonial rule of the island, gained momentum during this period. Demand for political autonomy frequently erupted in violence between police and the nationalists. The American chief of police was assassinated in 1936, and on Palm Sunday (March 21, 1937) demonstrations led to a struggle with the police; in this "Ponce Massacre" nineteen were killed.[36]

Amid this political and social crisis, enrollment at the Ponce school dropped from a high of 325 in 1934 to 225 in 1937 and down to around 190 in 1942. Post–World War II prosperity, augmented by families associated with new business initiatives from the mainland, fostered a continuous rise to well over seven hundred students in the 1950s. The construction of new buildings to accommodate this growth was the result of an architectural design by Brother Bernard Schad, a Ph.D. in engineering from the University of Michigan and an inspector of schools known for his far-sighted program of graduate education for the teaching brothers. Brother Thomas Dennman was assigned by the provincial to oversee the construction of the two-story structure that opened in 1949. Like most private schools, the Marianist school in Ponce was based on an extended collegiate system, kindergarten to twelfth grade, and was limited to the elite of the island. In 1938, Edwin Vincent Byrne, bishop of San Juan, asked the Marianists to staff a school in Río Piedras, a small town overlooking San Juan, which had been under the Trinitarians, who, because of the Depression and the impact of two hurricanes, decided to withdraw from their military academy. The Marianist school, Colegio San José, which was headed by Father Joseph Tetzlaff, was intended as a school for poor students, but there was a sizable enrollment from middle-class families. The growth of this school followed the trajectory of the Marianist school in Ponce, and both shared the professionalism of the Cincinnati Province: they were the first Puerto Rican schools approved by the Middle States Association of Colleges and Schools, an accrediting agency responsible for American schools along the eastern seaboard.[37]

Between 1940 and 1960 seven Puerto Rican boys from Ponce joined the Marianists, but each of them withdrew, most within a few years. One may cite the problems of minority status in a Society rather settled in its Eurocentric perspective as perhaps the principal reason for the "defections."[38] This was also a common phenomenon among African-American brothers in the St. Louis and Cincinnati Provinces: that is, the sense of family hospitality was not strong enough to allow minorities to feel at home in the Society of Mary. (The two schools are thriving in the 1990s, with the support of lay leadership formed in the post–Vatical II renewal.)

The Catholic University of Puerto Rico, founded in 1948, had a strong Marianist imprint. Three brothers were on the faculty, and William Ferree was the first Marianist president. While the wealthy would attend a private secondary school, they were drawn to the strongly academic character of the University of Puerto Rico. Those of middling and poor background attended the Catholic University.[39] Characteristic of Ferree's deep commitment to the apostolic life in specialized Catholic Action was his role as a founder of Pax Romana, the international Christian Student Association, as well as an influence in the early years of the National Federation of Catholic College Students. He, Ivan Illich, and the Jesuit sociologist Joseph Fitzpatrick, sponsored a conference on the care of Puerto Rican migrants. At the 1956 general chapter, Ferree was elected head of education in the general council and moved to Rome. He was replaced as president of the university by Father Thomas Stanley.[40]

The most diversified mission of the U.S. Marianists was in Peru: an elite Colegio Santa Maria (Lima) was founded in 1939 by the St. Louis Province.[41] To stem the advance of Protestantism in Peru, the Servants of the Immaculate Heart of Mary (I.H.M. sisters) of Philadelphia opened an English-speaking school (1922) in Lima, where the American Methodists had founded a school that appealed to the elite families of the Peruvian capital. A year later, John J. Burke, the Paulist secretary general of the NCWC, and William Kerby, priest-sociologist at the Catholic University of America, visited Peru in their travels for some much-needed rest after the NCWC had struggled for its existence against its arch-opponent, Cardinal William H. O'Connell of Boston. John J. Burke, former editor of the Paulist journal *The Catholic World*, told the sisters they should demonstrate to the Peruvians that "the United States is not a Protestant country" and that they should articulate a dynamic apologetic rooted in the American blend of "the natural and supernatural life."[42] Because the Peruvian church was in the hands of a generally apathetic clergy, Burke urged the sisters to be patient but to summon up American drive to show the Peruvians by example that the sisters represent a "people who are able to do things." He concluded that it was as members of the Body of Christ that the I.H.M. sisters should aim to bring the Peruvians to Christ: "The future of the Catholic Church in Peru depends upon the Catholics . . . [of] the United States . . . they have its salvation in their hands."[43] Such an idealistic and paternalistic portrayal of the responsibility and the burden of the American church was perhaps implicit in the first phases of the missionary movement in the 1920s and may have been active among the Marianists in Lima. However, they departed from the United States as World War II opened with Hitler's invasion of Poland on September 1, 1939.

The Marianist school originated among aristocratic men of Lima eager to have an English-speaking school for boys but one in which Peruvian culture would be cultivated. They had consulted the papal nuncio, who had known Archbishop Edward Mooney when he was in the Vatican diplomatic corps in Japan and in 1938 was chairman of the NCWC's Committee on Education. Since Mooney had been familiar with the work of the Marianists in Cleveland when he was at the Cathedral Latin School and in Japan when he was papal nuncio, he referred the Peruvians to the provincial of the Cincinnati Province, Father Walter Tredtin.[44] Ultimately Sylvester Juergens, the provincial of the St. Louis Province, responded affirmatively after Brother Eugene Paulin returned with a favorable report on the situation in Lima. In 1939 the Colegio Santa Maria opened with an original faculty of one priest, Bernard Blemker, and three brothers, Theodore Noll, Matthias Kessel, and Robert Buss. The school was originally funded as a corporation, with each parent required to buy a share of stock, the equivalent of four hundred dollars, as well as pay a high tuition. Eventually the Marianists gained control of the board of directors of the school, with the result that low-income students could attend the college with free-tuition scholarships.[45]

In his 1949 visit to Peru, Superior General Sylvester Juergens reported that the American sisters (i.e., I.H.M. sisters) "who conduct Villa Maria for girls in the same general section of Lima, were persuaded to open a school for boys, Inmaculado Corazón de Maria, to take the first four years as a preparatory for Santa Maria. That school is also completely filled."[46] The I.H.M. and the Marianist schools represented the need for the elite of Lima to educate their daughters and sons to fulfill their national aspirations to play a significant role in the world economy.

The Colegio San Antonio, also founded in the port city of Callao near Lima, became a Marianist school in 1943. Enrolling students from the poor and the lower middle classes, it was actually a parish school of the principal church in the area; enrollment figures climbed to more than two thousand male students within a short time.[47]

In the tradition of Chaminade, who founded the first Marianist normal school, the men of the St. Louis Province opened Escuela Normal Rural in Chupaca, located in the highland region of central Peru. The school, which had been founded by the Maryknoll Brothers in 1943 became a Marianist mission in 1944. In 1949 there were fifty-two students, mostly indigenous men, though the school was Spanish-speaking. It was divided into two courses; an elementary school of six grades with two hundred students and a course for teacher training run by the government. Because of the unity of church and state, religion was a regular part of the curriculum.

In his 1949 report Juergens wrote that after a five-year effort under Marianist leadership, new school buildings with not only running water but also inside toilets had recently been constructed. "The whole set-up promises to be a show place for the entire mountain area of Peru," reported Juergens. He had visited with the minister of education, "who has asked that his son be enrolled in the American Sisters' school [Juergens never mentions the I.H.M.'s by name] . . . and he promised personal attention to making the 'Escuela Normal Rural de Chupaca' one of the outstanding schools of its kind in the nation." Juergens concluded: "I do not know of a single work of ours that calls for more religious stamina [two Marianist priests attended to the ministry of six missions in distant areas] than the noble mission of our three Marianists in Chupaca on top of the Andes in Peru."[48] However, with the majority of the faculties of both schools lay teachers, the Marianists eventually (1953) turned the schools entirely over to the government. By that time the Society had opened a parish in the Lima area in 1949, a postulate near Lima in 1951, and later, in 1957, a school in Trujillo. With the growth of native vocations Peru became a province in 1979.[49] In the late 1990s, about one-half of the members of the province are Americans, one of whom is Father Lawrence Jordan, a former principal of Chaminade College, St. Louis, Missouri.

The Marianist presence in Africa originated in 1957, when John Elbert, provincial of the Cincinnati Province, responded favorably to the priests of the Society of African Missions (S.A.M.) to teach at St. Patrick's College in Asaba, Nigeria. Elbert's decision was preceded by a visit to the area, an interview with the local bishop, a discussion with the S.A.M. priests, and a consultation with the recently elected superior general, Paul Hoffer of the French Province.[50] As the United States was entering a new phase in the civil rights movement, and as the Catholic Church had begun to desegregate its institutions in many dioceses, a new interest in Africa was beginning. By the mid-1950s the Congregation of the Holy Ghost, the "Spiritans" as they were called, had been for nearly a century committed to promoting missions in Africa and had initiated the Institute of African Studies at Duquesne University in Pittsburg in 1957.[51] Pius XII's encyclical *Fidei Donum* was dedicated to fostering missionary activity in sub-Saharan Africa. The encyclical stated: "The present situation in Africa, both social and political, requires that a carefully trained Catholic elite be formed at once from the multitudes already converted."[52] Influenced by these words of Pius XII, Elbert, whose Cincinnati Province was still the largest in the Society, enthusiastically responded to the call from Nigeria to staff a college to train prospective leaders in the West African nation. The pioneer Marianists in Nigeria were Fathers William Anderson and Joseph Bruder and Brothers Bernard Jansen and Raymond Streiff. In the 1960s the American Marianists expanded their presence in Africa to include schools in Kenya, Malawi, Zambia, and a second school in Nigeria.[53] An early pioneer, Brother George Dury had a considerable impact at Chaminade College in Malawi; during his later experiences in the 1980s he designed solar heating panels for a special outdoor cooking oven and grill in order to save the rapidly depleting wooded area.[54] The French Province established missions in Tunis, Libya, and Syria (1882), what was then the Congo (1946), and the Ivory Coast (1961); in the 1990s the Swiss Province was located in Togo. Later missions included the Pacific Province's schools in Korea and Australia in the early 1960s, though later the Cincinnati Province assumed control of the Australian mission. There was also a brief mission to Lebanon, while the Cincinnati Province established a mission in Ireland.

❧ IV ❧

THE MARIANISTS IN CALIFORNIA AND HAWAII WERE THE AMERICAN communities most resembling missions because of their distance from provincialates and the persistence of a frontier-like autonomy. During their journey to visit the missions in the Far East in 1948, Walter Tredtin and Sylvester Juergens discussed the problems entailed in governing the Western rim of the Cincinnati Province. After a visitation to Hawaii and California, Juergens agreed with Tredtin's proposal to establish a new province. In a circular letter to that effect issued May 16, 1948, Juergens established the Pacific Province (often referred to as the Province of the Pacific) and announced the appointment of Walter Tredtin as provincial and Brother James Wipfield as inspector.[55] According to Wipfield's memoirs, "There were rumors in the wind years before the establishment of the Province of the Pacific that something had to be done about Hawaii and California. With provincial visits occurring only at five-year intervals during the 1930s and 1940s many brothers were frustrated: "They don't care about us out here." "Why should we be supporting the houses back East?" "Any time we want to do something we have to write back there."[56]

Among the parish elementary and high schools in California and Hawaii staffed by the Marianists, none was owned by the Society. However, there were signs of vitality; construction was on the way for Riordan High School, which Archbishop John Mitty had designated for the Marianists; St. Louis College in Honolulu, a secondary school owned by the Society, was in the process of becoming a college of higher education. The details of boundaries were worked out prior to the official announcement of the establishment of the new province and included the states of Washington, Oregon, California, Idaho, and Nevada, and the territories of Alaska and Hawaii. Other areas in the Pacific were Australia, the Philippines, and the islands of the Pacific. There were 112 Marianists and eight schools in the province.[57]

Brother Wipfield, introduced to the Society while a student at St. Martin's School in Baltimore, had served in Hawaii for ten years. He was the principal of Chaminade High School in Dayton when he was named inspector— in actuality, inspector-treasurer. Father John A. Elbert succeeded Tredtin as provincial of the Cincinnati Province. It was at Tredtin's golden jubilee celebration of his first vows, held St. John's School for Boys in the Brooklyn diocese, that the new province was approved. Immediately prior to his appointment as provincial, Elbert was president of the University of Dayton. Whereas Tredtin was a native of Dayton, Elbert, born in New York City in 1895, entered the postulancy at the age of thirteen; he attended St. Barbara's School when the brothers took over the boys' school in 1907. One year later he traveled to Dayton to enter the Marianists. Awarded a Ph.D. in philosophy at the University of Cincinnati, he was president of Dayton University in the postwar boom in Catholic higher education. Elbert was a thoughtful man whose circular letters revealed a style of leadership that stressed the traditional rather than the transitional values of Marianist roles in the unfolding of modernity.[58]

Elbert agreed to transfer twenty-five members (volunteers) of the Cincinnati Province to the new Pacific Province on a basis of five a year. The new province was to compensate the Cincinnati Province two thousand dollars for each priest, teaching, or working brother, for the educational expenses of the transferee amounting to a total of fifty thousand dollars. Characteristic of the continuous financial hardship of the Pacific Province, in 1973 there was an indebtedness of twenty-three thousand dollars for the twenty-five Marianists transferred from the East. That year the debt was canceled.[59]

There were only two sites owned by the Society, St. Louis in Honolulu and the old Chaminade High School property in the Santa Cruz mountains. St. Louis College housed the new provincialate; in 1949 the postulancy was established at Santa Cruz, when a group of brothers cleared the property and renovated the buildings, including a new chapel.[60]

When the province held its first chapter in August 1949, there were thirteen priests, 110 teaching brothers, and two working brothers; there were only seven schools staffed by the Marianists, four in Hawaii and three in the San Francisco area. St. Louis College was staffed by thirty-three brothers; two priests were chaplains, and the president was Brother Herman J. Gerber. With a paucity of priests over the years, the rule was set aside for the Pacific Province. Bishop James J. Sweeney, consecrated first ordinary of Honolulu in 1941, promoted the high-school dimension with a strong vocational-education component, while Tredtin and Wipfield favored expanding the school to a junior college. Since Wipfield had experience in vocational training, he introduced an industrial arts program in 1950. In 1958 Chaminade College, with an independent, full four-year program, became a reality. St. Louis Elementary School for Boys closed in 1956, while the brothers withdrew from the Cathedral School for Boys as part of the general deemphasis on elementary education. St. Joseph's School in Hilo was referred to by Tredtin as coeducational but it was actually coinstitutional, that is, separate single-sex classes in the same building. "This condition is being tolerated for a short period of time in the greater interests of Catholic education."[61] After sixty-three years of service, the Marianists left St. Joseph School in the central section of San Francisco. Though they had attempted to terminate their commitment to St. James School in the city, they deferred to the "petulant aged pastor" and agreed "to staff the five upper classes of boys of the grade school for two more years. Prior to the opening of Riordan High School, the only viable school in the Bay area was St. Joseph's High School in Alameda.[62] Despite the 1946 general chapter's endorsement of the continuity of the Society's role in elementary education, four years later the three American provinces were limiting their education ministry to the secondary and collegiate levels. Had the parish elementary schools remained single-sex classes, it is likely the brothers would still be involved in that sphere of education. The 1949 chapter of the Pacific Province considered a proposal to maintain existing schools but "the religious . . . are not obliged to expose themselves to spiritual dangers necessarily connected with coeducational institutions." The withdrawal from the parish schools in San Francisco would have been required to staff five freshmen classes and "three upper classes" at Riordan High School. Also, a priest and four brothers were assigned to the postulate at Chaminade Preparatory School, on the Santa Cruz property.[63]

Wartime industry and the precipitous rise in population affected Catholic education and other ministries in the Archdiocese of San Francisco. Prior to the war, the parish high school was the dominant model; in 1933, 71 percent of the nearly six thousand Catholic students in secondary schools attended those schools. While women religious staffed most of these parish-based schools, the boys' central high schools were maintained by orders of men. Though the Marianists were to staff a new diocesan central high school in the mid-1930s, the Great Depression precluded such an investment.[64]

In contrast to the archdioceses in the Midwest and the Northeast, San Francisco did not develop a well-organized central office of education. Father Peter Yorke, educator, liturgist, editor of the *Monitor*, the archdiocesan newspaper, and labor priest, was Archbishop Riordan's most active educational leader during the 1890s when teachers institutes were held for centralized planning in curriculum, particularly religious education, grading, and administration.[65] Yorke, whose textbooks in religious education were a sophisticated improvement over the *Baltimore Catechism*, was never superintendent of education. That position was not created until 1915, when Archbishop Edward Hanna appointed Father Ralph Hunt as the first superintendent. Some centralized planning occurred. Hunt was assisted by the Scholastic Council, a policy-making board composed of seasoned teachers and administrators.[66] Later a team of educators, formed at the Catholic University of America and led by Edward A. Pace, psychologist and educationist, established institutes that led to a summer-school extension program that provided university credits leading toward a bachelor's degree. However, as Brother Lawrence Scrivani pointed out in his brief history of Catholic education in San Francisco, "It became apparent that the Catholic schools in the Archdiocese of San Francisco were more appropriately a system of schools than they were a school system. Systemization came only after a thriving infrastructure had been developed *ad hoc* by the combined efforts of pastors, parents and religious orders."[67]

The diocesan secondary schools of the 1950s were initiated by Father James T. O'Dowd, later auxiliary bishop. Named assistant superintendent in 1936, O'Dowd responded to the general demand for more secondary schools by presiding over the construction of "four central high schools, one for each of the four counties, San Francisco, Alameda, Marin and Santa Clara."[68] Riordan High School for Boys in San Francisco fulfilled a significant role; five years after its opening in 1949 it had an enrollment of 842 students and a Marianist faculty of seventeen brothers with two priests as chaplains. Since there were ten lay teachers on the faculty the ever-increasing numbers of vocations during this period did have a slight impact, but the proliferation of schools far exceeded the increase in brothers.[69] For example, in 1963 the enrollment was nine hundred, but there were thirty brothers and fifteen lay teachers.[70]

The first Marianist principal/director was Brother John McCluskey, who had received his master's degree from Case Western Reserve University in 1941 and was enrolled in the Ph.D. program at the University of California at Berkeley. After three years, a traditionalist faction, alienated by McCluskey's professionalism, brought about his resignation. He later succeeded Wipfield as the inspector of schools.[71] Brother John Samaha was the first archdiocesan superintendent of high schools and the first Marianist to be named to that position.[72]

During their "triumphal" tour of the province in 1949, Tredtin and Wipfield visited Fresno-Monterey. They knew Bishop Willinger, a Redemptorist, who as a young boy had attended a Marianist school in Baltimore. This was the same bishop who was instrumental in bringing the Marianists to Puerto Rico. Chaminade Preparatory School for Postulants was in the Santa Cruz section of Willinger's diocese, and Tredtin had hoped to staff another school in the diocese but there was no prospect of a new high school.[73]

Tredtin and Wipfield visited St. Monica High School in the Santa Monica district of the Archdiocese of Los Angeles, where the brothers had been located for only two years. After the pastor, Monsignor Nicholas Conneally, indicated his intention not to build a boys' high school but to maintain a coeducational high school, Tredtin asserted his opposition and "carried his case to Cardinal [Archbishop] James Francis McIntyre, a master builder of a vast array of institutions in the archdiocese numbering 830,000 Catholics in 1950."[74] McIntyre, well known for his traditionalism as both auxiliary bishop of New York and ordinary of Los Angeles, responded with characteristic certitude to Tredtin and "expressed total agreement for our position. I was amazed," said Wipfield. He went on to inform the Marianists of his plans to build three new high schools, one for the Mexican-American community, which would be "a well-equipped and well-staffed industrial school." Another high school would be in Gardena, "intended for white middle class with the usual blend of academic courses, supplemented . . . with shop courses."[75] The third was to be entirely academic. The Marianists successfully sought to run the Gardena school.

Brother Wipfield earnestly pursued a strong public-relations effort among the seventeen parish schools, potential feeders for Junipero Serra High School in Gardena, with nearly one hundred students enrolled. This was McIntyre's first school since he was appointed archbishop in 1948. Located on a twenty-acre plot in a relatively affluent area, the school reached an enrollment of six hundred students, with the faculty almost equally divided between brothers and lay teachers. Father Donald Bracht was principal; he was assisted by nine brothers and eleven lay teachers. By this time the Society had purchased land in Culver City and founded Chaminade High School for its postulants (moved from Santa Cruz) and day students. In this school there were eleven Marianists and only three lay teachers for the 244 boys enrolled in 1955, three years after its opening. St. Joseph's High School in Alameda outside San Francisco, enrolled 165 boys; there were six Brothers of Mary and one lay teacher, no doubt the coach, in 1955.[76]

The general dependence on lay teachers had been perceived by some as a compromise, as merely second-class adjuncts to the Marianist faculty. However, Brother Wipfield noted at the provincial chapter of 1956, "In recent years the lay teachers have assisted at the educational conferences of the Director, a distinct advance over previous practices of ignoring the laymen." Wipfield anticipated annual retreats sponsored by the dioceses. In the schools owned by the Marianists, the lay teachers were paid according to the scale of the public schools in the area. Despite his cautiously progressive views, Wipfield was convinced that the quality of lay teachers was generally "inferior to that of the Brothers. They lack a devotedness to the cause and stability in employment. They can not teach religion or even impart a religious tone to the secular branches. . . . They can not satisfactorily direct such activities as Sodalities, retreats, school papers, etc." Nevertheless, their presence was necessary if the Marianists were to "keep abreast of the extraordinary enrollments in Catholic school. There is much to be learned by us administrators about the selection, training, placing and remuneration and retention of lay teachers. Last summer the Brothers in California devoted an entire day of an institute to the study of this problem."[77]

A tabulation of the percentage of lay teachers on the faculty in 1955 ranged from 45 percent at Junipero Serra High School in Gardena to zero percent in the Wailuku elementary school and St. Louis junior college in Honolulu. Riordan High School lay faculty, at 30 percent, was the average for urban Catholic schools.[78] Brother James Wipfield was no impassioned liberal, but he was relatively enlightened on the need for a wage-and-benefits scale for lay teachers that was informed by the papal encyclicals on a living wage, or a "just salary" as he himself stated.[79]

The provincial inspector's reports to chapters and his correspondence placed Wipfield in the tradition of inspectors who were dominant figures in the history of the American Marianists—John Waldron, Eugene Paulin, Michael Schleich, George Sauer, and Bernard Schad. For example, in his report to the first chapter of the Province of the Pacific he identified a strong current of individualism among the teaching brothers:

> I am sorry to say [that] too many of our men are still 19th-century individualists, unwilling to cooperate with a group, unresponsive to a new idea or procedure, too complacent and self-satisfied; convinced that no improvement is possible beyond their present method. Others are individualists in the sense of being very parochial, limiting their interest to their own subject, failing to see the inter-relation to the rest of the curriculum or even to the broader aspects of the student's later life.[80]

Wipfield noted that this individualist attitude was most evident in the ways the faculty was responding to the rise in nonacademic students enrolled in Marianist high schools: "following a trend that is nationwide, we have as a group been slow to accommodate our curriculum offerings to these students." He referred to such a nonpolicy as "indefensible." Marianists must "adopt and support a policy of educating according to their needs all levels of intelligence, except the uneducable, because this is manifesting the mind of the Church, it is being true to the Mystical Body of Christ, and it will enable us to do our share in saving the working man for the Church." Associating the less academic with working-class families, Wipfield invoked the Marianist "constitutional prescription to have a special love for the poor (Art. 262)."[81]

Several Catholic social critics, who invoked the Mystical Body of Christ, were also reacting against the "social, scientific and other professionalized experts." Eugene McCarraher, a scholar of the "Cultural History of the Social Gospel in the United States, 1928–1975," has traced several "sacramental radicals" opposed to the rule of the experts, but he did not apply it to secondary education.[82] In a letter to Sylvester Juergens, Brother Wipfield illustrated his alienation with trends in education: "We in America are so enamored of the latest fad or 'group dynamics,' 'workshops,' 'opinions of the experts,' that religious superiors play a weak and pale secondary role, either as rubber stamps or mere advisors." He considered such procedures of relative value, "but often the secular point of view replaces the spiritual point of view." He supports McCarraher's thesis by referring to a "false spirit of democracy, the spirit of laissez-faire and independence that has unfortunately replaced the supernatural spirit of obedience. To invoke the 'intangible value' known as 'The Grace of God' was considered secondary to the tangible "values of the here and now."[83]

Social formation of the students in Marianist schools was the concern of many brothers and had been included in the statutes of the 1933 general chapter. In his 1956 report to the provincial chapter, Wipfield noted positive programs: a course in Catholic sociology and discussions on the social encyclicals. However, he deplored the students' narrow concept of social service, with no consideration of service to the "community at large. No attempt is made to put them into contact with the real poor." The inspector of schools concluded that if "we are sealed off from the real poor . . . we have no sense of responsibility for them." Parenthetically he remarked, "The only champion of the working class on the Hawaiian plantations is the Communist organizer."[84] Wipfield and a few other Marianists of the Pacific Province promoted the establishment of a labor school on the grounds of St. Louis College, which, according to the model established by the Jesuits in the Northeast and Midwest, would introduce workers to Catholic principles on the rights of labor to organize into unions and the significance of social justice in labor–capital relationships. With specific references to the anti-personalist bases of socialism and communism, the labor schools were engaged in direct competition with the communist organizers.[85]

Bishop Sweeney of Honolulu was reluctant to take a public stand on the labor schools or even give them his tacit approval. Wipfield told Juergens: "We have had a hard time understanding the bishop's attitude toward labor for many years. Proof abounds that the big ILWU is Commie dominated yet he has never opened his mouth or permitted others to." In a postscript in that same letter, however, Wipfield wrote enthusiastically that he had met a "Mr. Solomon K. an AFOL Business Representative," who told him that the bishop had consented to bringing a labor priest to Honolulu and that he was expecting St. Louis College to provide the facilities.[86]

The Wipfield-Juergens correspondence during the first half of the 1950s reveals the brother inspector's frustration with the erratic behavior of the provincial, Walter Tredtin. In December 1953 Wipfield indicated to Juergens his dismay with Tredtin's sudden announcement to the provincial council—"discontinuance (I don't think he said abandonment) of the junior college idea."[87]

Wipfield explained to Juergens another instance of Tredtin's alleged quixotic behavior, which entailed transferring the working brothers from St. Joseph to the teaching brothers' scholasticate at St. Mary's College (a Christian Brothers' institution) at Moraga, California. This move was made without consultation with the council and with Father Joseph Stefanelli, responsible for heading the programs of formation for the working brothers. "Sometimes," Wipfield lamented, "I feel unnecessary. I work to carry out instructions, only to see everything cancelled at the last minute. The temptation constantly arises: why make any effort at all? Everything will be undone."[88] A year later Walter Tredtin resigned as provincial. Though Juergens and Tredtin were close friends, the superior general was influenced by Brother Wipfield's correspondence and Brother Schad's report of his visitation to the Pacific Province. In any event, Leonard Fee was installed as the second provincial on October 7, 1956.[89]

Fee was one of only a few scholastics in William Ferree's study circle, and represented the ascending influence of this dominant figure. Ferree became president of the Catholic University of Puerto Rico in 1953, three years before Fee became provincial of the Pacific Province. Like Ferree, Fee was involved in formation; he was the first director of the Second Novitiate for the Cincinnati Province and continued in that position when all three provinces cosponsored the Institute for Marianist Studies. After three years in Beacon, New York, and a year in Galesville, Wisconsin, the Institute moved to a large country estate in Glencoe, Missouri, not far from St. Louis and close to the novitiate of the midwest province of the Christian Brothers. Designed for those perpetually professed brothers between the ages of twenty-six and thirty-five, the Institute was intended as a year of deepening Marianist identity both as religious and as teachers through independent study, formation classes, and research seminars that culminated in papers on topics in education, religion, or social problems. Fee entered the Society in 1927 and taught at Cathedral Latin in Cleveland for four years before entering the seminary in Fribourg. Immediately prior to his appointment to the Second Novitiate he was principal of Purcell High School in Cincinnati for several years. Though he transferred to the Pacific Province in 1949, he remained director of the Marianist Studies Institute until his appointment as provincial.[90]

Fee's policies represented a significant departure from Tredtin's traditionalism. He moved the provincialate to California; when St. Louis Junior College evolved into a four-year program and became Chaminade College in 1957, he moved the scholasticate to Honolulu despite the fact that the college also became coeducational that year. With several years of administrative experience, he implemented a 1951 chapter resolution that mandated a report from each Marianist community that was to include its mission statement and was to focus on its educational, apostolic, and religious life in light of that statement. Since several of these communities numbered over twenty brothers, Tredtin may have been reluctant to implement this measure because of his traditional notion of lines of authority. On the other hand, Fee had a confidence in local communities to generate initiatives and to assume responsibility to relate strategies to goals.

In his report to the 1957 chapter, Fee was quite candid in his evaluation of the communities' self-evaluation forms as well as the spirit of each community. For example, as a result of his visit to Junipero Serra High School in Gardena, California, Fee reported on the "realization of the school's Apostolic Mission Statement." He was gratified by the religious spirit manifested in "weekly observance of a particular point in the rule." Such a practice "may have been accountable for the fact that eight Serra boys were received by the novitiate." Nevertheless, regarding the Marianist faculty, Fee cited a "high percentage of difficult personalities, as well as poor teachers and disciplinarians."[91]

The largest high school in the province was St. Louis in Honolulu, with 1,015 students and a Marianist community of fifty-three members for both Chaminade College and St. Louis High School. According to the provincial, there was a notable "diminution of professional consciousness, and an excessive emphasis on athletics." Reports on these two schools were characteristic of the new provincial's critical approach to evaluations of the Marianist communities.[92]

In his "General Summation of the Condition of the Province," he listed four areas that were obstacles to progress. In the area of spirituality there was "a lack of a lively spirit of faith" with a corollary misunderstanding of the "virtue of obedience" and the need for "sacrifice demanded by our total dedication." The second obstacle was the lack of personnel; "the Province is spread itself much too thin." The shortage of priests, along with the prospect of only six additional clergy over the next few years, was the third barrier to progress. The Pacific Province had suffered from poor financial status almost from its origins. However, Fee concluded that on each of these four fronts there was a determination to make progress.[93]

The general direction and tone of Fee's report convey a positive understanding of his role as provincial in relationship with his confreres. Utterly free of moral exhortations and the traditional rhetoric of antipathy toward modernity as inherently opposed to the religious life, Fee's report reflects a trend toward a positive assessment of religious life, an attitude that may have been derived from the relatively idealistic ethos of the Institute for Marianist Studies. Brother Wipfield retired as inspector of schools, and Brother John McCluskey, his successor, issued his own report on the educational status of the province in 1957. Its first section was designed according to topics such as a Teachers' Institute for Marianists and was generally descriptive of school life and faculty development. Reports of individual schools included analysis as well as description.[94]

In his "Observations of the Retiring Inspector," Brother James Wipfield clearly articulated the historical trends of the province. He proudly noted that "the most healthy change in us as a teaching group" was the "emergence from the isolation of our jealous ghetto spirit" and the opening to cooperation with "professional groups," particularly "in such activities as standard testing, educational institutes, and conventions, subject-matter committees, research projects." He was gratified by the teachers' break from "rugged individualism" that made every brother a "sovereign in his own kingdom" and by the advance in a "willingness to learn from others." However, Brother Wipfield deplored the atmosphere of the schools, characterized by a lack of "serious study," by permissiveness, indeed by "hilarity and noise [that] are accepted as the order of the day." He criticized the "modern monk" as one who considered "class preparation as old-fashioned and unnecessary." Perhaps his deepest disappointment was the persistent neglect of gifted students while the "less gifted find themselves pushed, pulled and bludgeoned beyond their capability to reach a norm that was not intended for them." For many years Wipfield had been concerned with those students drawn to the arts, music, business, and mechanical trades who were frequently subjected to ridicule or opposition. "We simply cannot understand why anyone should be different. With us, mass education demands a standardized product."[95]

Characteristic of Brother Wipfield's commitment to creative teaching and the social apostolate was his perception of the Marianist life as analogous to a social cocoon.

> Our own life is one of professed uniformity by very definition; most of us are from the same comfortable middle class; we have been screened for a certain range of intelligence; we have experience with no other occupation than teaching; we are never confronted with the economic necessities and vicissitudes that worry lay people; we have no more than a theoretical knowledge of or interest in the dynamic social forces of our day, the good and bad labor unions, the giant competitive corporations, the government legislatures; we do not have women around to temper us with their outlook. We live in very narrow confines indeed! Is there any wonder then that we operate on a dead level of

standardization, inspire so few scholars, produce no creative writers either among ourselves, or our alumni—that we are not changing the world![96]

This remarkable critique is consonant with Wipfield's singular world-view. While Tredtin had lashed out at modernity as hostile to the interior life, Wipfield lashed out at modernity's impulse toward depersonalization, standardization, as well as middle-class mediocrity, all inhibiting the vitality of the Marianist apostolate. His earlier remarks were on the American penchant for the latest fads in education and "the opinions of experts." Nevertheless, he did conclude on a positive note with a nod to the effectiveness of the Marianist Education Institute for the province.[97]

The provincial leadership of Father Leonard Fee had made a significant impact in various spheres of Marianist life. Brother John McCluskey reflected the energy and commitment of his predecessor. The new office, Assistant Provincial for Zeal, was established in the Pacific Province in 1957 when responsibility for "zeal" was separated from the office of provincial that was in accord with the charism of Father Chaminade. Father Paul Kelley, the first head of zeal, issued a significant report in 1957 with an emphasis on the clerical conference and religious formation, continuing formation for the young members during the initial eight years in the Society, and a questionnaire on liturgy and the routine of prayers.[98]

At the 1957 provincial chapter, the delegates received a statistical table entitled "After Nine Years," with contrasting figures for 1948–1957. Membership increased from 115 to 177; the latter included 22 priests (100 percent increase), 141 teaching brothers (up from 105), and 14 working brothers (up from zero in 1948). The distribution of personnel represented the policies of Fee's administration: Hawaii was reduced from 80 to 70 members, while California rose from 21 to 97 Marianists. The deemphasis on elementary education was also quite significant: from 36 brothers in 1949 to 2 in 1957, while professionalization was emphasized: brothers with master's degrees rose from 15 to 32—far beyond the proportional increase in teaching brothers. The Pacific Province experienced sustained growth through the next ten years; in this process the working brothers were immersed in construction and renovation projects.[99]

❧ V ❧

GENERAL AND PROVINCIAL CHAPTERS HAD ADDRESSED THE IMPORTANCE of formation, education, and the overall dignity of the working brothers. Traditionally located on the farming property in each of the provinces, there was a greater diversification since the 1930s. There was also an increasing sense of solidarity among the working brothers, derived from their common experiences as "second-class" Marianists. The foundation of the Marianist journal *The Working Brother* in January 1946 was symbolic of the need for solidarity and was a revival of the founder's spirit for integrating the three categories in the Society, priests, teaching brothers, and working brothers. Each volume published articles on spirituality, reports of brothers' activities throughout the provinces, and the foundational role of Catholic Action. Edited by Brother John Soehnel, the journal restated its purpose in 1947: "to aim and work for the re-Christianization of labor. . . . The harmonic union into our Society of the three distinctive categories of persons, each of which is to excel in its own field, lends itself perfectly to the difficult task of the re-Christianization of labor."[100]

In *The Working Brother*, which was initially published by both provinces (prior to 1948), the writings of Chaminade were frequently cited; in his article "Hints at Holiness and Happiness as a Marianist Working Brother," Brother Aloysius Hochendoner told of his conversion experience. He was considering changing to a teaching brother, but then he began a five-year study of the *Spirit of Our Foundation*, a three-volume compilation of the writings of Chaminade and the first-generation Marianists.

> I read and reread the documents on the Working Brothers and the Society of Mary. I was fortunate to follow the religion course given to the Working Brothers by Father Ferree in '43 and '44. Mysteriously, the thought of changing categories just vanished like an ill-omened smoke. Mary was speaking to me through the Holy Spirit. There was definitely something lacking in my spiritual life. What I needed most was the Christ-life within me.[101]

Writing for confreres who were frustrated by "Superiors [who] don't understand us, [even] our fellow Brothers may slight us." Such misunderstandings were perceived as comparable to the marginalization of Mary's Son. This "Christ-life within us," and "the companionship of Mary were the sources of sustenance in the Working Brother's life."[102]

The rechristianization of labor, a theme derived from Pius XI's *Quadragesimo Anno*, was also related to the specialized Catholic Action originating with Canon Cardijn, and was organized as the Young Christian Workers (YCW). The latter was the title of Brother Ernest Avellar's article in *The Working Brother*. It was a brief account of the French branch of the YCW imported to Canada, the *Jeunesse Ouvrière Chrétienne (JOC)* or the *Jocists*. Avellar drew a historical analogy with Chaminade's "sodalities for all classes." He underscored the significance of the inquiry method, common to all specialized Catholic Action groups: "Observe, judge, act."[103] The U.S. Young Christian Workers were headquartered in Chicago and influenced by Monsignor Reynold Hillenbrand, who blended the Liturgical Movement, specialized Catholic Action, social justice, and pro-union activity into a significant social alliance.[104] Several working brothers formed a *Jocist* cell for personal sanctification, integrated the inquiry method into their workday, and developed a study program on the adaption of Chaminade's ideal working brother; the Marianist founder viewed the working brother as comparable to the Cistercian monk, who was separated from the apostolic work of the teacher but whose integrated prayers and work in the fields would be sources of grace for teaching brothers and priests.[105] Such reflection on their mission, their common life, and their role in the Society within the context of specialized Catholic Action, represents a proactive movement as well as the influence of William Ferree, the dominant figure in Marianist formation during this period.

In 1964 there were only fifteen working brothers in the Pacific Province in comparison with forty-one in the St. Louis Province. The provincial chapter of the latter province determined that all working brothers should be provided with education leading to an academic degree. This 1958 statute appears to have been the culmination of meetings held by working brothers representing the three provinces in 1955–1957. Brother Leo Slay of the St. Louis Province and Brother John Soehnel of the Cincinnati Province were energetic leaders of national seminars on working brothers' topics. Brother Slay, a chef, originated an annual Marianist culinary workshop in June 1961 at the new Vianney High School located on the grounds of the old Maryhurst Provincialate and formation center. These seminars and workshops were to the working brothers what the educational institutes were to the teaching brothers, and the clerical conferences were to the Marianist priests.[106] The Marianists' response to the class consciousness of the working brothers led to new programs that paralleled a positive response to African-American applicants to the Society.

❖ VI ❖

TO RECRUIT VOCATIONS AMONG THE AFRICAN-AMERICAN COMMUNITY had been considered unfeasible because white candidates would be deterred from entering an integrated Society. In the 1940s discrimination against black candidates began to break down. Under Archbishop John Mitty's leadership, the Archdiocese of San Francisco observed "Negro Week" in May

1944. In a letter to Father Francis J. Jung, vicar general of the Society, Brother John McCluskey, director of St. James High School, and Brother Charles Weiss, the community's annalist, noted that, "Until the war, San Francisco had very few colored people but they have flocked in to the defense industries and to the civilian positions vacated by whites; the Japanese [Americans] were evacuated early in the war, and Negroes now inhabit most of the section known as Japtown."[107] Apparently intended as St. James's observation of Negro Week, the school sodality "invited a Negro boy and girl to speak to the assembled students; the pastor (white) of the Negro mission church was present also." Some Catholic schools were integrated: "The girl, a Catholic attending a nearby Catholic high school" focused on the "religious aspect of the Negro question," that is, problems of prejudice and discrimination as violations of Christian principles and values. The boy, who was not Catholic, "gave an interesting account of the economic and social issues involved." The pastor, a member of the Society of Divine Word, responded to questions with "wholesome vigor and downright sincerity [that] proved to be inspirational for Brothers and boys alike." Since the Divine Word Seminary in Bay St. Louis was the only theological school for black Catholics aspiring to the priesthood, the pastor was in accord with the spirit of the order. The account of this interracial experience concluded on a characteristic note of optimism: "Few of the students will dare to say an unkind word about negroes in the future."[108]

This incident at St. James represented the strategy of the Catholic interracial movement founded by John LaFarge, S.J., and William Markoe, S.J., in 1932, when these two Jesuits broke with the Federated Colored Catholics (F.C.C.) under the leadership of Thomas Wyatt Turner. The F.C.C. was committed to the unity of black Catholics, to improve their status in the church, to expand opportunities for blacks within the Catholic school system, and to enlist many more black Catholics to struggle against racism in the church and society. Though LaFarge and Turner had worked together in ending Catholic racial injustice, LaFarge was convinced of the need to raise the consciousness of white Catholics as the principal path to that end; Turner was committed to raising black consciousness in the struggle against racial injustices in the church rather than "promote better race relations" in the church, as Markoe later stated. The Catholic Interracial Councils, composed of black and white leadership, gradually expanded, while Turner's F.C.C. pursued an end to discrimination at the Catholic University of America and in other areas of Jim Crow Catholicism.[109]

LaFarge had been a priest in Ridge, Maryland, a rural section in the southern part of the state. Composed of black and white parishioners LaFarge's parish was committed to advancing the education of black Catholics. In 1924 he and others formed the Cardinal Gibbons Institute, an agricultural school that, in his admiration for the moderate approach of Booker T. Washington, he frequently called the "Catholic Tuskegee." Ultimately this institution was closed because of financial indebtedness, exacerbated by conflicts between the black administrators Victor and Constance Daniel, who were advocates of Turner and his strategy, and the white board of trustees, particularly LaFarge.[110]

Ever the politician, John LaFarge was an aristocratic paternalist. In a 1921 article in *America*, he wrote, "The Negro is entitled to the best, the very best the white man may give him."[111] In 1926 he became editor of *America*, in which appeared many articles on the Catholic Interracial movement. His 1937 book *Interracial Justice* illustrated his deep commitment to the Mystical Body of Christ as the image of racial equality. In his biography of LaFarge, historian David Southern commends him for greatly expanding the moral conscience of the church and in the process preparing the church for the revolutionary black movement of the 1960s.[112]

Other leaders in the movement included Catherine de Hueck, a Russian émigrée who founded Friendship House in Harlem (1938), committed to interracial Catholic Action, and soon other Houses appeared in several urban areas. The idea proved attractive in other cities, which during the war experienced increasing black population as a result of waves of migration from the south as people sought jobs during and after the war years. Concerned about communist advances among alienated African-Americans, and religiously committed to making racial harmony work in Catholic Action projects, de Hueck became a good friend of the head of the Catholic Worker movement, Dorothy Day.[113]

William Markoe, S.J., a Jesuit of the Missouri Province, was an impassioned promoter of racial justice. As pastor of St. Elizabeth's, a black parish in St. Louis, Markoe lived the interracialism that was preached by LaFarge with rhetorical sophistication. According to David Southern, "Markoe was loud, bold, convivial, profane and charismatic; unlike the courteous New Yorker [LaFarge], he liked to shock people and keep provincials and bishops on edge." Markoe and his older brother, John, also a Jesuit, had dedicated their lives to the "salvation of Negroes."[114] William Markoe's strategies led to his exile from St. Louis because Archbishop John Glennon, a committed segregationist, was alienated by his brash style. William's brother, John, no less an impassioned interracialist, was involved in the 1944 desegregation of St. Louis University, a Jesuit institution. For this and other incidents, he was exiled as well. Hence, the interracialists, though not within the protest and confrontational style of the Federated Colored Catholics, were quite controversial in the white Catholic world, particularly that of Archbishop John Glennon.[115]

The archbishop of St. Louis applied his segregationist policies to all levels of Catholic education. When a few priests engaged in pastoral ministry to African-Americans formed as the St. Louis Clergy Conference for Negro Welfare (1943), one of their first initiatives was to support the breakdown of segregation at Webster College, a women's college run by the Sisters of Loretto. A highly qualified graduate of St. Joseph's Colored High School, staffed by the Sisters of St. Joseph of Carondolet, had applied to Webster College, but the mother superior of the Society sought Glennon's permission. The archbishop gave lip service to equal rights for black Catholics but stated that it must begin in the grade schools, and eventually changes in whites' social attitudes would permit higher levels of integration to occur. On the basis of Glennon's opinion, black students were not accepted at Webster College. Because he never sponsored a program of integration in the grade schools, his gradualist position was revealed as a de facto segregationist policy.[116]

Glennon's conservative position on the race question had been clearly defined in the early 1920s. In response to an inquiry from Archbishop Pietro Fumasoni Biondi, the apostolic delegate, on what the archbishop was doing for the black Catholic community, Glennon explained that the pursuit of equal rights in the church could not be realized in this southern city and if they attempted to overturn tradition and struggle against sentiment it "would lead to much destruction." He reminded the apostolic delegate that had it not been for the white Catholics there would be no schools for black Catholics, as the latter do not support the church. Glennon's policy was tested when he told one parent that she had no case against a Catholic school who refused to admit her son because he was black. She was informed of the dangers of racial mixing as inevitably leading toward miscegenation, obviously odious to Glennon.[117]

By this time he had been forty years archbishop of St. Louis. As recognition of his ecclesiastical service and long tenure as well as the importance of the archdiocese, John Glennon was elevated to the College of Cardinals, but he never returned to St. Louis. He died in Dublin on March 9, 1946. In July of that year, Joseph E. Ritter, archbishop of Indianapolis, succeeded Glennon.

Ritter, an Indiana native born in 1892 (in New Albany, across the river from Louisville), had promoted pastoral ministry among African-Americans and had integrated the schools in Indianapolis in the late 1930s. As one

Indiana black newspaper reported in 1944, "For many years Archbishop Ritter has been recognized as a champion of Negro rights, especially in education."[118] In the summer of 1947 the new archbishop of St. Louis announced that all pastors were to desegregate the schools in September of that year. Though there were four Marianist high schools in the archdiocese (in 1945 they had been assigned to teach the boys in the new Northside and later at DeAndreis High School) only the latter school and McBride were in areas with African-American Catholics in the neighborhood. In late 1947 Father Peter Resch, Juergens's successor as provincial of the St. Louis Province, wrote to Archbishop Ritter that the desegregation policies had progressed well at McBride High School, which, incidentally, was across from a small recreation park where there had been a race riot in the immediate postwar era. Indeed, later that year there was a severe backlash against desegregation, which included a parents' group of McBride High School. Without receiving any encouragement from the Brothers of Mary at the school, the parents turned to the apostolic delegate, Archbishop Amleto Cicognani, who responded unsympathetically, while Archbishop Ritter threatened excommunication on the basis that these groups were obstructing the policy of their ordinary to fulfill the exercise of his office.[119]

Resch, who had been novice master for thirteen years, was a prolific writer in the popular media. He was very active in the U.S. Mariological Society and wrote several works on Mary. He was one of the many Marianists who eagerly supported Pope Pius XII's definition of Mary's Assumption as an official dogma of the church in 1950. In 1939, the St. Louis Province had indicated its interest in pastoral ministry to African-American Catholics.[120] As early as August of 1945 Sylvester Juergens accepted Quincy Foster, an African-American from New Orleans, into the novitiate of the St. Louis Province with Father John G. Leies as novice master. Though he represented the first to break the traditional color line in any congregation of brothers, Quincy Foster became ill and returned to New Orleans. His fellow novices corresponded with Foster; but he relied upon his friend Matthias Newell from Panama, a Sodalist from Xavier College, to respond for him. Newell was so impressed with this display of empathy that he eventually entered the Marianist novitiate. Though Newell had written to many brotherhoods only the Marianists invited him to enter their Society in August 15, 1949. Brother Matthias Newell was the first black religious brother to profess first vows in a religious congregation in twentieth-century America.[121]

Shortly after he was professed, Newell and a group of brothers were in the downtown St. Louis area to attend a convention of the National Catholic Educational Association. They stopped for lunch in a popular cafeteria,

Miss Hullings. When Newell was refused service, his confreres immediately left the restaurant with him in protest against the policy of discrimination initiated by the Catholic owner of the restaurant.[122]

The year Newell professed first vows (1949), C. Vincent Gray, an African-American from Detroit, wrote to Peter Resch a "letter of application for entrance into the novitiate." A member of Holy Family Parish and a junior at Sacred Heart High School, Gray had consulted with Brother Vincent Brand, "when he was principal of Holy Redeemer," and with Brother Francis Greiner. Gray had heard of Newell's entrance to the Society and was obviously encouraged by the news that "a colored boy from the South would enter the novitiate." He was also impressed by the Marianist vocation pamphlet *The Making of Leaders*, which was composed by Father Raymond Roesch of the Cincinnati Province. (This book had attracted several young men to the Society; among them were Brother Raymond Fitz, president of the University of Dayton, and Superior General David Fleming.) These two incidents converged and Gray sought admission for the next year. He entered the novitiate in July of that year. He later noted the crucial experience with Brother Vincent Brand at Holy Redeemer, "who told me a number of interesting things about the Society and its devotion to our Blessed Mother. I consider it a work of grace that I made the visit to Holy Redeemer when I did."[123]

Brother Vincent Gray became a very popular social studies teacher at McBride High School, considered one of the first integrated Catholic boys' secondary schools. He soon became head of the department. After attending the Second Novitiate at Glencoe, Missouri, he was assigned to teach at Vianney High School, which had opened in 1960. During this period he also chaired the Archdiocesan Council on Social Studies. He was a professor of education at St. Mary's University in 1961, ten years after he enrolled there as the first African-American student. Gray held two master's degrees—in history from DePaul University and in education from St. Louis University. By this time Brother Newell had left the community to join the Trappists, so Gray became the senior black Marianist. Assigned director of the Maryhurst formation program in 1963 he remained there until his death from a heart attack on December 14, 1967; he was just thirty-seven years of age. An activist in several urban affairs and civil rights movements, this Marianist brother achieved significant prominence in religious and civic spheres. His contributions were memorialized when the Marianists founded the Vincent Gray Alternative High School in East St. Louis, Illinois. Intended to "provide an opportunity to high school dropouts to acquire academic skills, vocational experiences and spiritual and social traits necessary for self-esteem and the power to contribute to a better society," the school opened in 1980. Diplomas were granted by Assumption High School, a diocesan school run by the Marianists.[124]

By the time of Brother Gray's death, the African-American Marianists were immersed in the civil rights movements of the 1960s—a topic that will be considered in the next chapter. It is significant that Gray's assignment to various positions beyond McBride High School illustrates a commitment toward gradual racial integration of the St. Louis Province.

In 1951, San Antonio's Central Catholic High School, under the leadership of Brother Henry Ringkamp, admitted its first black student, a significant milestone in this southern community.[125] As late as 1957, however, Daniel Sharpe, director of Don Bosco High School in Milwaukee confided to Resch's successor, Father J. Glennon McCarty, "There seems to be a possibility that the Archbishop [i.e., Albert G. Meyer] would welcome a Negro Brother. . . . It is not an easy situation here, you know, but with time and preparation designed as a target date, there are those who believe the problem possible of solution."[126] In a later letter, Sharpe told McCarty that it would take "eighteen months to pave the way" for the archbishop to approve the appointment of an African-American brother to Don Bosco High School.[127] Though relatively reserved and distant, Archbishop Meyer was no segregationist. On the contrary, when he was appointed to Chicago to replace Samuel Stritch, "Meyer swung the prestige of his office behind a forceful policy of interracial justice. His words and actions brought an end to an era of timidity in racial matters."[128] Sharpe's allusion to the archbishop's reluctance was therefore ambiguous. He may have been referring to the auxiliary bishop, Roman R. Atkielski, who was conservative on urban social policy, but had little authority in the Archdiocesan Office of Education. Hence, it appears as if the Marianist community in Milwaukee favored a policy of gradualism. Eventually, Don Bosco became an integrated school.

In St. Louis, Glennon's personalist style for over forty years appeared anachronistic in light of such postwar trends as progressive modernization, professionalism, and increase in the number of administrators. To impose financial accountability and a standardized administration process, Ritter, Glennon's successor, appointed diocesan priests to the post of administrator in each of the diocesan high schools, including those run by Marianists. The increasing number of lay teachers and the need to promote vocations to the diocesan priesthood, led Ritter to assign many priests to high school faculties, particularly to departments of religion. Though not intended as a criticism of the brothers' command of the field of catechetics, it was nevertheless a blow to the *raison d'être* of Marianist education, as every teaching brother received a diploma in religious education.[129]

❧ VII ❧

THEMATIC TO THE CORRESPONDENCE BETWEEN MARIANIST PROVINCIALS and archdiocesan superintendents was the gap between the archdiocese's demand for more teaching brothers to keep pace with increasing enrollments and with the reduction in class size mandated by accrediting agencies. Because postwar enrollments at the Marianist colleges had increased at a rapid pace, there was an increasing need for brothers with graduate degrees suitable for the requirements of college and university. Expanding mission endeavors also drew upon the personnel resources of the provinces: the English-speaking school in Japan was staffed by members of each of the U.S. provinces; the proliferation of schools in Puerto Rico (Cincinnati Province) and Peru (St. Louis Province); new missions in Nigeria, Malawi, and Zambia (Cincinnati Province) and Korea (Pacific Province). Despite the increase in vocations, the high schools were compelled to rely increasing upon lay teachers throughout the 1950s and beyond.

In 1945 low enrollments were characteristic of all Catholic institutions of higher education. Marianist universities were no exception: at St. Mary's University there were 549 students in 1945, up from 504 in 1944. The community was composed of "5 priests, 2 retired Brothers, 4 Working Brothers, 1 librarian, 22 Brother Professors, and officers. . . . St. Mary's seems definitely on the up-grade, though the personnel is not taxed to capacity."[130] Sylvester Juergens continued his report of the university—so-called because of its law school—by remarking on the low scholarly productivity of the faculty. Morale also seemed low; faculty complained about intellectual and spiritual leadership yet "a strong group of religious has not been cooperative religiously. There is something essential lacking either in our general methods of preparing University professors, or we have chosen the wrong men to do the work down there."[131] Ten years later Father Peter Resch reported to chapter delegates that St. Mary's enrollment had reached "a surprising all-time high: 1712. Four extra Brothers were stationed here."[132]

At the core of the curriculum in the Catholic college and university was the neoscholastic philosophy and theology dependent upon St. Thomas Aquinas. The humanities were intended to provide for the formation of the whole person, while the natural law basis of neo-Thomism integrated science and the humanities by the objective order of truths. This included the proofs for the existence of God and the teaching that, with the light of faith, the foundational creed may be explained rationally as the supernatural structure rooted in natural-law epistemology. Required courses in philosophy and theology provided students with the intellectual armament to combat secularism, materialism, and Marxism.[133]

In a 1953 address to the Serra Club of Dallas, Texas, Father Walter J. Buehler, S.M., president of St. Mary's University, responded to contemporary educationists who were committed to preparing students only for careers.[134] These educators, stated Buehler, said that "man should do something rather than become something." In contrast to the "prevalent skepticism . . . and educational pragmatism," he stressed that "our perennial philosophy says there are values as hard and objective as reality. They are in the true and good. Our revealed religion says so, too. Faith carries us up rapidly to Him who is the Way and the Truth and to Him who is the Good."

The principal aim of a Catholic college was perceived in tandem with the "ministry of truth exercised in the pulpits of our Catholic parish church. Nowhere is the ministry of truth exercised with greater frequency and greater benefit of so many hungry Catholic minds as in the Catholic schools." In its theology courses "it lays bare the reasonableness of the divine deposit of faith." Portions of Buehler's address appear to reflect the ideas of John Newman, the subject of his dissertation, but more significantly the integral humanism of Jacques Maritain, which envisioned a Christian unity of art, music, literature, and liturgy. The Catholic college preserves the past through its perennial philosophy, "which . . . ranks after theology in the academic [priority] of values. Hence, it appreciates the thought of Judaism, Islam and Christianity and thereby fosters" the finest example of democracy in human thought. The neo-Thomistic synthesis imposes order on "conflicting claims of a multitude of modern art and science."[135]

Buehler expanded on neo-Thomism as an enlightened response to the intellectual challenge of the era, and the Catholic college's commitment to organize its curriculum through a synthesis of reason and faith, the natural and the supernatural, the material and the spiritual. Though most Catholic colleges had embraced neoscholasticism in the 1930s, it seems to have taken on vitality in the 1950s as Catholic culture flourished in all its forms—specialized Catholic Action, the Liturgical Movement, popular piety. The English departments were proponents of the Catholic literary revival, featuring such notable figures as Gerard Manley Hopkins, Léon Bloy, Paul Claudel, Georges Bernanos, G. K. Chesterton, and Hilaire Belloc, with the latter two on the lecture circuit as well.[136]

The promotion of Catholic culture in colleges and universities permeated secondary education. No Marianist was more committed to this endeavor than Brother George Schuster of the St. Louis Province, who founded the Living Catholic Authors series in 1940. Perhaps influenced by Calvert Alexander's *Catholic Literary Revival* (1935), Schuster certainly discerned a vital school market for Catholic literary works. What began as a periodical became in its second year a high school textbook; in 1945 and 1946 the junior edition for grades 7–9 and a senior edition for grades 10–12 were published. Orders soon reached 240,000, and eventually other Marianists contributed to teachers' manuals. Catholic Authors' Press published individual books with manuals; the first of the "Crown Books" as they were entitled, was G. K. Chesterton's *Ballad of White Horse*, "the world's one great Marian epic" wrote Brother Gerald J. Schnepp. Many of the publications were illustrated by Brother George Schuster's blood brother, Brother Louis. So successful was this publishing effort, promoted through the NCEA and other venues, that the Marianists of the St. Louis Province made a deep imprint upon the Catholic culture during the 1940s to 1970s; indeed, as late as the late 1990s Catholic Authors' Press was fulfilling individual orders.[137]

As St. Mary's and Dayton Universities were expanding at a rapid pace, Trinity College, a Marianist institution in Sioux City, Iowa, closed in 1949. Joseph Tetzlaff, provincial from 1928 to 1938, presided over the largest province in the Society, with 407 brothers and 22 priests. It expanded into Puerto Rico; Mineola, Long Island; and Sioux City in 1939. Opened in 1912 as a diocesan college under the direction of the Third Order Regular of St. Francis (Sacred Heart Province in Loretto, Pennsylvania), Trinity College became a secondary school and a four-year college.[138] Though Trinity was located in the St. Louis Province, Tetzlaff made an arrangement based on his design to pursue a second college apostolate unsuitable for the smaller province in the Midwest. Bishop Edmund Heelan was pleased with Tetzlaff's decision to assume responsibility of the college. The Diocese of Sioux City agreed to help defray the expenses by contributing fifty thousand dollars, based on a parish assessment. Trinity became the minor seminary for the diocese, but even before that time the college was designated for "aspirants to the priesthood." Indeed, Heelan perceived Trinity as a center of Catholic life and thought.

> Knowing what I do about the Society I am confident that the best traditions of Trinity College will be upheld under its direction. These Fathers and Brothers come to us with over a century of splendid educational achievement to their credit and there is no doubt but that their activities here will redound to the good of the whole diocese. Without question they will give the young men who come to them an excellent education, not alone in secular matters but in those

of religion as well, and, through organizations promoted at the College, such as the Apostleship of Prayer, the League of the Sacred Heart, the Sodality of the Blessed Virgin Mary, the Holy Name Society, and the Student's Mission Crusade will prepare them for active participation in all Catholic endeavors.[139]

The only Catholic college for men in northern Iowa, Trinity introduced a bachelor of science in rural leadership, a blend of agricultural studies and Catholic rural-life principles. The curriculum included four courses in theory, history, and practice of cooperation in agriculture. Besides courses in dogma and ethics, there were religion courses in worship and organization and two in current problems in religion. The required liberal arts courses did not include philosophy, a departure from the general commitment to neoscholasticism.[140] Walter Tredtin was president of Trinity until he became provincial in 1938. Coincidentally, Tredtin's successor at Trinity, John A. Elbert, also succeeded him as provincial in 1948. Enrollment at the college when Elbert became president was 260 full-time students. The faculty included nineteen brothers, six priests, and one lay professor.[141] The source of these statistics, the *Catholic Directory*, did not specify the high school program, but in 1947 the student enrollment at the college was 70 while the high school was 324.[142]

By this time Elbert had returned to teach at the University of Dayton; Father Francis Friedel succeeded him as president. Later that year (1947), the provincial chapter noted that the "GI Bill of Rights" contributed a large increase of enrollment at the University of Dayton. "Trinity College still runs a very limited program, mainly for seminarians and nursing students."[143] Since Marianist high schools generally averaged about nine hundred students, the investment of twenty Marianists at Trinity High School appeared to be a drain. Hence, in 1949 the Marianists departed from Sioux City; Trinity High School closed and was replaced by a diocesan institution, Heelan High School. Trinity College was a significant source of vocations; John McCluskey, the second inspector of schools and founder of the mission in Australia in the Pacific Province, first encountered the Society at the college.[144]

Enrollment at the University of Dayton increased at a pace even greater than that of St. Mary's in San Antonio. When Brother Elmer Lackner became registrar in 1945, the enrollment was nine hundred; two years later it was 2,400, half of whom were veterans. This obviously required faculty housing; the university was fortunate to receive government surplus buildings [Quonset houses] for almost no cost from Wright Patterson Air Force Base in the Dayton area. With low rent to pay for maintenance, this arrangement went on into the mid-1950s.[145]

Until the foundation of the St. Louis Province's scholasticate at St. Mary's in the late 1950s, American Marianists enrolled at Dayton for the bachelor's degree. The minutes of the 1948 provincial council included two notable statistics related to the University of Dayton: "Three percent of the student body is colored [ca. 75 students of a 2,500 total enrollment] and fifty-nine percent are Catholic."[146] Since many Catholic colleges and universities were still segregated in this period, the integration of Dayton appears to have been gradual, with no noticeable event to mark a beginning of integration. The presidential reports of the 1950s did not break down the enrollment by race and religion. However, those figures highlight the shift to its highly cosmopolitan character. The stated purpose of the university reflected the neo-Thomistic synthesis:

> . . . the University of Dayton professes to provide an academic atmosphere in which Christian principles of thought and action are essential integrating and dynamic forces impelling the student to pursue, to cherish, and to disseminate what is true, good and beautiful.[147]

Appearing in the 1959 president's report, by the Very Reverend Andrew T. Seebold, S.M., these remarks also reveal his own graduate work as a theologian. During his six years as president, the university's enrollment increased from 3,915 to 6,074 students, a figure that led to a parallel increase in full-time faculty, 142 to 217, 30 percent of whom held the doctoral degree.[148]

The commitment to Thomism was most explicit in the religion department, which featured four courses in the *Summa* of St. Thomas. Though Jacques Maritain's *True Humanism* had moved far beyond the medievalism of the *Summa*, the commitment to reading the original sources was quite unusual for undergraduate training in theology. In the fall of 1959 the department provided a major and a minor in theology, which would include courses on scripture, the encyclicals, and other topics relating to "practical application of theology to problems current in modern society."[149]

Responsible for directing and coordinating religious life on campus was the Religious Activity Council, the campus ministry program of later years. Representative of the traditional religious devotions were the Legion of Mary, the Mariology Club, and the Catholic Students Mission Crusade. Infused in these traditional associations was the spirit of Catholic Action that often included interracial activity and other forms of social-justice endeavors. The Religious Activity Council sponsored a Rosary Rally in October 1958.[150]

Father John Dickson, who began teaching theology at the university in

1957, despite the fact that he had a doctorate in sociology, noted, "These were the days of faith when you took an assignment and did the best you could with it." Dickson's academic career coincided with the postwar acceleration of new students and faculty. While he was head of the Provincial Sodality Office located at North Catholic High School in Pittsburgh (a thriving school with over one thousand students), he attended Duquesne University and received a master's degree in sociology. To pursue the doctorate he attended St. John's University in Jamaica, New York, and stayed at the Marianist Boys' Home in Rockaway Park. In 1957 he was not only professor of theology but also chair of the religion department and chaplain of the university. He noted that "St. Thomas, of course, was the basis of our theology; moral, doctrine, sacraments, the life of Christ." There were other courses "to fill out the particular core course," such as communism, marriage, and one Dickson created on "the theology of lay life."[151] Dickson was a Marianist influenced by William Ferree, and his course no doubt reflected the Catholic Action model prevalent in the sodality and perhaps bore the imprint of Yves Congar, O.P., the principal theologian of the laity in the pre–Vatican II period.

As chaplain of the university, Dickson initiated two reforms: "First of all we managed to change the rule of compulsory chapel service. When I first came here every student had to go to Mass once a week on a certain day at a certain time. Actually they passed out little cards to have the student sign."[152] Dickson's other initiative related to the advancement of the sodality movement on campus, which was, according to Ferree's model, the unification of personal growth and apostolic action. John Dickson became the first provincial of the New York Province in 1961.

In those years there did not appear to be any conflict between the shift in authority from traditional mandates for mass attendance to that of individual initiative. The Marianist sodality movement was congenial to the blend of personalism, social radicalism, and traditional piety of Dorothy Day and the Catholic Worker Movement. Indeed, the sodality of the Cathedral Latin School in Cleveland sponsored its own House of Hospitality for the homeless in the late 1940s. Brother John Jansen, director of the Sodality of Cathedral Latin, was a Ferree protégé and also was influenced by Dorothy Day.

On October 9, 1958, Pius XII died, and soon John XXIII became pope. As the historian Emile Poulat has observed: "Pope Pius XII was closer to Pius IX (1846–1870) than he was to his immediate successor, John XXIII."[153] The optimism among American Catholics of the 1950s was affected by some vestiges of anti-Catholicism, by the frustration of the Korean conflict, and by the advances of the Soviet Union in science and nuclear armament, but the apparent vibrancy of the Catholic subculture, Catholic Action, and even aspects of the Liturgical Movement were positive signs of the times. This attitude appears in the circular letters of the provincials of this period: John Elbert, Peter Resch, and Leonard Fee. Gone were the attacks on a modernity that could only be fought with the traditional asceticism of monastic routine and the old formulas for the "life of perfection." The tone and content of these circulars reflected a moderately positive anthropology. These provincials had achieved advanced degrees, were relatively cosmopolitan, and were conscious of the need to adapt to the professionalism and modernism of the time. The provincials were activists with an instinctive understanding of the need to integrate conflicting demands of the high school and those of the religious life. Regardless of whether they held William Ferree in high esteem, he was the major force in the formation of scholastics of the St. Louis and Cincinnati Provinces, many of whom later became leaders of the Pacific and New York Provinces. Hence, his accent upon the synthesis of the apostolic life and the commitment to the value of the interior life appears to have made a significant impact. His spiritual talks to the scholastics (1947–1953) were considered the intellectual and spiritual high points of the week. In a sense the 1950s represented the ascendancy of the Ferree generation, not only among the teaching brothers but especially among the working brothers. William Ferree, the positive forces in American Catholicism, and the cosmopolitanism of the American provincials profoundly affected the Marianist tradition to that point when the occasions of grace appear to have prevailed over the occasions of sin.

CHAPTER EIGHT

Reform, Renewal, and Reaction
1960–1980

❈ I ❈

AS A POLITICAL-CULTURAL PHENOMENON, THE 1960S ORIGINATED when the civil rights movement and the Students for a Democratic Society (SDS) were in varying phases of ferment. In 1958 the American bishops condemned racism, the first pastoral response to the most significant social issue of the era. In a 1957 work, *Religion in America*, three Jesuits—John Courtney Murray, Walter J. Ong, and Gustave Weigel—contributed essays that presaged the spirit of the 1960s. Murray focused on the historical forces converging on the church's recognition of religious pluralism rooted in religious liberty and the separation of church and state. Walter Ong urged Catholics to adopt the personalism of Martin Buber and Gabriel Marcel, since it was more congenial to the bonds of affection animating the democratic spirit. Gustave Weigel warned Catholics of the potential danger of secularism coopting the moral authority of the church and thus compelling religious people to take to the streets in protest. He stressed the social activism of St. Francis of Assisi rather than the cloistered vision of St. Thomas Aquinas.[1] Since pluralism, personalism, and protest became dominant trends in the culture, these essays are situated in the prologue to the dramatic 1960s. The Liturgical Movement, identified with *Worship* magazine, edited by Godfrey Diekmann, O.S.B., of St. John's Abbey, Collegeville, Minnesota, had achieved great momentum in promoting the vernacular, in uniting the theological and the aesthetic, and in focusing on the eucharistic celebration as generating solidarity and social justice.[2]

Though the traditional subculture that characterized devotions and novenas within the "household of the faith," by parish missions, and by eucharistic piety, was thriving during the 1950s, religious separatism, within which this subculture flourished, was experiencing the strains of the rise of suburbia, of the college-educated laity, and of the Americanization of second-generation immigrants from southern and eastern Europe. Alternative sources of spirituality emanated from Dorothy Day's Houses of Hospitality, Catherine de Hueck's Friendship Houses, the Christian Family Movement, the Young Christian Students, the Young Christian Workers, and the Sister Formation Conference. The latter promoted continuous higher education for sisters rather than time-consuming summer-school programs; the Conference also fostered new religious, theological, and liturgical understanding that was in opposition to Catholic separatism and its devotional subculture.[3] These trends in Catholic life prepared a portion of the Catholic community for the period of renewal and reform of the Second Vatican Council and for subsequent reform "chapters" or the "constitutional conventions" of religious communities charged with updating the governance, spirituality, and ministry of their congregations. The context of the 1960s profoundly affected communities of religious women and men. Hence, the changes associated with Vatican II converged with social changes identified with pluralism, personalism, and a call to transform church, society, and the academy; this convergence generated a burst of new consciousness that affected the activists in religious communities. Alternative ministries, experiments in new forms of community, and the adoption of a prayer life grounded in scripture, experience, and communal reflections on charism and identity, characterized the life of religious in the 1960s. Reform and renewal in these contexts generated reactions, generation gaps, and polarizations based on views of the relationship between authority and personal development.[4]

To narrate the story of the Marianists as they passed through this dynamic period entails analyzing the activism of the late 1950s, the process of change symbolized by foundation of the New York Province in 1961 (the year before the opening of the Second Vatican Council). But by 1965 reforms had generated reaction. There were charges of heresy in the philosophy department at the University of Dayton; the black power movement affected African-American Marianists; and there was an impassioned reaction against reforms in the New York Province that related to the meaning of Marianist identity and that culminated in the formation of the new Meribah Province in 1976, centered in the Chaminade Community in Mineola.

⋇ II ⋇

AS HEAD OF THE CINCINNATI PROVINCE, JAMES M. DARBY WAS appointed provincial in 1958. A Harvard Ph.D. in English literature with a dissertation on T. S. Eliot, Darby represented a blend of intellectual sophistication and religious activism, with a strong commitment to missionary expansion in Africa. Dated September 5, 1958, Darby's first circular letter opened with a tribute to "the feastday of especial significance for the modern Marianist, Our Lady Queen of the Apostles." The term "modern" was related to the recent designation of the feast day by Pope Pius XII, the Marian pope, so dear to the Marianists; but because this is the first positive usage of "modern" in a circular letter, it may signify at least an unconscious acceptance of the spirit of the times. Darby invoked Chaminade's notion of mission and extended it to an ever more forceful level. "My dear Brothers, let us look confidently, from the start, to the happy outcome of such Christocentric apostolicity, that is, to the spreading of God's kingdom among our students."[5] Darby has been criticized as a rather blustery, overconfident, dictatorial, and controlling provincial, but he articulated a positive spirituality; he perceived the collective expression of building the kingdom in the apostolic work of all the brothers. The apparent revitalization of spirituality and ministry was not as clearly articulated as William Ferree's, nor was it an integration of the two, grounded as they were in an incarnational understanding as expressed by Joseph Simler. However, Darby appears to have been dependent on that understanding as he invoked the founder with familiarity and ease.

Even before the Second Vatican Council, Pius XII had encouraged women and men religious to retrieve their founders' vision and to discern the essentials from the accidentals in their traditions.[6] Students of the Marianists were familiar with Chaminade, as they had celebrated a special founder's day—January 22—since the early twentieth century. Generally, he was not as well known as St. John Baptist de la Salle, whose feast was on the liturgical calendar. No doubt American Marianists were particularly delighted to welcome an article on the founder in the popular, illustrated, and progressive monthly, *Jubilee*.[7]

The author of the piece was Richard Gilman, a "Jewish-Atheist" who had converted to Catholicism some five years earlier. An intellectual, well versed in the cultural tradition of Western Europe and attracted to François Mauriac, Georges Bernanos, Etienne Gilson, and other voices of the Catholic revival, Gilman was consciously drawn to Catholic "certitude" to compensate for his complex webs of sexual fantasies, desires, and ambiguities. Catholic mysteries, the blend of popular and high culture, the "mantra" prayers of the rosary mystically linking the community and the Mystical Body of Christ—all were both appealing and repelling to him, but he perceived and integrated these experiences with fresh insights of the Catholic faith. His memoir, *Faith, Sex, Mystery*, is a moving story of the passages through Catholic life and thought authentically narrated, memories that convey a life still affected by those Catholic times: the chiaroscuro of the routine days and the dark nights of the soul. Having read of Thomas Merton's conversion, Gilman appears to have unselfconsciously modeled his conversion on the journey of the Trappist monk.[8]

He had an abiding interest in journalism from his youth and was, coincidentally, connected to Edward Rice and Robert Lax, friends of Thomas Merton and editors of *Jubilee*. Soon he was on the staff. Gilman's article on Chaminade reveals a fine command of his life; one suspects he was introduced to John Garvin's history of the Marianists in the United States and the 1950 historical material published on the centennial of the University of Dayton and on the death of the founder. Reflecting *Jubilee's* commitment to strengthening the role of the laity in the church, Gilman was clearly impressed with the foundation period, 1800 to 1817, when the Sodality of Bordeaux flourished in the rechristianization of the parishes made dormant by the French Revolution. Indeed, Gilman said that Chaminade "is frequently hailed today as the father of the lay apostolate."[9] He well understood the source of the founder's commitment to the laity comparable to the model of the early church "in which priests and laymen [and laywomen] mingled on a footing of perfect equality." Gilman evaluated the foundational sodality as a "radical idea in the early nineteenth century."[10] In his relatively detailed biographical sketch, he traces Father Chaminade from his birth through his experiences as an underground priest in Bordeaux, his exile in Spain, his devotion to the Lady of the Pillar, and his return to France in 1800. He also accurately portrayed him as a royalist, but he refers to Chaminade as departing from his confreres who worked for the restoration of the monarchy "in a conspiratorial manner." He also noted Chaminade's refusal to be associated with the restorationists' agenda to return to a period of "rigid social stratification, . . . or sense of outraged privileges or . . . aristocratic nostalgia." Gilman rightly stressed the social diversity of the Sodalities of Bordeaux that generated controversy and conflict among social conservatives: "the traditional fate of the founder whose vision outstrips that of his contemporaries."[11]

Gilman perceived the foundation of the Society of Mary and the Daughters of Mary as "marked by the same democratic qualities that had distinguished their predecessors," the sodalities. The *Jubilee* writer, perhaps indebted to Joseph Simler's French biography of the founder, was fully aware of the conflict between Chaminade and those brothers who overemphasized the Society's apostolate to education, as well as of Georges Caillet's dismissal of Chaminade as having "outlived his usefulness."[12] Though he did not name Caillet, he did understand his animus and clearly supported the founder's abiding spiritual leadership of the Society. With remarkable insight into the significance of Chaminade and the Society of Mary, Gilman rendered the life of the founder as if he were a "cradle Catholic" rather than a recent convert. Though Gilman would gradually become distracted from Catholicism within a year, by the time he wrote his memoir on his Catholic period he had been drama critic for *Commonweal*, *Newsweek*, the *New Republic*, and *The Nation*, and a professor at the Yale Drama School.[13]

Though Gilman had also written on St. John Baptist de la Salle, founder of the Christian Brothers, his article on Chaminade for a progressive journal edited by laymen and committed to the lay apostolate represented an American Catholic appropriation of the founder, the first such portrait outside Marianist publications. From various Marianist points of view this article must have been greeted with enthusiasm, particularly as a vital source for vocations.

❧ III ❧

JAMES DARBY MAY BE CHARACTERIZED AS *THE* "VOCATIONS PROVINcial"; as early as January 22, 1959, he announced the goal of gaining forty novices on a twice-a-year basis; the postulancy passed on graduates in January and new postulants entered in August.[14] Eleven months later he announced that the goal had been surpassed. Though the expansion of the province—Moeller High School in Cincinnati and Chaminade High School in Hollywood, Florida (September 1960)—required an increase in vocations, the prospective division of the Cincinnati Province, initiated in 1959 by Paul Hoffer, the superior general, provided significant impetus for Darby's emphasis on recruitment.[15]

Unlike Sylvester Juergens's speedy decision to establish the Province of the Pacific, Hoffer allowed the Cincinnati Province ample time to consider all the ramifications entailed in the creation of the New York Province, officially established on November 18, 1961.[16] Father John Dickson, the chaplain at the University of Dayton and a former head of the Province's Sodality

Secretariat, was named provincial; Brother John T. Darby, the blood brother of James, was appointed provincial inspector of schools, a position he held in the Cincinnati Province.[17]

Dickson clashed with the Darby brothers' relatively authoritarian styles of leadership. Hence, many considered the presence of Brother John Darby as symbolic of Father Darby's determination to shape the development of the New York Province.[18] John Darby had been director/principal of Chaminade in Mineola, Long Island, since 1945, until appointed inspector for the Cincinnati Province in 1959. Of the 716 brothers and priests in the Cincinnati Province, 211 were located in the ten houses that became the New York Province. The balance of 505 (75 priests and 430 brothers) were located in the houses of the Cincinnati Province. Shortly after the formation of the new Province, Father Paul Landolfi became head of the Office of Zeal; Father William Anderson was appointed head of the newly created Office of Apostolic Action; and Brother Patrick Hance was head of temporalities.[19]

The new provincialate was located in an old mansion near the largest school, St. James High School in Chester, Pennsylvania; situated in the Philadelphia archdiocese, St. James enrolled 1,691 students in 1961. The faculty included ten diocesan priests, twenty-six Marianists, and eighteen lay teachers. In contrast to this modern facility, there was an old parish high school in Brooklyn, Holy Trinity, with an enrollment of 650 students drawn from the region. Brother John Darby noted large class sizes; fifty students "was not uncommon." The biology lecture room—there was no laboratory—"would challenge both a magician and a competent teacher. The incumbent is neither." The report concluded with some doubt as to the future of the school because of the competition of new high schools "and the effect of the overwhelming influx of Puerto Ricans in the neighborhood."[20]

Also in the Brooklyn diocese was St. John's Home for Boys in Rockaway Park, Queens, New York. It was under the supervision of the Catholic Child Care Society of Brooklyn, a division of Catholic Charities, an agency directed by Father Francis J. Mugavero, later bishop of Brooklyn. Twelve Marianists supervised and taught the 124 boys, some of whom attended special education classes in public schools. Brother Darby noted the increased number of residents admitted through the courts and a few more released from mental-health facilities. There was a need for the professionalization of the young brothers, while two who were counsellors were assigned for a summer of work and observation at Boys Town, "that famed institution" in Nebraska.[21]

The jewel of the province, Chaminade High School in Mineola, was in the new Diocese of Rockville Centre, and as the former principal/director at Chaminade, Darby composed a rather detailed report. Analogous to Cathedral Latin School in Cleveland with a rigorous academic program, Chaminade had an enrollment of thirteen hundred; it "continues to set the pace in all phases of school life by reason of its faculty and select student body. . . . Seldom does a school, much less a single department, attract national renown for academic achievement as Chaminade's modern language department had done in the past three years." The science department also excelled. Darby proudly remarked that "College scholarships were in abundance. This year there are 62 N.Y. Regents scholarships won by the senior class." The Marianist commitment matched the Society's pride in this school: thirty-one brothers and four priests were assigned to Chaminade.[22]

Two recently opened high schools, Chaminade in Hollywood, Florida (1960), and Charlotte Catholic High School in Charlotte, North Carolina (1961), experienced periodic growing pains. Chaminade was a private high school in the Miami diocese that opened with a freshman class. In 1962 there were only 114 students in the first two years; the faculty was composed of five brothers and two lay teachers. Brother Darby reported that the classes were held in "sparkling new buildings" that were both "attractive in appearance and functional in design." It held the promise of developing in the tradition of excellence of other schools owned by the Marianists: Chaminade, Mineola, Cathedral Latin School in Cleveland, Chaminade, St. Louis; and St. Louis, Honolulu.

Bishop Hafey Memorial High School in Charlotte, a Raleigh diocesan school, was, according to Brother Darby, a "Home Mission" school. With virtually the entire state in the diocese, Bishop Vincent N. Waters—the first southern bishop to racially integrate his schools—was active in the National Catholic Rural Life Conference. The director and the assistant director of the diocesan Home Missions were priests in residence at the Cathedral. Hence, Waters was very supportive of the Glenmary Home Missioners. One percent of the population of North Carolina was Catholic; 45,000 of the population of 4,556,000. With only seven Catholic high schools in the state, secondary education was symbolic of the entire Home Missionary character of the diocese. Since Darby made his visitation three weeks after the September 1961 opening of the school, his remarks on the schools' many problems, ranging from one brother's "frequent outbursts of fanaticism in the classroom" to "an occasional frantic telephone call to provincial headquarters," must be understood as the views of a former director of Chaminade-Mineola and one thoroughly unaccustomed to rural mission life.[23]

Darby's report on Colegio Ponceño in Ponce, Puerto Rico, was relatively positive. "There has been a steady upswing of community spirit, professional interest, and Marianist enthusiasm at Colegio Ponceño during these past years." He was impressed with the lay personnel and their edifying relationships with the Marianist faculty. Attitudes toward the students were somewhat different. With characteristic Irish-American biases Darby remarked: "The volatile Puerto Rican temperaments among the students are tempered firmly and gently by the excellent staff."

The other Puerto Rican school, Colegio San José, Rio Piedras, opened with a story of the brother director's "violent wrath [and] physical violence meted out" to one student. Though the brother "regretted his outburst of uncontrolled temper," he was immediately recalled to the states "for a cooling off program and a fresh start at St. James in Chester." His replacement brought vitality to a school "that was slowly becoming soul-less." Darby characterized Colegio San José as a "magnificent boarding-day school with its new additions, fine students and cooperative parents."[24]

The inter-province postulate, Marianist Prep in Beacon, New York, was in the new province. In 1961 the board of regents of the University of New York awarded a five-year renewable charter empowering the school to grant academic diplomas. The four-year program was completed within two and one-half years because of the eleven-month academic year. The novitiate at Marcy, New York, was followed by residency in the inter-provincial new scholasticate at Mount St. John, with a curriculum that included requirements for an undergraduate degree at the University of Dayton. Marianist Prep followed a modern high school model with field trips to history, art, and science museums, educational television programs, "student directed and controlled projects and operations—all nurtured in an excellent religious and aesthetic atmosphere."[25]

A Provincial Academic Council established in 1962 was charged with discussing, planning, and evaluating individuals and the course of studies in the formation programs from the postulancy through the scholasticate at the University of Dayton and into graduate study at a university, and/or at the Marianist Seminary in Fribourg, Switzerland. The modernization and professionalization processes, so characteristic of Marianist education, had become integral to the formation program as well. Despite the prevalence of modernization, the persistence of tradition was evident in the oldest school in the province, Immaculate Conception. With three brothers in Washington, D.C., in charge of the sixth through eighth grades in this parish school of ninety-seven boys, the fate of the school was precarious at best. Darby remarked: "No one knows what will happen first. A condemnation from the District and the closing of the school; or a condemnation [on grounds of dilapidation]." Darby's closing description captures the spirit of the school and community.

> Meanwhile, the Marianists struggle on, happily enduring miserable home conditions (the director cooks all the meals, except for school-day lunch when each member is on his own and enjoys the "distraction"; the community daily enjoys the fruit of distraction. The teaching conditions in the school, the general ability of the students, the quality of teaching are good. Relationships with the pastor and his assistants are excellent.[26]

The newest school in the province, opened after Darby's report to the 1962 provincial chapter, was Cardinal Gibbons High School in Baltimore, which was built on the 131-acre site of the old St. Mary's Industrial School, where orphans and wards of the court, including Babe Ruth, were assigned to study for job training and a high school diploma. The Xaverian Brothers, who were in charge of Mount St. Joseph's College about two miles north of Gibbons, had been responsible for St. Mary's School. Archbishop Francis P. Keough had planned a model contemporary high school with the latest designs for academic, artistic, and athletic facilities. However, his successor, Lawrence J. Shehan, presided at its opening in 1963. When it reached full four years in 1967, there were twenty-one brothers, three priests, and twenty-two lay teachers on the faculty responsible for 930 students. It must have been a gratifying experience to return to Baltimore, where the Marianists had been so vitally immersed in the education in the German-American parishes, St. Michael's, St. James, and St. Alphonsus and the Irish-American parish, St. Martin, since nearly one hundred Baltimoreans had entered the Society.[27]

In 1966 the provincialate moved to the Roland Park area of Baltimore, where the province purchased an antiquated nursing home for women, Kirkleigh Villa, staffed by the Daughters of Charity. A year prior to the move, Brother Anthony Isparo was appointed assistant superintendent of schools by Cardinal Lawrence Shehan, while Brother Carroll Wentker, was assistant director of the Archdiocesan Retreat House in Baltimore. Father Dickson informed the province of these appointments and remarked that Wentker's "main work will be the development of the Cursillo-type retreat for public school boys [aimed at forming deep commitments to Christian leadership]. The prospects are really thrilling and exciting."[28] Hence, by 1966 the New York Province's associations with Baltimore extended into several new spheres of missionary activity, representing departures from the teaching apostolate.

As mentioned earlier, John Dickson was more experienced as a leader in the sodality movement than in education. In his role as director of religious activities at the University of Dayton he leaned toward moderate reform, preferring individual initiative over the imposition of required mass attendance.[29] A thirty-one-page circular letter (October 12, 1963) was the "official statement of Policy of the Sodality Council of the New York Province of the Society of Mary" signed by the entire provincial council. There are quotations from William Ferree's work and that of Brother John Totten, who promoted the sodality in the St. Louis Province. Dickson was deeply influenced by Ferree and defined the mission of the Marianist community as encompassing the creation of an apostolate that entailed participation "in Christ's mission to redeem mankind," a mission that "continued now in the Church, Christ's Mystical Body." The specialized apostolate is the Marianist school, and within the school are the student sodalities identified also by apostolate. "The Family of Mary is . . . an organic unit with many parts all interrelated."[30] Ferree is cited to substantiate the integrity of the Family of Mary, particularly the several "states of perfection," which were like paths to holiness, "including the married state."[31] Actually, Ferree's letter presages the "call of the whole church to holiness," chapter 5 §40 of *Lumen Gentium*: "Thus it is evident to everyone that all the faithful of Christ of whatever the rank or status are called to the fullness of Christian life and to perfection of charity. By this holiness a more humane way of life is promoted in this earthly society."[32] Historian Patricia Byrne, C.S.J., captures the meaning of this chapter of *Lumen Gentium* for religious, "The Council thus spelled the end of two-story Christianity, of the theology that supported a privileged status for vowed religious."[33]

As if he were anticipating the demise of a two-story Christianity, John Totten, an expert on sodality in the St. Louis Province, interpreted Chaminade's method as the image of "concentric Marian societies centered in filial piety [to Mary]" with the Society of Mary "of utter consecration" to the Mother of Jesus.[34] Hence, the ideals of Ferree, Dickson, and Totten, derived from the charism of William Joseph Chaminade, are supportive of the one-story Christianity based on the historical experience of dwelling in a society of priests, teaching, and working brothers, proceeding from a sodality that was also related to the horizontal Family of Mary. As will be explored in the epilogue, the Family of Mary notion of sodality would evolve into the lay-Marianist model so central to the *aggiornamento* of Chaminade.

William Ferree was the first general assistant for apostolic action, a position that has its origin in Ferree's influence at the general chapter of 1961. The chapter also committed the Society to "the foreign student apostolate and the training of lay missionaries," areas of ministry identified with the vision of Ferree. He wrote to all the American provincials that the general administration "had engaged the services of an experienced layman . . . Mr. Edward J. Kirchner, Vice President of the Association of International Development (AID), an organization of lay missionaries, and a permanent representative of Pax Romana at the United Nations."[35] Since the late 1940s Ferree had been involved in Pax Romana, an international organization of Catholic students, founded in Switzerland in 1921.[36] As one of the early organizers of the National Federation of Catholic College Students (founded in 1937) he was introduced to the student apostolate when he was associated with Pax Romana during his years in the seminary at Fribourg, Switzerland (1933–1937); he became chaplain general soon after his appointment as assistant general of education (1956–1961).[37]

In a letter to John Dickson dated March 16, 1962, William Ferree encouraged the provincial to enter the apostolate of international student housing, particularly because without an institution of higher education the New York Province would be attracted to this ministry. Also it would not entail a large capital investment nor the placement of numerous brothers, but rather the property could be rented and only three brothers would be needed. Dickson and others in the provincial chapter met with Edward Kirchner "to outline plans for future apostolic developments in the Province," but such endeavors were more evident in Puerto Rico. Father Albert Schmidt's parish activity in Mission Noell, responsible for twenty-two square miles of severely underdeveloped mountainous area, did become a training center for religious and lay missionaries.[38]

The Cincinnati provincial, James M. Darby, responded with alacrity to the 1961 chapter directive. On April 23, 1962, he announced the foundation of the "Marianist Missionary Institute to train priests, Brothers and Sisters as well as laymen [sic] for their impending assignment or reassignment to mission lands." Headed by Father Joseph McCoy, who had had missionary experience in China, the Institute was related to the sociology department of the University of Dayton, with additional courses in psychology and missiology. A special lay missionaries program, Chaminade Auxiliaries from North America (CANA), was directed by Father Philip C. Hoelle. A twelve-month program, it was "equivalent to a sort of novitiate," wrote Darby. "Problems of adaptability to foreign cultures and mentalities, the spiritual life of the lay missioner and language study form the nucleus of the formation." Hoelle was also a local director of the Papal Volunteers for Latin America.[39] Pope John XXIII, who had been a national director of the Society for the Propagation of the Faith in Italy, had a strong interest in Latin America, indicated by the establishment of the Pontifical Commission for Latin America in 1959. Some two years later, the National Catholic Welfare Conference implemented a Vatican directive for lay missionaries by founding Papal Volunteers for Latin America. Since the general administration in Rome reflected this sentiment, and since Cincinnati still remained the largest province in the Society, it was appropriate that it assume the leadership role in the training of lay missioners.[40]

As director of PAVLA, Hoelle was "in close contact" with Monsignor Ivan D. Illich, head of the Inter-American Formation Center in Cuernavaca, Mexico. The Marianist at the Center, Brother Gerald Morris, was head of the language department.[41] In her book *The Missionary Movement in American History*, Angelyn Dries, O.S.F., describes lay-missioner life at the Center. "Participants had the opportunity to examine realistically their call to serve Latin America. Late-night discussions and invited speakers evoked heated and intense arguments about all aspects of mission life. Formation at Cuernavaca required persons to confront, sometimes painfully, their North American biases."

As mentioned in a previous chapter, William Ferree, Joseph Fitzpatrick, S.J., and Ivan Illich had edited a symposium on social and religious problems in Puerto Rico. As president of the Catholic University of Puerto Rico, Ferree had been one of the founders of the Catholic Bureau of Inter-America and was active in several Inter-American Catholic Congresses. At the Second Vatican Council, Ferree was a consultor of the Commission on the Lay Apostolate and Social Justice.[42]

It had been over ninety years between the First and Second Vatican Councils; the former was brought to a precipitous closure in 1870 when the Italian state took possession of Rome; the council had declared the pope infallible even outside of an ecumenical council. Pius IX had promulgated the dogma of the Immaculate Conception; major Papal events and publications occurred on the feast day, December 8.[43] Though the bishops and theologians were immersed in the ecclesiological controversy over infallibility, the Catholic community, particularly in the United States, was primarily an immigrant church caught up in the concerns of jobs, home, family, and parish.[44] These are necessary, perennial preoccupations, but, as pointed out earlier, there was an increase in college-educated middle-class Catholics who would be absorbed in the Second Vatican Council, brought into their homes through television as well as the print medium. John F. Kennedy, a Harvard-educated Catholic, exemplified the Americanization that had been in the ascendancy in the postwar period and was characteristic of the assimilated Catholics, no longer a minority group. Pope John XXIII, whose personal style of leadership demythologized the distanced formalism of the papacy, proclaimed the prospective Second Vatican Council as entailing a process of *aggiornamento*, an updating of the Church in accord with the "language of modern thought."[45]

The first session in the fall of 1962 was characterized by a struggle on the agenda between traditionalists in the curia and the majority of bishops, motivated by the spirit of Pope John's optimism. Pope John died before the opening of the second session; however, when Cardinal John Baptist Montini was elected Pope under the name Paul VI, he immediately announced the continuation of the council. The three subsequent sessions (September 29–December 4, 1963; September 4–November 21, 1964; and September 14–December 8, 1965) yielded sixteen documents: Revelation, Liturgy, the Dogmatic Constitution on the Church, the Church in the Modern World, Communications, Eastern Churches, Bishops, Priestly Formation, Religious Life, Laity, Priests, Missions, Education, Ecumenism, Non-Christians, and Religious Freedom. Theologian/historian Patrick W. Carey captures the general significance of these documents, which "revitalized [the] understanding of the Church's nature and mission in the modern world." He also noted that they reflected not only the "neo-scholastic theological orientation of the immediate past but also the new biblical, historical, and existential theology that had been developing in France and Germany since the First World War." Hence, there was emphasis on the historical in the articulation of Revelation, salvation, and ecclesiology. "This historical view of human and Christian existence helped to produce a new consciousness of the Church's presence in the world. . . . The Council fathers furthermore fostered a spiritual renewal, reform and change."[46]

In the United States, concurrent with the reforms and renewal of the church were the rapidly accelerated social and cultural changes of the 1960s: the civil rights movement culminating in black power protests; the student life movement culminating in seizures of administrative offices in protest against the exclusive governance structures of colleges and universities; the youth-culture movement culminating in Woodstock and new lifestyles; the anti-war movement culminating in break-ins to destroy draft records; the women's movement culminating in the National Organization of Women (NOW), the recognition of women's political, social, and economic rights and cultural freedom of expression; and several phases of other movements directed at improving the poor through literacy, housing, and employment.[47]

Patrick Carey elaborates on the relationship between religious change within the context of these movements: "The implementation of the Second Vatican Council's liturgical and structural reforms and the corresponding transformation of American Catholic consciousness that accompanied them took place at a time of revolutionary change . . . when continued, the religious and cultural reformations produced a period of unprecedented turmoil and change." During the council many religious were involved in social-justice ministries outside of their regular school responsibilities. The young were particularly drawn to the civil rights movement. They were responding to the call basic to *Gaudium et Spes*:

> The joys and the hopes, the griefs and the anxieties of the men [sic] of this age, especially those who are poor or in any way afflicted, these too are the joys and hopes, the griefs and anxieties of the followers of Christ. Indeed, nothing genuinely human fails to raise an echo in their hearts.[48]

Perfectae Caritatis, the decree on the Appropriate Renewal of the Religious Life (October 28, 1965), according to Paul J. Philibert, O.P., was interpreted by many "as an invitation to clean house or to renovate the structure." The significant lines of the decree are:

> The appropriate renewal of religious life involves two simultaneous processes: (1) a continuous return to the source of all Christian life and the original inspiration behind a given community and (2) an adjustment of the community to the changed conditions of the times.[49]

Since *Gaudium et Spes* and Pope John's *Pacem et Terris* had urged Christians to discern the "signs of the times," many religious interpreted the renewal of religious life within a general reform spirit. They fastened on to conciliar statements as "the suppression of outmoded regulations" and "antiquated trappings."[50] A *motu proprio*, *Ecclesiae Sanctae*, included directives on the implementation of the decree on Renewal of Religious Communities, such as the mandate to hold a general chapter "within two or three years."[51] These "constitutional conventions" aimed at incorporating the principles of renewal and adaptation could be held in two separate sessions but not separated by more than one year.

During the Vatican Council, the Marianists reflected the general trends in church and society. Provincial circular letters and the various chapter meetings abound with comments on the documents. From the late 1960s there was a rapid decline in vocations and a rise in brothers and priests withdrawing from the Society. There was little or no tension over the changes in the liturgy, particularly the adoption of the vernacular and the directive to set aside traditional Marianist prayers such as the Little Office of the Immaculate Conception and to adopt in an abbreviated form the Divine Office or the Liturgical Hours of the church. There were conflicts within local communities over the introduction of what were referred to as folk-guitar liturgies, which reflected the growing polarization in the interpretation of Vatican II within the culture of the 1960s.

The provincials articulated the new theology, particularly the emphasis on scripture, the new ecclesiology, and the universal call to holiness of all baptized people of God. Though the leadership echoed the dominant theological movements associated with the Second Vatican Council, there were variations on the themes and a general concern for the traditional integrity of community life and the structures of governance; but, despite experimentation, renewal, and the commitment to dialogue, there was an attempt to hold the line on individualism or, as it was referred to in the 1960s and 1970s, personalism.[52]

As provincial of the New York Province, John Dickson represented the drive to integrate the apostolic and the monastic so characteristic of his friend and mentor, William Ferree. In a circular of September 5, 1966, he referred to the fragmentation, not between the monastic life and the apostolate, but between the school and new apostolates.[53] By this time the impact of *Gaudium et Spes* was quite evident; Archbishop Rembert Weakland put it this way:

> The Church sees itself as having a common history with the world. The perspective is more ecumenical, but, in its own way also more evangelical. . . . It leaves its isolation behind and takes up the role of witness while being sacrament to the world. Religious were very much caught up with this perspective and embraced it eagerly and totally. . . . Some of the older terminology that came from the monastic tradition about "separation from the world" was abandoned by religious as inappropriate and meaningless in the new context. Orders that had an apostolic impulse from their origins saw in Vatican Council II a new way of bringing into focus their apostolic involvement with the world. They saw their charism vindicated by the council.[54]

The abandonment of the old monastic language was most evident among the younger brothers socialized during the period of ferment, 1958–1968. As a sodality leader, Dickson straddled the generational fence; he tended toward the new terminology but governed in the traditional style.

Dickson's criticism of the school–social apostolate conflict as disastrous to a local community was followed by a commentary on "Social Temperance," which Ferree lifted from a work on "Industrial Management," whereby members of a group pool individual interests and "the common interests of the group will be achieved. Social temperance, therefore, has the common good as its object by keeping the desires and interest of the group members on a high altruistic level avoiding selfish and undue emphasis upon private interests." Dickson augmented Ferree's idea with a citation from the superior general, Paul Joseph Hoffer, "Collaboration requires sacrifice." Against those brothers and priests who "were doing their own thing" or pursuing spheres of self-fulfillment, the leadership of all provinces was mounting an attack.[55] Ferree's strategy as head of apostolic action was to provide a modern model for promoting the common good, while others employed more direct didactic approaches.

James Darby, provincial in Dayton, was president of the Conference of Major Superiors of Men (CMSM) from 1962 to 1967, a position that required considerable time. He was also a founding member and vice president of Center for Applied Research in the Apostolate (CARA), a research arm of the American bishops, with such projects as the church's role in the inner city. After the completion of his second term as provincial (1968), Darby became the executive director of CARA until his death on April 21, 1969. In contrast to the soft-spoken Dickson, Darby was a forceful leader.

A circular letter dated January 22, 1966, Founder's Day or Chaminade Day, was Darby's first communication with members of the province since the close of Vatican Council II on the previous December 8. With theological sophistication, it stressed the need for a Marianist dialogue on the apostolate with a strong emphasis on theory but with few references to the controversies of the time except the need for light and the reduction of heat. His thesis was to reintegrate the traditional Marianist apostolate of education within aspects of contemporary theology. The subtext appears to be that the current of individualism or personalism must be subsumed into the larger church's role as missionary. "[T]he theologian tells us it is the Church that is missionary; *not* the missioner or the educator, but the *Church.* Thus the expert [i.e., theologian] aims at putting each one of us in his proper place, a risky business amidst the burning fevers of personalism."[56]

The contemporary ecclesiological discourse is quite evident in the provincial's further elaboration of the larger church's role as missionary. "We are all missionaries, apostles of the world, but precisely only insofar as we are Church, the people of God, baptized in the living Christ. . . . Thus the *redeemed* are redemptive; the people of God are in mission or they are nothing. Their very activity must be the Church living and giving fruitful, formative missionary presence." To ignore this missionary quality or to fail to respond to the call to be a church in mission indicates that one is immersed in "too much self, too much of the merely temporal and the profane."[57]

Though the individual "may offer a variety of kinds of witness . . . [for] redemptive effect," Darby separated natural goodness from "the sacredness of . . . labors." The old monastic dichotomy of the separation from the contagion of the world is evident in Darby's contention that those who are living virtuous lives "but not supernaturally living the missionary life" surrender the "whole [of the] interior life to the unredeemed rhythms of the world, where universal hedonism appears imminent and the economy, the law and politics generally recognize no God." Darby's separationist mentality, regardless of his nod to contemporary notions of ecclesiology, appears to rationalize not an incarnational spirituality abundant with graced experiences in the world, but rather an identification of the missionary as "synonymous with saint." The missionary saint recognizes the Virgin Mary as "the preeminent example of everything that [he] is called upon to be as Church. Her presence to us is Church. She is for us a formative and redeeming fact. Thus, we love and honor her as the Church personified and in doing so generate the perfection of the Church in our persons."[58] This notion of the traditional missionary saint does not exclude an incarnational spirituality, but its association with a separationist mentality appears to mean that Darby was not fostering an incarnationist understanding.

As provincial, Darby was *ex officio* chairman of the Board of Trustees of the University of Dayton, which had reached an enrollment of ten thousand students by 1966 and had embarked on master's level courses in theology. Father Raymond Roesch, president of the university, is identified with the shift from a modest institution to a burgeoning center of modernized administration, professionalized faculty, and sophisticated academic program. A highly charged controversy symbolic of the decline of neoscholasticism occurred within the philosophy department. Its complexity almost defies a simplified narrative treatment; but because it gained national notoriety, it is necessary to briefly narrate the story in the Marianist context.

There was an increasingly tense and polarized situation in the philosophy department during 1965–1966. Prior to the crisis's culmination in a letter to Archbishop Karl Alter, ordinary of Cincinnati, two Marianists, Fathers Thomas Stanley and Charles Lees, provosts of the university, had been discussing with two professors their lectures and writings which emphasized historical and developmental models in opposition to the ahistorical neoscholasticism that had been the regnant school of philosophy and theology prior to the Second Vatican Council. The provost, Father Lees, appointed Dennis Bonnette to the Academic Council to advise him on the department of philosophy.[59] A series of talks on campus by two philosophy professors, John M. Chrisman and Eulalio R. Baltazar, in the spring of 1966 and on October 11, 1965, by Professor Lawrence Ulrich, of the philosophy department, and those of Randolph F. Lumpp of the theology department, prompted Dennis Bonnette to inform Archbishop Alter of the "rapidly developing situation which is now at the point of doing great harm to the faith and morals of the entire university community." The first two speakers, wrote Bonnette, "publicly endorsed situation ethics in precisely that form which had been condemned by the Holy See." The talks by Ulrich and Lumpp also on "situation ethics" were "subjective in tone and during its entirety no positive affirmation of the traditional teaching on natural law was uttered." He also reported that Chrisman justified abortion "in some cases."[60] He later accused Baltazar of denying the existence of purgatory (three years later Baltazar's book *Teilhard and the Supernatural* was cited by Bernard Lee, S.M., a process theologian of the St. Louis Province).[61] He urged Alter to initiate a "comprehensive investigation of the grave spiritual harm which is now occurring here"; he warned the archbishop that the "Catholic consciences [of those professors sympathetic to Bonnette's position] . . . have been compromised too long already [and] will resign in protest." He reminded the archbishop that the ideas advanced by these heterodox professors are the very themes "condemned in Cardinal Ottaviani's famous letter of July 24, 1966." Bonnette closed his October 15 letter with the remark that if Alter does not take action he would "freely sacrifice the security of . . . [his] position to the service of the cause of Christ."[62]

A carbon copy of this letter was sent to Archbishop Egidio Vagnozzi, the apostolic delegate, who was not unsympathetic to Cardinal Ottaviani, prefect of the Sacred Congregation for the Doctrine of the Faith (CDF). Bonnette's brief against the allegedly heterodox professors generated an October 20 phone call from Karl Alter to Raymond A. Roesch informing him of Bonnette's accusations and the Vagnozzi directive that Alter "look into it."[63]

With a strong commitment to investigate Bonnette's charges, Roesch and his administrative council decided on this course of action:

1. Call the principals and find out what was happening.
2. Ask Bonnette to acquaint all with the charges.
3. Request Bonnette to substantiate the charges.
4. Direct each of the four accused to answer the charges.
5. Two possible outcomes could eventuate:
   a. Bonnette could admit error and publicly retract;
   b. Bonnette could persist in the charges.
6. If the latter, we would set up an ad hoc committee to investigate the details of the case.[64]

Over the next week Bonnette and the accused professors, who were surprised by the charges, agreed to these procedures. Though there had been unanimity on the need for confidentiality, the case was leaked first to the campus newspaper and was soon picked up by the *National Catholic*

Reporter (NCR). Philip Gleason described the highly politicized atmosphere:

This [case] immediately plunged the university community into strife; faculty and student groups held meetings, drew up manifestoes, issued reprimands, and in general filled the air with charges and counter-charges for several months. As the case attracted national attention from both liberal and conservative factions, it more and more clearly reflected the post-counciliar breakdown of the Catholic consensus on matters of doctrine and discipline.[65]

Ironically, in Lawrence P. Ulrich's explanatory letters to Roesch he included an article by Philip Gleason in the *Catholic Mind*, "The Crisis in Catholic Universities: An Historical Perspective," published in the September prior to the outbreak of the University of Dayton controversy. This learned piece is too complex to elucidate in this space, but Gleason's contention that academic freedom, despite its evocation of a quasi religion of humanity traditionally in opposition to Catholicism, is all the more necessary at the present moment characterized by "flux and uncertainty. . . . [W]ithout the fullest liberty to explore new perspectives we can never hope to arrive at a satisfactory resolution of these profound issues of faith and knowledge."[66]

Consciously departing from the objective order of systematic natural-law ethics, two of the professors, Lawrence Ulrich and Randolph Lumpp, were engaged in elucidating the intersubjectivity referred to by some as situation ethics. Lumpp preferred Karl Rahner's term, "formal existential ethics." In his conclusion to the address cited by Bonnette in his letter to Alter, Lumpp noted "the historical impact of the Christian stress on intersubjectivity, interpersonal encounter as the basis of moral behavior. It is, in light of this, a reaction not against Christianity but against an overly abstract impersonalized non-Christian or pre-Christian worldview. It demands not selective interpretation but total personal involvement."[67]

The influence of Karl Rahner and other theologians was most evident in the theological language abundant with references to human development in light of Christ's self-revelation. Such ideas alienated moral philosophers or theologians who were trained in "legalistic versions of moral theology" and articulated their foundational ideas in an abstract, ahistorical language.[68] Hence, the incongruity of the two forms of discourse—historical and abstract—led to controversies within philosophy and theology departments.

Bonnette's reference to Ottaviani's letter may have had its basis in a September 1965 article by John Cogley, religion editor of the *New York Times*, who reported on Cardinal Alfredo Ottaviani's letter to episcopal leaders throughout the world listing ten "widespread abuses in interpretation of Council teachings." Because the letter was to be kept confidential and was enveloped in secrecy, "its exact contents are not known." However, Cogley had access to specific information as he listed the alleged abuses. Of the ten abuses listed in the letter, two, as articulated by Cogley, relate to this case:

> There are widespread denials of the objectivity and immutability of truth. Relativism is being endorsed and the idea is put forth that every truth is the product of conscience and history. . . .
>
> In moral theology, some deny any objective basis at all to morality. They do not accept natural law and hold that wrongness and righteousness are established by moral situations in which people find themselves.[69]

To cite Ottaviani in 1966, four years after his attempt to steer Vatican II in a rightward direction had been frustrated by the consensus of the council, did not serve Bonnette's cause.

From October 20 to December 2, 1966, Roesch pursued the agreed-upon procedures, held several meetings of the Ad Hoc Committee, and met with the archbishop, who told him he was only concerned with those alleged statements on abortion and purgatory. The four professors were cleared of all charges, a decision accepted by Alter on December 2. However, eight professors dissented from the decision and were supported by six pastors in Dayton, a movement which, Roesch stated, "threw the entire affair back into the ecclesiastical realm."

Despite the acrimony that gave rise to Alter's fact-finding committee, its decision confirmed the decision of the Ad Hoc Committee. In his *Statement Relative to the Controversy Touching Academic Freedom and the Church's Magisterium,* Raymond G. Roesch indicated his commitment to academic freedom and to welcoming professors with positions from all points on the spectrum with two qualifications: "those who speak should confine themselves to their competence and that appropriate respect must be paid to the proper role of the Church's magisterium. Just how that respect is to be acknowledged is part of the task facing the *Ad Hoc* Committee."[70] By the time this committee issued its report on academic freedom it asserted the university's independence of "all outside authority," but, as Philip Gleason remarks, "presumably because the individuals who composed it were conscientious Catholics, it could claim to respect the teaching authority of the local bishop. It was not clear how this formulation would apply in a dispute" such as the one generated by Bonnette. The report also asserted the university community's commitment to secularization;

that is, "to come of age . . . means a new freedom for men to perfect the world in a non-religious way." Gleason describes this section of the report as a vaporous discussion of the faculty as a "new *gemeinschaft*."[71]

As mentioned earlier, James Darby was chairman of the university's Board of Trustees. In an article in *America* entitled "Reflections on the Dayton Situation," Darby defended the reports of Roesch's Ad Hoc Committee, noted that Bishop Fulton J. Sheen "has recently assigned one of the accused professors to teach Teilhard de Chardin in the Rochester Seminary next year (1967–1968), and that another accused professor was granted a sabbatical to complete his dissertation under Leslie Dewart, author of *The Future of Belief*." In response to those who criticized the interference of the archbishop of Cincinnati, Darby simply stated that even Alter's fact-finding committee merely acknowledged what the Ad Hoc Committee had stated in its report with additional remarks on the need to understand the role of the magisterium and a commitment to academic freedom as stated in the report.[72]

Though Darby's reflections were characteristically ambiguous, there was no doubt of his loyalty to Roesch and the university. With student sit-ins, anti-ROTC demonstrations, and some civil rights protests, student life at the University of Dayton followed a national pattern, but the so-called heresy incident elicited more media attention than student movements. It also revealed the ideological tensions in church, academy, and society.

⋈ IV ⋈

THE CIVIL RIGHTS MOVEMENT PROFOUNDLY AFFECTED AMERICAN society and all religious denominations. In 1958 the Catholic bishops had proclaimed the church's impassioned opposition to racism and had indicated their commitment to desegregation. As Cyprian Davis has pointed out, "They injected a note of timid caution by seeking to draw a balance between what they saw as 'a gradualism that is merely a cloak for inaction' and a 'rash impetuosity that would sacrifice the achievements of decades in ill-timed and ill-considered ventures.'"[73] For several reasons Catholics were not in the front ranks of the civil rights movement: there were few black priests and none in leadership positions in the early sixties; priests and religious were discouraged by their superiors from demonstrations as if they violated certain behavioral codes. The famous mass demonstration at the Lincoln Memorial on August 23, 1963, featuring the historic "I have a dream" speech by Dr. Martin Luther King, Jr., drew some Catholic organizations, including some Marianists. Archbishop Patrick O'Boyle, who had desegregated the schools in the Archdiocese of Washington, D.C., in 1947, was on the platform and delivered the invocation immediately before Dr. King's address. Cyprian Davis noted that this was the first time the Catholic Church "was significantly present for a massive public demonstration under the leadership of a black civil-rights leader."[74] Catholics also responded to Dr. King's call to participate in the demonstration in Selma in March 1965. The numbers of priests, brothers, and sisters who converged in Selma were quite impressive by any standards, except those of the bishop of Birmingham, who disapproved of the demonstration.

Three years after Selma there were periodic eruptions of violence, such as in the Watts area of inner-city Los Angeles; in 1965 Malcom X was assassinated, and the Black Panthers had begun their drive for control of the programmatic and political dimensions of the movement. The assassination of Martin Luther King, Jr., on April 4, 1968, resulted in the black community's eruption of "fury, frustration and despair. Riots broke out in areas already ravaged by fire and in areas never before touched by black frustration," stated Cyprian Davis.[75]

Shortly after these tragic events, during a scheduled meeting of the Catholic Clergy Conference on the Interracial Apostolate, a special caucus of around sixty black priests and brothers met at the suggestion of Father Herman Porter, a black priest of the Diocese of Rockford, Illinois. The statement issued at the last meeting of the caucus reflects the agonizing discussions of personal and institutional responsibility during this exceedingly critical period: "The Catholic Church in the United States, primarily a white racist society, has addressed itself primarily to white society and is definitely a part of that society." The statement also challenged the church to respect the current trends in the black community affected by the civil rights and black power movements. The statement also affirmed that the church must recognize militant forces seeking rights and control of Catholic institutional presence in the black community; because of the white church's ineffectiveness in the community, it "is rapidly dying. . . . In many areas there is serious defection on the part of black Catholic youth. . . . The black community no longer looks to the Catholic church with hope."[76] The caucus became a permanent organization and issued nine demands to the American hierarchy that were related to black clergy being placed in policy-making positions in those organizations dealing with the black community, and in positions of formation of white priests in "black thinking" and in programs of black ministry. It called for a department of African-American affairs in the United States Catholic Conference (USCC), for black men to receive training in leadership, and for some of them to be chosen for the permanent diaconate program.

Cyprian Davis writes:

> The calling of the Black Catholic Clergy Caucus was a milestone in the history of the black Catholic community. It created a solidarity among the black Catholic clergy that had never previously existed. It was a return to the tradition of black Catholic initiative that had marked the black Catholic lay congresses and the Federated Colored Catholics. The one significant change was that this time it was the clergy that had seized the initiative. The demands of the clergy became a program that was implemented or has been in the process of implementation. It was, finally, the beginning of a change of direction on the part of the American Catholic church. No matter how one may view the assertion that the Catholic church in the United States was a "white racist institution," it is remarkable that the church as an institution opened itself with a minimum of resistance to the needs of its black members in most areas.[77]

Among the African-American Marianists, Brother Joseph Davis was the most active in national movements. He attended the initial meeting of the caucus, became its secretary, and was the first executive director of the National Office of Black Catholics. A native of Dayton, he entered the novitiate after graduation from high school in 1955 and received his education at the University of Dayton and at the Catholic University of America. His provincial, James Darby, appointed him to teach in Nigeria; he eventually became principal of St. Patrick College, a secondary school and junior college located in Asaba. He returned to Dayton's Chaminade High School in 1967 and later became principal of St. James Parochial School (1969–1970) shortly after the pastors of the city agreed on a busing plan to achieve racial balance.[78]

Davis attended a mid-November caucus meeting of the Black Catholic Clergy Conference in Washington, D.C., just seven months after its foundation in Detroit. At a social action seminar sponsored by the Ohio State Council of the Knights of Columbus, Davis reflected the spirit and direction of the caucus. He referred to the "missionizing" and "colonial" ethos that dominated the Catholic church's relationship with black Catholicism and black America. He told the Knights that the church has been influenced by "those blacks who will say the things church leaders want to hear . . . and will not disturb the peace and listen to them." Within this traditionalist context the church will not thrive in the black community. Davis obviously shared the deeply felt statement of the caucus to the bishops: "Until such time as black Catholics will have the chance to assume the responsibility of the Church in their own communities and can feel the weight of that responsibility, the Church will not only fail to prosper there, but the programs will remain inadequate and ineffective." He urged the Ohio Knights not to "form commissions, or committees to study the situation. . . . Please don't feel satisfied with paying the tuition of a black Catholic in a high school or in a university. . . . Rather marshall your reserves to confront the problems head-on and in the most necessary places and that can be done by working under the leadership of black Catholics in your organization." Since the Knights of Columbus had only recently promoted integration, it is likely that there were not many black members to lead such social action. It would not be out of character for Brother Davis to be ironic in his call for black Knights to become leaders of a grass-roots movement in Ohio.[79]

Joseph Davis's leadership, his rhetorical gifts, and his commitment to the spirit and agenda of the caucus led to his appointment as executive director of NOBC in 1970. When he returned to Dayton for an address, a local newspaper referred to him as a "Leader of Militants." In an interview, Davis criticized the University of Dayton as "hopeless. It is a haven for bigoted, racist attitudes and they had some bad situations there. . . . Its soul is sold to the business community of Dayton and their glorious alumni on whom they depend for money." He also subjected the American bishops to a barrage of criticism. He noted that the NOBC had refused a grant of $50,800 from the NCCB, a figure significantly lower than the NOBC had requested and one that was presented as non-negotiable. He noted that with the church's emphasis on the needs of white ethnic Americans, blacks received little from the bishops' Campaign for Human Development. Though the collection for Catholic Missions for Colored People and Indians exceeded $2.5 million, the fund is administered by three white bishops and a white executive secretary. "Blacks are viewed by the hierarchy . . . as not totally in the church—a pagan, backward people who have to be taken care of like little children."[80]

One of the purposes of the NOBC was to reverse the ways black Catholics disrespected and devalued themselves. "What NOBC is about and is saying is it's time for that foolishness to be over. If we are going to be in the church —and that's a question—we're going to be in it as equals. [I] am more and more convinced that there are few if any bishops who would lose a night's sleep if the black community were written off."[81]

The Cincinnati provincials were supportive of Brother Davis's ministry in NOBC. In February of 1976 he appealed to Father William Behringer, who had succeeded William Ferree as provincial, for a one-thousand-dollar contribution to help reduce the deficit. Because "the Bishops [had] determined that NOBC had to be financially self-sufficient," explained Davis, "we had to go into deficit spending in order to offer services and keep the movement alive." As early as 1972 NOBC had established the Black Catholics Concerned program to raise funds, but the proceeds had to be shared with "the Black Clergy Council, Black Sisters Conference, Black Lay Catholic Caucus, as well as local caucuses, who are the backbone of the fund-raising project." Though NOBC had cut expenses, the deficit was still quite large. In his letter to Behringer, Davis noted that he had relied on the province's "generosity and also your sensitive understanding of the contributions this office is making to the whole church. I have a deep faith that as God has enabled us to survive these past five years, so His providence will be with us in the future."[82] Six weeks later Davis acknowledged the contribution. The deficit persisted, however, and because this proved to be such a drain upon Davis's energies he resigned in 1977.[83]

Davis's leadership in NOBC was appreciated by a broad consensus, particularly because his qualities were vitally needed in the 1970s. His successor, Cyprian Lamar Rowe, substantiated the evaluation:

> Joseph Davis, S.M., had been one of the founding members of the NOBC and had served as the first vice-president of the National Black Catholic Clergy Caucus. He had been a prolific writer in those early days of the "movement" and those writings had a profound influence on its direction. Davis was powerfully charismatic in style and visionary in substance. He aspired to shape a markedly different role for people of color within the Church and built, often with just the force of his prophetic imagination, a movement that brought far more light and heat on to the ecclesial scene than had been seen and heard in many Black Catholic lifetimes. It was full of sound and fury and it signified much for Blacks, Hispanics, and others of color who needed to feel that the Church belonged to them.[84]

Brother Davis returned to Africa for several years before embarking on studies for the priesthood. A year after his ordination he died of cancer.[85] Though a controversial figure who alienated some Marianists, no one doubted his deep loyalty to the Society.

Father Paul Marshall, also of the Cincinnati Province, was also active in African-American movements. Ordained in the early 1970s, he has served primarily in parish ministry. A significant witness to the desperate need for an end to racism, Marshall is the only African-American Marianist in the Cincinnati Province in 1999. St. Louis Province had the largest contingent of African-American brothers; ten professed vows during the 1950s to 1970s. The correspondence of Albert Glanton is illustrative of the movement of black power and the consciousness of the Black Catholic Clergy

Conference. In a September 1968 reflection on his recent experiences with an "Upward Bound" program, one that he apparently circulated among some Marianists in the province, Brother Glanton stated that he "was confronted with attitudes which seem to indicate that Christianity is largely irrelevant to much of the Black community." After living in the white Marianist community for seventeen years he "discovered again what it means to be Black in America."[86]

Glanton commented on the relationship between black consciousness and the Brothers of Mary.

> From all appearances it means practically nothing to the major portion of the St. Louis Province. True, the Province has elevated Black Brothers to administrative positions; it has engaged in "inner city" work. It has opened Maryhurst property to Black youth; it has accepted Black youth in some of its schools; it has a few Brothers in "Upward Bound" programs; but the majority of the Brothers have no connection with these works.

Glanton explained that the Brothers were "secluded in their semi-cloistered communities . . . concerned with . . . changes in the Mass, our prayer life, authority and obedience, the pill, etc. . . . [and] have no idea what is going on in the minds and hearts of Black people . . . Black students . . . , or even of the Black Brothers of Mary."[87]

To solve these problems of seclusion, ignorance, and racism, Glanton, abhorring the traditional white patriarchal approach, suggested that the white brothers of the province should "admit that they are the victims of the same racial myths which have influenced their parents." Hence, he urged them "to spend less time on petty problems" and "begin to read books and articles written by Black men who are trying to face the racial issue in America." On his "Book List" were authors such as James Baldwin, Richard Wright, Ralph Elison, Martin Luther King, and Malcolm X.[88]

In response to this letter, Brother James F. Gray, who was assistant provincial of education, emphasized the need for placing Christianity into black American forms, what would be referred to today as the theology of inculturation. "Your paper is great in the sense that it speaks of and preaches concern and awareness. But . . . it does not seem to focus sharply or with any distinctions on the avenues to be pursued. It has a tone of almost hopelessness or negativism about the role of Christianity in the Black community."[89]

Glanton's response to Gray is not extant in the archives, but there is a letter explaining his professional status. He had been acting director of the Upward Bound program at Webster College until May 1970, when the college hired someone on a full-time basis. Glanton had applied for the position. After explaining his association with a former director who had alienated the president of the college, Glanton said he told the president he "did not intend to crawl in order to get any position."[90]

Glanton also lashed out at the Archdiocese of St. Louis for its decision to close Providence Junior High School, a Catholic institution of recent origins for black male students: "I consider this action racial discrimination of the worst sort because this decision affecting young Black Males and their future was made without any consultation with Black people who have been working with these youngsters."[91]

Glanton served principally in black programs but ended his teaching career in the English department of Serra High School in the Archdiocese of Los Angeles, which was staffed by the brothers of the Pacific Province. With an enrollment of five hundred students, 99 percent black and 85 percent Catholic in 1979, there were eight brothers on a faculty of thirty. Besides Brother Glanton there was one other African-American brother from the St. Louis Province, Edwin Johnson, who had been principal of the province's largest black Catholic high school, St. Michael's in Chicago, whose closure prompted his desire to teach at Serra.[92] Brother Johnson, who transferred to the Pacific Province, was involved in campus ministry at West Hills. Brother Glanton had died, and the first African-American Brother, Matthias Newell, was a priest of the Diocese of Richmond in 1998. In late 1983 Newell explained why it is difficult to recruit African-American candidates for the Society: "[We] do not wish to subject today's youth to the institutional prejudice and racism [we] . . . suffered as Marianists."[93]

⚔ V ⚔

THE YEAR 1968 MARKS THE PASSAGE TO A MORE CYNICAL PHASE OF the 1960s: the tragic assassinations of Martin Luther King, Jr., and Robert Kennedy; the rise of the Black Panthers and the illegal retaliations of the F.B.I., such as publishing a bogus Panthers' publication of a comic book encouraging hate and violence against local law enforcement officers, thereby delegitimating the leadership of Bobby Seale and others; the My Lai massacre and the Tet offensive in Vietnam; the break-in of the Selective Service office in Catonsville and the destruction of records by Daniel and Philip Berrigan and seven others who formed the Catonsville Nine anti-war activists; the promulgation of *Humanae Vitae*; and the subsequent public incidents of dissent by Charles Curran and others.

For the Marianists, 1968 was the year marked by William Ferree's appointment as provincial of the Cincinnati Province; the initiation of preparatory measures for the general chapter's consideration of a new constitution; the appointment of John Mulligan as provincial of the New York Province (to take effect in January 1969) and the continuous polarization between his provincial council and the leadership of the Marianist community at Chaminade High School in Mineola on Long Island; and the persistence of a spirit of renewal and reform generated as much from the climate of the 1960s as from the conciliar documents. Because of the severe decline in vocations and the rise in those brothers and priests choosing forms of Christian life outside of religious communities, the discussion of renewal and reform, the school apostolate, and the increasingly diverse lifestyles are placed within changing cultural contexts.

Renewal was identified with divergent lifestyles, with the popularity of the psychologists who were identified with exploring the need for personal fulfillment—Josef Goldbrunner, Adrian Van Kaam, and others—and with the need to abandon traditional authority structures. From the point of view of some critics, the drive toward personal freedom and dissent, and the movement toward small communities, nontraditional ministries, and in general new lifestyles were perceived as rampant individualism. Experimentation did often generate rather bizarre behavior among religious in general and some Marianists. The adoption of secular dress led to wide-ranging diversity of styles; abuses of personal freedom alienated moderate community-minded young brothers and priests; the dynamic of renewal seemed even to the promoters of change to have gained such rapid momentum that the motivation of those committed to personal freedom was questioned by older and more conservative Marianists. Among most communities of men and women religious, renewal discussions and workshops on sensitivity training, particularly in formation programs, exacerbated the tensions and generational conflicts frequently represented by opposing views in three principal areas: traditional authority and personal development; structural prayer life and faith-sharing in small communities; and the totality of the school apostolate and the movement of Christian peace and justice. Add to this mix popular music, films, and the need for grappling with intimacy so characteristic of the youth culture of the 1960s, and the result was tension and conflict.

Shortly after he became provincial, William Ferree altered the patterns of provincial administration; he emphasized visitations to local communities by all members of the provincial council on a half-time basis—one week in the office, one week visitation in a local house. Rather than issue decrees, he was committed to local conversations and democratic discernment of the needs of the province. After serving in the general administration from 1956 to 1966, five years as assistant for education, five years as assistant for apostolic action, and two years in Honolulu as president of Chaminade College, he realized the need for such dialogue on the local level. It is important to recall his commitment to individual responsibility of scholastics for their own formation when he was director of Mount St. John Scholasticate. Referred to by many as a rather unselfconscious person gifted with an extraordinarily brilliant mind and given to relatively dispassionate analysis, Ferree came into a province that had begun to decline in numbers and morale during the late Darby years.

In an outline of Ferree's May 1969 address to the Cathedral Latin School community, he referred to the death or "disappearance" of the province if the "present beliefs, attitudes, aspirations and self-image . . . continue just as they are now." He cited the statistics on "Perseverance," which were "disastrous." During 1967 and 1968 ninety-nine members of the Cincinnati Province left the religious life. The recruitment figures confirm an equally precipitous decline in the province: from seventy-five novices in 1965 to twenty-four in 1968. (Had it not been for the recruitment efforts of St. Joseph's High School in Cleveland, Ferree said the 1968 novices would have been around five.) With the decrease in personnel and because of "experiments in new life-styles, and the double-costs of decentralizing formation and setting up small communities" the $25,000 deficit of 1968 "which wiped out the cash reserve . . . will probably triple this year."

Under the rubric "Roots of the Problem" Ferree listed three factors within the Cincinnati Province and four "tendencies of the post-Conciliar Church" that were particularly related to such change. According to Ferree, the Cincinnati Province, the largest in the Society, was not prepared for "the general wave of disorientation." Since 1960, 352 novices had made vows and formed more than half of the province after the foundation of the New York Province. Two-thirds of the ninety-nine members who left the Marianists were of this group, while the remaining thirty-two were perpetually professed brothers and priests. The dynamic for these departures to lay life, according to Ferree, was the predominance of the "free-wheeling workshops of renewal" because they "provided a *ready made forum for this instability*" (emphasis in Ferree's text). The third factor in the province was leadership, which "seems to have been *overrun by the suddenness and the pervasiveness* of the disorientation," and tended to no more "than watch things go by once the storm broke."

The four tendencies in the postconciliar church were: the affirmation of secularity as a positive value; the emphasis on self-fulfillment, that is, abuses of personalism; the "reaching out" for new philosophies; and fostering "dissent, protest, and confrontations." The affirmation of the value of secularity was not intended for those committed to the religious life. Ferree approved of the Vatican II call *"to meet the secular world,"* but criticized those "'experts' in renewal" who were preaching the need "to become secular itself. . . . Similarly, the 'spirituality of the secular life' (spirituality of incarnation, spirituality of possession) which Vatican II did so much to promote *for the laity*, was never intended to replace the *already* developed 'spirituality of the religious life.'" The "evangelical counsels," so basic to the religious life, and the spirituality of the laity are both "valid ways to God, but for different states of life."[94]

Ferree embraced personalism as an essential antidote to the bureaucratization of contemporary life. However, when the emphasis is on self-fulfillment as an end rather than "the result of self-transcendent service . . . then all values are subverted. By the process of making 'fulfillment' an *end*, we succeed in making everything else and everyone else a *means*. Unless we fully reinstate a personalism that is self-transcendent in service, we will not be able even to imagine common purposes [as if he were responding to the famous quip by Timothy Leary, 'Tune in, turn on, and drop out.']" Ferree noted that there are tendencies to *drop out* of secularization rather than to "vitalize it"; the role of "conscience is being used to drop out of law instead of applying it; dissent . . . justifies dropping out" of common purposes instead of promoting the means to achieve unity; dialogue is synonymous with dropping out of authority rather than providing input for good leadership; lastly, "freedom is being invoked to drop out of responsibility."[95] In accord with his philosophical training, Ferree concluded by noting "that the vertiginous and *ever-increasing rate of growth and change* which is the most striking characteristic of modern developed civilization has simply frightened large masses of people into 'wanting out.' There is, of course, no place to go; so they have to content themselves with dissent and protest, a fairly common 'adolescent' reaction." This adolescent reaction illustrates the crisis in civilization, a crisis "from which it is extremely easy to drop out. We must learn to seek our answers first within our own commitment."[96]

Ferree noted that the philosophies of "existential phenomenology" and "the more solidly-based process philosophies" are supportive of dissent and encourage many religious to question the permanence of their commitment, as if their existence at the point of profession of vows and their existence at some future junction will be so different as to make that profession no longer binding. "Without full personal commitment religious life is not only unworkable—it is unthinkable."[97]

"The strategy of TURN-AROUND" entailed seven points: (1) In opposition to secularity, "*reassert the essential value system of religious life*" and (2) *reintegrate all the Marianist options of consecration* [i.e., Marianist religious, those with a "state" commitment, and lay Marianists]. (3) As a counter to personalist inadequacies, "it is necessary to practice *good administration*." (4) To redirect the "mindless thrashing about for 'relevance' that abandons Chaminade's vision," it is necessary to "revive interest in the Marianist Foundations." (5) Rather than merely grinding out "former students" as members of the Society, it will be necessary to "complete our Marianist Apostolate" by working with adults in apostolic action. (6) "Turn the 'Mission complex' of denouncing what others are trying to do into *an honest effort to build what is claimed to be better*. Work for less moral indignation which, when sustained over long periods by sinners, is always suspect and usually phony." (7) Allow the moral indignation about practices and opinions in the Society to engender "a certain pluralism of *life-styles* once common goals had been reinstated. An example might be the structured, personal, personalist and charismatic styles . . . or the division of the largest communities into smaller, more homogeneous units." Such a strategy would allow those who were "strongly committed to a style," to prove the feasibility of their plan rather than being merely "morally indignant about the past."[98]

In his summation of the "OVER-ALL PROBLEM" that the present crisis yielded, he stated: "we are seeing more clearly that the positions we assume are positions of faith and commitment on our part; and that we, and under God's grace are responsible for them." With consistency and clarity he remarked that "in the profound crisis like the present one, we can be quite sure that no matter what or how widespread the *occasions* are for the disorientation, we, and, we alone are the *cause*. And, of course, by the same token, we can be the cure."[99]

Ferree's analyses of the many dimensions of the problems in society, church, and the Marianists were based less on a year's experience as provincial than on the many years he had been considered the Marianists' Marianist. His emphasis on disorientation in the contemporary church harks back to the late 1930s, when he wrote in opposition to the separation between the monastic and the apostolic and proffered a positive integration of the two. He was committed to Chaminade's vision of the sodality and of the Family of Mary, a vision that precluded individualism and promoted the self-transcendent service of humanity. He proposed that "once common goals have been reinstated," and there is a general agreement on the sub-stantive purpose of the Society, then experiments "in pluralism based on life-styles and small communities may be the most appropriate means to generate commitment and consensus."[100]

As the leader of the Cincinnati Province, Ferree allowed the formation of small communities, perhaps as much to reduce the intensity of polarization in large school-based communities as to allow the younger generation the opportunity to promote new models for the religious life. However, he remained deeply concerned about contemporary trends; his first two cir-cular Letters were eighty-nine pages, nearly equally divided between "Theological Opinions Today" (circular no. 1) and the "Theology of the Evangelical Counsels," (circular no. 2) with the writings of Hans Urs von Balthasar on one page and commentaries by Ferree on the opposite page. They were intended to engender serious dialogue, serious in the sense that both sides of the dialogue agree on common goals, particularly "self-transcendent service." He referred to those Marianists who represented the "Church effervescent" based on "the presupposition that the new ideas (any new ideas) would send the old ideas back into the woodwork as irrelevant, so that the bright future would need nothing more than a sort of sensitivity-session accommodation among the bright new ideas." Committed to "tough-minded confrontation in dialogue" Ferree revealed some cynicism about the ability of the advocates of new lifestyles to be tough-minded. Nevertheless, he closed the second circular with the embrace of the con-temporary age: "It is open, it is dynamic, it is alive and full of hope."[101]

He yearned for an honest dialogue between the prophets, some of whom "dance to their own drums," and the administrators dedicated to achieving results. Unfortunately, he concluded, there are far too many Marianists with the self-image of prophets, but few real prophets and even fewer good administrators. "My own suggestion, constantly reported, is that we start talking to one another about the things that are important."[102]

The year following these 1969 circular letters Ferree suffered a heart attack; after his recovery he was immersed in preparation for the 1971 gen-eral chapter, charged with completing a new constitution. Even had he been well, it is doubtful that serious dialogue would have ensued. His intellec-tual power and his strong Marianist presence, despite his unassuming and unpretentious personality, inhibited the emergence of dialogue partners among the proponents of change. He tended to speak in nondialogical terms: for example, his invocation of von Balthasar was to the authoritative theologian who perceived the evangelical counsels as based on the awareness of the crucified Christ and the assent of Mary to the Cross. The 'spirit' of the Evangelical Counsels is quite simply the Spirit of the Church. Whoever has the mind of the Church has the mind of *Agape*—i.e. self-renouncing love which seeks not its own, bears all, hopes all, suffers all to the end (1 Cor 13:5.7.). . . . Living the Counsels does not mean setting any example of one's own before the Church, but keeping awake the memory of the archetypal obedience of the Son of God."[103]

Von Balthasar and Ferree articulated their theological reflection in the language of mystery, self-transcendence, a Christology of the cross and a complementary Mariology of obedience. In contrast, younger Marianists would use the language of mystery, but with the emphasis on immanence, the humanity of Jesus and the relational Mary, the nurturing mother who provides sustenance to the young Marianist. There are anthropological bases to each of these languages, but they are not simply negative and positive. Indeed, to transcend self assumes a positive quality; however, the affirmations of a graced humanity reveal a positive Christ-centered humanism. If the world is repudiated, then transcendence of self may be the most appropriate means of the religious life. If the world is not threatening, then stress on immanence and humanism is a more feasible strategy for religious life. However, because the 1960s were tumultuous and given to polarization on a vast array of issues, the two theological languages reflected the tension and anxiety, idealism and cynicism of the era.[104]

Nowhere was the struggle over Marianist identity more volatile than in the New York Province. As noted earlier, John Dickson had been a close associate of William Ferree, and as provincial he had consulted Ferree on prospective circular letters, several of which were positive commentaries on the documents of Vatican II. Though he consistently identified the educational or school apostolate as at the core of Marianist commitment, Dickson was also immersed in promotion of the sodality with a wide perspective on alternative apostolates among alumni and associates of Marianist schools. Hence, he was flexible on the issue of brothers engaging in non-school apostolates on the weekends, such as the four brothers involved in programs of the Confraternity of Christian Doctrine (CCD) classes in an inner-city parish.[105]

Unlike James Darby of the Cincinnati Province, Dickson was not authoritarian but rather tended to be dialogical in his governing style, despite his occasional expression of sarcasm. On one occasion in early 1966, as he related in a letter to Ferree, Dickson was subjected to Darby's emotionally charged tirade against the New York Province in which he said "[we were] shabby in our dealings with him, that we were not honest and sincere, that we were working behind the scenes" regarding the New York Province's decision to close the postulancy program at Beacon.[106] Though there were several layers of complexity involved in this dispute, it simply reveals a long-standing conflict rooted in differences of personality and styles of governance. The following year Dickson assigned four of the twelve scholastics to the scholasticate of the St. Louis Province at St. Mary's University in San Antonio, while the remainder went to the interprovincial scholasticate, Mount St. John, attached to the University of Dayton, a move that symbolized Dickson's independence from the traditional deference to the Cincinnati Province. Brother Stephen Glodek, who became the second American brother to be appointed provincial (New York Province), was assigned to St. Mary's University, and after two years he received word that if he was accepted at Columbia University he could complete his education as a scholastic in this secular university and live in the Brooklyn community at Holy Trinity Parish High School.[107] Such a departure from traditional formation represents Dickson's accommodation to modernity and could be rationalized in terms of several conciliar documents. In a circular April 1, 1966, Dickson underscored "the efforts of Vatican Council II" to revitalize "the Church's sense of mission—of being sent by Christ to the people, of meeting them where they are, of meeting their needs as they exist in a given institutional and structured place . . . . The laity, the people of God, who in reality are the Church, must be involved."[108] It would not be difficult to apply these principles to new modes of formation, a blend of the local community-based residence with an education at Columbia University.

American Marianist seminarians, who had attended St. Meinrad's School of Theology during the war, returned to Fribourg in 1947. Because of the disenchantment with its rigid Thomism and because of widespread preference for American religious and secular culture, the Marianist provincials abandoned the Fribourg seminary and an interprovincial house was opened adjacent to St. Louis University, where the Marianist seminarians were enrolled at the Divinity School in 1967. Father John Mulligan, former spiritual director at Fribourg and novice director of the New York Province, was the first director of the program, the American Marianist Seminary. Renewal and reform characterized the program, which emphasized collegiality with the Servites and other religious communities attending the Divinity School. When John Mulligan was appointed provincial of New York Province in early 1969, he was replaced by Father John Bolin of the Pacific Province. The Marianist enrollment hovered around thirty. Because of a crisis in the administration, which led the Jesuits to transfer their seminarians in 1973, the Marianists decided to move their programs to St. Michael's College, the Basilian school, one of the seven cluster schools of theology at the University of Toronto. Father George Montague of the St. Louis Province, who was committed to the charismatic movement, was the transitional director at St. Louis and St. Michael's (1974–1975).[109]

Father George Cerniglia, who attended Chaminade High School in Mineola, became novice director and later assistant provincial of the New York Province; he enthusiastically recalled his experience in the program in St. Louis.[110] Both the Columbia University and the St. Louis University programs symbolized new directions in the religious life of the New York Province, which when blended with other experiments in renewal were easily adopted departures from the monastic routine that was once so large a part of the Marianist tradition. That tradition was revived at Chaminade High School in Mineola.

Philip Eichner and John McGrath had formed a close relationship from their high school days at Chaminade. Patrick Tonry met them in Fribourg; Eichner and McGrath were ordained to the priesthood in 1966; Tonry preceded them by a year. He and Eichner were together as priest-faculty members at Chaminade, while McGrath pursued graduate studies at the University of Nijmegen to study under Edward Schillebeeckx. According to Tonry, when he and Eichner returned to the United States after four years in Fribourg, they became deeply alienated by the trends in Marianist religious life, particularly the pluralistic lifestyles, individualism, the breakdown of monastic routine of meditation, prayer, Eucharist, and the New York provincial's complicity with these trends.[111] Philip Eichner, director of the religious community and later president at Chaminade, who became the most highly articulate of these traditionalists, also perceived a rise of anti-institutionalism and a concomitant decline in a commitment to the school apostolate. Since Chaminade was the most prestigious school in the province, Eichner's position as an impassioned advocate of Marianist monastic tradition was rooted in an institution highly regarded by the Catholic families of Long Island as a school of academic excellence, traditional Catholicism, and discipline.

Eichner embodied these qualities. An excellent student in every phase of his education, he was highly regarded for his powers of analytical reasoning and for his excellent teaching. His Catholic self-understanding was expressed in a philosophical certitude; he was a disciplined leader who could preside with energetic and effective authority. As a Marianist, he did not respect provincials who did not argue their cause with clarity, certitude, conviction, and the traditional charism of their office. Nor did he respect collegiality and pluralistic lifestyles, because of their deviation from his view of Marianist identity. Pluralism appeared to him as a betrayal of the central truths of Marianist tradition.[112]

In a letter to Dickson, Eichner explained his disappointment with the chapter of 1967, to which he had been elected: "At none of the three sessions were issues openly and honestly on the table." He was disappointed that Dickson stated at the chapter of 1967, "I have never conceived a policy being a matter for the Chapter." He said he was still waiting for reports of several houses and minutes of the provincial council. Actually, the purpose of this letter was to elaborate on why he resigned from the prospective 1968 chapter. "I accept your desire to run the Province without the Chapter and therefore I have resigned out of deference to your determined and effective policy." It was not to be considered "a personal move against yourself or any member of the Provincial Administration, but rather a capitulation to that which I can't change." He did not intend "to create another camp. I do not believe in revolution in religious life. . . . While I may disagree profoundly with a number of Provincial procedures and programs, I will not organize in any way active resistance against you or them." He cited Dickson's remarks that the 1967 chapter was "a terrible emotional experience" and the election of 1968 was "an organized movement against the Provincial Administration." Though he stated that his resignation "is not substantially or initially due to any Provincial decision regarding Chaminade,"[113] it is difficult to separate Eichner from the high school. In any event, polarization was obvious, and shortly after the chapter of 1968 Dickson resigned.

In January of 1969 John Mulligan, who had been in formation ministry for several years, became provincial. Like Dickson, he was accustomed to dialoguing with small groups, and in his correspondence he was reluctant to engage in argumentation. One of the electric charges in the polarized atmosphere was financial; a portion of the cash reserves of Chaminade was turned over to the provincial administration, a portion of the school's income in what was called in the Marianist lexicon, *boni*. Over the years provincial funds were used to support Chaminade High School in Hollywood, Florida, and Rose Hill Novitiate in Charlottesville, Virginia. In the late 1960s Chaminade was seeking funds for capital improvements. Philip Eichner expected to receive a very low interest loan from the provincial administration, but neither Dickson nor Mulligan would accede to such a request, which, of course, exacerbated the tension between the provincial and the president.[114]

Amid the widening gap of trust, the traditionalist lifestyle of the Chaminade community was becoming an issue of outsider versus insider, of minority versus majority, of periphery versus core. In this volatile situation, Eichner and his confreres became convinced that to maintain their integrity as a community it was necessary to start their own formation program. The issue was no longer criticizing the lifestyles of the province, but defending the traditionalist lifestyle of the Chaminade community.

In an October 1969 nine-page single-spaced letter to Mulligan, Eichner reflected on the situation as it had developed over the past two weeks. Eichner informed him that despite Mulligan's attempt to preempt an open discussion between the Mineola community and the official Visitors, by informing the latter of Eichner's lack of cooperation, Father Hoffer, the superior general, gave public approval, support, and "official approbation of our lifestyle, the first and only time a major superior has given public approval to what we are doing." Hoffer encouraged Eichner to work within the provincial structure "but not at the price of what we have." Eichner told Mulligan that Hoffer was concerned about the formation program of the province; perhaps an allusion to the scholastics at Columbia University as symbolic of an unraveling of formation. Eichner did not inform Hoffer of his own formation proposal.[115]

When Eichner heard that Mulligan had told William Ferree that the men of the Mineola community were separatists, Eichner accused the provincial of separating the province itself from the "traditional concept of the SM community life, common life, and prayer life. If there is separation who has separated from whom? Who is it that has promoted pluralism in the Province over the past five years or who is it that has allowed pluralistic lifestyles to become not only *desiderata* but also *facta*." He pointed to the St. Louis Seminary, where "common meditation was abolished . . . the religious habit was eliminated in favor of the more secular accommodation to the University milieu," and where daily Eucharist was "abolished in favor of a more 'plural' Eucharistic experience because they belong to . . . the University and parish communities." He also criticized the education of scholastics at Columbia University and the provincial's rationale that Marianist schools "are too confining for our candidates." He told Mulligan that Ferree made a surprise, yet "refreshing" visit to the Mineola community.[116]

The Cincinnati provincial may not have discouraged the stress upon the monastic structure at the Chaminade community. Indeed, he may have perceived it as representative of legitimate pluralism. Because of this apparent convergence of the views of Eichner and Ferree, this section of the letter demands a lengthy quote:

> We spoke for about five hours. He came to see if we were just prophets, that is, stating a position without wanting to fight for it; and to see how deep we

thought the crisis was. We both agreed that the crisis is quite profound, more so than most people want to admit, and that it will take much work to deal with it. On the character and depth of the crisis, on the nature of religious life and all related points, we agreed very much. He feels that much that is passed off as religious life today is not viable in the real order. We discussed his circular on the contemporary question of religious life. To remedy the malaise he suggested the following procedure: he would legitimately recognize the pluralism that already exists, and structure the Province according to it, and then start a dialectic between the various styles. This, he felt, would at least stop the effervescent from keeping the rest of the Province from doing what they want to do. He listed four levels of life-styles, two of which he does not consider viable (nor do I), but which have to be considered so in order to flush the thrush from the brush. I agree completely with the descriptions and judgements regarding these life-styles. The two viable ones would form the Right Anchor: the Structured and the Personal. The other wing would be the Left Flap: The Apostolic Effervescent and the Charismatics. I mentioned to him that Father Keenan has attempted to effect the same recognition of pluralism by his meeting with the Provincial Council some weeks previous but had gotten nowhere. Therefore, I welcomed his attempts to recognize the de facto situation, and by recognizing it to pull it out of the underground and thereby be able to deal with it face to face instead of the guerilla warfare which is now the tactical mode. I promised him our full cooperation with this plan.[117]

In his response to Eichner's long letter, which conveyed a sense of achievement among the leadership of the society—Hoffer and Ferree—Mulligan explained his prior consultation with Hoffer and Ferree as simply providing information and not intended to influence their assessment of Chaminade's position within the province. "Father Hoffer wrote to me from Chaminade to say how much he enjoyed his visit there. That doesn't disappoint me or make me angry. I'm glad his visit was, as you indicate, a morale boost." He told Eichner that he had suggested to Ferree that he visit Chaminade on the way to his visit to Washington, D.C. "Ferree's insight and counsel means a lot to me. . . . He has problems in his province and we have problems too. I saw him last week in Dayton and he spoke about the four levels of life-styles that he discussed with you." As to the other issues in Eichner's letter, he postponed a response until the provincial council would meet with him and "the House Council of Mineola."[118]

In contrast to Father Eichner's letters, Mulligan's were rather brief and dispassionate. Hence, the material on the Chaminade-Mineola case is quite animated and extensive, while the provincial documentation tends to be official reports and chronicles of significant events. There was a brief period of *détente* generated by an agreement on the need for structural pluralism;

within the framework of the province that would entail recognition of diverse styles, including what was considered the traditional Marianist way of life.

This position was first outlined in a paper dated December 1, 1969, unsigned but from the office of the president (Philip Eichner) of Chaminade High School. In its recommendation of pluralism, the Mineola community recognized its de facto situation in opposition to the principle of pluralism as "an absolute good"; indeed, the "proponents of this paper have worked against pluralism in religious life (concrete Marianist life)." However, by establishing plural structures it "protects the healthy element"—non-pluralists in principle, from the unhealthy element.

The position paper projected pluralism "in attitude, in actual religious expression, in a concrete anthropology, in education, in formation." It proposed a reorganization of the province "on the basis of a confederation of houses each responsible for its own life-style (pluralism). Provincial authority has become so diffuse; it has replaced decision by consensus, and directive by exhortation." Hence, since the Mineola community considered most decisions to be made at the local level, proponents perceived their proposal as legitimating this de facto self-determination.[119]

The confederation principle precluded the need for a provincial council, while the provincial chapter, representative of the houses, was to be the only deliberative policy-making body. Father Thomas Stanley, general assistant for apostolic life, had proposed the foundation of a new province composed of those in the Cincinnati and New York Provinces who shared a common commitment to Marianist identity that would have subsumed the local autonomy proposed by the Mineola community.[120] Intended to remedy polarization in both provinces, Stanley's proposal was unrealistic, as it would move brothers and priests on an ideological chessboard.

The very evening that this proposal was dated, John Mulligan presented to the Mineola community his bulletin No. 16 on Structured Pluralism. In this significant "Provincial Bulletin" (or circular) Mulligan noted William Ferree's idea "of establishing certain communities with a specific thrust, e.g. personalist, structured [i.e. monastic], charismatic, etc." (This was incorporated into Father Stanley's proposal.) Since the New York Province was already pluralistic, Mulligan's proposal involved "structuring our present *de facto* situation." It was based on three "presuppositions":

> 1. We are in crisis; the question is one of corporate survival. In some of our communities it is at least questionable whether the life-style will survive into another generation.

2. The provincial administration is made to feel responsible for the future of the province, but it is not in a position to effect the structures nor to inspire the unity necessary to meet the crisis.

3. In some local communities those who are making the decisions that affect our future are not made to feel personally responsible for the long-term consequences of their decisions. We have suffered from the vast diffusion of responsibility.

With obvious reference to Chaminade-Mineola, Mulligan noted a Marianist-style "love it or leave it . . ." expressed with bumper-sticker succinctness. The proposal would change the provincial chapter to a representation of houses based on subsidiarity. It was only a proposal, however, one that would be considered by the provincial council.[121] In a memo to the provincial council, Eichner stated that Mulligan's summary of his proposal was "clear, forthright and unequivocal. The community sensed a Provincial directness and readiness to make decisions which would restore us to greater health as a Province. . . . Both in mode and content, it expresses well the dimensions of the religious crisis in which we find ourselves."[122]

The mutual commitment to the principle of structured pluralism was short-lived. As John McGrath explained it, Mineola emphasized structural pluralism in terms of local autonomy, and the province emphasized that the structural character meant that all decisions regarding pluralism had to be approved by the provincial council, which maintained a degree of central authority.[123] However, it did endorse the principle of local authority in formation, particularly the formation program of Chaminade-Mineola. As an example, John McGrath, as assistant for religious life, wrote to Philip Eichner approving the summer program of brothers in his community. McGrath's assertion of authority elicited a five-page, single-spaced letter to John Mulligan in which the president of Chaminade-Mineola elaborated on the differences between power and authority, the abdication of provincial power in deference to conciliar power. "I find this reversion to a former structure in 'approving' summer programs somewhat 'anachronistic' because it is a throwback to an era prior to the agreements on pluralism." The polarization between the community of Chaminade-Mineola and the Province of New York had so widened that Father Eichner wrote to Father Mulligan on November 30, 1969, referring to recent correspondence, apparently from Father John McGrath, and Brother William A. Abel, director of finances; such correspondence "represents a full renunciation of structural pluralism . . . my disillusionment is complete and I feel that the betrayal is gigantic." Signed by six other members of the community, Eichner's letter also indicated that "our patience with your programs, committees, procedures, papers, formularies, statues [*sic*] has reached a limit. We will deal with you and with you alone on these issues, and all ask for a meeting at your earliest convenience."[124]

Mulligan's commitment to team governance with the provincial council obviated an official meeting alone with the Chaminade community. Because he considered that the provincial council had affirmed the legitimacy of Mineola's formation program, its traditional structure and its commitment to the school apostolate, and was willing to negotiate the settlement of the loan problem, Mulligan evaluated Eichner's letter as a symbol of the province's failure to achieve a *modus vivendi* with the Mineola community. After consulting with the council and with members of the chapter by phone he wrote to Paul Hoffer, superior general, and included correspondence between him and Eichner that clearly established "unmistakably our consistent inability to exercise effective or fruitful leadership in regard to Chaminade. . . . Whatever efforts we have made at structured pluralism have not really altered anything. . . . Efforts to exercise an evaluative role in their behalf are judged as over-reaching our bounds."[125]

He told Hoffer of his respect for the quality of religious expression at Chaminade as actually "admirable. In fact, we had hoped that the strong elements here would speak positively to others in the Province." However, the Mineola "community has effectively closed itself off in such a way that the image is not at all attractive to other religious." Ironically, Mulligan and his council's attempt to recognize Mineola within the commitment to pluralism had been viewed by many in the province as a sign of the administration's "pro-Mineola bias in our decisions and policies. However, correspondence from Chaminade consistently asserts the opposite."[126]

Because the provincial administration over the past two years had been unable to "guide, lead or serve Chaminade in any constructive way," Mulligan and his council, with the support of his administration, "formally and urgently" requested the appointment of an official "visitor" to the Chaminade community. "The visitor should be empowered with Provincial authority" in Chaminade's regard and "should exercise line authority between the Superior General and the director of the community. Administratively it would remove Chaminade from any dealings with the present provincial administration." Though Mulligan did not explicitly state that the Mineola community should be severed from the Society, the following remark was interpreted by Hoffer and through him by Philip Eichner, as tantamount to dismissal from the Society. "The principal aim of the visitation would be to help Chaminade work out its autonomy from the rest of the province," wrote Mulligan.[127]

Rather than send this letter to Rome, Mulligan personally delivered it to Hoffer, who immediately telephoned to ask Eichner to travel to Rome for a consultation. He and Father Francis Keenan—who after experiencing disillusionment with the trends in the province over several years was assigned to Mineola—met with the superior general and the general council. The separation from the province became official, but Mineola preferred not a visitor but rather open negotiations with Hoffer as arbiter. The general council enforced the decree of separation and from that time (1970) on Chaminade-Mineola remained directly under the authority of the general administration until after the general chapter of 1976, when it became the Meribah Province.[128]

A detailed account of the several crises over the years would not only be beyond the scope of this work but, because there are many facets to the various visitations among the general administration and the Sacred Congregation for Religious, the documentation is incomplete. The extant material does indicate that, despite the opposition of Father Stephen Tutas and Father John Mulligan, and the majority of the 1976 general chapter in favor of less than provincial status, the Sacred Congregation for Religious, particularly after the visitation of its prefect, Archbishop Mayer, decided that the Mineola community at Chaminade should be established as an independent province, the Meribah Province.[129] The Mineola community, which, according to Philip Eichner, had not had a positive relationship with Father Tutas, saw this denouement as the only decision that could provide them with security to maintain their traditions. Of course, the province lost its most prestigious institution.[130] Not to have achieved its reintegration was a severe blow to the province; the foundation of Meribah was perceived as the vindication of its notion of traditional Marianist identity.

Throughout this period the Chaminade-Mineola community perceived itself to be a besieged minority struggling against what it saw as the abandonment of a century of tradition in favor of new forms of what it considered to have been the diffusion of authority—the commitment to nonschool apostolates, the dominance of individualism, and the dissolution of the common life. Concurrent with the creation of the Meribah Province were analogous developments in other communities of men and women religious. For example, in opposition to the liberal drift of the New England Province of the Sisters of Notre Dame de Namur, a conservative province was established, which also had its motherhouse in Massachusetts.

John Mulligan was not simply a liberal, nor did Philip Eichner fit neatly the conservative mold. Instead, they represented two opposing views of the religious life. Mulligan's experience was in formation and, in the tradition of William Ferree, he encouraged novices and later seminarians to assume responsibility for their own formation according to Chaminade's directive to be in permanent mission. Influenced by the significance of psychology, the need for personal growth, and the inhibiting tendencies of traditional monastic structures to the development of authentic spirituality within an active apostolate, Mulligan was open to facilitating the personal, spiritual, ministerial, and professional growth of young Marianists.

This new generation was socialized as Marianists during the 1960s and in a sense was affected by protest, dissent, the drive for authenticity, and, of course, by Vatican II and subsequent developments in ecclesiology, scripture studies, and later liberation theology, which tended to emphasize pluralism, historical methodologies and perspectives, and the preferential option for the poor. In this sense it was only appropriate and hardly that adventurous to allow scholastics to attend Columbia University, and for Marianist seminarians to include in their formation prayer and liturgical experience with other religious communities, and to attend parish liturgies at St. Louis University's chapels. No doubt John Mulligan and others in formation would have followed the same path had they had the opportunity. In short, monastic routine did not have a strong hold upon them. Mulligan's openness to the new theological developments prompted him to pursue Marianist identity within his collaborative style of leadership.

In contrast, Philip Eichner was very academic, gifted with a facility in languages and with a sense of his intellectual authority. In a recent interview he said that the climate of Mount St. John during his time in the scholasticate was formulaic, rigorist, and anti-intellectual. He became a dedicated teacher, well known for inspiring vocations, including Father James Heft, the widely known and highly regarded chancellor of the University of Dayton. Though he thrived in the classroom, Eichner was not an extrovert. He entered the seminary at the beginning of Vatican II and was open to changes in the liturgy but was more influenced by the Thomism of the Dominican professors at the university than by the contemporary existential and historical Thomism of theologians such as Karl Rahner, S.J., and Bernard Lonergan, S.J. Eichner's close associate at Mineola, Francis Keenan, was also steeped in traditional Thomism, which provided him with philosophical certitude. Since Keenan also studied Karl Barth at Union Theological Seminary, he blends the antimodernity of neo-Thomism with the ecumenism of Barth. Keenan was drawn to preaching, while Eichner was attracted to teaching, philosophical reflection, and dialectical argumentation. Had he not felt compelled to defend both the school apostolate and the traditional integrity of Marianist life at Mineola, he would have pursued doctoral studies. At heart he was a restorationist, critical of the culture of the 1960s, which appeared to him to be without philosophical or religious anchor; he was certainly averse to the current Marianist way of life, which he considered to be long on psychology, team governance, and experimentalism and short on traditional authority, the monastic life, and the school apostolate.[131]

In contrast to the restorationists of the school apostolate, William Ferree, who served only one term as provincial of Cincinnati Marianists, was open to new apostolates, a position in accord with his longtime commitment to social justice and Catholic Action. In response to the generational and ideological gaps within the province, compounded by a loss of roughly fifty members a year, Ferree proclaimed the theology of the religious life according to Hans Urs von Balthasar. Von Balthasar fostered the restoration of tradition by his creative Christ-centered theology of the evangelical counsels. Ferree's strategy of pluralism was actually a reluctant accommodation to contemporary developments. Sympathetic to pluralism and therefore to both Eichner and Mulligan, Ferree was caught between the decline of the old and the rise of a new Marianist identity. Had he become provincial in 1958 rather than in 1968, Ferree would have been a more effective leader. As mentioned earlier, from the late 1930s Ferree had advocated a Marianist identity based on an integration between interior spirituality and the active apostolate. The Meribah Province had a self-image of blending the monastic and the school apostolate with a strong emphasis on authority as essential to maintaining Marianist traditions. In contrast to Ferree's notion of the school as a kind of sodality engaged in redeeming the world, Chaminade-Mineola did not explicitly extend its commitment to social-justice issues in the Ferrean sense. Those who promoted the new Marianist identity based on an appropriation of the 1960s as a positive experience of growth—intellectually, spiritually, and professionally—tended to relate to social-justice issues and to integrate Marianist commitment to varieties of ministries including teaching. They would be confined by the monastic structure of the Meribah Province and would perceive Ferree's synthesis as representing ideals that needed to be transposed to a new era.

Recall Ferree's dictum for those in religious formation, which, according to George Montague, was radical for its day (1940s and 1950s); rather than just proclaim the characteristics of a good Marianist, Ferree urged scholastics to take charge of their own formation. This "empowering process," in accord with the ideals of Chaminade's Sodality of Bordeaux, was adopted in varying degrees by several Marianists involved in formation, the sodality, and provincial leadership; examples of the latter are John Dickson, John

Mulligan in the New York Province, and Bertrand Clemens and Joseph Ste-fanelli in the Province of the Pacific.

As the younger Marianists tended to embrace measures for renewal on the basis of personal responsibility, and promoted reforms of the governance structure along the lines of collegiality and subsidiarity, they were supported by those leaders indebted to Ferree and his positive anthropology. Hence, many Marianists were prepared for the changes in the church and the academy and were favorable to renewal and reform. In each community there were those in varying degrees of reaction, not necessarily to renewal and reform but to the culture of the sixties. In a real sense these tensions among the Marianists, so endemic to religious communities, represent the dynamic of this work: self-understanding of authority, spirituality, and ministry are profoundly affected by developments in church, academy, and society. The overarching thesis of this work is that from the origins of the Society there have been periods of integration and fragmentation between the monastic and the apostolic dimensions of Marianist life. William Joseph Chaminade, Joseph Simler, William Ferree, and others articulated a synthesis between spirituality and ministry: Chaminade's integration of prayer and the apostolic mission of the Sodality and the Society of Mary; Simler's revival of the Sodality, his biography of the founder, and his incarnational spirituality; and Ferree's retrieval of Chaminade's documents on the Family of Mary and the presence of God in the Sodality, the state, and various forms of apostolic life.

These notable Marianists perceived the common life or the monastic as not the boundary within which spirituality was cultivated but rather one sphere interacting with the sphere of ministry to form the vital center of Marianist apostolic spirituality. During times of fragmentation when the rigorists dominated and their negative anthropology polluted the common life, the apostolates were the only sources of spirituality.

The Second Vatican Council's call for renewal and reform was steeped in an incarnational spirituality and a notion of the sacramental character of the church in mission. This became the ecclesiological rationale for an updated synthesis of Marianist spirituality and ministry, energizing the dynamic relationships of society, academy, church, and Marianist ways of life.

CHAPTER NINE

Epilogue
Convergences: Past, Present, and Future

❧ I ❧

INTRINSIC TO THE METHODOLOGY OF RESEARCHING AND WRITING about the recent past is the shift from the perspective of the historian to that of the journalist. To capture the salient trends of the recent Marianist past, it is necessary to rely on published circulars, reports, and other documents, particularly because of the confidential character of contemporary correspondence. To discern the many instances of personal witness to events and their meanings, I relied on provincial letters and articles by prominent Marianists as they related to real problems, genuine aspirations, the sense of mission, and the role of Mary in their lives. The principles for selecting materials are the following: reflective character and insights on the significance of carrying on with the low numbers of active brothers and priests; their clarity in rendering distinctive historical self-understanding; the cogency of their insight on Marianist charism; and the depictions of "deep stories" past, present, and future. This material is augmented by some oral interviews, providing a third dimension to the topics. This chapter is also dependent on the general narrative of religious communities in the post–Vatican II era, a period of malaise and ennui in the social and political life of the nation. Indeed, some would say that in this contemporary culture "to cope is a cardinal virtue."

By way of background material I provide a brief statistical account of the membership in the Society of Mary in America. The total membership during the ten-year periods between 1965 and 1995 is: 1,372, 1,101, 821, and 746. Since there was a significant drop in novices, from 116 in 1965 to 16

282

in 1995, the average age of the Society has increased considerably. Because these numbers include members of American missionary regions, the number of those living in the United States is lower than these figures. Though these statistics are comparable to most apostolic communities, the Marianist working brothers decreased from over one hundred in 1965 to fewer than twenty in 1995, a drop that has not been adequately analyzed. Several reasons are proffered for the decline in membership in religious congregations: the attraction of the life of lay ministry, alienation derived from generational and ideological conflicts, the drive for self-fulfillment associated with marriage and a career, and the general confusion of identity of religious life.

One set of statistics reveals a narrowing of the ratios between priests and brothers: in 1965 there were 217 priests and 1,115 brothers; in 1995 the figures were 197 and 549. This ratio does not account for those in retirement, nor was there a significant rise in priestly vocations during this period. The church's need for priests may be a factor, but the priestly ministries appear to be more significant to the Society as well. In 1995 many served as campus ministers at the three Marianist universities and the seventeen Marianist schools. However, since there were twenty Marianist parishes in 1995, there was an obvious need for priests. Because brothers are members of pastoral teams in schools, universities, and parishes, priests were still living in community with brothers.

Hence, the proportional increase in priest members did not entail the clericalization of the Society of Mary. In 1995 two brothers were provincials; a brother was president of the University of Dayton; and the novice master of the interprovincial novitiate was a brother. Therefore, the historical egalitarian spirit still characterizes the mixed character of the Marianists in America.[1]

❖ II ❖

THE SUPERIOR GENERAL DURING THE 1970S, THE SECOND AMERICAN to serve in that capacity, was Stephen Tutas of the Province of the Pacific. Elected at the general chapter of 1971, Tutas was, as mentioned in the last chapter, responsible for helping to forge a solution to the thorny problem of Chaminade-Mineola and its status in the Society. With wide administrative experience at Chaminade College in Honolulu—acting president and later academic dean—as rector of the Marianist Seminary in Fribourg and as a member of the provincial council, Tutas was so well organized that he could easily continue his role as superior general with active participation in the Union of Superiors General in Rome. After he returned to the United States in the early 1980s he became president of the American Conference of Major Superiors of Men (CMSM) for nearly five years. Committed to the principles of subsidiarity and collegiality adopted at the 1971 general chapter, he was associated with the continuity of renewal in the 1970s and 1980s.[2]

In an article in the first number of the 1983 *Review for Religious*, entitled "Signs of Hope in Religious Life Today," Tutas based his positive assessment on many conversations and meetings with superiors in Rome and his contacts with Marianists in thirty-one countries on all the continents (recall the Pacific Province's mission in Korea headed by Father James Mifsud and the mission in Australia transferred from the Pacific to the Cincinnati Province), and his encounter with religious in the United States. He discerned "Ten Signs of Hope," many of which were traced in the last chapter, but he injected a notable commitment into his commentary. In abbreviated form these ten signs include: (1) Radical departure from the negative notion of the consecrated life: for example, there is "on-going renewal" related to a "positive understanding of celibacy as a way of loving not a simple renunciation of marriage and a family." (2) "A rediscovery of the relevance of the founding charism." (3) "New direction in Evangelization." (4) A greater and deeper role of religious in the life of the local church. (5) An increasing commitment for promoting justice and peace. (6) "Promotion of the laity." (7) There is a brief commentary on the prevalence of collaborating for vocations among religious. (8) New patterns in formation and governance that "assure the best conditions for human development," such as "affective maturity," personal freedom and responsibility, subsidiarity and collegiality. (9) An appreciation of new trends among the religious communities in non-Western churches. (10) The embodiment of hope within the leadership of religious communities.[3]

Tutas closes this article with an exhortation for religious "to look beyond the day-to-day struggles, the evident failures and shortcomings, to see God at work in our lives and to share the experience with each other."[4] Though not all that was happening may be attributed to the movement of the Holy Spirit, with cautious discernment that movement "is evident in religious life." In accord with the published work (1979)[5] of other Marianists— Lawrence Cada, Raymond Fitz, and Thomas Giardino—on the cycles of religious life, Tutas perceives the present (1983) as one of "transition as we experience the death of much of what was familiar and as we experience the birth of a new era in the history of religious life."[6]

John McGrath, who succeeded John Mulligan as provincial in the New York Province, was a realist; yet he too commented on the signs of hope. As provincial assistant for religious life (1969–1977) he experienced the severe polarization between Chaminade-Mineola and the provincial council. He committed his administration to be "inspired by the Gospel and in accord with our consciences and . . . our Marianist community . . . to work with the Meribah Province. . . . This will be no lark or a moment's work, but we are determined to do it." In his first "Provincial Bulletin" (June 29, 1977) McGrath reflected on the past, present, and future of the province. His perception of the past was "with great veneration, humility and many questions." He extolled "greatness, wisdom and holiness of men; thoughts and movements of centuries." He considered the present "as a time of richness and growth when we are compassionate and realistic." To live without such realism "is to live a fiction and choose an imaginary and thus disastrous path to the future." The effect of an unsympathetic view of the present would be "to paralyze confidence and to chill love and courage." For the future he stresses the need for "exhilaration, adaptability, commitment, a long reach, and ideals."[7]

The periodic tension within each of the provinces was generated between the school men and those either aloof from the traditional apostolate or committed to peace and justice issues. McGrath appears to have sought a consensus by stressing the need to "test . . . whether Christianity and our Marianist spirit actually affect the philosophy, policy, activities, students and teachers in our schools . . . ? Are they communities of faith?" For those in "adult apostolates" and in "foreign cultures" (Puerto Rico, Nigeria, Zambia, and Kenya) he emphasized the need for the Marianist spirit of adaptation.[8] As a Ph.D. in historical theology (St. Michael's College, University of Toronto) with an emphasis on the study of modernism, McGrath was able to appreciate the relationship between past, present, and future with a sense of distance and a stress upon "development" as an operative term in the life of the church, society, and the Marianists. Moreover, his administration was deeply committed to programs in peace and justice.

According to custom dating back to the early years of the Society of Mary, the provincial assistant for temporalities was responsible for allotting funds for the poor and needy. At the 1961 general chapter, the assistant for apostolic action was established with the duty to evaluate social-justice projects worthy of support. By 1977 that office, which never achieved unambiguous status nor a general consensus, was dissolved and the social-justice ministry, a minor aspect of the office, was returned to the office of temporalities.

Within the post–Vatican II context, programs in peace and justice were increased in quantity as well as quality, which placed a burden on the office of temporalities, headed in the New York Province by Brother William

Abel. Hence, the provincial council of New York appointed Richard Ullrich, then vice principal of Cardinal Gibbons High School, staffed by the Marianists, to work in the area of peace and justice. Charged with assisting the council with socially responsible investments, and representing a new "model of leadership in the area of social justice concerns in the province," Ullrich had a ten-month provisional contract (October to August 1977–1978) that has been renewed over the years. As late as 1998 Ullrich was heading this office, which had become a basis for an ad hoc peace-and-justice network through the Archdiocese of Baltimore as well as the New York Province, the only Marianist Province that has established such a position.[9] As early as 1995, however, at the suggestion of Brother James Facette of the St. Louis Province, a gathering of Marianists, including representatives of lay communities, met to discuss common concerns. From this emerged the Marianist Social Justice Collaborative in 1998, aimed at a nationwide Marianist campaign for responsible investments and to identify areas for social action.[10]

Marianists in Puerto Rico celebrated the fortieth anniversary of Colegio San José in 1978. Among those Marianists invited to reflect on their experiences at the high school, Brother Joseph Jansen composed a brief memoir that focused on social-justice issues during his leadership. In his first administration of the Colegio San José (1964–1967) Jansen drew on his prior experience at Colegio Ponceño, another Marianist high school, and the thought of William Ferree, who "had an impact on my thinking." Rather than "yoke the school to . . . sophisticated organizational structures that would complicate matters," he involved lay teachers, parents, and other lay people in the school's direction "by means of structures that facilitated collegiality and subsidiarity."[11] He was also influenced by the conciliar documents and the leadership of Popes John XXIII and Paul VI in areas of peace and justice, renewal and reform. This generated programs in social service, catechesis, the environment, and renewal for the religious in the diocese. Assistant provincial for education during the critical period of Chaminade-Mineola's reaction to the post–Vatican II developments in the Province, Jansen attempted to build a bridge of understanding but was committed to the team approach of provincial government and was supportive of John Mulligan. After ten years as general assistant for education, he returned to Puerto Rico and eventually wrote a history of the Marianists on the island.

The evolution of the term "pluralism" during the 1970s, so divisive in the New York Province's relationship with the Chaminade-Mineola community, became quite evident in the St. Louis Province under Father James A. Young (1961–1971) and was well articulated by his successor, Father

Quentin Hakenewerth (1971–1979). Hakenewerth had a master's degree in psychology and had been involved in formation ministry prior to his appointment as provincial in 1971; he noted that pluralism "causes a real anxiety in many good religious of diverse persuasions. . . . We must be able to handle the basic differences in our individual and our community life to make pluralism an enriching rather than a divisive experience."[12]

He listed five areas of differences: worship, work, community living, administration, and poverty. Worship was perceived as the regular observance of the religious exercises in contrast to the emphasis on "faith sharing as the core of community worship. . . . Both positions can be authentic, but only as an emphasis and not as an exclusion of the others. In the area of work, the division is between those who gain satisfaction from 'performance,' that is doing things for others, getting the job done, producing things, earning a living. Others stress the 'prime emphasis' [of] personal welfare. They believe they are of more help to others by being someone for them rather than doing a service. . . . They are more comfortable with personal relationships than with work skills."

Community living entails two distinctive approaches: there are those dedicated to the common observance of the rule as a "norm for community living." They emphasize "common tasks, sports, physical togetherness, etc." The other approach holds that community "begins with dialogue, with a commitment of members to one another for the sake of the Gospel as the basic unifying element." The differences of administration follow a pattern etched above; administrative decisions are from above "directing and controlling group behavior" as opposed to decisions developed in dialogue. Views on poverty differ in the use of material goods to effect good in the work vis-à-vis "those who view poverty as austerity, frugality, simple life styles, of not having things which the poor do not have."[13]

Quentin Hakenewerth perceived a positive character in each of these values; "the more we develop a balanced integration of these values the more we approach the wholeness of maturity." The chapter and the administration drew up a list of guidelines which Hakenewerth summarized:

- Kneel down together with those with whom we differ and pray with them for unity.
- Admit to each other what our differences really are—what we want the other to change and what we are withholding from him.
- Take care of one another's personal needs, but do not make them into principles of religious life.
- Be honest about what we resist because of cultural uneasiness and be willing to give up the security of the familiar for the sake of renewal.

- Be uncompromising with revealed truth, but open to new systems of intellectual expression.
- Bring our differences to the level of faith: to what we believe about God's presence and power in concrete situations.
- Make our differences a real expression of care for one another.[14]

Conscious of the relationships between the evolution of both secular and religious cultures and their impact on the religious life and trends in Marianist life, Hakenewerth's letters also touched on the perceived conflict between school and Family of Mary, commitments which he considered as relating in an integral rather than a divisive way. When he was superior general (1991–1996), Hakenewerth became a major leader in the movement of lay Marianists within the context of the Family of Mary.

Father James Fitz of the Cincinnati Province, who later became provincial, was a delegate to the general chapter of 1981 and was one of six Marianists to present their views on developments over the past fifteen years. John McGrath summarized Fitz's two dominant currents: pluralism and affluence.

He saw pluralism supported by Vatican II's emphasis on individual freedom, human dignity and personal authority. Pluralism needn't be destructive but can be an enrichment of the traditional notion of authority. Christ's authority is now seen as mediated by a series of authorities; e.g., Scripture, the Marianist tradition, the individual conscience, the directives of authority. Affluence has caused a loss of cultural sense and a lessening of real interest in the past or the future. All of this affects the Society of Mary, even in its practice of all the vows and in our common life. There has been a shift in emphasis from work to community and the witness of community. Affluence naturally affects also our life and witness of justice.[15]

James's blood brother, Brother Raymond Fitz, a Ph.D. in engineering and longtime president of the University of Dayton, articulated Marianist identity at the university as clearly as his brother's commentary on pluralism and affluence. After Patrick Tonry's term as provincial of the New York Province, he became rector at the university, a sort of vice president for Marianist mission effectiveness; Father James Heft, a theologian, articulated the vitality of the Catholic intellectual tradition and Marianist identity at the university during the 1980s and 1990s.

Father Hakenewerth's successor as provincial of St. Louis was David Fleming, a former English professor at St. Mary's University and assistant provincial for religious life. While he was attending the University of

Chicago in the mid-1960s he lived with the St. Michael's community. He had actually completed his Ph.D. in English literature before attending the seminary, reversing the historical pattern. Though identified as a progressive on social and religious issues as both provincial (1979–1987) and as superior general (1996–) he defies facile labels. In 1987, toward the end of his second term as provincial, Fleming reflected on the recent past (ca. 1967–1987), which he perceived as "a Paschal Experience." He said that "once we began to realize and accept that religious life was changing, that numbers were decreasing, that we were collectively aging, our initial reactions tended to anger and blame. We looked for someone to accuse of infidelity that must have been at the root of this situation." Though few would have contested the fact that the Society was witnessing a new birth of what it meant to be "Catholic, Religious and Marianist," there was no way of discerning the "kind of child this 'new birth' will be." Rather than dwell on this condition of decline with anxiety and fear, Fleming urged his readers to "see our experience as a participation in the paschal mystery." Just as the disciples felt anger, blame, and fear after the death and resurrection of Jesus, and soon began anticipating the end time, the province must travel the road of the early church; a shift from gazing back "to looking ahead and working for the coming of God's reign." Fleming perceived the immediate past in terms of a graced passage to a phase characterized by a "stronger sense of fraternity, trust and mutual support, a growth of 'healthy pluralism' and steps toward spiritual renewal."[16]

A sense of realism also prevailed; according to Fleming, the province was able to confront the problems of "alcoholism, the kind of anger that poisons attitudes and outlooks, other self-destructive patterns." The nemesis of idealistic people, that is, many Marianists, was cynicism, but Fleming considered the brothers and priests ready to support or help each other deal with these problems. Realism and a "resignation" characterized the pervasive attitudes of 1987. As Fleming put it: "We seem to exist in a quiet but unenthusiastic acceptance of our current situation. Of course we have creative individuals and groups, many dynamic and corporate accomplishments . . . [yet there is] too much talk about death, not enough about our resurrection." To apply the paschal metaphor to this experience, he stated: "The image of Holy Saturday seems to capture some of our experience: hopes and loves shaken, a quiet, uncertain time, waiting for some new movement and wondering if it will come, knowing that it can only come through the Lord." After reflecting on Chaminade's call for a vow of stability and for a new mission to be grounded in "happiness, joy and thankfulness" despite the "dark vision of his time," Fleming cited the "Rule of Life" (1981): the vow of stability "supports our fidelity and thus leads to depth in maturity and fervor in love."[17]

The provincial's final exhortations included: to "choose life" today; to not worry forever; to respond to the call for transformation—we run out of the ability merely "to cope"—to focus on the Family of Mary and to cultivate the myriad ways to serve Mary: "Mary lives, often in an implied, even hidden way, at the heart of [our] vocation. We intuit a charm in the person of the Virgin of Nazareth. . . . We are Marian by the creative fidelity to our way of life."[18]

At the end of his second administration, David Fleming volunteered for the missions in India and Nepal founded in 1980 after Father William Christensen had initiated his own rural program in the north of the Bihar Province in 1979. There were persistent problems with visas to remain in India for a lengthy stay. The visa problem was eased when the Jesuits in Kathmandu, Nepal, enabled such Marianists as Brothers James O'Hara, Joseph Sheehan, and Stephen Erspamer, and Father Gerald Hammel to get their own visas on the rationale that they would teach at their school on a part-time basis; two years later George Montague, who had published works on, and participated in, the charismatic renewal, became the first novice master in Nepal when houses of formation were established.[19] Gifted with a remarkable facility for learning languages, Fleming was soon able to communicate in Hindi. Hence, as novice master from 1988 to 1993 and as regional superior of the Marianist region of India, he was an effective leader, particularly of Hindi-speaking members of the region. He was elected superior general at the general chapter of 1996. In each of the American Provinces many of those attracted to the missions were Marianists whose self-understanding was integrated along a continuum from the synthesis of William Ferree to the social thought of John XXIII and Paul VI, blended with the conciliar documents and the culture of the 1960s. Of course, the Marianists have revealed a strongly practical zeal over the years that has been evident in the missions.

Another reflection on past, present, and future was published as a "Provincial Letter" by Father James Fitz of the Cincinnati Province in March of 1992. In his consideration of the tensions between the "Common Mission and Individual Journey" he noted its analogue in the cultural conflict between the individual good and the common good. In Marianist history, during the period prior to 1968 "many felt that the community had all the rights and the individual had all the obligations." Though many recalled their strong sense of loyalty to the Society, "there were also memories of the lack of respect for the individual." The renewal chapter strengthened "sub-sidiarity and respect for local and cultural differences." On the other hand, continued James Fitz, "we have lost a significant number of our members and some of the *esprit de corps*; some feel the delicate balance . . . has tipped heavily in the other direction" of individual rights.

Among those community or corporate decisions related to the directives of the *Rule of Life* (1981) and those of the general chapter of 1991, he stressed "Apostolic availability," steeped in an incarnational spirituality: "Like Mary we are called to be instruments of the incarnation of the Word of God." Apostolic availability requires discernment of the needs of the cul-ture in order "to be a leaven in its midst and to resist its negative influences in our religious living."[20]

Fitz applied the principles of community and solidarity as counter-symbols in the human environment of the world beset with nationalism, racism, and other forms of "other" bashing. The call to community among the Marianists requires the commitment to respond to God's grace and "to be living witnesses of the gospel. . . . The world communities are of one mind and one heart today—the world needs a concrete living gospel as a sign of hope." Many religious communities expressed a self-understanding, as an eschatological sign of hope in a world out of joint in its tendencies to live only for the moment. Fitz avoided a theological reflection and implied the need for Marianists to set aside their own individualism and live the gospel with a blend of realism, Christian idealism, and an updated Mariol-ogy. Fitz's provincial letter is characteristic of the general trends in church and society; a sense of the limits and a modest agenda.[21]

Under the direction of Father Thomas Thompson, S.M., and Father Johann Roten, S.M., of the Swiss Province, the Marian Library, which occu-pies an entire floor in the seven-story Roesch Library at the University of Dayton, remains the world's largest collection of books, manuscripts, and of Mariana in classical, folk and popular arts and crafts. Father Roten per-ceives Mary as the "woman . . . facilitator. She teaches 'relationality' because everything in her is in reference to the Father, the Spirit, Jesus, of course, but also to the church and the world. . . . Mary teaches us Christian *Kenosis* which is nothing else but our becoming faithful in the service of Christ's mission."[22]

Father Bertrand Buby, S.M., provincial of the Cincinnati Marianists (1981– 1989), a scripture scholar who has published several books, wrote on "The Biblical Prayer of Mary" for the *Review for Religious* in 1980. In the form of an exegesis of Luke 2:19, 51, "As for Mary, she treasured all these things and pondered them in her heart," the article includes no references to the Marianist relationship to Mary. However, in his second provincial letter he comments on several themes of the *Rule of Life* (1981), including "our vow of stability." With a strong sense of history he refers to William Chaminade, Joseph Simler, and even goes back to the custom in the Marianist schools to recite the three-o'clock prayer invoking Jesus and Mary at the time of Christ's death on Calvary. He also referred to Emil Neubert, S.M., the traditional Marianist writer on devotion to Mary, who wrote *Our Gift From God*. In contrast to the contemporary understanding such as Mary as the model for cooperation in the incarnation, Neubert stressed the filial love as that of a "child towards a loving mother."[23]

Provincial letters were abundant with positive exhortations and exegeses of the *Rule of Life*; Buby seems to have avoided referring to problems. In an interview, however, he stressed the significance of the many personal problems among the communities, particularly depression and alcoholism. His predecessor as provincial, William Behringer (1973–1981), also revealed a positive spirit, but on the more practical level processed many official forms for those Marianists of the Cincinnati Province who chose to leave the Society. Like some Marianists who have wished to sustain the spirit of reform and renewal, William Behringer served in mission areas of Africa. Bertrand Buby, the scripture scholar, teaches at the University of Dayton and responds to students as he did to his own Marianists during his terms as provincial.[24]

Of those Marianists immersed in the life and times of Father Chaminade, Vincent Vasey and Joseph Stefanelli are the most prominent. Vasey, who received doctorates in canon law, in jurisprudence, and in early Christian studies, was vice rector and rector of the seminary in Fribourg (1951–1965) and procurator general of the Society in Rome (1966–1974) before embarking on full-time research and writing a life of William Chaminade. In an interview published in the *Marianist Heritage Series* (ca. 1980) Vasey commented on the Marianist family spirit derived from its origins. He cited a law professor at the University of Dayton who had taught at several universities but had never encountered before "a community and a spirit of openness, consultation and intercommunication among and between faculty, students, staff and administration." Vasey's biography of Chaminade, which restored the founder to his rightful historical role, related this idea of family to the Society's dedication to Mary. His interpretation of Chaminade's charism as embodied in his faith was also applied to Mary. Vasey noted that many perceived her in terms of "a kind of miraculous existence and did not have to live by faith, which is not true. She should be presented as the gospel presents her, a woman of faith."[25]

Joseph Stefanelli's experience in formation and his exposure to William Ferree led to his immersion in the documents on the origins of the Society of Mary. When he was provincial of the Pacific Province (1973–1981) he attempted to promote the Family of Mary, particularly the lay Marianists. After researching and writing for nearly five years, Stefanelli completed his biography (1989) of Adèle de Batz de Trenquelléon, who, with the assistance of Father Chaminade, founded the Daughters of Mary a year before the Society of Mary was founded. Stefanelli has also written a biography of *Mlle de Lamourous*, who, under the inspiration of Adèle and Chaminade, established the Bordeaux Miséricorde. Marie Thérèse Charlotte de Lamourous is known as "the Saint of Bordeaux."[26] Hence, Stefanelli's work is integral to what Bernard Lee has referred to as the "deep story" of the Family of Mary.[27] The Daughters of Mary Immaculate, the Marianist Sisters founded by Adèle, numbered around four hundred in 1998, with nearly twenty in the United States; their ministries include education, retreats, social centers, and campus ministry (University of Dayton, Chaminade University, and St. Mary's University). The United States Province, based in San Antonio, celebrates its fiftieth anniversary in 1999, the sesquicentennial of the Society of Mary in the United States.[28]

There are several lay groups in the Family of Mary: The Marianist Voluntary Service Communities entails a one-year commitment to live in a community of simplified life and ministry to the poor and neglected in urban areas of the Cincinnati and New York provinces. High school students and young adults involved in L.I.F.E. groups (Living in Faith Experiences) foster commitment to a Christian service, mutual support, and personal choice for Christ. Marianist Associates, principally in the East, gather together as families and single people dedicated to prayer, social activities, and family programs aimed at enrichment in the ideals of the Society of Mary. Marianist Lay Communities are historically autonomous, and therefore they vary programmatically and in styles of prayer and service; most have a social-justice dimension or a commitment to permeate the marketplace with Marianist values, but all are communal in shared responsibility for Christian living. Marianist Affiliation is a spiritual bond with the Society or Daughters of Mary and entails living according to the spirit of the *Rule of Life*, devotion to Mary, dedication to her mission, and living the gospel; affiliation is considered a Marianist vocation. Marianist League, co-workers, and a Miriam Guild—the latter are single women who aim to blend spirituality and work, while the others, originating as parents of Marianists, engage in promoting vocations and in raising funds for the Society; there are few active groups in the late 1990s. Then there are the many co-workers with the Marianists who are in varying phases of commitment to the Marianist spirit, ministry, and affiliation with the Society. Over the years, the lay Marianists have evolved national and international structures. Though their governance is independent, their spirituality and ministry are inspired by and in collaboration with brothers, priests, and sisters of the Marianist religious groups.[29]

The L.I.F.E. program originated in the Marianist high schools as an analogue to the sodalities but more proactive and animated by a contemporary incarnational spirituality, which Joseph P. Chinnici, O.F.M., has referred to as a Christocentric humanism, blended with pilgrim people of God ecclesiology.[30] The historical conflict between those who stress the school ministry and those who press for the proliferation of lay Marianist communities persisted in the 1990s but in rather muted terms. Of course, the Meribah Province is committed to the traditional school apostolate; in 1987 it added Bishop Kellenberg Memorial High School to its province, and later added to Kellenberg a "junior high" school, the Brother Joseph Fox Latin School. Active in the Marianist Conference composed of provincials and assistant provincials, the Meribah leadership and the entire province have been gracious in their hospitality to members of other provinces.

Brother William Bolts of the Pacific Province is a forceful proponent of developing the Marianist spirit among the laity solely within the school context. In a position paper that he discussed in an interview with me, Bolts explained what he considered to be the diffusive and relatively unfocused lay Marianist thrust of the past thirty years. With over twenty years in school ministry, eight years as assistant provincial and director of education (1982–1990), and with a doctorate in history, he has formed a distinctive perspective on the promotion of the Marianist élan within the schools. Through workshops with lay teachers in the high schools, such as Riordan in San Francisco and St. Louis in Honolulu, in tandem with Marianist heritage weeks and various religious programs for the alumni, Bolts's plan envisions a vital Marianist presence in the institutional context. Though Joseph Stefanelli and others recalled their commitment to develop lay Marianist communities outside of the schools, the movement never gained the necessary momentum despite Stefanelli's development of provincial structures to support this commitment. While Stefanelli attributed this failure to form vital lay communities to the strong resistance among school men, Bolts laments the deemphasis on the schools over the years. Though he has been involved in campus ministry at the University of California at Santa Cruz, in parish ministry, and has written a history of St. John's parish in San Francisco and a history of Riordan High School, he remains a strong voice for Marianist mission-effectiveness in the schools of the Pacific Province.[31]

Most Marianist educators, such as the general assistant for education in the 1990s, Brothers Thomas Giardino, Peter Pontolillo, and James Gray of the New York and St. Louis Province respectively, have been identified with a synthesis of school-based and independently formed lay Marianist communities. Brothers Stephen Glodek and Joseph Kamis, provincials of the New York and Cincinnati Provinces, and Joseph Uvietta of the St. Louis Province, also represent that synthesis.

Father Adolf Windisch, former president of Vianney High School in St. Louis, represents the link between the large Marianist vision of his mentor, William Ferree, and the leadership of the schools. His Family of Mary commitment found a congenial residence when he joined the North American Center for Marianist Studies (NACMS) in Dayton in 1995. Since the 1970s he has been involved in the Marianist Studies Program founded in 1970, two years after Ferree became provincial of the Cincinnati Province. The content of Marianist Studies is, according to a 1992 Discussion Guide, entitled "State of Marianist Studies," a body of knowledge that has developed over the years principally related to the Society's charism both historical and lived, as well as spirituality, mission, and history of the Society since 1800. From its origin, the Studies Program was associated with the Marianist Resources Commission (MRC) under the direction of Brother Giardino.

In 1983 NACMS was founded by a national conference of provincials and assistant provincials in the United States that later became the Marianist Conference. The directors have been Father Robert Ross (1983–1986) followed by Lawrence J. Cada (1986–1993), on the staff since the foundation, and Carol Quinn (1993–); a Marianist sister, Anna Huth, F.M.I., and three Marianist priests, Joseph Lackner, Joseph Stefanelli, and Adolf Windisch, have been on the team. NACMS continues the work of the MRC, publishes works in the Studies area, and sponsors courses and workshops in Marianist Studies in the various provinces. It has initiated two periodical-style publications, *The Bulletin* and *Things Marianist*, has developed a Marianist Research Library, and has established a network with Marianist writers throughout the world and similar groups among non-Marianist communities.[32] Central to its identity is the study of Mary within the Society's self-understanding, past, present, and future.

At the origins of the Bordeaux Sodality, Mary Immaculate was Father Chaminade's banner to restore faith and purity to the secular age defiled by anti-Catholicism. The filial relation to Mary was the personal dimension of the vowed life, blending the Holy Family with the Society's Family of Mary. Father Leo Meyer, on the eve of the 1848 revolutions in Europe, was guided by an "ecstatic woman" who had conversed with Mary, urging him to embark on a mission to the United States, where he established an American home for the sons of Mary and the Brothers of Jesus at "Nazareth," where he nurtured the first formation center, the first school owned by the Society in the United States, and the motherhouse of the U.S. Marianists. Though Marianists promoted the shrines of Mary's appearances from Lourdes to Medjugorje, their own devotion was manifested in their recitation of the Little Office of the Immaculate Conception, and in schools, sodalities, and eventually among the alumni.

Converging with the Nazareth symbol of the Holy Family is the long-standing devotion to St. Joseph, the quietly heroic protector of Mary and Jesus, the model for the Marianists' male protector image. In contrast, Simler articulated the need to cultivate the feminine, maternal zeal of meekness and benevolence in accord with Mary's "universal motherhood." Hence, there is an androgynous character to the Marianists congenial with the Joseph-Mary inspiration. With the Americanization of the Marianists' schools and the proliferation of structures, devotion to Mary became more routinized in the monastic environment, a refuge from the tension with the modern high school movement. The revival of interest in Father Chaminade, initiated by Joseph Simler, the second founder of the Society, and later by William Ferree, arguably the "second founder" of the American Marianists, promoted the development of Mary's role in the Incarnation, a role that achieved a synthesis in the post–Vatican II trends in ecclesiology, spirituality, and renewal in religious life. To be sons and daughters of Mary in the 1990s has evoked the following descriptions published in *Things Marianist*:[33]

It is to the chanting of a new Magnificat that we are called: the celebration of God's action in our world and our response in faith. This response in faith must be a careful, critical discernment of both "yes" and "no." It needs to be a response of "yes" to the uplifting of God's people to God and a response of "no" to all that impedes or works against that uplifting.

—Stephen Glodek, S.M.

. . . Any Marianist community that prays daily Mary's Magnificat as its own prayer will have an enviable passion for the transformation of unjust social situations.

—Bernard Lee, S.M.

As Marianists, we believe in the effectiveness of Mary's presence. We believe that we are called to bring the influence of her presence everywhere, but especially to those people most in need and to those situations that most demand support or transformation. We believe in the power of her presence, since it guarantees the active presence of the Holy Spirit. So we dedicate ourselves to communicate Mary's presence in everything, whether we are cooking a few beans for supper or working to change the world's economic structures which oppress the poor.

—Quentin Hakenewerth, S.M.

The slow, patient, tolerant but persistent work of a mother is connatural to the Marianist charism. Our way is that of entering into the heart of any human community and seeking to transform it, with full participation, with acceptance, affirmation, and love from within. . . . This patient, formative, nurturing thrust is prophetic. It challenges our culture and meets a deep-felt need.

—David Fleming, S.M.

This woman, with her openness to God incarnating and continuing to work through her, is the person Chaminade chose . . . as model and inspiration, as leader. Her mission of responsiveness to allowing God to become incarnate through her, Chaminade claims as the mission of the entire Family of Mary.

—Anna Huth, F.M.I.

These remarks reveal the convergence of a traditionally accessible Mary with the companionship of a democratized Mary who is embodied in the contemporary Marianist in various ways; in his feminine and masculine and Magnificat dimensions, in the immanence of God, in David Fleming's notion of the Holy Saturday companionship in the Paschal mystery awaiting the resurrection, or in Elizabeth Johnson's advent image, waiting for the birth of a new Society of Mary in accord with the postmodern age.

Afterword

THE SESQUICENTENNIAL OF THE PRESENCE OF THE SOCIETY OF MARY in the United States coincides with the church's celebration of a new millennium. Reading 150 years of Marianist history at this time illuminates important patterns in our past experience and also stimulates reflection about the future.

Dr. Christopher Kauffman ably shows us how members of the Society of Mary during the past 150 years played a lively part in key trends of American Catholic history. In the earliest phase the principal concern was implanting church structures and preserving immigrant faith. Later Marianists focused, with the mainstream of American Catholic culture, on issues such as inculturating and Americanizing immigrant communities, creating the Catholic school system, attaining educational excellence, moving out of the "ghetto," overcoming racial discrimination, entering into realms of social justice and pastoral care, founding lay communities, collaborating with laypeople, and developing a global missionary outreach. Kauffman shows us how periods of fragmentation and integration between the "monastic" and the "apostolic" dimensions of our heritage have regularly alternated throughout our history, sometimes in creative tension, but often in a more sterile opposition. During the immediate past, we have been preoccupied with the new approaches to spirituality, community, and mission that appeared in the wake of the Second Vatican Council, and have found ourselves sometimes confused and discouraged, sometimes exhilarated and empowered, by visions of the future that we still but dimly perceive. In all this, our experience as Marianist religious has paralleled that of the majority of Catholic religious, offering a good case study in the long-term evolution of religious life in the United States.

At the same time, members of the Society of Mary have contributed something of their own uniqueness to American Catholic history. Our educational heritage and our ministry to young people have often nudged us in the direction of progressive innovation, and our educational institutions have on the whole been marked by tolerance, "family spirit," and the need to prepare successive generations of students for adaptability and change. Despite all the varieties of educational style and the idiosyncracies of individual Marianist educators, elitism and a rigid, militaristic discipline have never characterized our institutions. Our "mixed composition" of priests and lay members working together in the same works and communities, mostly under nonclerical leadership, has made its quiet but significant contribution to the evolution of a collaborative and somewhat egalitarian attitude in the American church. The concern for developing lay leadership and supporting lay spirituality, derived from our origins, has taken on new prominence in the years since Vatican II. Our Marian spirituality has perhaps not been sufficiently popularized in the United States, and it tends to appeal principally to well-educated Christians; nonetheless, Marianists have made important contributions to a dynamic, theologically sound understanding of Mary that impels a significant number of religious and laypeople into apostolic service. From the time of Damian Litz on, a series of distinguished and creative American Marianists have made significant contributions to the development of Catholic thought and life on the regional and national levels. Marianist participation and leadership have been striking in national Catholic educational and religious organizations. Without the Marianist contribution, American Catholic history would have been different in many subtle ways over these 150 years.

In his final chapter, Dr. Kauffman summarizes Marianist probings about the future. Few doubt that the new millennium marks a significant turning point in world history and in the mission of the church. Even though the shape of the future is still far from clear, most of us Marianists feel that certain elements are central:

- We continue to be moved as we probe into the riches of our unique heritage; we know that we have a future only insofar as we stand faithfully and creatively on that foundation.
- Collaboration with laity, individually and in small communities of faith, is a significant part of our heritage and also a key to our future. The unique contribution of vowed religious in an increasingly lay-

oriented church still needs further exploration, but issues of religious witness and identity take on a new importance in our time.

- We are challenged, perhaps more than ever, to offer the gift of a deep and perceptible spirituality to a world in search of transcendence. For us, this spirituality must be grounded in a Chaminadean fascination with the mystery of the Incarnation.

- A global outlook and solidarity with the poor and marginalized, locally and internationally, are a key element for meaningful religious witness and vitality.

- A community life that goes beyond mere structures and prompts us to authentic sharing of prayer, possessions, ministries, and life experiences is a difficult but essential element for our future.

- Education and youth ministry, in both old and new forms, remain a hallmark of our identity.

- In all of this, an attitude of dialogue and ever-broadening collaboration—among provinces, religious communities, and with all who share similar ideals—is essential as we look to the road ahead.

Our founder designated Mary as the one "in whose name and for whose honor we have embraced the religious life." May she continue to guide and inspire the American Marianists of coming centuries in fidelity to their rich heritage.

David Joseph Fleming, S.M.
Superior General
Rome, September 12, 1998

Marianist Leadership

Compiled by Lawrence Cada, S.M.

PROVINCIALS OF THE NORTH AMERICAN PROVINCES

American Province (1855–1908)

1855–1862	Leo Meyer (1800–1868)
1862–1864	John Courtès (1809–1870)
1864–1886	John Nepomucene Reinbolt (1824–1895)
1886–1896	Landelin Beck (1842–1935)
1896–1906	George Meyer (1850–1939)
1906–1908	Joseph Weckesser (1856–1934)

St. Louis Province

1908–1916	Joseph Weckesser (1856–1934)
1916–1926	Louis A. Tragesser (1866–1942)
1926–1936	Joseph C. Ei (1875–1961)
1936–1946	Sylvester P. Juergens (1894–1969)
1946–1956	Peter A. Resch (1895–1956)
1956–1961	J. Glennon McCarty (1912–1977)
1961–1971	James A. Young (1915–)
1971–1979	Quentin Hakenewerth (1930–)
1979–1987	David A. Fleming (1939–)
1987–1995	Joseph Uvietta (1931–)
1995–	Timothy Dwyer (1935–)

Cincinnati Province

1908–1918	George Meyer (1850–1939)
1918–1923	Bernard P. O'Reilly (1874–1955)

1923–1928	Lawrence A. Yeske (1880–1960)
1928–1938	Joseph A. Tetzlaff (1884–1968)
1938–1948	Walter C. Tredtin (1881–1972)
1948–1958	John A. Elbert (1895–1966)
1958–1968	James M. Darby (1917–1969)
1968–1973	William J. Ferree (1905–1985)
1973–1981	William R. Behringer (1931–)
1981–1989	Bertrand A. Buby (1934–)
1989–1997	James F. Fitz (1946–)
1997–	Joseph H. Kamis (1946–)

Pacific Province

1948–1956	Walter C. Tredtin (1881–1972)
1956–1964	Leonard Fee (1909–1976)
1964–1973	Bertrand E. Clemens (1917–1989)
1973–1981	Joseph M. Stefanelli (1921–)
1981–1989	John F. Bolin (1925–)
1989–1997	Timothy Eden (1945–)
1997–	John Russi (1939–)

New York Province

1961–1969	John G. Dickson (1916–1985)
1969–1977	John D. Mulligan (1929–)
1977–1985	John A. McGrath (1935–)
1985–1993	Patrick J. Tonry (1934–)
1993–	Stephen M. Glodek (1948–)

Independent Region of Canada

1964–1972	Gabriel Arsenault (1927–)
1972–1980	François Boissonneault (1933–)
1980–1988	Raymond Roussin (1939–)
1988–1994	Gustave Lamontagne (1936–)

Meribah Province

1976–1984	Francis T. Keenan (1932–)
1984–1992	Philip K. Eichner (1935–)
1992–	George E. Endres (1954–)

INSPECTORS AND ASSISTANT PROVINCIALS OF THE NORTH AMERICAN PROVINCES

Inspectors of the American Province (1869–1908)
1869–1886   John B. Stintzi (1821–1900)
1886–1905   John B. Kim (1849–1909)
1905–1908   Michael Schleich (1860–1945)

St. Louis Province
1908–1924   John A. Waldron (1859–1937)
1924–1929   Gerald Mueller (1870–1939)
1929–1948   Eugene A. Paulin (1882–1962)
1949–1959   Theodore Hoeffken (1904–1982)
1959–1964   Edwin Goerdt (1909–1990)
1964–1974   James Gray (1922–1980)
1974–1979   Vincent Wayer (1938–)
1979–1987   Daniel Sharpe (1923–)
1987–1992   Anthony J. Pistone (1935–)
1992–   Jerome Bommer (1933–)

Cincinnati Province
1908–1909   Michael Schleich (1860–1945)
1909–1938   George N. Sauer (1865–1940)
1938–1946   Bernard Schad (1885–1968)
1946–1959   Paul A. Sibbing (1897–1987)
1959–1961   John T. Darby (1913–1986)
1961–1971   John J. Jansen (1916–)
1971–1974   Stanley G. Mathews (1922–)
1974–1979   Robert J. Brisky (1932–)
1979–1987   George A. Deinlein (1927–)
1987–1991   Thomas F. Giardino (1943–)
1991–1997   Joseph H. Kamis (1946–)
1997–   Joseph H. Lackner (1942–)

Pacific Province
1948–1957   James Wipfield (1905–)
1957–1962   John McCluskey (1912–1998)
1962–1967   Maurice Miller (1911–)
1967–1974   Roger D. Richter (1935–)

1974–1982 Edward L. Gomez (1938–)
1982–1990 William Bolts (1935–)
1990–1995 William Campbell (1944–)
1995– Gary Morris (1946–)

New York Province
1961–1965 John T. Darby (1913–1986)
1965–1967 Louis J. Faerber (1909–1981)
1967–1971 Joseph G. Jansen (1927–)
1971–1976 William A. Abel (1935–)
1976–1981 Anthony J. Ipsaro (1931–)
1981–1986 Francis M. Ouellette (1936–)
1986–1993 Stephen M. Glodek (1948–)
1993– George J. Cerniglia (1939–)

Independent Region of Canada
1964–1969 Dollard Beauduin (1928–)
1969–1977 Dominique Martineau (1931–)
1977–1985 Raymond Boutin (1932–)
1985–1990 Lucien Julien (1930–)
1990–1994 Irénée Breton (1933–)

Meribah Province
1976–1977 Lawrence Oleksiak (1936–)
1977–1985 Edward T. Smith (1942–)
1985–1992 Robert A. Fachet (1942–)
1992– Thomas A. Cardone (1955–)

Marianist Communities in North America

Compiled by Earl Leistikow, S.M.

INTRODUCTION

This appendix includes communities in five provinces but not small communities of Marianists identified only by an address and committed to diverse ministries; nor does it incorporate missionary communities in Latin America, Africa, Asia, and Australia. Each of the provinces was formed from the Cincinnati Province (before 1908 the American Province), except for the Canadian Province, whose original communities were in the St. Louis Province.

I. THE CINCINNATI PROVINCE
Formerly the American Province, established in 1855

ALBION, MICHIGAN
St. John's Grade School, 1971–1992

CENTERVILLE, OHIO
Franciscan at St. Leonard, 1993– . Healthcare facility.

CHILLICOTHE, OHIO
St. Peter's Grade School, 1882–1888

CINCINNATI, OHIO
Elder High School, 1912–1928. Began as St. Lawrence High School.
Holy Trinity Grade School, 1849–1854

Purcell High School, 1928– . Now called Purcell Marian.

Moeller High School, 1960–

St. Aloysius Orphanage, 1854–November, 1855

St. Anthony's Grade School, 1868–1922

St. Augustine's Grade School, 1871–1931

St. Joseph's Grade School, 1861; 1879–1903

St. George's Grade School, 1899–1928

St. Mary's Grade School, 1852–1938

St. Paul's Grade School, January 2, 1854–April 1858. Accepted in 1853, opened in 1854.

St. Philomena's Grade School, 1857–1860

St. Xavier's Grade School, 1902–1935

All Saints Parish School, 1972–1979

CLEVELAND, OHIO

Cathedral Latin High School, 1916–1980. Evolved from St. John's Cathedral School.

St. Bridget's Grade School, 1880–1889

St. Columba's Academy, 1881–1891

St. John's College, 1858–1859. A small boarding and day school.

St. John's Grade School, 1857–1889. Evolved into Cathedral Latin High School.

St. Joseph High School, 1950– . Merged with Villa Angela.

St. Mary's Grade School, 1858–1922

St. Patrick's Grade School, 1856–1879

St. Peter's Grade School, March 1863–1922.

St. Stephen's Grade School, 1903–1921

St. Malachy's Grade School, 1978–1981

COLUMBUS, OHIO

Holy Cross Grade School, 1872–1909

COVINGTON, KENTUCKY

Covington Catholic High School, 1925–1979. Evolved from St. Joseph's Grade School.

St. Joseph's Grade School, 1885–1927

DAYTON, OHIO

Chaminade High School, 1927– . Chaminade-Julienne after merging.

Emmanuel Parish School, February 1853

Holy Trinity Grade School, 1869–1927

Immaculate Conception Parish, 1838–1955

Mount St. John Normal School, 1915– . Purchased the necessary additional property in February 1912. Became the motherhouse of the Cincinnati Province. Property in late 1990s contains Bergamo retreat center, novitiate, Meyer Hall community, and Queen of Apostles parish.

Mount St. John Novitiate, 1911– . Same property as Mount St. John Normal. Used as a postulate and retreat house; became novitiate again in 1969.

Our Lady of the Rosary Grade School, 1903–1958

St. Joseph's Grade School, 1862–1863; 1882–1891

University of Dayton, 1850– . Originally called Nazareth; included the Marianist residence and boarding school until 1871, when they became separate communities. Residence was later moved to Mount St. John (1915). Boarding school became St. Mary's Institute (1871), St. Mary's College (1912), the University of Dayton (1920).

HAMILTON, OHIO
Catholic High School, 1909–1947

HUNTSVILLE, OHIO
Governer's Island Summer Residence and Retreat Center

KALAMAZOO, MICHIGAN
Hackett High School, 1964–

LOUISVILLE, KENTUCKY
St. Martin's Grade School, 1892–1917

LOUISVILLE, OHIO
Mission and school, 1855–1858

MEMPHIS, TENNESSEE
Catholic High School, 1966–

OSBORN, OHIO
Mary, Help of Christians Parish, 1934–1955. A "mission" church of St. Mary's Institute since 1873, it was canonically erected a parish in 1934. City called Fairborn in 1950.

PHILADELPHIA, PENNSYLVANIA
St. John the Baptist High School, 1922–1956
West Philadelphia Catholic High School, October 1916–1926

PITTSBURGH, PENNSYLVANIA
North Catholic High School, 1939– . Also called Boy's Catholic High
   School.
St. Mary's Grade School (Allegheny), 1871–1939
St. Michael's Grade School, 1882–1934
St. Philomena's Grade School, 1859–1883
St. Joseph Grade Church, 1973–1976

PORTAGE, MICHIGAN
St. Catherine of Sienna Parish School, 1976–

RUSSIA, OHIO
St. Remy Mission and School, January 1854–1855

SANDUSKY, OHIO
Holy Angels Grade School, 1859–1861
St. Mary's Grade School, 1860–1864

SIOUX CITY, IOWA
Trinity College, 1930–1949. Although in St. Louis Province territory, it was
   run by the Cincinnati Province. College and high school from the
   beginning, college dropped in 1947. The name changed to St. Joseph
   High School, 1926–1979.

II. THE ST. LOUIS PROVINCE
Established in 1908

BELLEVILLE, ILLINOIS
Cathedral High School, 1905–1964. St. Peter's High School, 1905–1929.
   Cathedral High School, 1929– 1964.

CHICAGO, ILLINOIS
St. Aloysius Grade School, 1892–1932
St. Francis Grade School, 1882–1906
St. Michael's Grade School, February 1874–1923. High school, 1923–1978.
   Full high-school course in 1923. Closed in 1978.

CLAYTON, MISSOURI (in the St. Louis area beyond the constricted boundary of Clayton)
Chaminade College Preparatory School, 1910– . Property acquired in 1907.
   College and normal school at first. Normal school moved to Maryhurst in 1922.

Our Lady of the Pillar Parish, 1938–. Parish began at Chaminade, then moved to a new building on adjacent property.

COMFORT, TEXAS
Boy's Camp, 1937–1951. Run by the St. Louis Province.

DENTON, TEXAS
Marianist Community, 1990– . Campus ministry for surrounding universities, now includes a parish.

DETROIT, MICHIGAN
Holy Name Institute, 1915–1922. A grade and high school.
Holy Redeemer High School, 1916–1944. In 1937 transferred from the Cincinnati to the St. Louis Province. Brothers also taught seventh and eighth grade the last several years there.

DUBUQUE, IOWA
St. Mary's Commercial School, 1906–1929

DURAND, WISCONSIN
Maryhill Postulate, 1931–1935

DYERSVILLE, IOWA
St. Francis Xavier High School, 1902–1932

EAST ST. LOUIS, ILLINOIS
Central Catholic High School, 1929–1952. Changed to Assumption.
Assumption High School, 1952–1989
Vincent Gray House, 1971–1975
Vincent Gray High School, 1981–1994. An alternative high school still in operation in 1999.
Marianist Community, 1994– . Engaged in family ministry to the poor.

EL PASO, TEXAS
St. Joseph High School, 1958–1962

FERGUSON, MISSOURI
Villa St. Joseph, 1907–1922. Postulate (1908), novitiate (1910). After a fire in 1914, a new building was erected. A postulate again in 1917.

FORT WORTH, TEXAS
Our Lady of Victory High School, 1961– . Name changed to Nolan High
School in 1964.
St. Mary of the Assumption Parish, 1981–

GALESVILLE, WISCONSIN
Marynook Novitiate, 1941–1973. Transferred here from Maryhurst. A community remained as part of an ecumenical center for some time after
1973. The last SM member left in 1993.

GERMANTOWN, WISCONSIN
Mission and school, January 1856–1858

GLENCOE, MISSOURI
Marycliff, 1951–1966. A second novitiate.
Marianist Apostolic Center, 1967– . Built on the same property as Marycliff,
now called Marianist Retreat and Conference Center.
Marianist Novitiate, 1973–1977. St. Louis Province novitiate.
Marianist Provincialate, 1966–1974. Moved from here to St. Louis.

HELOTES, TEXAS
Our Lady of Guadalupe Parish, 1942– . Begun as a mission served by SM.

HOUSTON, TEXAS
Marianist Community, 1993– . Youth, faith community ministry.

KIRKWOOD, MISSOURI
Eugene Coyle High School, 1939–1960. A coinstitutional school. The Marianist faculty and staff resided at Maryhurst.
Maryhurst Normal School, 1918–1969. Property bought in 1916–1917.
Motherhouse of the province. Building demolished, part of the property leased, the rest used by Vianney, Marianist Art Studio, and province cemetery.
Maryhurst Novitiate, 1919–1941. Property and house bought in 1917. Began
in 1918 and transferred to Marynook in early 1941.
Vianney High School, 1960– . Successor to Eugene Coyle High School, but
limited to boys.
Chantilly Postulate, 1969–1970. Five apartments were used for a single
year.
Jefferson House, 1974–1985. Small community served various ministries.

LASALLE, ILLINOIS
St. Patrick's Grade School, 1882–1909

MILWAUKEE, WISCONSIN
Messmer High School, 1944–1945
Don Bosco High School, 1945–1972
Thomas More High School, 1972. Successor to Don Bosco; Marianists withdrew in 1989.

MOUNTAIN HOME, TEXAS
Tecaboca, 1951– . A boy's camp, successor to Comfort camp, but a new facility with expanded ministry.

NEW HAVEN, MISSOURI
Maria Vista, 1965–1978. A retreat house, second novitiate 1966–1968.

NEW ORLEANS, LOUISIANA
Liguori High School, 1916–1925
St. Alphonsus Grade School, 1878–1896
St. Mary's Grade School, 1869–1882
Verrina High School, 1915–1926
Madeleine House, 1991– . Community with various ministries.

OKLAHOMA CITY, OKLAHOMA
McGuinness High School, 1976–1981. A diocesan school partially staffed by Marianists.

OMAHA, NEBRASKA
Daniel J. Gross High School, 1968–1992

PEORIA, ILLINOIS
Spalding Institute, 1899–1933

PUEBLO, COLORADO
Roncalli High School, 1964–1971

ST. LOUIS, MISSOURI
De Andreis High School, 1942–1952. Originally named North Side Catholic High School. Faculty and students shared McBride building, 1946–1947. New building in 1947.

McBride High School. Originally named Kenrick High School, 1911–1924. Changed to the new name and opened the new school in 1924. Closed in 1971.

St. Anthony's Grade School, 1901–1922

St. Mary's High School, 1933– . Named South Side until 1947.

SS. Peter and Paul Grade School, 1897–1940

SS. Peter and Paul High School, 1897–1911; it became Kenrick High School, 1911–1924

North Side High School, 1942–1947

Marianist Seminary, 1967–1974. In buildings occupied by provincial administration in late 1990s.

St. Louis Provincialate, Maryland Avenue, 1974–

SAN ANTONIO, TEXAS

Central Catholic High School, 1852– . Originally named St. Mary's Institute, then St. Mary's College. Changed to St. Mary's Academy (1923–1932). Acquired present name and new building on the present site in December 1931, and started classes there in January 1932. Original site changed name in 1932 to St. Mary's College and was the downtown school of St. Mary's University.

Mission Concepcion, 1855–1869. Acquired formal ownership only in 1859. Property was used as a farm from the beginning, then as a house for training candidates, 1864–1866.

St. Mary's University, 1894– . A branch of the original St. Mary's College. Acquired property on the outskirts of town in 1892 and opened in 1894 under the name of St. Louis College. Changed to St. Mary's College (1923) and then to St. Mary's University in 1927.

San Fernando Grade School, 1888–1927, for Mexican-Americans.

Holy Rosary Parish and School, 1948– . Adjacent to St. Mary's University.

Charles Francis Hall, 1951–1967. Scholasticate building at St. Mary's University until Treadaway Hall was opened in 1967.

St. Louis Province Formation Community, 1983–1997. Formation house for student brothers; house changed name [Woodlawn Marianist Community] and mission in 1997.

St. Joseph Community, 1983– . Health center for the St. Louis Province, added as a wing of Faculty Residence that opened in 1960.

SOMERSET, TEXAS

St. Mary's Mission Parish, 1933–1964

VICTORIA, TEXAS
St. Joseph High School, 1906–1970. St. Joseph College 1906–1926.

VON ORMY, TEXAS
Sacred Heart Mission Parish, 1935–1937

WICHITA, KANSAS
Cathedral High School, 1926–1932

III. THE PACIFIC PROVINCE
Established in 1948

ALAMEDA, CALIFORNIA
St. Joseph High School, 1935–1970

CANOGA PARK, CALIFORNIA
Chaminade Preparatory, 1961– . City now called West Hills

CUPERTINO, CALIFORNIA
Provincial Administration, 1968– . Headquarters of the Pacific Province.
Villa St. Joseph, 1975– . Retirement and health center.
Marianist Center, 1981– . Formation center at the beginning, in the late
    1990s a retreat center.

FRESNO, CALIFORNIA
St. John's High School, 1926–1933. Changed name and new building to St.
    Columba High School in 1928.

GARDENA, CALIFORNIA
Junipero Serra High School, 1950–1994

HILO, HAWAII
St. Mary's Grade School, 1885–1951
St. Joseph's Church, 1984–

HONOLULU, HAWAII
Cathedral Grade School, 1933–1956
St. Louis College, 1883– . A grade and high school. New building on present
    site opened in 1928. In December 1941, the U.S. army used the build-
    ings for a hospital and returned it in the fall of 1946. During the war,
    classes were held in various schools in the city. Changed name to
    Chaminade University in 1955.
Holy Family Church, 1950–1986

LOS ANGELES, CALIFORNIA
Chaminade High School, 1952–1961

MARYSVILLE, CALIFORNIA
St. Mary's Grade School, 1884–1886

RUTHERFORD, CALIFORNIA
St. Joseph's Agricultural Institute, 1911–1916

SAN FRANCISCO, CALIFORNIA
St. James Grade and High School, 1906–1950
St. Joseph's Grade School, 1886–1949
Archbishop Riordan High School, 1949–

SAN JOSE, CALIFORNIA
St. Joseph's Grade School, 1898–1935. Also high school 1907–1935.
Archbishop Mitty High School, 1964–1990
Queen of Apostles Parish, 1985–

SANTA CRUZ, CALIFORNIA
Chaminade High School, 1924–1940. Property purchased in 1924 and called
    "Villa." Some brothers taught at the village school 1928–1930. Cham-
    inade started in 1930. The building and property were leased out in
    1940 and reoccupied in May 1949–1952 as a postulate; novitiate,
    1952–1978. Villa St. Joseph, working brothers' scholasticate,
    1954–1960.

SANTA MONICA, CALIFORNIA
St. Monica High School, 1946–1948

STOCKTON, CALIFORNIA
St. Mary's Grade and High School, 1884–1931. Began with commercial
    courses and grade school. In 1911 grades only. High school courses
    added in 1927.

WAILUKU, HAWAII
St. Anthony's Grade and High School, 1883– . Graduated a commercial high
    school class in 1927 and its first full four-year class in 1942.
St. Anthony Parish, 1975–

WALLA WALLA, WASHINGTON
De Sales High School, 1970–1988

IV. THE NEW YORK PROVINCE
Established in 1961

BALTIMORE, MARYLAND
St. Alphonsus Grade School, 1872–1879
St. James Grade School, 1873–1947
St. Martin's Grade School, 1880–1928. Also called St. Martin's Academy.
St. Mary, Star of the Sea Grade School, 1885–1892
St. Michael's Grade School, 1870–1956
Cardinal Gibbons High School, 1962–1995
St. Mark's Grade School, 1982–1991

BEACON, NEW YORK
Marianist Preparatory, 1922–1950. Acquired property in December 1921.
    Began as postulate, became novitiate in 1940. Acquired adjoining Villa
    St. Joseph property in June 1937. Closed in 1950.

BROOKLYN, NEW YORK
Holy Trinity Grade School, 1904–1972. High school in 1920.
St. Barbara's Grade School, 1907–1938
St. John's Home, 1937– . Rockaway, 1948–
St. Michael's Grade School, 1910–1941

CAPE MAY POINT, NEW JERSEY
Retreat Center, 1972–

CHARLOTTE, NORTH CAROLINA
Charlotte Catholic High School, 1961–1969

CHESTER, PENNSYLVANIA
St. James High School, 1956–1993

CUMBERLAND, MARYLAND
St. Patrick's Grade School, 1882–1888

HOLLYWOOD, FLORIDA
Chaminade High School, 1960– . Since 1988 Chaminade-Madonna.

MARCY, NEW YORK
Chaminade Preparatory, 1947–1981. Postulate 1948–1949.

NEW YORK, NEW YORK
Holy Redeemer Grade School, 1873–1888
Our Lady of Sorrows Grade School, 1879–1896
St. Boniface Grade School, 1879–1882
St. John the Baptist Grade School, 1876–1931

PATTERSON, NEW JERSEY
Cedar Hill, February 1875–1884. Thirty-three acres intended for formation
    and other purposes. Abandoned without a viable identity.
St. Bonaventure's Grade School, 1879–1882
St. Boniface Grade School, 1880–1885
St. John the Baptist Grade School, 1880–1885

ROCHESTER, NEW YORK
St. Joseph's Grade School, 1861–1899
SS. Peter and Paul Grade School, 1865–1887

WASHINGTON, D.C.
Chaminade Institute, 1915–1918. House of higher studies in the orbit of the
    Catholic University of America.
Immaculate Conception Grade School, 1890–1965
Marianist House of Studies, 1926–1965. Originally named Chaminade College, changed in 1942. Residence changed several times.
Marianist Seminary, 1941–1942

YOUNGWOOD, PENNSYLVANIA
Marianist Apostolic Center, 1970

V. THE MERIBAH PROVINCE
Established in 1976

MINEOLA, NEW YORK
Chaminade High School, 1930–

MUTTONTOWN, NEW YORK
Chaminade Retreat House, 1979–

UNIONDALE, NEW YORK
Bishop Kollenberg Memorial High School, 1993–

VI. THE INDEPENDENT REGION OF CANADA

CAP ROUGE, QUEBEC
St. Augustine, 1965– . A student residence. Name was changed in late
  1990s.

LAUZON, QUEBEC
Maison Chaminade, 1978–

LEVIS, QUEBEC
Villa Chaminade, 1944–1965. Postulate

MASHAM, QUEBEC
SS. Cecile de Masham, 1959–1961

ST. ANSELME, QUEBEC
Institut Ste. Marie, 1948–1973
St. Anselme School, 1938–1961
Postulate, 1940–1948
Ecole Provencher, 1962–1967
Parish, 1973–

ST. DAVID, QUEBEC
Ecole St. David, 1952–1961

ST. BONIFACE, MANITOBA
Provencher School, 1899–1972
Louis Riel School, 1968–1974
Louis Riel High School, 1971–1976

ST. JEAN BAPTISTE, MANITOBA
St. John's School, 1917–1940, formerly a postulate

WINNIPEG, MANITOBA
St. Mary's School, 1880–1917
St. Joseph's School, 1883–1887

TORONTO, ONTARIO
Chaminade College School, 1963–1977

Notes

◆ *Introduction* ◆

1. Paul J. Philibert, O.P., ed., *Living in the Meantime: Concerning the Transformation of Religious Life* (New York: Paulist Press, 1994); Elizabeth Johnson, C.S.J., "Between the Times: Religious Life and the Postmodern Experience of God," *Review for Religious* (January–February 1994): 6–27.

2. Bernard Lee, S.M., "A Social-Historical Theology of Charism," *Review for Religious* (January–February 1989): 130–31.

3. Lawrence Cada, S.M., Raymond Fitz, S.M., Gertrude Foley, S.C., Thomas Giardino, S.M., Carol Lichtenberg, S.N.D.deN., *Shaping the Coming of Age of Religious Life* (New York: Seabury Press, 1979); John W. Padberg, S.J., "In the Midst of the Times: Religious Life and the Ever-Present Experience of the World," *Review for Religious* (March–April 1994): 167–79.

• Chapter One •

1. The biographies consulted for this chapter are the following: Henry Rousseau, S.M., *William Joseph Chaminade, Founder of the Society of Mary*, trans. John E. Garvin, S.M. (Dayton, Oh.: Brothers of Mary, 1914); Joseph Simler, S.M., *William Joseph Chaminade, Founder of the Marianists*, trans. Joseph Roy, S.M. (Dayton, Oh.: Marianist Resources Commission, 1986); Vincent R. Vasey, S.M., *Chaminade, Another Portrait*, ed. Lawrence Cada, S.M., and Joseph Stefanelli, S.M. (Dayton: Marianist Resources Commission, 1987).

2. Simler, *William Joseph Chaminade*, 5.

3. Vasey, *Chaminade*, 45–50.

4. Christopher J. Kauffman, *Tradition and Transformation: The Priests of St. Sulpice in the United States, 1791 to the Present* (New York: Macmillan, 1988), 3.

5. Vasey, *Chaminade*, 41.

6. Ibid., 45.

7. Jean Claude Délas, S.M., *History of the Constitutions of the Society of Mary*, Monograph Series, 19 (Dayton, Oh.: Marianist Resources Commission, 1995), Appendix, 17–18.

8. Quoted by Kauffman, *Tradition and Transformation*, 7 (emphasis added).

9. Délas, *Constitutions*, Appendix, 18.

10. Simler, *William Joseph Chaminade*, 28.

11. John McManners, *The French Revolution and the Church* (London: SPCK, 1969), 14 (emphasis added).

12. Ralph Gibson, *A Social History of French Catholicism, 1789–1914* (London: Routledge, 1989), 16–17.

13. Simler, *William Joseph Chaminade*, 12.

14. Vasey, *Chaminade*, 44.

15. Gibson, *French Catholicism*, 26.

16. For analysis of the French Revolution and the church, see Crain Brinton, *A Decade of Revolution* (New York: Harper & Row, 1959); Adrien Dansette, *Religious History of Modern France*, vol. 1, trans. John Dingle (New York: Herder & Herder, 1961); François Furet and Mona Ozouf, eds., *A Critical Dictionary of the French Revolution* (Cambridge, Mass.: Harvard University Press, 1989); Gibson, *French Catholicism*; Herbert Jedin and John Dolan, eds., *History of the Church* (New York:

Crossroad, 1981), Vol. 7 of *The Church Between Revolution and Restoration*, by Roger Aubert et al., trans. Peter Becker; McManners, *French Revolution*.

17. McManners, *French Revolution*, 28–30.

18. Ibid., 30–37.

19. Ibid., 38.

20. Ibid., 56.

21. Vasey, *Chaminade*, 54.

22. McManners, *French Revolution*, 45; see also Vasey, *Chaminade*, 56.

23. Simler, *William Joseph Chaminade*, 24.

24. Ibid., 24–25.

25. McManners, *French Revolution*, 67.

26. Ibid., 88.

27. Vasey, *Chaminade*, 89.

28. Phillipe Pierrel, S.M., *A Missionary Journey with William Joseph Chaminade, Founder of the Marianists* (Dayton, Oh.: Marianist Resources Commission, 1986), 21–22.

29. Quoted by Gibson, *French Catholicism*, 48.

30. Ibid., 47. Also see McManners, *French Revolution*, 140–50.

31. Simler, *William Joseph Chaminade*, 88–96.

32. Gibson, *French Catholicism*, 55.

33. Quoted by Edmund Baumeister, S.M., *Secondary Education of the Society of Mary in America* (Dayton, Oh.: Marianist Press, 1940), 10.

34. Quoted by Pierrel, *Missionary Journey*, 42.

35. Quoted by Adolf M. Windisch, S.M., *The Marianist Social System According to the Writings of William Joseph Chaminade 1761–1850* (Fribourg, Switzerland: St. Paul's Press, 1964), 98.

36. Vasey, *Chaminade*, 110-11.

37. Joseph Verrier, S.M., *The Sodality of Father Chaminade*, 2 vols. (Dayton, Oh.: Marianist Resources Commission, 1986), 1:297.

38. Vasey, *Chaminade*, 112.

39. Verrier, *Sodality*, 1:211.

40. Quoted by Rousseau, in *William Joseph Chaminade*, 93–94. This book's principal author was not Rousseau but Louis Cousin, S.M., who, because of his involvement in the Sillon movement, which had been condemned by Pius X in 1910, was considered too controversial to be identified publicly as the author. The Society published the biography as the work of Rousseau. Michael Schleich to George Meyer, March 20, 1992, 30.3.12, ASM (CIN).

41. Rousseau, *William Joseph Chaminade*, 95–103.

42. Quoted by Vasey, *Chaminade*, 102.

43. Charles S. Phillips, *The Church in France* (New York: Russell & Russell, 1966), 93.

44. Verrier, *Sodality*, 2:76.

45. Phillips, *Church in France*, 158ff.

46. Dansette, *Religious History*, 186.

47. Vasey, *Chaminade*, 42–43; Verrier, *Sodality*, 2:327–42.

48. For a thorough study of the "State" in the writings of Chaminade, see Francisco José García de Vinuesa Zabala, *Relations of the Society of Mary With the Sodality State* (Dayton, Oh.: Marianist Resources Commission, 1977).

49. Simler, *William Joseph Chaminade*, 259–60.

50. Quoted by Vasey, *Chaminade*, 148.

51. Simler, *William Joseph Chaminade*, 268.

52. Quoted in Simler, *William Joseph Chaminade*, 262.

53. Délas, *Constitutions*, Appendix T: "The Institute of Mary" (1818), 59.

54. Article 19, 1839 Constitutions as cited in *Chaminade's Letter to the Retreat Masters of 1839*, trans. Lawrence J. Cada, S.M. (Dayton, Oh.: Cincinnati Province of the Society of Mary, 1989).

55. Délas, *Constitutions*, "Institute of Mary," 59.

56. Ibid., 60. Also see Windisch, *Marianist Social System*, 190.

57. Kauffman, *Tradition and Transformation*, 22–23.

58. Délas, *Constitutions*, "Institute of Mary," 60.

59. Ibid., 61.

60. Ibid.

61. Ibid.

62. Ibid., 40.

63. Baumeister, *Secondary Education*, 74.

64. Simler, *William Joseph Chaminade*, 49.

65. Vasey, *Chaminade*, 158.

66. Quoted by Vasey, *Chaminade*, 160.

67. Délas, *Constitutions*, "Institute of Mary," 61.

68. Cardinal Giacomo Giustiniani to Chaminade, April 27, 1839, quoted by Simler, *William Joseph Chaminade*, 499.

69. *Chaminade's Letter to the Retreat Masters*, 8; Délas, *Constitutions*, 49–55.

70. *Chaminade's Letter*, 7.

71. Ibid., 5.

72. Ibid., 4–5.

73. Quoted by Vasey, *Chaminade*, 138.

74. *Chaminade's Letter*, 7.

75. Ibid., 6.

76. Ibid., 6–7.

77. Ibid., 13–14.

78. Ibid., 14.

79. Ibid., 15–16.

80. *The Spirit of Our Foundation According to the Writings of Father Chaminade and the Original Documents of the Society* (Dayton, Oh.: Mount St. John Normal School, 1920), 3:67–68.

81. Ibid., 3:68–69.

82. Joseph J. Panzer, S.M., *Educational Traditions of the Society of Mary* (Dayton, Oh.: University of Dayton Press, 1965), 137.

83. Simler, *William Joseph Chaminade*, 153–55; see also Vasey, *Chaminade*, 151.

84. Quoted by Panzer, *Educational Traditions*, 39.

85. Ibid., 60.

86. Ibid., 59–60.

87. Baumeister, *Secondary Education*, 31.

88. Panzer, *Educational Traditions*, 51.

89. Vasey, *Chaminade*, 123–25.

90. *Spirit of Our Foundation*, 3:353.

91. Ibid., 359.

92. Quoted by Baumeister, *Secondary Education*, 165.

93. Panzer, *Educational Traditions*, 156.

94. *Spirit of Our Foundation*, 3:345–46.

95. D. Scheuer, "Para du Phanjas, François," in *The Catholic Encyclopedia* (New York: Robert Appleton, 1911), 11:470.

96. *Spirit of Our Foundation*, 3:346.

97. Dansette, *Religious History*, 1:194–95.

98. Simler, *William Joseph Chaminade*, 115–16.

99. *Spirit of Our Foundation*, 3:176–77.

100. Dansette, *Religious History*, 1:178–203.

101. Quoted by Simler, *William Joseph Chaminade*, 422.

102. Ibid., 424–25.

103. Ibid., 425.

104. Ibid., 424.

105. Ibid., 423.

106. David Blackbourne, *Marpingin* (New York: Alfred A. Knopf, 1994), 23. For an exploration of the cultural meanings of apparitions of Mary, see Thomas Kselman, *The Miraculous in Nineteenth Century France* (Brunswick, N.J.: Rutgers University Press, 1983); Barbara Carrodo Pope, "Immaculate and Powerful: The Marian Revival in the Nineteenth Century," in *Immaculate & Powerful: The Female in Sacred Image and Social Reality*, ed. Clarissa Atkinson, Constance H. Buchanan, and Margaret Miles (Boston: Beacon Press, 1985), 173–200; Sandra L. Zimdars-Swartz, *Encountering Mary from La Salette to Medjugorje* (Princeton, N.J.: Princeton University Press, 1991).

107. Sister Daniel Hannefin, D.C., *The Daughters of the Church: A Popular History of the Daughters of Charity in the United States, 1807–1987* (Brooklyn: Foculare Press, 1989), 50–60. Also see Ann Taves, *Household of Faith: Roman Catholic Devotionalism in Mid-Nineteenth Century America* (Notre Dame, Ind.: University of Notre Dame Press, 1986).

108. Vasey, *Chaminade*, 205.

109. Simler, *William Joseph Chaminade*, 425.

110. For an exploration of Napoleon's reaction to royalists, see chapter 1 in Frederick B. Artz, *Revolution and Reaction, 1814–1832* (New York: Harper & Row, 1934).

111. Panzer, *Educational Traditions*, 80. For works on the liberal Catholic movement in France, see Roger Aubert, *Le pontificat de Pie IX* (Paris: Bloud & Gay, 1952); Jean Leflon, *La crise révolutionnaire 1789–1846* (Paris: Bloud & Gay, 1949); Phillips, *Church in France*; Bernard Reardon, *Liberalism and Tradition* (Stanford: Stanford University Press, 1970); Peter Steinfels, "The Failed Encounter: The Catholic Church and Liberalism in the Nineteenth Century," in *Catholicism and Liberalism*, ed. R. Bruce Douglas and David Hollenbach (New York: Cambridge University Press, 1994), 19–44; Alec R. Vidler, *Prophecy and Papacy: A Study of Lamennais, the Church and Revolution* (London: SCM Press, 1954).

112. Quoted by Simler, *William Joseph Chaminade*, 426–27.

113. Phillips, *Church in France*, 301.

114. Vasey, *Chaminade*, 209.

115. Simler, *William Joseph Chaminade*, 432–444.

116. Vasey, *Chaminade*, 220.

117. Annabelle M. Melville, *Jean Lefebvre de Cheverus 1768–1836* (Milwaukee: Bruce, 1958), 336.

118. Vasey, *Chaminade*, 220.

119. Ibid., 227.

120. Ibid., 231.

121. Ibid. 262.

122. Ibid., 288–89.

123. Ibid., 307.

124. Paul Tillich, *Theology of Culture*, ed. Robert Kimball (New York: Oxford University Press, 1959), 42.

125. Vasey, *Chaminade*, 207.

✦ *Chapter Two* ✦

1. Among the numerous works on the German-American Catholic experience, see Colman J. Barry, O.S.B., *The Catholic Church and German Americans* (Milwaukee: Bruce, 1957); Jay P. Dolan, "Philadelphia and the German Catholic Community," in *Immigrants and Religion in Urban America*, ed. Randall M. Miller and Thomas D. Marzik (Philadelphia: Temple University Press, 1977); Theodore Roemer, "The Leopoldine Foundation and the Church in the United States 1829-1839," United States Catholic Historical Society Monograph Series (New York, U.S. Catholic Historical Society, 1953), 145–211; Stephen Joseph Shaw, "Chicago's Germans and Italians, 1903–1939: The Catholic Parish as a Way-Station of Ethnicity and Americanization" (Ph.D. diss., University of Chicago, 1981).

2. Joseph P. Chinnici, *Living Stones: The History and Structure of Catholic Spiritual Life in the United States* (Maryknoll, N.Y.: Orbis Books, 1996).

3. The most detailed study of DuBourg is Annabelle M. Melville, *Louis William*

DuBourg, 2 vols. (Chicago: Loyola University Press, 1986). For DuBourg's Sulpician roles, see Christopher J. Kauffman, *Tradition and Transformation in Catholic Culture: The Priests of St. Sulpice in the United States, 1791 to the Present* (New York: Macmillan, 1988), 46–53, 75–91.

4. Vincent R. Vasey, S.M., *Chaminade, Another Portrait*, ed. Lawrence Cada, S.M., and Joseph Stefanelli, S.M. (Dayton, Oh.: Marianist Resources Commission, 1987).

5. Quoted by Peter A. Resch, S.M., *Shadows Cast Before, The Early Chapters of the History of the Society of Mary in St. Louis County* (Kirkwood, Mo.: Maryhurst Press, 1948), 40–42.

6. Ibid., 147–48.

7. For a detailed account of Leo Meyer and his American experience, see John G. Graves, *Father Leo Meyer's 13 Years at Nazareth* (Dayton, Oh.: North American Center for Marianist Studies, 1996). For Leo Meyer's early years in Alsace, see ibid., 1–5. Also see the English translation of French correspondence in the following collection: "American Marianist Letters and Source Material, 1840–1865" (hereafter cited as AML, located in the Archives of the Society of Mary, Cincinnati Province, cited as ASM (CIN)).

8. I am indebted to Brother Donald J. Hebeler, S.M., for his research on this person.

9. Graves, *Leo Meyer*, 2–3.

10. Ibid.

11. Leo Meyer to Father Chevaux, October 25, 1846, AML, ASM (CIN).

12. Meyer to Chevaux, April 12, 1847, and June 16, 1847, AML, ASM (CIN).

13. Meyer to Chevaux, June 11, 1848, AML, ASM (CIN).

14. Meyer to Chevaux, July 14, 1848, AML, ASM (CIN).

15. M. A. Varga, "Elizabeth Eppinger," *The New Catholic Encyclopedia* (New York: McGraw-Hill, 1967), 5:496.

16. Meyer to Chevaux, July 14, 1848, AML, ASM (CIN).

17. Henry Rousseau, S.M., *William Joseph Chaminade, Founder of the Society of Mary*, trans. John E. Garvin, S.M. (Dayton, Oh.: Brothers of Mary, 1914), 464.

18. Meyer to Chaminade, August 24, 1848, AML, ASM (CIN).

19. Ibid.

20. Meyer to Chevaux, August 4, 1848, AML, ASM (CIN).

21. Graves, *Leo Meyer*, 9.

22. Meyer to Chevaux, May 31, 1848, AML, ASM (CIN).

23. Bishop John Timon, C.M., to Leo Meyer, December 25, 1848, located in the correspondence of April 15, 1849, AML, ASM (CIN).

24. Ibid.

25. Caillet to Meyer, April 23, 1849, AML, ASM (CIN).

26. Graves, *Leo Meyer*, 15–16.

27. "Cincinnati," *The Metropolitan and Catholic Almanac and Laity's Directory* (Baltimore, 1850), 141.

28. R. Edmond Hussey, "John B. Purcell," in *Patterns of Episcopal Leadership*, ed.

Gerald P. Fogarty, S.J. (New York: Macmillan, 1989). Also see Anthony H. Deye, "Archbishop John Baptist Purcell of Cincinnati: Pre-Civil War Years" (Ph.D. diss., University of Notre Dame, 1959); Mary Agnes McCann, "Archbishop Purcell and the Archdiocese of Cincinnati" (Ph.D. diss., The Catholic University of America, 1918); Joseph M. White, "Cincinnati Germans" (Ph.D. diss., University of Notre Dame, 1981); John H. Lamott, *History of the Archdiocese of Cincinnati* (Cincinnati: Frederick Pustet, 1921).

29. Hussey, "John B. Purcell," 90.

30. On Bishop Henni and the German Catholic experience in Milwaukee, see Kathleen Neils Conzen, *Immigrant Milwaukee, 1836–60: Accommodation and Community in a Frontier City* (Cambridge, Mass.: Harvard University Press, 1976). Also see Bayard Still, *Milwaukee: The History of a City* (Madison, Wis., 1848).

31. Peter Leo Johnson, *Stuffed Saddlebags: The Life of Martin Kundig, Priest, 1805– 1879* (Milwaukee: Bruce, 1942). For an account of the cholera epidemic in Detroit, see Christopher J. Kauffman, *Ministry and Meaning: A Religious History of Catholic Health Care in the United States* (New York: Crossroad, 1995), 58. Also see Leslie Woodcock Tentler, *Seasons of Grace: A History of the Archdiocese of Detroit* (Detroit: Wayne State University Press, 1990).

32. White, "Cincinnati Germans," 212–15.

33. Barry, *Catholic Church*, 9–10.

34. Deye, "Archbishop John Baptist Purcell."

35. Leo Meyer to John B. Purcell, August 2, 1849, AML, ASM (CIN).

36. Ibid.

37. Meyer to Chevaux, August 10, 1849, AML, ASM (CIN).

38. John E. Garvin, *The Centenary of the Society of Mary: Historical Sketch of the Brothers of Mary in the United States* (Dayton, Oh.: Brothers of Mary, 1917), 113.

39. Ibid., 123.

40. Ibid., 131–33.

41. Ibid., 137.

42. Meyer to Chevaux, February 27, 1850, AML, ASM (CIN).

43. Ibid.

44. Meyer to Purcell, August 24, 1850, AML, ASM (CIN).

45. Garvin, *Centenary History*, 173.

46. Ibid., 174.

47. "Cincinnati," *The Catholic Directory* (Baltimore, 1853), 86.

48. Ibid.

49. Ibid. (1855), 142.

50. Ibid. (1856), 130.

51. Ibid. (1860), 343.

52. St. Mary's College Catalogue 1879, IAA, Archives of the University of Dayton (hereafter AUD).

53. Meyer to Chevaux, February 11, 1851, AML, ASM (CIN).

54. Ibid.

55. Meyer to Chevaux, January 12, 1859, AML, ASM (CIN).

56. Ibid.

57. Chevaux to Meyer, March 26, 1851, AML, ASM (CIN).

58. Ibid.

59. Meyer to Chevaux, November 3, 1851, AML, ASM (CIN).

60. Chevaux to Meyer, December 21, 1851, AML, ASM (CIN).

61. Caillet to Meyer, January 21, 1852, AML, ASM (CIN).

62. Caillet to Purcell, January 22, 1852, AML, ASM (CIN).

63. Meyer to Chevaux, January 27, 1852, AML, ASM (CIN).

64. Meyer to Chevaux, April 10, 1853, AML, ASM (CIN).

65. Edel to Caillet, Ascension Day, 1852, Texas Letters (hereafter cited as TL). Originals of all Texas Letters are in the Texas Catholic Historical Archives, Austin. Copies are located in ASM (CIN).

66. Garvin, *Centenary History*, 180–83.

67. Meyer to Caillet, November 29, 1853, AML, ASM (CIN).

68. Ibid.

69. See "Data from the Archives of St. Aloysius Orphanage, Cincinnati, Ohio," AML, ASM (CIN).

70. Henri Lebon, S.M., *Our First Century, 1817–1917*, trans. John Dockter, S.M. (Dayton, Oh.: Marianist Resources Commission, 1975), 69–72.

71. Damian Litz to Chevaux, August 17, 1855, AML, ASM (CIN).

72. Meyer to Caillet, March 1, 1856, AML, ASM (CIN).

73. Stintzi to Caillet, February 6, 1859, AML, ASM (CIN).

74. Ibid.

75. Meyer to Caillet, June 27, 1862, AML, ASM (CIN).

76. George Meyer, "Annals of the American Province," 20, ASM (CIN).

77. Quoted by Graves, *Leo Meyer*, 230.

78. Meyer to Bishop Henni, August 21, 1855, AML, ASM (CIN).

79. Brother Edward Gorman, "Memoirs," p. 5, ASM (CIN).

80. Garvin, *Centenary History*, 204. Of course, Garvin revealed some biases in his description, but his characterizations are generally well accepted.

81. Ibid., 202–3.

82. Zehler to Superior General (Caillet), April 17, 1862, AML, ASM (CIN).

• *Chapter Three* •

1. M. V. Geiger, "School Sisters of Notre Dame," *The New Catholic Encyclopedia* (New York: McGraw-Hill, 1967), 12:1175.

2. For the Philadelphia experience, see Michael Feldberg, *The Philadelphia Bible Riots of 1844: A Study of Ethnic Conflict* (Westport, Conn.: Greenwood Press, 1975); and Vincent P. Lannie and Bernard Diethorn, "For the Honor and Glory of God: The Philadelphia Bible Riots of 1844," *History of Education Quarterly* 8 (Spring 1968): 44–106. For New York and other areas of conflict, see Vincent P. Lannie, *Public Money and Parochial Education: Bishop Hughes, Governor Seward and the New*

York School Controversy (Cleveland: Press of Case Western Reserve, 1968); Richard V. Shaw, *Dagger John: The Unquiet Life and Times of Archbishop John Hughes* (New York: U.S. Catholic Historical Society, 1977). On Catholic education, see Harold A. Buetow, *Of Singular Benefit: The Story of U.S. Catholic Education* (New York: Macmillan, 1970); James A. Burns, *The Growth and Development of the Catholic School System in the United States* (New York: Benziger Brothers, 1912); Niel G. McCluskey, ed., *Catholic Education in America: A Documentary History* (New York: Bureau of Publications, Teachers College of Columbia University, 1964); F. Michael Perko, ed., *Enlightening the Next Generation* (New York: Garland, 1988); Timothy Walch, *Parish School: American Catholic Parochial Education from Colonial Times to the Present* (New York: Crossroad, 1996).

3. Joseph P. Chinnici, *Living Stones: The History and Structure of Catholic Spiritual Life in the United States* (Maryknoll, N.Y.: Orbis Books, 1989).

4. Jay P. Dolan, *Catholic Revivalism: The American Experience, 1830-1900* (Notre Dame, Ind.: University of Notre Dame Press, 1978), 69.

5. Ibid.

6. Joseph Lackner, S.M., "St. Ann's Colored Church and School, Cincinnati: The Indian and Negro Collection for the United States and Reverend Francis Xavier Weninger, S.J.," *U.S. Catholic Historian* 7 (1988): 145–56.

7. James Talmadge Moore, *Through Fire and Flood: The Catholic Church and Frontier Texas, 1836–1910* (College Station: Texas A & M Press, 1992), 109–10.

8. James F. Connelly, *The Visit of Archbishop Gaetano Bedini in the United States of America, June 1953–January 1854* (Rome: Gregorian University Press, 1960), 200 n. 69.

9. John E. Garvin, S.M., *The Centenary of the Society of Mary: Historical Sketch of the Brothers of Mary in the United States* (Dayton, Oh.: Brothers of Mary, 1917), 139.

10. Bishop Amadeus Rappe to the Very Rev. Georges Caillet, S.M., Archives of the Marianists in Rome, December 11, 1860 (hereafter cited as AGMAR) 122.8.1 (translated by Lawrence Cada, S.M., Spring 1978, Rome).

11. Rappe to Caillet, November 28, 1861, AGMAR 122.8.6, and February 3, 1862, AGMAR 122.8.7 (translated by Lawrence Cada, S.M., February 1992.)

12. Henry B. Leonard, "Ethnic Conflict and Episcopal Power: The Diocese of Cleveland, 1847–1850," *Catholic Historical Review* 62 (July 1976): 397. Also see Rev. John F. Lyons, *The Life and Times of Bishop Louis Amadeus Rappe* (Cleveland: Cleveland Catholic Diocese, 1997).

13. Ibid.

14. Garvin, *Centenary*, 189.

15. *History of St. Patrick's Parish, 1853–1903: Memorial of the Golden Jubilee* (Cleveland: St. Patrick's Parish, 1903), 49.

16. Garvin, *Centenary*, 131–32.

17. Jean-Marie Odin to Georges Caillet, December 16, 1851, TL, ASM (CIN).

18. Jean Chevaux to Leo Meyer, December 21, 1851, AML, ASM (CIN).

19. Joseph William Schmitz, S.M., Ph.D., *The Society of Mary in Texas* (San Antonio: Naylor Company, 1951), 31–35.

20. Patrick Foley, "Jean-Marie Odin, Missionary Extraordinaire," *Texas Catholic History & Culture* 1 (January 1990): 34.

21. "Galveston," *Catholic Almanac and Laity's Directory* (Baltimore: Lucas Brothers, 1855), 216.

22. Ibid., "Cincinnati," 143.

23. Ibid., "Galveston," 216.

24. Ibid., "Cincinnati," 142.

25. Schmitz, *Society of Mary*, 32.

26. Timothy M. Matovina, "Sacred Space and Collective Memory, San Fernando Cathedral, San Antonio, Texas," *U.S. Catholic Historian* 15 (Winter 1997): 38.

27. Schmitz, *Society of Mary*, 31–32.

28. Ibid., 42.

29. Matovina, "Sacred Space," 39.

30. Moore, *Through Fire and Flood*, 112–13.

31. Ibid., 115.

32. Stephen Ochs, *Desegregating the Altar: The Josephites and Their Struggle for Black Priests* (Baton Rouge: Louisiana State University Press, 1990), 33. Also see Cyprian Davis, *The History of Black Catholics in the United States* (New York: Crossroad, 1991), 118.

33. Moore, *Through Fire and Flood*, 113.

34. Edel to Caillet, November 27, 1854, TL, ASM (CIN).

35. Odin to Caillet, December 20, 1858, TL, ASM (CIN).

36. Clouzet to Meyer, March 14, 1858, TL, ASM (CIN).

37. See Texas Letters, 1852, TL, ASM (CIN).

38. Caillet to Meyer, May 6, 1858, TL, ASM (CIN).

39. Meyer to Caillet, December 17, 1859, TL, ASM (CIN).

40. Odin to Caillet, October 10, 1858, TL, ASM (CIN).

41. Beyrer to Caillet, 1865, TL, ASM (CIN).

42. Sr. Mary Clarence Friesenhahn, "Catholic Education in the Province of San Antonio" (M.A. thesis, Catholic University of America, Washington, D.C., 1938), 29.

43. Ibid., 30.

44. Reinbolt to Caillet, November 1, 1866, TL, ASM (CIN).

45. Dubuis to Caillet, March 17, 1854, TL, ASM (CIN).

46. Schmitz, *Society of Mary*, 52–57.

47. Ibid., 114–16, 121.

48. Ibid.

49. *The Catholic Directory* (Baltimore: Lucas Brothers, 1892), 395.

50. Matovina, "Sacred Space," 40–41.

51. Kim to Simler, March, 1899, TL, ASM (CIN).

52. Ibid.

53. Schmitz, *Society of Mary*, 121–37.

54. *Catholic Directory* (1892), 395.

55. Quoted by Schmitz, *Society of Mary*, 140.

56. *The Catholic Directory* (Baltimore: Lucas Brothers, 1898), 456.

57. Ibid.

58. Schmitz, *Society of Mary*, 148.

59. Religious history of the Hawaiian Islands includes only a few critical works. For the Catholic dimension I have relied on Robert Schoofs, SS.CC., *Pioneers of the Faith: History of the Catholic Mission in Hawaii 1827–1948*, revised by Fay Wren Midkill (Waiksane, Hawaii: Boeynaems, 1978); and Daniel Joseph Dever, "The Legal Status of Catholic Schools Under the Constitutional and Statutory Law of Hawaii" (M.A. thesis, Catholic University of America, 1952).

60. Schoofs, *Pioneers*, 14.

61. Dever, "Legal Status," 5–7.

62. Schoofs, *Pioneers*, 52.

63. Eugene Paulin, S.M., and Joseph Becker, S.M., *New Wars: The History of the Brothers of Mary in Hawaii 1883–1958* (Milwaukee: Bruce, 1959), chapters 1 and 2.

64. Annals of St. Louis College, Honolulu, September 3, 1893, 1F-1, Folder 1.1, Archives Society of Mary, Pacific Province, Cupertino, California (hereafter cited as ASM [PAC]).

65. Sydney E. Ahlstrom, *A Religious History of the American People* (New York: Doubleday, 1975) 2:342.

66. Paulin and Becker, *New Wars*, 3–17.

67. Annals of St. Louis College, 1F-1, Folder 1.1, ASM (PAC).

68. Ibid., 1895, ASM (PAC).

69. Quoted by Reginald Yzendorn, SS.CC., *Guide to the History of the Catholic Mission* (Honolulu: Honolulu Star Bulletin, 1927), 213. Also see Paulin and Becker, *New Wars*, 28.

70. Paulin and Becker, *New Wars*, 28.

71. Annals of St. Louis College, September 4, 1900, 1-F, Folder 1.1, 3, ASM (PAC).

72. Paulin and Becker, *New Wars*, 94.

73. Annals of St. Louis College, November 6, 1900, 1-F, Folder 1.1, ASM (PAC).

74. Paulin and Becker, *New Wars*, 33.

75. Annals of St. Louis College, March 7, 1887.

76. Minutes of the Provincial Council, Dayton, February 1, 1892, Provincial Council Files, ASM (CIN).

77. Ibid., January 6, 1903, ASM (CIN).

78. Bertram to Meyer, March 14, 1905, St. Louis College-Provincial correspondence, ASM (CIN).

79. Joseph Simler, Circular No. 28, December 28, 1883 Circular Letters to the Society of Mary, 20, NACMS.

80. *The Catholic Directory* (Baltimore: Lucas Brothers, 1885), 218.

81. Vincent Steele, S.M., "The Society of Mary in California, 1884–1956" (M.A. thesis, University of San Francisco, 1958), 13–14. Copy, ASM (PAC).

82. Ibid., 15

83. Ibid., 27

84. *The Catholic Directory* (Baltimore: Lucas Brothers, 1902), 169.

85. Quoted by Dieter Cunz, *The Maryland Germans: A History* (Princeton, N.J.: Princeton University Press, 1948), 184.

86. Thomas W. Spalding, *The Premier See: A Bicentennial History of the Archdiocese of Baltimore* (Baltimore: Johns Hopkins University Press, 1989), 32.

87. Ibid., 104.

88. Cunz, *Maryland Germans*, 185.

89. Spalding, *Premier See*, "Introduction."

90. Ibid., 128. Also see Michael J. Curley, C.SS.R , *The Provincial Story: A History of the Baltimore Province of the Congregation of the Most Holy Redeemer* (New York: The Redemptorist Fathers, Baltimore Province, 1963), 54–60.

91. Thomas W. Spalding, C.F.X., "German Parishes East and West," *U.S. Catholic Historian* 14 (Spring 1996): 38.

92. Spalding, *Premier See*, 138.

93. John E. Garvin, S.M., treats the Redemptorist–Marianist connection in *Centenary*, 143–44, 196, 223, 237.

94. Annals of St. James School, 1873–80, ASM (CIN).

95. Ibid., 1878, p. 7.

96. Ibid., 1883–84, p. 12.

97. Ibid.

98. *The Catholic Directory* (Baltimore: Lucas Brothers, 1881), 69.

99. Annals of St. James School, May 3, 1883, p. 9, ASM (CIN).

100. Ibid., May 23, 1883, p. 9.

101. Annals St. Alphonsus, Baltimore, p. 6, and St. Martin's, Baltimore, August 31, 1872, 1961, ASM (CIN). Since the Marianist community moved from St. Alphonsus to St. Martin's, these annals are in one book. Because the specific date is not always provided, page number is significant.

102. Ibid.

103. Ibid., August 23, 1872, p. 4.

104. Ibid., August 31, 1872, pp. 7–8.

105. See the Annals of St. Alphonsus for the years 1872–1875, pp. 3–14.

106. Ibid., December 18, 1878, p. 26.

107. Ibid., no date, ca. spring 1878, p. 27.

108. Ibid., pp. 27–29.

109. Annals of St. Alphonsus Parish, Archives of the Redemptorist Fathers and Brothers, Baltimore Province, Our Lady of Good Counsel Residence, Brooklyn, New York. Thanks to Father Carl W. Hoegerl, C.SS.R., for his assistance and hospitality.

110. Brother Julius of Mary, "The District of Baltimore," unpublished manuscript, pp. 26–27. Archives of the Christian Brothers, LaSalle University, Philadel-

phia. Thanks to Brother Joseph Grabenstein, F.S.C., for his kind assistance in providing me photocopies of this chronicle of events at St. Alphonsus.

111. Annals of St. Alphonsus, Baltimore, and St. Martin's, Baltimore, 1961, ASM (CIN).

112. *The Catholic Directory* (Baltimore: Lucas Brothers, 1880).

113. Annals of St. Martin's, Baltimore, pp. 30–31, ASM (CIN).

114. Ibid., p. 32.

115. Ibid., pp. 32–33.

116. See *Catholic Directories* for this period, 1886–1895.

117. Annals of St. Martin's, Baltimore, p. 36, ASM (CIN).

118. Quoted by Jean Claude Délas, S.M., *History of the Constitutions of the Society of Mary*, Monograph Series, 19 (Dayton, Oh.: Marianist Resources Commission, 1975), 148.

119. *History of St. Martin's Church, Baltimore, 1865–1895* (Baltimore, 1895), 212–43.

120. Ibid., 41–45.

121. Ibid., "Introduction."

122. Ibid., 39.

123. Stonewall [*sic*], "Columbus Celebration in Baltimore," *The Catholic News* (Washington, D.C.), October 22, 1892, p. 2.

124. Christopher J. Kauffman, "Christopher Columbus and American Catholic Identity," *U.S. Catholic Historian* 11 (Spring 1993): 93–110.

125. Susan G. Davis, *Parades and Power: Street Theatre in the Nineteenth Century* (Berkeley: University of California Press, 1988).

126. Donald Kinzer, *The American Protective Association* (Seattle: University of Washington Press, 1964).

127. Quoted by Christopher J. Kauffman, *Faith and Fraternalism: A History of the Knights of Columbus*, revised edition (New York: Simon & Schuster, 1992), 91.

128. "Catholic Education Exhibit," Preface, *The World's Columbian Catholic Congresses and Educational Exhibit* (New York: Arno Press, 1978), 36–38.

129. Ibid.

130. "Our Education Exhibit," *The Catholic Mirror* (Baltimore), May 15, 1893, p. 1.

131. Ibid., p. 7.

132. *The World's Columbian Catholic Congresses and Educational Exhibit*, 35.

• *Chapter Four* •

1. Jean Claude Délas, S.M., *History of the Constitutions of the Society of Mary*, Monograph Series, 19 (Dayton, Oh.: Marianist Resources Commission, 1975), 76.

2. Ibid., 50–57.

3. Quoted by Délas, *History*, 77.

4. For the American episcopal reaction to Pope Pius IX's declaration of the dogma of the Immaculate Conception, see James Hennesey, "A Prelude to Vatican I: American Bishops and the Definition of the Immaculate Conception," *Theological Stud-*

ies 25 (1964): 409–19. For Hennesey's contributions to theology and history, see the entire issue of the *U.S. Catholic Historian,* essays in honor of James Hennesey, S.J., 16 (Fall 1996): 1–170.

5. Délas, *History,* 80–85.

6. Ibid., 88–89.

7. Ibid., 93ff.

8. Quoted by Délas, *History,* 94.

9. Ibid., 95ff.

10. Georges Joseph Caillet, Circular Letter No. 71, June 25, 1863. English translation, in Early Circular Letters, NACMS, "Various Documents," 1840, 1863–1885.

11. Jean Joseph Chevaux, Circular Letter No. 16, May 15, 1872, Early Circular Letters, NACMS.

12. Louis Gadiou, S.M., and Jean Claude Délas, S.M., *Marianists in a Continuing Mission,* trans. Robert Sargent, S.M. (Dayton, Oh.: Marianist Resources Commission, 1973), 83–84.

13. Délas, *History,* 130ff.

14. Ibid.

15. Ibid.

16. Reverend Henri Lebon, S.M., *Our First Century, 1817–1917,* trans. John Dockter, S.M. (Dayton, Oh.: Marianist Resources Commission, 1975), 132.

17. Ibid.

18. Joseph Simler, S.M., "Filial Piety in Christian Life," Circular Letter No. 10, June 28, 1878, English translation in Circular Letters of Simler (Dayton, Oh.: St. Mary's Institute, 1881).

19. Gerald A. McCool, *Catholic Theology in the Nineteenth Century* (New York: Seabury Press, 1977).

20. Simler, "Filial Piety," 9.

21. Ibid., 83–93.

22. Very Reverend Joseph Simler, "Instruction on the Characteristic Features of the Society of Mary on the Occasion of the First Century of its Origins," Circular Letter No. 62, July 10, 1894, English translation (Dayton, Oh.: St. Mary's Community, 1895), 69.

23. Ibid., 94.

24. Ibid., 122.

25. Records of the Sodality of the Holy Angels, 6 SR (1), AUD.

26. Ibid., 8-11.

27. Ibid., 12ff.

28. Ibid., May 10, 1876, 22.

29. Ibid., May 10, 1876, 23.

30. Records of the Sodality of the Immaculate Conception, February 10, 1899, 17, 6 SR (2), AUD.

31. Ibid., February 25, 1899, 19, AUD.

32. Edmund J. Baumeister, S.M., *Secondary Education in the Society of Mary in America* (Dayton, Oh.: Mount St. John Press, 1940), 230.

33. Oral interview, William Wohlleben, S.M., January 6, 1958. McMahon Tapes, copy 1M(2), Folder 12, AUD.

34. Very Reverend Jean Chevaux, "Instruction on Diverse Points Relating to Religious Discipline and Christian Education," Circular Letter No. 7, November 30, 1869. English translation in Early Circular Letters, NACMS, 9.

35. Baumeister, *Secondary Education,* 243–45.

36. John M. Reinbolt, S.M., "Supplement to the Instruction Given in the Retreat of 1879," Provincial Circulars of John Reinbolt, ASM (CIN).

37. Ibid., 7–10.

38. Mathias Leimkuhler to Joseph Weckesser, March 14, 1907, Provincial Papers, Joseph Weckesser, ASM (CIN).

39. Brother Robert Holzmer, letter included in ibid.

40. *Constitutions of the Society of Mary, 1839,* trans. Herbert G. Kramer, S.M. (Honolulu: Pacific Province, 1967), art. 253, p. 31.

41. Ibid., arts. 261–62, p. 32.

42. Ibid., art. 267, p. 34. The 1891 Constitution refers to these principles and methods in articles 261–78, *Constitutions of the Society of Mary* (Dayton, 1937), 66–71. This 1937 publication was the 1891 document with a few revisions to conform to the norms established by the revised code of canon law of 1918. These revisions support a thesis of this book, as they underscored the significance of the enclosure.

43. *Manual of Christian Pedagogy for the Use of The Brothers of the Society of Mary* (Dayton, Oh.: Nazareth, 1899). See Baumeister, *Secondary Education,* 163–66, for a brief commentary on the origin of the *Manual.* Not available until the first decade of the twentieth century were several works for novices composed by Marianists: Christian Christ, *Catechism of the Religious State* (Dayton, Oh.: St. Mary's Convent, 1906); Emil Neubert, *A Study of the Interior Life According to the Spirit of the Society of Mary* (Dayton, Oh.: Nazareth, n.d.); idem, *The Devotion to the Blessed Virgin in the Society of Mary* (Ferguson, Mo.: Villa St. Joseph, 1913); idem, *The Spirit of Our Foundation,* 3 vols. (Dayton, Oh.: St. Mary's Convent and Mount St. John Normal School, 1911–20).

44. *Manual,* 14.

45. Ibid., 22.

46. Ibid., 29–34.

47. Ibid., 39–43.

48. Ibid., 44–54.

49. Ibid., 57–58.

50. Ibid., 58.

51. Ibid., 63–64.

52. Ibid., 65–67.

53. This lengthy treatise on methodology is in manuscript form. See "Manual of Christian Pedagogy for Use in the Society of Mary, Second Part," translated and reproduced in the Scholasticate of Mary, 1885, ASM (CIN).

54. Ibid., 3–4.

55. *Management of Christian Schools* (New York: de la Salle Institute, 1887), Archives of the Christian Brothers, Midwest Province, Memphis, Tennessee.

56. *Manual* (part one), 58–67.

57. *Management of Christian Schools*, 304.

58. "Provincial's Report," Reverend George Meyer, S.M., 1899, Provincial Chapters, ASM (CIN).

59. Ibid.

60. "Provincial's Report," Reverend George Meyer, S.M., 1900, Provincial Chapters, ASM (CIN).

61. John E. Garvin, S.M., *The Centenary of the Society of Mary: Historical Sketch of the Brothers of Mary in the United States* (Dayton, Oh.: Brothers of Mary, 1917).

62. Dieter Cunz, *The Maryland Germans: A History* (Princeton, N.J.: Princeton University Press, 1948), 359 n. 100. Also see Carl Wittke, *The German Language Press in America* (New York: Haskel House Publishers, 1973).

63. Cunz, *Maryland Germans*, 356–58.

64. Ibid., 360.

65. Rory Connelly, "Arthur Preuss, Journalist and Voice of German and Conservative Catholics in America, 1871–1934" (Ph.D. diss., Catholic University of America, 1996), 228.

66. The literature on Americanism and its opponents is extensive. See Philip Gleason, "The New Americanism in Catholic Historiography," *U.S. Catholic Historian* 11 (Summer 1993): 1–19. Also see Patrick H. Ahern, *The Life of John J. Keane, Educator and Archbishop 1839–1918* (Milwaukee: Bruce, 1954); Colman J. Barry, O.S.B., *The Catholic Church and German Americans* (Milwaukee: Bruce, 1957); Robert Emmett Curran, *Michael Augustine Corrigan and the Shaping of Conservative Catholicism in America* (New York: Arno Press, 1978); Gerald P. Fogarty, S.J., *The Vatican and the American Hierarchy* (Wilmington, Del: Michael Glazier, 1982); Philip Gleason, *The Conservative Reformers: German-American Catholics and the Social Order* (Notre Dame, Ind: University of Notre Dame Press, 1968); Thomas T. McAvoy, *The Great Crisis in American Catholic History* (Chicago: Regnery, 1957); Marvin R. O'Connell, *John Ireland and the American Catholic Church* (St. Paul: Minnesota Historical Society Press, 1988.

67. Anthony L. Saletel, "Damian Litz and the German-American Press" (M.A. thesis, Catholic University of America, 1937), 100–102.

68. Christopher J. Kauffman, "Christopher Columbus and American Catholic Identity," *U.S. Catholic Historian* 11 (Spring 1993): 93–110.

69. Oral Interview William Wohlleben, S.M., January 16, 1958, p. 28, McMahon Tapes, copy 1M(2), Folder 12, AUD.

70. *The Catholic Directory* (Baltimore: Lucas Brothers, 1904), 149.

71. Wohlleben interview, p. 30.

72. Gleason, *Conservative Reformers*, 47

73. Garvin, *Centenary*, 213.

74. John Lancaster Spalding, *Education and the Higher Life* (Chicago: McClurg, 1890); David Francis Sweeney, *The Life of John Lancaster Spalding, First Bishop of Peoria, 1840–1916* (New York: Herder & Herder, 1965).

• *Chapter Five* •

1. Philip Gleason, *Speaking of Diversity* (Baltimore: Johns Hopkins University Press, 1992), 282.

2. Philip Gleason, *The Conservative Reformers: German American Catholics and the Social Order* (Notre Dame, Ind.: University of Notre Dame Press, 1968); idem, "American Identity and Americanization," in *Harvard Encyclopedia of American Ethnic Groups*, ed. Stephen Thernstrom et al. (Cambridge, Mass.: Harvard University Press, 1980), 31–58.

3. Robert H. Wiebe, *The Search for Order, 1877–1920* (New York: Hill & Wang, 1968), XIV. In its thirty-third printing in 1995, this work is obviously a standard text for both undergraduate and graduate students of history.

4. Elizabeth McKeown, "The National Bishops' Conference: An Analysis of Its Origins," *Catholic Historical Review* 65 (1980): 565–83. Also see her *War and Welfare: American Catholics and World War I* (New York: Garland, 1988).

5. For an overview, see Robert Anderson, "The Conflict in Education" in *Education and Morals*, ed. Theodore Zeldon (London: George Allen & Unwin, 1970), 61; Joan Coffey, "Of Catechisms and Sermons: Church-State Relations in France, 1890–1905," *Church History* 66 (March 1997): 57–66; Ralph Gibson, *A Social History of French Catholicism, 1789–1914* (London: Routledge, 1989).

6. Anderson, "Conflict in Education," 70.

7. Charles J. T. Talar, "Conspiracy to Commit Heresy: The Anti-Americanist Polemic of Canon Henri Delassus," *U.S. Catholic Historian* 11 (Summer 1993): 77–92.

8. Gibson, *Social History*.

9. Roger Price, *A Social History of Nineteenth Century France* (New York: Holmes & Meier, 1987), 318. Also see Adrien Dansette, *Religious History of Modern France* (New York: Herder & Herder, 1961) 2:187–206.

10. The complexities of the secularization issue and anti-clericalism are considered in Henri Lebon, S.M., *Our First Century, 1817–1917* (Dayton, Oh.: Marianist Resources Commission, 1975), 191–99.

11. Joseph Simler, Circular Letter No. 94, November 8, 1904, in Very Reverend J. Simler Circulars 60–94, pp. 6–8, NACMS.

12. Dansette, *Religious History*, 2:271–73. Lebon states that Simler, as late as 1902, was sympathetic to Sangnier (*Our First Century*, 160).

13. Dansette, *Religious History,* 283.

14. Harry W. Paul, *The Second Ralliement: The Rapprochement Between Church and State in France in the Twentieth Century* (Washington, D.C.: Catholic University of America Press, 1967), 20. For a splendid work on American modernism, see R. Scott Appleby, *Church and Age Unite: The Modernist Impulse in American Catholicism* (Notre Dame, Ind.: University of Notre Dame Press, 1992). For an excellent study of French education in relation to Marianist service, including the roles of the alumni of the Collège Stanislas in the French military and the bureaucracy, see Maurice Larkin, *Religion, Politics and Preferment in France Since 1890: La Belle Epoque and Its Legacy* (New York: Cambridge University Press, 1995).

15. Michael Schleich to George Meyer, March 30, 1912, ASM (CIN), 30.3.12.

16. John Kim to George Meyer, April 1, 1907, John Kim Correspondence, ASM (CIN).

17. Lebon, *Our First Century,* 205–12.

18. Schleich to Kim, September 19, 1906, AGMAR 081.6.15.

19. Ibid., December 28, 1905, AGMAR 081.6.25.

20. Eugene Joseph Sohm, S.M., "The History of the Society of Mary in the St. Louis Area" (M.A. thesis, St. Louis University, 1948), 20–43.

21. Michael Schleich to John Kim, February 1, 1907, AGMAR 082.1.133.

22. John Waldron to John Kim, January 26, 1908, AGMAR 082.1.

23. Gerald J. Schnepp, S.M., *Province of St. Louis, 1908–1983: The First Seventy-Five Years* (St. Louis: Society of Mary, Province of St. Louis, Marianist Press, 1985), 17–18.

24. John Waldron to Joseph Hiss, October 13, 1908, AGMAR 082.1.2.

25. Schleich to Kim, 1908, AGMAR 082.1.142.

26. Paul C. Goelz, "John Waldron, The Man and The Educator" (M.A. thesis, University of Dayton, 1945), 1–21.

27. Inspector's Report, Inspector's Files, Archives of the St. Louis Province at St. Mary's University, San Antonio, Texas (hereafter ASM [St. L]).

28. Ibid., 4.

29. Ibid., 6.

30. Ibid.

31. Ibid.

32. Quoted by Edgar Patrick McCarren, "The Origin and Early Years of the National Catholic Education Association" (Ph.D. diss., Catholic University of America, 1966), 129.

33. Philip Gleason, *Contending With Modernity: Catholic Higher Education in the Twentieth Century* (New York: Oxford University Press, 1996), 21–46.

34. Goelz, "John Waldron," 134–35.

35. Ibid., 135–43.

36. Ibid., 128–30.

37. Timothy Walch, *Parish School: American Catholic Parochial Education From Colonial Times to the Present* (New York: Crossroad, 1996), 111.

38. Brother John Waldron, S.M., "Methods in Teaching Bible History," *The School Journal* 6 (April 1907): 321–26.

39. Gerald P. Fogarty, *American Catholic Biblical Scholarship: A History From the Early Republic to Vatican II* (San Francisco: Harper-Collins, 1989).

40. Gleason, *Contending with Modernity*, 47.

41. Ibid.

42. Ibid.

43. Brother Joseph Gallagher, S.M., "The Organization of Our Educational Work," *Bulletin of the NCEA* 15 (1918): 528–60; Brother John Waldron, S.M., "How Many Grades Should There Be In An Elementary School," *Bulletin of the NCEA* 7 (1910): 541–44.

44. Gleason, *Contending with Modernity*, 87.

45. Walch, *Parish School*, 119–24.

46. Joseph Hiss, "Acts of the General Chapter," Circular Letter No. 18, August 18, 1910, 89-90. Hiss Circulars I, 1905–1913, NACMS.

47. Ibid., 90–92.

48. Ibid., 94.

49. Ibid., 95–97.

50. John Waldron, "Reports of the Inspector of the St. Louis Province," 1919, 2. Reports of the Inspector, ASM (St. L).

51. Waldron, "Reports of the Inspector," 1911, 2, ASM (St. L).

52. Quoted by Harold A. Buetow, *Of Singular Benefit: The Story of U.S. Catholic Education* (New York: Macmillan, 1970), 196.

53. Waldron, "Reports of the Inspector," 1911, 4, ASM (St. L).

54. Ibid.

55. John Waldron, "Reports of the Inspector," 1912, ASM (St. L).

56. Ibid.

57. Waldron, "Reports of the Inspector," 1916, ASM (St. L).

58. Ibid.

59. Ibid.

60. George Meyer, S.M., Provincial's Report, July 22, 1904, Provincial Chapters, ASM (CIN).

61. Schleich to George Meyer, March 22, 1912, ASM (CIN) 22.3.12.

62. George Sauer, S.M., "On Vocations To the Teaching Brotherhood," *Bulletin of the NCEA* 18 (1921): 301–11.

63. Ibid., 302.

64. Ibid., 303.

65. Ibid.

66. Ibid., 304–5.

67. Ibid., 305–6.

68. Ibid., 308.

69. Ibid.

70. Ibid., 310.

71. Ibid., 310–11.

72. Ibid., 312. One teaching community, the Brothers of Holy Infancy, was founded in Buffalo in 1855.

73. "Provincial Chapter, Province of Cincinnati 1919," AGMAR 080/08/082.

74. "Provincial Chapter, Province of Cincinnati, 1922," AGMAR 08.2.3.

75. Ibid., n. 73.

76. Ibid., "Provincial Chapter, Province of Cincinnati, 1924," AGMAR 0.80.2.5.

77. Ibid.

78. Lawrence Yeske to Cardinal Denis Dougherty, January 16, 1924, AGMAR 084.1.32.

79. Ibid.

80. George Meyer to Michael Schleich, January 3, 1919, AGMAR 083.3.15.

81. George Deck to Michael Schleich, 1919, AGMAR 083.3.35.

82. John Waldron File, ASM (St. L). On the confidentiality of Waldron's removal, see George Sauer to Michael Schleich, March 22, 1925, AGMAR 084.5.14; and Ernest J. Sorret to M. H. Lebon, July 25, 1924, AGMAR 087.3.19. Sorret writes that Waldron's "accident in Milwaukee" may have been the result "of an abuse of strong liquors." Sorret told Lebon of his discussion with Waldron: "I pointed out to him very forcefully that danger of alcohol on his health."

83. Eugene A. Paulin to Michael Schleich, March 9, 1930, AGMAR 093.1.15.

◆ *Chapter Six* ◆

1. James A. Burns, C.S.C., *The Growth and Development of the Catholic School System in the United States* (New York: Benziger Brothers, 1912), 116–17.

2. Brother Thomas E. Oldenski, S.M., "Marianist Beginnings in Secondary Education" (Cincinnati Province, 1989, privately circulated), appendix, ASM (CIN).

3. For extensive treatment of Marianist high schools, see Edmund Baumeister, S.M., *Secondary Education of the Society of Mary* (Dayton, Oh.: University of Dayton Press, 1940).

4. Norbert Brockman, S.M., "The Marianist Contribution to the American Experiment," privately circulated, Document 31, *MRC Bulletin*, Vol. 7, No. 1 (February 1976): 1–15, copy, NACMS.

5. Quoted by Baumeister, *Secondary Education,* 141.

6. Quoted by Paula S. Fass, *Outside In: Minorities and the Transformation of American Education* (New York: Oxford University Press, 1989), 198.

7. Ibid., 194.

8. Baumeister, *Secondary Education,* 80–113.

9. Ibid., 112.

10. Ibid., 142.

11. Ibid., 146.

12. Paula M. Kane, *Separatism and Subculture: Boston Catholicism 1900–1920* (Chapel Hill: University of North Carolina Press, 1994), 1–7.

13. Ibid., 90.

14. Harold A. Buetow, *Of Singular Benefit: The History of U.S. Catholic Education* (New York: Macmillan, 1970), 261–62.

15. For fraternal societies, see Christopher J. Kauffman, *Faith and Fraternalism: A History of the Knights of Columbus,* revised edition (New York: Simon & Schuster, 1992).

16. Edgar Patrick McCarren, "The Origins and Early Years of the National Catholic Education Association" (Ph. D. diss., Catholic University of America, 1966), 202.

17. Ibid., 203.

18. Quoted by William Barnaby Faherty, *Dream by the River: Two Centuries of St. Louis Catholicism* (St. Louis: Piraeus Publishers, 1973), 144.

19. Eugene Joseph Sohm, S.M., "The History of the Society of Mary in the St. Louis Area" (M.A. thesis, St. Louis University, 1948), 74.

20. Quoted by Sohm, "History," 75.

21. Ibid., 76–77.

22. Quoted by Sohm, "History," 80.

23. Quoted by Faherty, *Dream,* 149.

24. On Denis O'Connell, see Gerald P. Fogarty, S.J., *The Vatican and the Americanist Crisis: Denis J. O'Connell, American Agent in Rome, 1885–1903* (Rome: Gregorian University Press, 1973) and Colman J. Barry, O.S.B., *The Catholic University of America 1903-1909, The Rectorship of Denis J. O'Connell* (Washington, D.C.: Catholic University of America Press, 1950).

25. Faherty, *Dream,* 140–45; see also Sohm, "History," 81.

26. Faherty, *Dream,* 151.

27. Sohm, "History," 81.

28. Treasurer's Report, Chapter of the St. Louis Province, 1925, Chapter Files, ASM (St.L).

29. Quoted by Sister Agnes Claire School, O.S.B., "The Social Thought of John Lancaster Spalding" (Ph.D. diss., Catholic University of America, 1944), xix.

30. Robert N. Barger, *John Lancaster Spalding, Catholic Educator and Social Emissary* (New York: Garland, 1988), 221.

31. Quoted by Barger, *John Lancaster Spalding,* 223.

32. Ibid.

33. This anecdote originated with Brother Gerald Mueller cited in an August interview with Mary E. Henthorne ("The Career of Rt. Rev. John Lancaster Spalding" [Ph.D. diss., University of Illinois, 1930]), in Barger, *John Lancaster Spalding,* 240.

34. Prospectus of Spalding Institute, Peoria File, ASM (CIN).

35. Barger, *John Lancaster Spalding,* 224.

36. Ibid., 246.

37. Edmund M. Dunne to George Meyer, November 4, 1910, Peoria File, ASM (St.L).

38. Joseph Weckesser to John Waldron, November 12, 1911, ASM (St.L).

39. Brother Albert Hollinger to Joseph Weckesser, November 19, 1911.

40. T. J. Jordan (vicar general) to Joseph Ei, S.M., telegram June 27, 1937, ASM (St.L).

41. Hollinger to Ei, July 23, 1933, ASM (St.L).

42. Ei to Schlarman, September 29, 1933, ASM (St.L).

43. David Salvatore, "Deep Are the Roots," in *Seed Harvest: A History of the Archdiocese of Dubuque*, ed. Sister Mary Kevin Gallagher, B.V.M. (Dubuque: Archdiocese of Dubuque, 1987), 57.

44. Msgr. J. J. Wolfe to Rev. L. A. Tragesser, April 10, 1926, Dubuque Papers, ASM (St.L).

45. Brother Paul A. Roesner to Very Reverend Joseph Ei, May 27, 1928, Dubuque Papers, ASM (St.L).

46. Ibid., June 18, 1928.

47. Michael Schleich to Gerald Mueller, February 25, 1929, Dubuque Papers, ASM (St.L.).

48. For an overview of enrollments, see "New Orleans," *The Catholic Directory* (New York: Benziger Brothers, 1926).

49. Brother Francis Wohlleben to Louis A. Tragesser, June 29, 1926, New Orleans Papers, ASM (St.L).

50. Wohlleben to Tragesser, June 20, 1926 and July 5, 1926, New Orleans Papers, ASM (St.L).

51. Archbishop Shaw to Wohlleben, July 6, 1926, ASM (St.L).

52. Quoted by Gerald J. Schnepp, S.M., *Province of St. Louis, 1908–1983: The First Seventy-Five Years* (St. Louis: Society of Mary, Province of St. Louis, 1985), 42.

53. Charles Shanabruck, *Chicago's Catholics: The Evolution of An American Identity* (Notre Dame, Ind.: University of Notre Dame Press, 1981), 15.

54. St. Michael's, Chicago, Illinois, Annals, 1877–1884, p. 32, Archives of the Redemptorists of the St. Louis Province, Glenview, Ill. (hereafter cited as AR [St.L]).

55. Copy of the annals is included in *Marianists in Chicago 1874–1974*, Chicago Files, St. Michael's School, ASM (St.L).

56. Ibid.

57. Shanabruck, *Chicago's Catholics*, 17.

58. Quoted by James W. Sanders, *The Education of An Urban Minority, Catholics in Chicago, 1833–1965* (New York: Oxford University Press, 1977), 65.

59. Edward R. Kantowicz, "The Beginning and End of An Era: George William Mundelein and John Patrick Cody in Chicago," in *Patterns of Episcopal Leadership*, ed. Gerald P. Fogarty (New York: Macmillan, 1989), 205.

60. Edward R. Kantowicz, *Corporation Sole: Cardinal Mundelein and Chicago Catholicism* (Notre Dame, Ind.: University of Notre Dame Press, 1983).

61. Ibid., 13–15.

62. "Souvenir Program, St. Michael's Central High School Dedication, May 30, 1929," Chicago, St. Michael's Files, ASM (St.L).

63. Rev. John P. Miller to Very Rev. E. K. Cantwell, April 13, 1928, and May 11,

1929, Houses in the Province, House Correspondence, St. Michael's, Volume 1, 1880–1925, AR (St.L).

64. Miller to Cantwell, May 26, 1930, AR (St.L).

65. Cantwell to Miller, May 27, 1930, AR (St.L).

66. Henry Oenning to Thomas M. Palmer, Chicago I, St. Michael's, Chicago Letters, 1936-56, No. 1, 1937, AR (St.L).

67. For the general effects of the Great Depression on Catholic education, see Sanders, *Education,* 183–86.

68. Quoted by Sanders, *Education,* 187.

69. Miller to Cantwell, January 12, 1932, AR (ST.L).

70. See "Chicago," *The Catholic Directory* (New York: P. J. Kenedy & Sons, 1929), 48; (1930) 51; (1935) 53.

71. Oenning to Palmer, July 4, 1941, AR (St.L).

72. Martin Loveny to Edward Fastner, September 15, 1943, AR (St.L).

73. Schnepp, *Province of St. Louis,* 134.

74. "Chicago," *The Catholic Directory* (New York: P. J. Kenedy & Sons, 1950), 34.

75. Interview Father Francis Friedel, January 27, 1958, McMahon Tapes, 1M(2), Folder 3, AUD.

76. "Detroit," *The Catholic Directory* (New York: P. J. Kenedy & Sons, 1950), 64.

77. Interview Father Francis Friedel, January 27, 1958, McMahon Tapes, 1M(2), Folder 3, AUD.

78. Provincial Chapter, Province of Cincinnati, 1937, January, 1933, AGMAR 080.3.8.

79. Sylvester Juergens, Report of the Provincial, Province of St. Louis Chapter, November 1937, p. 3, Provincial Chapter Files, ASM (St.L).

80. Ibid., November, 1940, p. 4.

81. For an excellent description and analysis of Bishop Gallagher's administration and the significance of Coughlin, see Leslie Woodcock Tentler, *Seasons of Grace: A History of the Archdiocese of Detroit* (Detroit: Wayne State University Press, 1990), 297-351.

82. "Holy Redeemer High School for Boys Diocesan School Report, 1940," School Reports for years 1940–44, Archives of the Archdiocese of Detroit (hereafter AAD).

83. Leon Swaskiewicz to Brother L. J. Meinhardt, January 29, 1940.

84. School Report, 1940.

85. Sylvester Juergens, Visitation Report, March 15, 1943, Detroit Files, Holy Redeemer High School, ASM (St.L).

86. E. S. Wolaver to Brother Vincent Brand, December 8, 1943, School Reports, 1940–1944, AAD.

87. Edward Malloy to Sylvester Juergens, February 18, 1944, Detroit Files, Holy Redeemer High School, ASM (St.L).

88. Sylvester Juergens, Memorandum of a discussion with Edward Malloy, Redemptorist Rector, Holy Redeemer Parish, March 9, 1944, Detroit Files, ASM (St.L).

89. Eugene Paulin to Michael Schleich, April 6, 1944, AGMAR 094.2.39.

90. Edward Malloy to Carroll F. Deedy, AAD.

91. Ibid.

92. Vincent Gray to Sylvester Juergens, Vincent Gray File, ASM (St.L).

93. Sylvester Juergens, Report of the Provincial, November 23, 1940, Province Chapter Files, ASM (St.L).

94. Ibid.

95. Schnepp, *Province of St. Louis*, 69–90. Also see the correspondence between Joseph Duventester and Sylvester Juergens, 1929–1940, ASM (St.L).

96. Provincial Inspector's Report, Provincial Chapter, Cincinnati Province, August 9, 1941, AGMAR 080.4.2.

97. Provincial's Report, Provincial Chapter, Cincinnati Province, August 7, 1947, AGMAR 080.4.2.

98. "History of Cathedral Latin," Record of Consulters, Volume 2 (old Volume 3), April 13, 1922, p. 78, ADC.

99. Bernard O'Reilly to Bishop Joseph Schrembs, March 30, 1923, ADC.

100. See Sorret's 1924 correspondence during his visitation and other letters, ASM (CIN).

101. Joseph A. Tetzlaff to Bishop Joseph Schrembs, August 24, 1924, ADC.

102. Tetzlaff to Monsignor Joseph Smith, Vicar General, August 27, 1925, ADC.

103. Tetzlaff to Smith, May 13, 1924, ADC. For Schrembs's role in NCWC, see Elizabeth McKeown, "The National Bishops' Conference: An Analysis of its Origins," *Catholic Historical Review* 65 (1980): 565–83.

104. Tetzlaff to Rt. Rev. Monsignor J. McFadden, May 12, 1928, ADC.

105. L. A. Yeske to Schrembs, July 1, 1931, ADC.

106. Schrembs to Yeske, July 7, 1931, ADC.

107. Yeske to Schrembs, ca. August 1937, ADC.

108. John A. Elbert, Provincial, to Monsignor John L. Krol, March 28, 1953, Agreement September 8, 1953, ADC.

109. Provincial Chapter, Province of Cincinnati, June 1928, AGMAR 080.2.9.

110. Joseph Tetzlaff, Circular, January 1, 1931, AGMAR 081.2.2.

111. Ibid., January 14, 1931, AGMAR 081.2.2.

112. Provincial Chapter, Province of Cincinnati, July 30, 1937, AGMAR 080.3.3.

113. Ibid., July 31, 1937, AGMAR 080.3.8.

114. Sylvester Juergens to Very Reverend Francis J. Jung, April 1, 1945, AGMAR 094.2.80.

115. Philip Gleason, *Speaking of Diversity* (Baltimore: Johns Hopkins University Press, 1992), 285.

116. John W. Shaw to Rev. Pastors of New Orleans, November 9, 1925, Administrative Reports and Correspondence Prior to 1935, Subject, Catholic Schools, AANO.

117. On the Oregon school case, see Kauffman, *Faith and Fraternalism*, 297–301.

118. Gleason, *Speaking of Diversity*, 285.

119. On Catholic responses during the Great Depression, see James Fisher, *The*

Catholic Counterculture (Chapel Hill: University of North Carolina Press, 1994); George O. Flynn, *American Catholics and the Roosevelt Presidency* (Lexington: University of Kentucky Press, 1968); David J. O'Brien, *American Catholics and Social Reform: The New Deal Years* (New York: Oxford University Press, 1968); idem, *Public Catholicism* (New York: Macmillan, 1989). Also see two issues of the *U.S. Catholic Historian* on "Labor and Lay Movements," 9 (Summer and Fall 1990).

120. Ernest Joseph Sorret, "Instruction on the Proceedings of the General Chapter of 1933 and Promulgation of Said Chapter," Circular No. 3, January 29, 1934, p. 37, Circulars of Sorret, NACMS.

121. Ibid., 178–83.

122. William Ferree, "Principles Governing the Roles of Sodality in Our Secondary Schools," *Apostle of Mary* 19 (Sept.–Oct. 1938): 150–51.

123. Ibid. (November, 1938): 190.

124. Ibid., 30 (January 1939): 15. This article, by P. Broutin, S.J., was in the April 1938 issue of *Nouvelle Revue Théologique,* referred to by Ferree on pp. 4–8 of this article in January 1939. An English translation of Broutin's article was published by the *Apostle of Mary Documentary Series* in March 1949.

125. William Ferree, "First Aim of Sodality: Personal Sanctification," *Apostle of Mary* 30 (April 1939): 101.

126. Ibid., 29 (September–October): 157.

127. Ibid., 158.

128. Ibid., 30 (April 1939): 102–3.

129. Joseph P. Chinnici, O.F.M, "Culture and Prayer: Towards a History of Contemplation in the Catholic Community in the United States," *U.S. Catholic Historian* 15 (Fall 1996): 1–16.

130. Curriculum Vitae of William Ferree, S.M., NACMS.

131. Province of Cincinnati, September 4, 1944, Provincial Chapter, AGMAR 080.4.5.

132. Province of Cincinnati, June 29, 1945, Provincial Chapter, AGMAR 080.4.6.

133. Province of St. Louis, Provincial Chapter, Provincial Chapter Files, ASM (St.L).

134. Sylvester Juergens to Francis Jung, March 29, 1946, AGMAR 094.2.80.

135. Eugene Paulin, S.M., and Joseph Becker, S.M., *New Wars: The History of the Brothers of Mary (Marianists) in Hawaii, 1883–1958* (Milwaukee: Bruce, Catholic Life Productions, 1959), 111–22.

• *Chapter Seven* •

1. For works on these dioceses, see Timothy Dolan, *Some Fell On Good Ground: Edwin Vincent O'Hara* (Washington, D.C.: Catholic University of America Press, 1982); William Barnaby Faherty, S.J., *Dream by the River: Two Centuries of St. Louis Catholicism* (St. Louis: Piraeus Publishers, 1973). For the story of black migration, see John T. McCreevy, *Parish Boundaries: The Catholic Encounter With Race in Twentieth Century Urban North* (Chicago: University of Chicago Press, 1996).

2. Steven Avella, *This Confident Church* (Notre Dame, Ind.: University of Notre Dame Press, 1992).

3. Louis Faerber, S.M., "Provisions for Low Ability Pupils in Catholic High Schools" (Ph. D. diss., Catholic University of America, 1948), xxiii–xxv. Cited by Paula Fass, *Outsiders In: Minorities and the Transformation of American Education* (New York: Oxford University Press, 1989), 206.

4. Will Herberg, "Religion and Culture in Present Day Culture," in *Roman Catholicism and the American Way of Life*, ed. Thomas T. McAvoy (Notre Dame, Ind.: University of Notre Dame Press, 1960), 4.

5. Will Herberg, *Protestant, Catholic and Jew: An Essay in Religious Sociology* (Garden City, N.Y.: Anchor Books, 1960).

6. Herberg, "Religion and Culture."

7. John Tracy Ellis, *American Catholics and the Intellectual Life* (Chicago: Heritage Foundation, 1956).

8. Sylvester J. Juergens, S.M., Circular No. 2, October 2, 1946, pp. 1–3, 15–16, Circular Letters of Juergens, NACMS.

9. Ibid., 16.

10. Ibid., 29.

11. Provincial Inspector's Report, Provincial Chapter, Cincinnati Province, August 9, 1941, AGMAR 080.4.2.

12. Juergens, Circular No. 2, October 2, 1946, 35, NACMS.

13. Henri Lebon, S.M., *Our First Century, 1817–1917*, trans. John Dockter, S.M., (Dayton, Oh.: Marianist Resources Commission, 1975), 226.

14. Joseph M. White, *The Diocesan Seminary in the United States* (Notre Dame, Ind.: University of Notre Dame Press, 1989), 401.

15. Juergens, Circular No. 2, 37-41, NACMS.

16. Ibid., 41-42.

17. Ibid., 53.

18. Ibid., 30.

19. Ibid., 31–34.

20. Ibid., 58–59.

21. Louis Gadiou, S.M., and Jean Claude Délas, S.M., *Marianists in a Continuing Mission*, trans. Robert Sargent, S.M. (Dayton, Oh.: Marianist Resources Commission, 1973), 96.

22. Ibid., 97–98; Juergens, Circular No. 6, 113, 122, NACMS.

23. Angelyn Dries, O.S.F, *The American Mission Experience* (Maryknoll, N.Y.: Orbis Books, 1998).

24. Sylvester J. Juergens, S.M., Circular No. 6, January 6, 1948, 115, NACMS.

25. Ibid., 129–31.

26. Ibid., 131–32.

27. Dries, *American Mission*, 137.

28. Joseph McCoy, S.M., *Advice From the Field* (Baltimore: Helicon, 1962).

29. Juergens, Circular No. 23, 1953, 362–63, NACMS.

30. Jaime R. Vidal, "The American Church and the Puerto Rican People," *U.S. Catholic Historian* 9 (Winter/Spring 1990): 124.

31. Juergens, Circular No. 23, 1953, 367, NACMS.

32. Lebon, *Our First Century*, 226.

33. Dries, *American Mission*, 67–92.

34. Ibid., 93.

35. Ibid., 95.

36. Joseph Jansen, S.M., "A History of the Society of Mary in Puerto Rico," Colegio San José, Río Piedras, PR, appendix, SMA (N.Y.).

37. Ibid., 2.

38. Ibid., Appendix No. 2.

39. Vidal, "The American Church and the Puerto Rican People."

40. *The Spiritual Care of Puerto Rican Migrants: Report on the First Conference Held in San Juan, Puerto Rico, April 11th to 16th, 1955*, ed. William Ferree, Ivan Illich, Joseph P. Fitzgerald (Cuernavaca, Mexico: Centro Intercultural de Documentation [1955]).

41. Gerald J. Schnepp, S.M., *Province of St. Louis , 1908–1983: The First Seventy-Five Years* (St. Louis: Marianist Press, 1984), 264.

42. Margaret M. Reher, "Mission of America: John J. Burke in Peru," *U.S. Catholic Historian* 15 (Fall 1997): 90.

43. Ibid., 91.

44. For Bishop Mooney's background, see Gerald P. Fogarty, S.J., *The Vatican and the American Hierarchy* (Wilmington, Del.: Michael Glazier, 1982), 242; and Leslie Woodcock Tentler, *Seasons of Grace: A History of the Archdiocese of Detroit* (Detroit: Wayne State University Press, 1990), 329–31.

45. Schnepp, *Province of St. Louis*, 265.

46. Juergens, Circular No. 9, 157, NACMS.

47. Schnepp, *Province of St. Louis*, 265.

48. Juergens, Circular No. 9, 160, NACMS.

49. Schnepp, *Province of St. Louis*, 266–67, 272.

50. John Elbert, S.M., Circular No. 61, October 2, 1957, NACMS.

51. Dries, *American Mission*, 163–64.

52. Quoted by Dries, *American Mission*, 163.

53. For a summary of the African missions, see James M. Darby, S.M., Provincial Report, Provincial Circular No. 48, "Our African Apostolate," 329–30, NACMS.

54. Brother George Dury, interview with the author, 1996.

55. Sylvester J. Juergens, S.M., Circular No. 7, May 16, 1948, 135, NACMS.

56. "Brother Wipfield Remembers," The Birth of the Pacific Province, 1, ASM (PAC).

57. Ibid., 2.

58. Charles Boglitz, S.M., *The Expanding World of Chaminade: A History of the Province of the Pacific* (Gardena, California, 1981, privately circulated, 1923), ASM (PAC).

59. Report of Provincial, Chapter of the Pacific Province, ASM (PAC), C183, 1973. Also see Boglitz, *Expanding World*, 16–19.

60. Report of the Provincial, Chapter of the Pacific Province, 1973, p. 4, C1, 8C, 1949, ASM (PAC).

61. Ibid., 4.

62. Ibid.

63. Ibid.

64. Brother Lawrence Scrivani, "Some Trends in the Bay Area Catholic School Movement," 22, copy, AASF.

65. Ibid., 16.

66. Ibid., 17.

67. Ibid., 19–20.

68. Ibid., 23.

69. "San Francisco," *The Catholic Directory* (New York: P. J. Kenedy & Sons, 1955), 242.

70. "San Francisco," *The Catholic Directory* (New York: P. J. Kenedy & Sons, 1963), 266.

71. Boglitz, *Expanding World*, 45.

72. Scrivani, " Some Trends," 24.

73. Wipfield, "Memories," 20–21, ASM (PAC).

74. Ibid., 22. For a detailed description of McIntyre's education policy, see Msgr. Francis J. Weber, *His Eminence of Los Angeles James Francis Cardinal McIntyre* (Mission Hills, Calif.: St. Francis Historical Society, 1997) 2:245–89.

75. Ibid., 22.

76. "San Francisco," *The Catholic Directory* (New York: P. J. Kenedy & Sons, 1956), 110.

77. Brother James Wipfield, Report of the Inspector 1955, p. 9, 13D, Folder 1.6, ASM (PAC).

78. Ibid., 10.

79. Ibid.

80. Ibid., 1949, p. 1, 13D, Folder 1. 6, ASM (PAC).

81. Ibid., 2.

82. Eugene McCarraher, "American Gothic, Sacramental Radicals and the New Medieval Social Gospel, 1928–1948," *Records of the American Catholic Historical Society of Philadelphia* 105 (Spring-Summer, 1995): 9.

83. Wipfield to Juergens, August 14, 1953, 2D, Folder 5.4, ASM (PAC).

84. Brother James Wipfield, Inspector's Report, 13D, Folder 6.1, ASM (PAC).

85. Joseph McShane, S.J., "The Church Is Not For the Cells and the Cave: The Working-Class Spirituality of the Jesuit Labor Priests," *U.S. Catholic Historian* 9 (Summer 1990): 289–304.

86. Wipfield to Juergens, February 2, 1953, 2D, Folder 5.4, ASM (PAC).

87. Wipfield to Juergens, December 1, 1953, 2D, Folder 5.4, ASM (PAC).

88. Ibid., August 15, 1955.

89. Boglitz, *Expanding World*, 86.

90. Ibid., 92–97.

91. Leonard Fee, Provincial's Report, Provincial Chapter, August 19, 1957, C1, 8C, ASM (PAC).

92. Ibid.

93. Ibid.

94. Ibid.

95. James Wipfield, "Observations of a Retiring Inspector," Provincial Chapter, August 20, 1957, 1, C1, 8C, ASM (PAC).

96. Ibid.

97. Ibid.

98. Rev. Paul Kelley, Report of the Head of Zeal, Provincial Chapter, 1957, C1, 8C, ASM (PAC).

99. "After Nine Years," Provincial Chapter, 1957, C1, 8C, ASM (PAC).

100. "Statement of Purpose," *The Working Brother* 2 (January 1947): 3.

101. Brother Aloysius Hochendoner, "Hints of Holiness and Happiness as a Marianist Working Brother," *The Working Brother* 2 (April 1947): 11.

102. Ibid., 12.

103. Ernest Avellar, "The Young Christian Worker," *The Marianist Working Brother* 3 (January 1948): 11.

104. Avella, *This Confident Church*, 151–67.

105. Avellar, "Young Christian Worker."

106. Schnepp, *Province of St. Louis*, 91. Also see Philip Melcher, S.M., "The History of the Working Brothers in the United States" (an unpublished manuscript located in NACMS).

107. Brother John McCluskey and Brother Charles Weiss to Very Rev. Francis J. Jung, Monday of Holy Week 1945, AGMAR 0151.18.

108. Ibid.

109. Cyprian Davis, O.S.B., *The History of Black Catholics in the United States* (New York: Crossroad, 1991), 225. Also see Marilyn W. Nickels, *Black Catholic Protest and the Federated Colored Catholics 1917–1933: Three Perspectives on Racial Justice* (New York: Garland, 1988).

110. Ibid., 226. Also see Cecilia Moore, "'To Be of Some Good to Ourselves and Everybody Else': The Mission of the Cardinal Gibbons Institute 1922–1934," *U.S. Catholic Historian* 16 (Summer 1998): 45–66.

111. Quoted by David W. Southern, "But Think of the Kids: Catholic Interracialists and the Great American Taboo of Race Mixing," *U.S. Catholic Historian* 18 (Summer 1998): 67–93. Also see David W. Southern, *John LaFarge and the Limits of Catholic Interracialism 1911–1963* (Baton Rouge: Louisiana State University Press, 1996).

112. Ibid.

113. McCreevy, *Parish Boundaries*, 63–67.

114. Southern, "But Think of the Kids."

115. Ibid.

116. Faherty, *Dream*, 155.

117. Southern, "But Think of the Kids."

118. Quoted by Faherty, *Dream*, 186.

119. Ibid., 187.

120. Provincial's Report, Provincial Chapter 1939, Provincial Chapter Files, ASM (St.L).

121. Schnepp, *Province of St. Louis*, 131.

122. Adolf Windisch, S.M., interview with the author, August 1995.

123. C. Vincent Gray to Peter Resch, May 1, 1949, Gray Files, ASM (St.L).

124. Ibid.

125. Schnepp, *Province of St. Louis*, 146.

126. Daniel Sharpe to J. Glennon McCarty, October 13, 1957, Don Bosco Files, ASM (St.L).

127. Ibid., January 2, 1958.

128. Avella, *This Confident Church*, 13.

129. This evaluation of Archbishop Ritter's school policies is derived from my own experience as a teacher at Mercy High School, a diocesan school in St. Louis, Missouri, from 1958 to 1966.

130. Sylvester Juergens, Report of the Provincial, Provincial Chapter 1945, Provincial Chapter Files, ASM (St.L).

131. Ibid.

132. Peter Resch, Report of the Provincial, Provincial Chapter 1957, ASM (St.L).

133. Philip Gleason, *Contending With Modernity: Catholic Higher Education in the Twentieth Century* (New York: Oxford University Press, 1996).

134. Walter J. Buehler, S.M., Address to the Serra Club of Dallas, St. Mary's University Files, ASM (St.L).

135. Ibid.

136. Gleason, *Contending with Modernity*, 151. Also see Arnold Sparr, *To Promote, Defend and Redeem: The Catholic Literary Revival and the Cultural Transformation of American Catholicism 1920–1960* (Westport, Conn.: Greenwood Press, 1990); and Calvert Alexander, S.J., *The Catholic Literary Revival: Three Phases In Its Development* (Milwaukee: Bruce, 1935).

137. Schnepp, *Province of St. Louis*, 214–17.

138. Historical material found in a newspaper clipping from the *Catholic Globe*, the official publication of the Diocese of Sioux City, 1961 T73-Sioux, ASM (CIN).

139. Edmund Heelan to the Clergy and Laity of the Diocese of Sioux City, April 22, 1930, ASM (CIN).

140. Typed copy of "Bachelor of Science in Rural Leadership," ASM (CIN).

141. "Sioux City," *The Catholic Directory* (New York: P. J. Kenedy & Sons, 1938), 556.

142. Ibid. (1947), 728.

143. Province of Cincinnati, 1947, Provincial Chapter, AGMAR 080.417.

144. In 1957 the Salvatorian Fathers opened a minor seminary (i.e., a four-year high school and two-year college) for their own postulants and for those of the diocese. Newspaper clipping ASM (CIN).

145. Brother Elmer Lackner, oral history interview with Margaret Becker, June 14, 1977. Transcription, 1H Box 2, Folder 27, AUD.

146. Provincial Chapter of the Cincinnati Province, 1948, copy in AGMAR 080.

147. "Six Years In the Process of Achieving: A Report of the President of the University of Dayton, Very Reverend Andrew L. Seebold, S.M., 1953 to 1959," p. 3, presidents papers, 1DC (16), AUD.

148. Ibid., 5–10.

149. Ibid., 20.

150. Ibid.

151. Reverend John Dickson, S.M., oral history interview with Margaret Becker, 1H Box 1, Folder 12, AUD.

152. Ibid.

153. Quoted by Joseph Komonchak, "Modernity and the Construction of Roman Catholicism," a paper presented to the Working Group on Roman Catholic Modernism at the annual meeting of the American Academy of Religion, Kansas City, Missouri, November 11, 1981, p. 11, in *Modernism as a Social Construct*, ed. George Gilmore, Hans Rollman, and Gary Lease. For a copy write to George Gilmore, Spring Hill College, Mobile, AL 36608.

◆ *Chapter Eight* ◆

1. John Cogley, ed., *Religion in America* (New York: Harper & Row, 1957).

2. For works on Virgil Michel and the Liturgical Movement, see R. W. Franklin and Robert L. Spaeth, *Virgil Michel: American Catholic* (Collegeville, Minn.: Liturgical Press, 1988); Paul V. Marx, *Virgil Michel and the Liturgical Movement* (Collegeville, Minn.: Liturgical Press, 1957). On the fiftieth anniversary of Michel's death, *Worship* did a special issue on his historical significance (*Worship* 62 [May 1988]).

3. Debra Campbell, "The Struggle to Serve: From the Lay Apostolate to the Ministry Explosion," in *Transforming Ministry*, ed. Jay P. Dolan (New York: Crossroad, 1989), 203–80.

4. For a comprehensive sociological study of religious life, see Patricia Wittberg, *The Rise and Fall of Catholic Religious Orders: A Social Movement Perspective* (Albany: State University of New York Press, 1994).

5. James M. Darby, S.M., Circular No. 1, September 5, 1958, Darby Circulars, NACMS.

6. Wittberg, *Rise and Fall*, 210–12.

7. Richard Gilman, "Father Chaminade," *Jubilee* 6 (September 1958): 38–43.

8. Richard Gilman, *Faith, Sex and Mystery* (New York: Penguin Books, 1988), 13–98.

9. Gilman, "Father Chaminade," 39.

10. Ibid., 40.

11. Ibid., 42.

12. Ibid., 43.

13. Gilman, *Faith, Sex and Mystery*, identification of the author in the front matter.

14. James H. Darby, Circular No. 5, January 22, 1959, Darby Circulars, NACMS, 29.

15. James M. Darby, Circular No. 12, December 11, 1955, Darby Circulars, NACMS, 75.

16. Ibid., 77.

17. James M. Darby, Circular No. 21, December 8, 1960, 130, Darby Circulars, NACMS.

18. Several interviews with brothers of the New York Province.

19. Brother John T. Darby, S.M., Schools in the New York Province, "Report to the Provincial Chapter, 1962," ASM (NY).

20. Ibid.

21. Ibid.

22. Ibid.

23. Ibid.

24. Ibid.

25. Ibid.

26. Ibid.

27. John T. Darby, in John G. Dickson, S.M., Circular No. 1, November 27, 1961, ASM (NY Prov), 7–9.

28. John G. Dickson, Circular No. 26, June 13, 1965, ASM (NY), 289.

29. See chap. 7, n. 151.

30. John G. Dickson, Circular No. 12, October 12, 1963, ASM (NY), 127–32.

31. Ibid., 132.

32. Quoted by Patricia Byrne, C.S.J., "In the Parish But Not Of It," in *Transforming Parish Ministry*, 158.

33. Byrne, "In the Parish," 158.

34. Quoted by Dickson, Circular No. 12, ASM (NY).

35. Quoted by Dickson, Circular No. 4, May 15, 1962, 6–7, ASM (NY).

36. C. W. Albright, "Pax Romana," *New Catholic Encyclopedia* (New York: McGraw-Hill, 1967), 11:35.

37. M. Treacy, "National Federation of Catholic College Students," *New Catholic Encyclopedia* (New York: McGraw-Hill, 1967), 10:236.

38. Dickson, Circular No. 4, 7–11, ASM (NY).

39. James M. Darby, Circular No. 25, April 23, 1962, 246–47, ASM (NY).

40. Angelyn Dries, O.S.F., *The Missionary Movements in American Catholic History* (Maryknoll, N.Y.: Orbis Books, 1998), 179–200.

41. Darby, Circular No. 35, 247, ASM (NY).

42. Ibid., 198.

43. James L. Heft, S.M., "From the Pope to the Bishops: Episcopal Authority from Vatican I to Vatican II"; and William L. Portier, "Church Unity and National Traditions: The Challenge to the Modern Papacy" and "The Papacy: The Power, Authority and Leadership," in *The Papacy and the Church in the United States*, ed. Bernard Cooke (New York: Paulist Press, 1989).

44. Patricia Byrne, "American Ultramontanism," *Theological Studies* 56 (June 1995): 307–26.

45. Jay P. Dolan, *The American Catholic Experience* (Garden City, N.Y.: Doubleday, 1985), 424.

46. Patrick Carey, *The Roman Catholics in America* (Westport, Conn.: Praeger, 1996), 43.

47. David O'Brien, *Public Catholicism* (New York: Macmillan, 1989).

48. Quoted by Byrne, "In the Parish," 158.

49. Paul J. Philibert, O.P., "Editor's Introduction," in *Living in the Meantime: Concerning the Transformation of the Religious Life*, ed. Paul J. Philibert, O.P. (New York: Paulist Press, 1994), 3.

50. Ibid., 4.

51. Quoted by Gerald J. Schnepp, S.M., *Province of St. Louis, 1908–1983: The First Seventy-Five Years* (St. Louis: Marianist Press, 1985), 138.

52. Brother Charles Boglitz, S.M., *The Expanding World of Chaminade: A History of the Province of the Pacific* (Gardena, California, 1981, privately circulated), 159–73, ASM (PAC); Schnepp, *Province of St. Louis*, 137–56.

53. John T. Dickson, Circular No. 33, September 5, 1966, 362–63, ASM (NY).

54. Rembert G. Weakland, "Religious Life in the U. S.: Understanding the Moment," in *Living in the Meantime*, ed. Philibert, 202.

55. Dickson, Circular No. 33, 363–64, ASM (NY).

56. James Darby, Circular No. 63, January 22, 1966, 423–24, ASM (NY).

57. Ibid., 424.

58. Ibid., 425.

59. Raymond G. Roesch, "Chronology of the Bonnette Case," presidents' papers, 1DC (17), AUD.

60. Dennis Bonnette to Archbishop Karl Alter, October 15, 1966, copy, presidents' papers, 1DC (17), AUD.

61. Bernard Lee, S.M., "The Spring Wants to Come: A Study in Community," *Review for Religious* 22 (Fall 1968): 596–603.

62. Bonnette to Alter, October 15, 1966. For a discussion of the crisis see Philip Gleason, *Contending with Modernity: Catholic Higher Education in the Twentieth Century* (New York: Oxford University Press, 1995), 310–12. Also see David O'Brien, *From the Heart of the American Church: Catholic Higher Education and American Culture* (Maryknoll, N.Y.: Orbis Books, 1994), 53–54.

63. Roesch, "Chronology," AUD.

64. Ibid.

65. Gleason, *Contending with Modernity*, 310.

66. Clipping of this article included in a letter from Randolf F. Lumpp to Rev. Raymond Roesch, S.M., November 21, 1966, presidents' papers, 1DC (17), AUD.

67. Ibid.

68. Ibid.

69. Quoted by John Cogley, "Ottaviani Lists Doctrine Abuses," *New York Times*, September 20, 1966, p. 20. Copy in presidents' papers, 1DC (17), AUD.

70. Raymond Roesch, *Statement Relative to the Controversy Touching Academic Freedom and the Church's Magisterium*, pamphlet, 10, president's papers, 1DC (17), AUD.

71. Gleason, *Contending with Modernity*, 311–12.

72. James M. Darby, S.M., "Reflections on the Dayton Incident," *America* (April 29, 1967): 650–52. For a further elaboration of this conflict at the University of Dayton, see Erving E. Beauregard, "An Archbishop, a University, and Academic Freedom," *Records of the American Historical Society of Philadelphia* 93 (March–December, 1982): 25–39. In 1967 Dennis Bonnette joined the philosophy department at Niagara University.

73. Cyprian Davis, O.S.B., *The History of Black Catholics in the United States* (New York: Crossroad, 1990), 255.

74. Ibid., 256.

75. Ibid., 257.

76. Ibid., 258.

77. Ibid., 258–59.

78. Newspaper clipping, Brother Joseph Davis File, ASM (CIN).

79. Newspaper clipping, Joseph Davis File, *Catholic Telegraph*, November 21, 1968, 11, ASM (CIN).

80. Newspaper clipping, Joseph Davis File, ASM (CIN).

81. Ibid.

82. Joseph Davis to William Behringer, February 6, 1976, Joseph Davis File, ASM (CIN).

83. Ibid., Davis to Behringer, March 18, 1976, ASM (CIN). For a detailed summary of his experiences with the NOBC, see Joseph M. Davis, S.M., and Cyprian Lamar Rowe, F.M.S., "The Development of the National Office of Black Catholics," *U.S. Catholic Historian* 7 (Spring-Summer, 1988): part 1, 1970–1978, pp. 265–75. This article was divided into two parts. Davis covers the period 1970–1978 and Cyprian Rowe, 1978–1987.

84. Ibid., Rowe, 277.

85. Joseph Davis File, ASM (CIN).

86. Albert Glanton, reflection paper, September 21, 1968, Albert Glanton File, ASM (St.L).

87. Ibid.

88. Ibid.

89. James F. Gray to Albert Glanton, October 4, 1968, Albert Glanton File, ASM (St.L).

90. Glanton to Gray, July 9, 1970, Albert Glanton File, ASM (St.L).

91. Gray to Glanton, July 30, 1970, Albert Glanton File, ASM (St.L).

92. Rev. George Montague, Visitation Report, September 21, 1970, Albert Glanton File, ASM (St.L).

93. Schnepp, *Province of St. Louis*, 130.

94. "Address to the Latin Community," May, 1969, copy, William Ferree File, ASM (NY). Also see same, ASM (CIN).

95. Ibid.

96. Ibid.

97. Ibid.

98. Ibid.

99. Ibid.

100. Ibid.

101. Circular Letter of William Ferree, Ferree Files, 1045C1, 87, Fn. 41, ASM (CIN).

102. Ibid., 89.

103. Ibid., 103–4.

104. I am indebted to Joseph P. Chinnici for his insights on the relationships between anthropology and the spirituality of the religious life gleaned from our conversations over the years. However, I am responsible for these remarks based on my understanding of these complex relationships.

105. John G. Dickson, Circular No. 30, April 1, 1966, 340, ASM (NY).

106. John G. Dickson to William Ferree, February 14, 1966, correspondence files, William Ferree, ASM (NY).

107. Interview with Brother Stephen Glodek, May 1998, ASM (NY).

108. John G. Dickson, Circular No. 30, April 1, 1966, 337–38, ASM (NY).

109. Schnepp, *Province of St. Louis*, 83. Interview with George Montague, January, 1988.

110. Interview with George Cerniglia, May 1998, ASM (NY).

111. Interview with Patrick Tonry, June 1998, ASM (NY).

112. Interview with Philip Eichner, June 1998, ASM (NY).

113. Philip Eichner to John G. Dickson, May 3, 1968, Mineola File, ASM (NY).

114. See Dickson–Eichner and Mulligan–Eichner correspondence 1967–1971, Mineola File, ASM (NY).

115. Eichner to John Mulligan, October 28, 1969, Mineola File, ASM (NY).

116. Ibid.

117. Ibid.

118. Mulligan to Eichner, November 5, 1969, Mineola File, ASM (NY).

119. Position paper on Structured Pluralism, December 1, 1969. Copy in the Mineola File, ASM (NY).

120. Ibid.

121. John Mulligan, Provincial Bulletin No.16, November 29, 1969, ASM (NY).

122. Memo, Philip Eichner to the Provincial Council of the New York Province, December 1, 1969.

123. Interview with John McGrath, December 1997, ASM (NY).

124. Eichner to Mulligan, November 3, 1970, Mineola File, ASM (NY).

125. Mulligan to Paul Hoffer, December 19, 1970, Mineola File, ASM (NY).

126. Ibid.

127. Ibid.

128. See Philip Eichner, "Chaminade-Mineola—A Chronology" 1968–1974. This is a twenty-one page chronicle of events with ninety-two letters cited to document his construction of events.

129. Interview with Father Joseph Stefanelli and the letters of Stephen Tutas in ASM (NY). The selection of the name Meribah has two meanings. In the Hebrew Bible the Meribah was the site of refuge for those discontented with Moses' inability to provide sustenance of bread and water. However, Psalm 95 states: "Do not grow stubborn, as your fathers did in the wilderness, when at Meribah and Massah they challenged me and provoked me although they had seen all my works."

130. Only reluctantly did John Mulligan accept the establishment of the Meribah Province. Interview with John Mulligan, September 1996.

131. Francis Keenan and Philip Eichner, interview with the author, June 1998, ASM (NY).

• *Chapter Nine* •

1. For these statistics on the Marianist membership, see *The Official Catholic Directory* (New York: P. J. Kenedy & Sons, 1966), 931. In the 1991 edition, see pp. 1, 407. Since these statistics are compiled a year before publication I cited the figures for 1965 and 1995.

2. Interview with Stephen Tutas, January 1998.

3. Stephen Tutas, S.M., "Signs of Hope in the Religious Life Today," *Review for Religious* (January–February 1983): 4.

4. Ibid., 5.

5. Lawrence Cada, S.M., Raymond Fitz, S.M., Gertrude Foley, S.C., Thomas Giardino, S.M., Carol Lichtenberg, S.N.D.deN., *Shaping The Coming Age of Religious Life* (New York: Seabury, 1979).

6. Tutas, "Signs of Hope," 5.

7. John McGrath, Provincial Bulletin No. 1, January 29, 1977, ASM (NY).

8. Ibid.

9. John McGrath, Provincial Bulletin No. 5, September 25, 1977, ASM (NY).

10. Interview with Richard Ullrich, June 1998.

11. Personal reflections of Brother Joseph Jansen, quoted in John McGrath, Provincial Bulletin #18, April 13, 1978, ASM (NY).

12. Quentin Hakenewerth, Provincial Circular No. 11, December 15, 1977, Report on the Interim Chapter of November 3–5, ASM (St.L).

13. Ibid.

14. Ibid.

15. Quoted by John McGrath, Provincial Bulletin No. 72, August 3, 1981, ASM (NY).

16. David Fleming, Circular No. 22, April 12, 1987, "Choose Life: Marianist Stability Today," ASM (St.L).

17. Ibid.

18. Ibid.

19. Schnepp, *Province of St. Louis*, 269–71.

20. James Fitz, Provincial Letter, March 1992, ASM (CIN).

21. Ibid.

22. Quoted in *Things Marianist*, October 1992, NACMS.

23. Bertrand Buby, S.M., "The Biblical Prayers of Mary," *Review for Religious* (July–August 1989): 576–80.

24. Bertrand Buby, SM, Circular No. 26, September 12, 1984, ASM (CIN).

25. Vincent Vasey, *Marianist Heritage Series* (ca. 1980) AUD.

26. Joseph Stefanelli, S.M., *Adèle* (Dayton, Oh.: Marianist Resources Commission, 1987); and *Mlle de Lamourous* (Dayton, Oh.: NACMS, 1998).

27. Bernard Lee, S.M., "A Socio-Historical Theology of Charism," *Review For Religious* (January–February 1989).

28. "Who Makes Up the Marianist Family?" *Things Marianist*, 1989, NACMS.

29. Ibid.

30. Joseph P. Chinnici, *Living Stones: The History of Catholic Spiritual Life in the United States* (Maryknoll, N.Y.: Orbis Books, 1996). See the preface to this second edition.

31. Interview with Brother William Bolts, January 1998.

32. Report on the history of the North American Center for Marianist Studies, October 1992, NACMS.

33. *Things Marianist*, October 1992, NACMS.

Index

Abel, William A., 276, 285–86, 304
Africa. *See* Cincinnati Province
African Americans
    black power movement and, 238
    early ministry to, 73
    racial justice and, 225–30
    Marianists and, 194, 223–25, 259
Ahern, Patrick H., 334n. 66
Ahlstrom, Sydney E., 329n. 65
Albert, George, 93
Albright, C. W., 350n. 36
Alemany, Joseph S., 93
Alexander, Calvert, 232, 348n. 136
Alphonsus Liguori, St., 35, 96
Alter, Karl, 253–57, 351nn. 60, 62
Americanism, 132
    in postwar era, 198
Americanization, 3, 74, 189–90, 197–98
    of Marianists, 135–62
    secularism and, 199
    World War II and, 195, 198, 248
American Protective Association (A.P.A.), 104, 107
American Province, 71, 87
    inspectors and assistant provincials of, 303
    provincials of, 301
Anderson, Robert, 335n. 5
Anderson, William, 210, 242
anti-Catholicism
    American Protective Association (A.P.A.) and, 104–5, 107
    in the U.S. in 1800s, 72, 78–79
    in the U.S. in 1920s, 189
    and anti-Mexican sentiment, 78–79
anticlericalism
    in France, 137–38
    reaction of Marianists to, 138

Appleby, R. Scott, 336n. 14
Aquinas, Thomas, 3, 116, 230, 234, 237
Arsenault, Gabriel, 302
Artz, Frederick B., 323n. 110
Association Catholique de la Jeunesse Française, 140
Atkielski, Roman R., 229
Aubert, Roger, 323n. 111
Auguste, Brother, 40, 42
Avella, Steven, 344n. 2, 347n. 104, 348n. 128
Avellar, Ernest, 222, 347nn. 103, 105

Bachelot, Alexis, 87
Baldwin, James, 262
Baltazar, Eulalio, 253, 254
Baltimore, Maryland
    German Americans in, 95–97
    Redemptorists in, 96, 98
    St. Alphonsus School, 97, 98, 99, 101, 119
    St. James School, 97, 101, 103, 106, 159, 183
    St. Michael School, 97, 99, 101, 103, 130, 159, 183
Barger, Robert N., 171, 339nn. 30–32, 35, 36
Barry, Colman J., 55, 323n. 1, 325n. 33, 334n. 66, 339n. 24
Barth, Karl, 279
Baudoin, Louis Marie, 15–16, 22
Baumeister, Edmund, 165, 320n. 33, 321n. 63, 322nn. 87, 92, 333nn. 32, 35, 43, 338nn. 3, 5, 8–11
Beauduin, Dollard, 304
Beauregard, Erving E., 352n. 72
Beck, Landelin, 86, 92, 301
Becker, Joseph, 329nn. 63, 66, 69, 70, 72, 74, 343n. 135
Becker, Margaret, 349n. 145

356